CONTEMPORARY ECONOMIC PROBLEMS AND ISSUES

FIFTH EDITION

THOMAS J. HAILSTONES
Dean, College of Business Administration
Professor of Economics
Xavier University, Cincinnati

FRANK V. MASTRIANNA
Associate Professor of Economics
Xavier University, Cincinnati

 Published by
SOUTH-WESTERN PUBLISHING CO.

CINCINNATI   WEST CHICAGO, ILL.   DALLAS   PELHAM MANOR, N.Y.   PALO ALTO, CALIF.

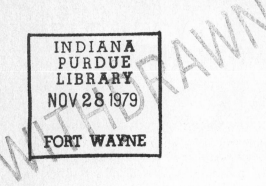
Copyright © 1979
by
South-Western Publishing Co.
Cincinnati, Ohio

ISBN: 0-538-08390-5

Library of Congress Catalog Card Number: 78-57155

1 2 3 4 5 **D** 3 2 1 0 9

Printed in the United States of America

Preface

Students successfully completing a good introductory course in economics develop an understanding of the workings of the American economic system and the use of basic tools and techniques in economic thinking. But because of the comprehensive scope of principles texts, only a relatively small segment of the text can be devoted to socioeconomic problems and issues. In many texts, treatment of such issues is confined to mini-readings or concluding comments within each chapter. To the student, readings and abbreviated applications within the text often seem superficial and lacking in depth. When one considers that most students' formal education in economics begins and ends with the principles course, all too often the unfortunate result is a lack of insight into the major problems of the day.

The basic goal of this text is to fill this need by presenting fifteen major problems and issues in a manner which the student finds both interesting and enlightening. Our approach is to present the chronological development or evolution of each problem, along with the current facts necessary for proper understanding of the problem. The text contains an economic analysis of the alternate solutions that have been suggested. In most cases, however, the decision as to what should be done is left to the reader. It is hoped that after the reader has marshaled the facts, analyzed the alternatives, and weighed the merits of proposed solutions, decisions can be rendered and supported on what should be done about the various problems and issues.

Topics covered in this text are presented within a four-part framework. Part One concerns general problems and issues and contains chapters dealing with unemployment, inflation, wage and price controls, and a guaranteed annual income. Part Two explores more specific problems of the American economy and consists of such topics as Social Security, national debt, national health insurance, and farm problems. Part Three is an urban-oriented section in which the problems of air pollution, crime, mass transit, and revenue sharing are probed. Finally, Part Four presents problems of a multinational scope with chapters on international economics and the dollar, the energy problem, and the population explosion.

In each chapter, the student should recognize the application of important economics concepts, such as supply and demand, opportunity cost, and cost-benefit analysis. In order to avoid unnecessary repetition, graphic models are utilized selectively with the belief that students can readily apply these tools in chapters in which such concepts are presented in descriptive form. The main thrust of each chapter, however, is to emphasize the trade-offs individuals and society as a whole must make in order to achieve a desired end.

In evaluating economic policy, students should keep in mind the political realities of a democratic society such as ours. Frequently it may appear that solutions proposed by economists are both efficient and equitable and thus worthy of implementation. But public policy is largely determined by elected representatives who, in addition to seeking efficiency and equity in our economic system, are also very much concerned with the basic task of being reelected. Keeping this in mind, students can better understand why a significant number of public programs may provide substantial benefits in the present but even greater costs in the future.

Feedback from professors using previous editions indicates a variety of ways in which this book can be effectively utilized. In many cases the book is used as a supplementary text for the full-year principles course, while in others it is used for the one-term, problems and issues course. In still other cases, the text serves as the basic learning tool for upper-division courses in current economic problems and issues, with greater emphasis on student research and subsequent written or verbal presentations on particular aspects of a given problem.

The authors are again indebted to many individuals who aided in the development of the fifth edition of this book. We appreciate the contributions of students, colleagues, and other users of the first four editions who made valuable suggestions for the current revision. We would like to recognize particularly Dr. Bernard L. Martin and Dr. George A. Wing for their authorship on previous editions. An expression of thanks is also due to Mrs. Marjorie Schmidt and Mrs. Eunice Staples for typing various parts of the manuscript.

Thomas J. Hailstones
Frank V. Mastrianna

Contents

Unemployment — 1
Why and for How Long?

Of the domestic goals cited for our economy by Presidential commissions, Congressional committees, business organizations, private economic groups, and labor unions, the three that are most prominent are full employment, economic growth, and stable prices. It is especially desirous that we avoid serious unemployment because of its economic consequence for the total economy and the hardship it brings to individuals and families.

Although the current problem of unemployment, and that which occurred in the first half of the 1960s, does not match the catastrophic situation that prevailed in the Great Depression of the 1930s when one fourth of the labor force was unemployed and many others were partially unemployed, it is serious enough to merit considerable attention. The American economy was close to full employment for 17 years, 1941–1957, with the exception of short periods in the postwar recessions of 1949 and 1953–1954, in which unemployment barely reached 4 million. After the recession of 1958, however, we did not return to a full-employment level until the early part of 1966. Nagging unemployment, which was a condition in which unemployment exceeded the then tolerable 4 percent unemployment norm by 1.5 to 2.0 percentage points, was then replaced by so-called full employment. After a 3½-year period of full employment, which still contained 3–4 percent unemployment, nagging unemployment recurred in 1970 and averaged between 5 and 6 percent in 1971 and 1972. It eased below 5 percent in 1973, but was aggravated by the recession of 1974–1975 and reached 9.2 percent in the spring of 1975. Unemployment averaged 5.6 percent in 1974 and 8.5 percent in 1975. During the economic recovery, unemployment dropped to 7.7 percent in 1976 and averaged 7.0 percent in 1977. As late as March, 1978, however, unemployment was still over 6 percent.

The problem then is that, in spite of highly prosperous conditions and substantial growth in our economy, we have had hard-core unemployment in recent years. Naturally, questions arise. Why have we not had full employment? What do we mean by full employment? Who are the unemployed? How serious is the unemployment? Who are the hard-core unemployed? How do we compare with other nations in this respect? Is anything being done about it? What is the outlook for the future? Before analyzing the problem of unemployment, let us look at the definition, size, and composition of the labor force.

THE LABOR FORCE

In 1977 the total population in the United States was 216.7 million. Of this total, 158.6 million were in the category known as the *noninstitutional population*; that is, all persons 16 years of age or older, including members of the armed services but excluding persons in institutions. In 1977, of the noninstitutional population, 99.5 million were in the total labor force. The *total labor force* includes those in the noninstitutional population who are working or looking for work. Thus, it includes the unemployed as well as the employed. Furthermore, it includes proprietors, the self-employed, and members of the armed forces. The labor force, however, excludes all persons engaged exclusively in housework in their homes or attending school. Students, for example, are not members of the labor force unless they are working in addition to attending school. If they work or look for work during the summer vacation period, however, they become members of the labor force. Likewise, when they graduate, they generally become members of the labor force.

The Civilian Labor Force

If we subtract the number of persons in the armed forces from the total labor force, the remainder is known as the civilian labor force. By definition, the *civilian labor force* consists of all persons in the total labor force except members of the armed services. Since there were 2.1 million persons in the armed services as of 1977, the civilian labor force amounted to 97.4 million, and of this total 6.9 million, or 7.0 percent, were unemployed. The *unemployed labor force* includes all persons in the labor force seeking work, including those who are currently engaged in emergency relief work.

Employment and Unemployment

The *employed civilian labor force* is the difference between the civilian labor force and the unemployed. It is composed of all employed workers — including persons who did not work at all during the census week because of illness, bad weather, vacation, or labor dispute, but who had a job or business. It includes part-time as well as full-time employment. In 1977 the number employed was 90.5 million. Of this total, 3.2 million were in agricultural work while 87.3 million were in nonagricultural employment.

There were 59.1 million persons in the noninstitutional population who were not in the total labor force. Homemakers comprise 33.8 million of this group. Another 9.2 million of those not in the labor force were in school. There were 2.7 million who stated that they were unable to work. The remainder, 13.4 million, was composed of those who had retired, individuals who did not want to work, those who did not have to work, and those having other reasons for not working. A breakdown of the population and the labor force is shown in Table 1-1.

Table 1-1
POPULATION AND LABOR FORCE, 1977

Category	Millions
Total population	216.7
Noninstitutional population	158.6
Total labor force	99.5
Armed forces	2.1
Total civilian labor force	97.4
Unemployed labor force	6.9
Employed civilian labor force	90.5
Agricultural employment	3.2
Nonagricultural employment	87.3
Persons not in the labor force	59.1
Keeping house	33.8
In school	9.2
Unable to work	2.7
Other reasons	13.4

SOURCE: *Employment and Earnings* (January, 1978).

The bulk of the labor force is engaged in nonagricultural employment. The largest number, 19.6 million, is engaged in manufacturing. The second largest category, wholesale and retail trade, has 18.3 million workers. There are 15.3 million engaged in services, and government employment is a close fourth with 15.2 million workers, of whom 12.9 million work for state and local governments. The sources of nonagricultural employment are shown in Table 1-2. From another point of view, 70 percent of today's workers are employed in service-producing industries, compared to only 30 percent in goods-producing industries.

Labor Force Participation Rate

Although the labor force has been growing in size, the labor force participation rate has remained relatively stable over the past few decades. The *labor force participation rate* is the ratio of the labor force to the total population. It can be calculated as a percentage of either the total population or the

Table 1-2

EMPLOYMENT IN NONAGRICULTURAL ESTABLISHMENTS BY INDUSTRY DIVISION, 1977

Industry Division	Millions
Nonagricultural employment[1]	82.1
Goods-producing industries	
Manufacturing	19.6
Mining	.8
Contract construction	3.8
Service-producing industries	
Transportation, communication, and public utilities	4.6
Trade (wholesale and retail)	18.3
Finance, insurance, and real estate	4.5
Service	15.3
Government — federal, state, and local	15.2

SOURCE: *Employment and Earnings* (January, 1978).

[1]Excludes proprietors, self-employed, and domestic servants. Total derived from this is not comparable with estimates of nonagricultural employment of the civilian labor force reported in Table 1-1, which includes proprietors, self-employed, and domestic servants; which counts persons as employed when they are not at work because of industrial disputes; and which is based on an enumeration of population, whereas the estimates in this table are based on reports from employing establishments.

noninstitutional population. Since 1930, the percentage of noninstitutional population in the labor force has been between 52 and 60 percent. The labor force participation rate compared to the total population has been between 39.6 and 46.5 percent as shown in Table 1-3. It is presently 46 percent. The stability of the civilian labor force participation rate is even more remarkable, staying between 38.0 and 44.7 percent since 1930, including the war years. The fact that the total labor force participation rate does change over the years indicates that the labor force has some degree of elasticity.

The size and participation rate of the labor force also fluctuate annually. They have seasonal peaks and troughs. Consequently, actual labor force figures are usually adjusted for seasonal changes for purpose of analysis. It is a well-established pattern, for example, that rises in the size and participation rate of the labor force can be expected each June as millions of graduates and students on summer vacation enter the labor force seeking jobs. Likewise, in late spring and early summer there is an increase in the number of seasonal agricultural workers. (See Table 1-4 on page 6.)

A low point in the size of the labor force occurs in January and February as an aftermath of the pickup in the November-December Christmas rush. It must be remembered that these changes are not always evident in total labor force figures because the cyclical movements are superimposed on seasonal

Table 1-3

LABOR FORCE AS A PERCENTAGE OF TOTAL POPULATION, 1930–1977

Year	Total Population (Millions)	Total Labor Force (Millions)	Total Labor Force Participation (Percentage)	Total Civilian Labor Force (Millions)	Civilian Labor Force Participation (Percentage)
1930	123	50	40.8	49	40.0
1935	127	53	41.7	52	40.9
1940	132	56	42.5	55	41.6
1945	140	65	46.5	54	38.6
1950	152	64	42.1	63	41.5
1955	166	68	41.0	65	39.2
1960	181	72	39.9	70	38.6
1965	195	77	39.6	74	38.0
1970	205	86	42.0	83	40.5
1975	214	97	45.3	95	44.4
1977	217	100	46.0	97	44.7

SOURCE: *Employment and Earnings* (January, 1978.)

changes in the labor force. Seasonally adjusted data are necessary, therefore, for a proper interpretation of what is happening to the size and participation rate of the labor force as well as to the level of employment and unemployment. Note that Table 1-4 shows unadjusted and seasonally adjusted monthly data for the civilian labor force and unemployment. It can be observed, for example, that the seasonally adjusted unemployment for June, 1977, reads 6.9 million instead of the actual 7.5 million. Thus, seasonally adjusted figures show what is happening to the labor force exclusive of the seasonal changes that are taking place.

Age and Sex of Labor Force

Before leaving the structure of the labor force, the age composition of the labor force should also be noted. Table 1-5 shows that 9.3 million people in the labor force are in the 16–19 age bracket, while at the other extreme 3.0 million are in the over-65 age bracket. The largest number, 61.6 million, are found in the 25–54 age group.

Although not shown in the table, it might be noted for future reference that of the total 41.0 million women in the labor force approximately 60 percent are married, 16 percent are widowed or divorced, and the remaining 24 percent are single. Of the married women in the labor force, 88 percent of them have husbands present in the household.

Table 1-4

STATUS OF THE LABOR FORCE, 1973–1977

[Thousands of persons 16 years of age and over]

Period	Noninstitutional population	Civilian employment	Unemployment	Total labor force (including Armed Forces)	Civilian labor force	Civilian employment Total	Agricultural	Nonagricultural Total	Part-time for economic reasons[1]	Unemployment Total	15 weeks and over	Labor force participation rate (percent)[2]
		Unadjusted				*Seasonally adjusted*						
1973........	148,263	84,409	4,304	91,040	88,714	84,409	3,452	80,957	2,311	4,304	812	61.4
1974........	150,827	85,935	5,076	93,240	91,011	85,935	3,492	82,443	2,709	5,076	937	61.8
1975........	153,449	84,783	7,830	94,793	92,613	84,783	3,380	81,403	3,490	7,830	2,483	61.8
1976........	156,048	87,485	7,288	96,917	94,773	87,485	3,297	84,188	3,272	7,288	2,339	62.1
1977........	158,559	90,546	6,855	99,534	97,401	90,546	3,244	87,302	3,297	6,855	1,911	62.8
1976: Dec....	157,176	88,494	7,022	98,082	95,936	88,446	3,240	85,206	3,392	7,490	2,462	62.4
1977: Jan....	157,381	86,856	7,848	97,852	95,719	88,653	3,121	85,532	3,243	7,066	2,244	62.2
Feb....	157,584	87,231	8,109	98,457	96,320	89,047	3,164	85,883	3,441	7,273	2,168	62.5
Mar....	157,782	88,215	7,556	98,761	96,623	89,478	3,179	86,299	3,271	7,145	2,008	62.6
Apr....	157,986	89,258	6,568	98,878	96,746	89,877	3,256	86,621	3,192	6,869	1,828	62.6
May....	158,228	90,042	6,151	99,289	97,161	90,267	3,335	86,932	3,268	6,894	1,869	62.8
June...	158,456	91,682	7,453	99,681	97,552	90,648	3,330	87,318	3,390	6,904	1,788	62.9
July...	158,682	92,372	6,941	99,442	97,307	90,588	3,206	87,382	3,464	6,719	1,824	62.7
Aug....	158,899	92,315	6,757	99,751	97,614	90,793	3,224	87,569	3,253	6,821	1,800	62.8
Sept...	159,114	91,247	6,437	99,887	97,756	91,088	3,199	87,889	3,306	6,668	1,834	62.8
Oct....	159,334	92,230	6,221	100,205	98,071	91,383	3,243	88,140	3,263	6,688	1,848	62.9
Nov....	159,522	92,473	6,346	101,009	98,877	92,214	3,357	88,857	3,285	6,663	1,829	63.3
Dec....	159,736	92,623	5,880	101,048	98,919	92,609	3,323	89,286	3,220	6,310	1,797	63.3

SOURCE: Department of Labor.

[1] Persons at work in nonagricultural industries.
[2] Total labor force as percent of noninstitutional population 16 years of age and over.
Note: Seasonally adjusted data revised beginning 1973.

Table 1-5
TOTAL LABOR FORCE BY AGE AND SEX, DECEMBER, 1977
(In Millions)

Age	Total	Male	Female
16–19 years	9.3	5.1	4.2
20–24 years	15.2	8.5	6.7
25–54 years	61.6	37.1	24.5
55–64 years	11.6	7.1	4.5
65 and over	3.0	1.9	1.1
Total	100.7	59.7	41.0

SOURCE: *Employment and Earnings* (January, 1978).

THE MEANING OF FULL EMPLOYMENT

It is obvious that when we talk about full employment for our economy, we are not referring to a situation in which there is a job for everyone. Many are too young to work, and others are too old. Some do not want to work, and others are physically or mentally incapable of work. There are also about 35 million persons too busy with housekeeping chores to enter the labor force, and a large number of our youngsters are still in school. Thus, full employment is not a condition in which the entire population is employed. In fact, in our dynamic economy with its mobile labor force, it cannot be expected that everyone in the civilian labor force would be working. There will always be some workers quitting, others being discharged, and some moving to other positions. Furthermore, many persons upon completing vocational or skilled training are unable to find a job immediately at the particular occupation they desire and will refrain from accepting another position until they can find the type of work they want. In addition, we have a number of persons who want to work but have difficulty obtaining or holding a job because of physical or mental incapacities. Consequently, we can always expect some slack, or unemployment, in our labor force.

For nearly two decades it was generally accepted by reliable authorities, such as the President's Council of Economic Advisers, that full employment existed whenever 96 percent of the civilian labor force was employed. This allowed for 4 percent frictional unemployment, which was held to be consistent with full employment.

In the early and mid-1970s, however, it was suggested by various authorities that our full employment standard of 96 percent employment and 4 percent unemployment of the civilian labor force was outmoded. It was proposed that the composition of the labor force was changing and that a new full-employment unemployment rate might be more appropriate. There are currently in the labor force a larger number and percentage of youngsters, women, and minority workers than existed in the mid-1950s when we came to accept the 4 percent unemployment figure as being consistent with full employment. These groups historically have had higher unemployment rates than the labor force as a whole. Consequently, when more statistical weight is given to these categories in establishing a full-employment unemployment rate today, it will yield a figure in excess of 4 percent, perhaps something in the range of 4.5 to 5.5 percent. A 4.9 percent figure, for example, was calculated for the 1977 *Economic Report of the President*, with a proviso that if certain nonquantifiable factors were considered the figure may be as high as 5.5 percent.

It has been suggested by others that full employment should be near the point where the number of unfilled job vacancies is about the same as the number of unemployed. Unfortunately, up to the present time this is a difficult measurement, since the Department of Labor's count, or estimate, of unfilled job orders is less than precise.

Although there are some sources that think the full-employment unemployment rate should be a lower or higher number, it is reasonable to define full employment as a condition in which 5.0 percent or less of the U.S. labor force is unemployed.

Humphrey-Hawkins Bill

In the mid-1970s Senator Humphrey and Representative Hawkins authored a Senate Bill, S50, known as the Full Employment and Balanced Growth Plan bill. Congressional hearings have been held on the bill and it has been modified and revised in a number of ways. The bill is designed to provide job opportunities at fair pay as a right of all Americans sixteen years of age and older.

The bill, as revised, calls for a program to reduce unemployment of the *adult civilian labor force* (20 years of age and over) to 3 percent within a period of four years after enactment of the bill.[1] The bill would require that numerical goals be established each year regarding employment, production, and purchasing power. If unemployment were not reduced to the targeted figure of 3 percent at the end of four years, the government, through a program implemented by the Secretary of Labor, would serve as an "employer of last resort" and would provide public service jobs for the unemployed.

The bill calls for the use of accelerated public works, countercyclical grants for stabilization and needed growth of state and local budgets, skills training, community development programs, and public service jobs, as well as the use of conventional monetary and fiscal policies in seeking the goal of 3 percent unemployment.

The bill also recognizes inflation as a national problem. It calls for plans to prevent inflation from rising above the inflation rate at the time the bill is

[1] It should be remembered when analyzing the possible effects of this bill that adult unemployment usually runs about one percentage point less than the unemployment rate for the total civilian labor force. Thus, 3 percent adult unemployment would be equivalent to 4 percent unemployment of the total civilian labor force.

enacted and ultimately to achieve reasonable price stability. The bill abjures government control of production, employment, and the allocation of resources, except as otherwise authorized.

RECENT AND CURRENT UNEMPLOYMENT PROBLEMS

After experiencing severe unemployment in the 1930s when as much as 25 percent of the total labor force was unemployed in the depth of the Depression in 1933–1934 and 15 percent as late as 1940, we returned to full employment during the war years, 1941–1945. With the exception of the postwar recession years of 1949 and 1954, we remained at or near full employment until the recession of 1958. Thus, with minor exceptions we had a period of full employment for 17 years. Unemployment in 1958 reached 6.8 percent of the labor force for the year, which was the worst we had experienced since 1940. Whereas the economy recovered to a full employment level after each of the first two postwar recessions, we did not move back to a full employment level after the 1958 recession until the early part of 1966.

Nagging Unemployment (1958–1965)

From 1957 until 1966 unemployment was persistently higher than it was for the previous 17 years. For the decade prior to 1957, the unemployment rate averaged 4.3 percent of the civilian labor force and it exceeded 5 percent only during the recessions of 1949 and 1954. In the years 1958–1964, however, unemployment averaged 5.8 percent. It was below the 5 percent level in only 2 months during this period, and at times exceeded 7 percent. Fortunately during the first half of 1965 unemployment improved somewhat when it dropped below 5 percent. But it was not until January, 1966, that unemployment fell to 4 percent.

Full Employment (1966–1969)

During this period attention was centered on what is often referred to as hard-core unemployment. Early in 1969 the Department of Labor classified only 6 of 150 major areas in the United States as being areas of substantial unemployment, that is, over 6 percent unemployment. This was in sharp contrast to the 101 so classified in 1961 or the 35 still classified as having substantial unemployment as late as 1964.

Moreover, when an unemployment rate of 3.5 percent was reported for May, 1969, it did not tell the whole story. Published data showed that unemployment among experienced workers was only 3.2 percent. Among family breadwinners it was only 1.4 percent. On the other hand, the overall economically healthy labor force had some real sore spots. Unemployment among nonwhite workers, for example, was 6.5 percent. The unemployment rate among white teenagers was 10.8 percent and among nonwhite teenagers it was 28 percent; this latter rate was even higher among nonwhite teenage girls.

Unemployment (1970–1978)

Unfortunately the endeavors of the Administration to combat inflation in 1969 and 1970, along with other factors, led to a slowdown in the economy. Unemployment, which averaged 3.5 percent of the civilian labor force in 1969, rose to 6.2 percent by the end of 1970 and averaged 4.9 percent for the year. Thus, in 1970 we experienced the anomaly of having both inflation and recession simultaneously. In spite of the several measures employed by the Administration to reduce unemployment in 1971 and 1972, unemployment for 1971 averaged 5.9 percent and was 5.6 percent in 1972. Although the unemployment rate did drop to 4.9 percent in 1973, as a result of the 1974–1975 recession it rose again to 5.6 percent in 1974 and, after peaking at 9.2 percent in May, 1975, averaged 8.5 percent for that year. With the economic recovery, unemployment fell to 7.7 percent in 1976 and to 7.0 percent in 1977. As late as March, 1978, however, it was still above the 6 percent level. We might reflect upon the current problems of unemployment in many ways: Why did it take so long to return to full employment in the early 1960s? Why has unemployment stayed high among certain groups, such as teenagers and nonwhites, even in a full employment period? How can hard-core unemployment be eliminated or alleviated? What is causing the present state of unemployment? How is it possible to have unemployment and inflation simultaneously? On the other hand, we might ask, just how serious is unemployment?

Studies and Actions

In the late 1950s, 1960s, and early to mid-1970s, a number of important committees and organizations studied the problem of unemployment. Numerous Congressional acts, such as the Area Redevelopment Act (1961), the Manpower Development and Training Act (1962), the Economic Opportunity Act (1964), and the Appalachia Act (1965), all dealt with unemployment.

With the return to full employment in early 1966 efforts to reduce unemployment were not abandoned. The Department of Labor, the President's Council of Economic Advisers, and others began to refer to 4 percent unemployment as an interim goal and suggested that unemployment might be reduced to 3 or even 2½ percent. Consequently, existing acts and measures to reduce unemployment were continued and new ones, such as the Comprehensive Employment and Training Act of 1973, were introduced.

More recently, in 1974–1977, the return of unemployment brought about a shift in the Administration's emphasis from anti-inflationary measures to expansionary measures to reduce unemployment and generate an increase in production. Included among the measures to bolster the economy were accelerated depreciation for business, the enactment of a bill providing federal financing for an additional 200,000 jobs in the state and local governments for unemployed workers, extended unemployment compensation, Federal Reserve actions to liberalize the money supply and lower interest rates, the toleration of large federal deficits, and tax cuts to stimulate the economy.

WHO ARE THE UNEMPLOYED?

The question has often been asked in recent years: Who are the unemployed? Are they members of a particular group? Are they oldsters or youngsters? Are they skilled or unskilled? Are the same people continuously unemployed, or is there a turnover in the ranks of the unemployed? Let us try to answer a few of these questions.

Frictional and Structural Unemployment

Frictional unemployment arises from the normal operation of the labor market. It will occur even in periods of full employment. Workers are constantly being hired, fired, quitting, withdrawing from the labor force for special training, taking their time on entering or re-entering the labor force to search for the right job, and relocating, often interstate, from one job to another. This unemployment is usually short-term in nature. Much of the full-employment unemployment can be attributed to frictional unemployment.

Structural unemployment is caused by rigidities that create an imbalance between the skills and characteristics possessed by workers and those demanded in the labor markets. Structural unemployment tends to be long term in nature. To some extent it is argued that a substantial portion of our present unemployment is structural in nature insofar as we have imperfect adaptation of jobs and workers. It is pointed out, for example, that workers are rapidly displaced because of technological development and automation. New skills arise and old skills are no longer as important, or the demand for them no longer as great, as they once were. Consequently, displaced workers, usually 2 million or more annually, have difficulty finding new jobs. Some workers are unemployed because they lack proper training, others because they lack geographic mobility to take advantage of job opportunities. As a result, we always have unfilled jobs on the one hand and jobless workers on the other.

Current data from the Department of Labor indicate that the number of vacancies is substantial. Moreover, it has been suggested by some groups that perhaps in our growing, dynamic economy we ought to expect a higher rate of structural unemployment than we have been accustomed to in the recent past.

Cyclical and Induced Unemployment

Cyclical unemployment is the result of a less than full utilization of productive capacity due to a recession or depression. It is due to insufficient aggregate demand in the economy. If the aggregate demand can be strengthened by an increase in consumption, investment, or government spending, it is suggested that the level of business activity can be increased and the cyclical unemployment reduced. Much of the high rate of unemployment associated with the recession of 1974–1975 was cyclical in nature. Cyclical unemployment may be short term or long term, depending on the length of the recession.

Induced unemployment is a consequence of implicit and explicit subsidies built into public socio-economic programs. One source of induced unemployment is the unemployment compensation system in the United States. Although it serves as an automatic stabilizer and has many other benefits, it tends to increase unemployment. The tax levied on the employer, for example, is not in direct proportion to the employer's layoffs. Therefore, it may be more conducive for a firm to lay off workers than it would be if it had to pay the full cost of unemployment benefits. Secondly, in many cases the minimal difference between unemployed persons' non-taxable unemployment benefits and what they may be able to earn on another job may deter their search for a new job. Other programs such as welfare payments, food stamps, and rent subsidies can cause a similar upward bias on the rate or on the duration of unemployment.

Characteristics of the Unemployed

An analysis of employment data points out a number of the characteristics of the unemployed, which adds to the understanding of the problem.

Duration of Unemployment. The average length of unemployment for an idled worker generally varies with economic conditions. The period of unemployment is longer in a time of economic sluggishness or recession compared to a period of prosperity. For the period 1960–1965 the average duration of unemployment was about 14 weeks. Toward the end of the decade it decreased to 8–9 weeks. With the recession of 1970 the average duration of unemployment was extended to 11.5 weeks, and in the recession of 1974–1975 it reached 16–18 weeks. In 1977 it averaged 14.3 weeks. Long-term unemployment, persons seeking work for 15 weeks or more, generally tends to change correspondingly.

Long-term unemployment is usually prevalent among certain groups in the labor force, such as older workers, nonwhites, and workers laid off in industries manufacturing durable goods. Although stable employment seems to be more characteristic of white-collar workers, unemployment is found among professional and technical workers, craftsmen, clerks, and salesworkers, as well as skilled and unskilled workers.

Age and Color of Unemployed. The incidence of unemployment is usually high among teenage workers who are likely to change jobs frequently. The rate of unemployment among nonwhite male workers has been twice the rate for white male workers. This, of course, is due in large part to the fact that the nonwhite workers are concentrated rather heavily in the unskilled and semiskilled industrial occupations where unemployment rates are generally high. The number of unemployed by age can be seen in Table 1-6. Note that 46.1 percent of our total unemployed was in the 24 years of age or under category, and that 23.8 percent was in the 16–19 age bracket. In the 20–24 group it was 22.3 percent.

Table 1-6

UNEMPLOYMENT BY COLOR AND AGE,
OCTOBER, 1977 (Thousands)

Total unemployed	6,221	100.0%
Color:		
White	4,774	76.7
Nonwhite	1,447	23.3
Age:		
16 to 19 years	1,480	23.8
20 to 24 years	1,389	22.3
25 to 44 years	2,233	35.9
45 years and over	1,119	18.0

SOURCE: *Employment and Earnings* (November, 1977).

Table 1-7 shows the lowest rate, 3.7 percent unemployment, to be among married men. Teenage unemployment was over 17 percent, however.

At the other end of the spectrum, nearly 3 million elderly persons on pensions or Social Security worked and were counted as employed. On the other hand, about 146,000 people in this age group, or about 2.3 percent of the total unemployed, were seeking work and listed among the unemployed.

Table 1-7

UNEMPLOYMENT RATES WITHIN VARIOUS
CATEGORIES IN THE LABOR FORCE,
OCTOBER, 1977*

All workers	7.0
White	6.1
Male	4.5
Female	6.9
Black & other	12.7
Male	12.0
Female	13.5
Household heads	4.6
Married men	3.7
Teenagers (16–19 years)	17.3
White	14.8
Nonwhite	37.9

SOURCE: *Employment and Earnings* (November, 1977).

  *Seasonally adjusted

Secondary Breadwinners. Nearly 3.3 million, or 53 percent, of the unemployed are female. Since there are 40.2 million females in the civilian labor force, the unemployment rate among women in October, 1977, was 8.2 percent, noticeably above the national average of 7.0 percent. Other unemployment rates are given in Table 1-7.

Since nearly 60 percent of the women in the labor force are married, it can reasonably be assumed that married women will comprise a substantial percentage of our unemployment. Data for October, 1977, show this figure to be 20 percent. In fact, 1,163,000, or 85 percent of the unemployed wives in the civilian labor force, had husbands who were currently employed, and 41 percent of the unemployed husbands had wives who were working. In only a small fraction of the households were both husband and wife unemployed.

The Hard Core. Within the hard core are illiterates, the chronically ill, those physically and mentally incapacitated, alcoholics, and the like. The hard core generally is so demoralized that individual rather than mass treatment by job placement services is needed. Many existing government and other retraining programs are far beyond the capabilities of the hard core. These people form a highly singular class of unemployed and unemployables, socially and economically isolated.

It is suggested that even when the full employment goal of 5 percent unemployment is realized, there still is at the bottom 1 percent unemployable, in poverty and on relief. Studies indicate that the hard core has developed into a class of social outcasts, characterized by very low incomes, by residence in blighted areas, by living in isolation from the mainstream of life, and by their "attitude." The attitude found covers: (a) no feeling of obligation to the family; (b) deep dejection at inability to find work; (c) general loss of self-respect, and (d) mental imbalance. It was further revealed that many of these people do not know how to look for a job, fill out an application form, or market any skills and experience they may have.

MEASUREMENT OF UNEMPLOYMENT

There are many ways in which the employed and the unemployed can be measured. Usually employed figures are more reliable than those for unemployment, and at times much controversy can arise regarding the method utilized to count the unemployed.

The Survey Method

Information on the labor force is obtained by the Current Population Survey and is reported in the Department of Labor publication, *The Monthly Report on the Labor Force*, and elsewhere. Figures are gathered through a survey taken for one week, the week ending nearest the twelfth of the month. The sample is made up of 47,000 households in 461 areas throughout the nation, a sampling ratio of 1 in every 1,500 households in the United States. According to the survey, persons are classified into three basic groups: employed, unemployed, and not in the labor force. The survey is made by well-trained interviewers. Questions are asked carefully and skillfully in order not to influence the response of the interviewee. Any responsible person, usually the homemaker, may answer the questions concerning the working status of other members of the household who are not at home during the time of the interview.

Unemployed Classification. Regarding labor force activities, the first question the interviewer asks is, "What was the person doing most of last week?" Of course, if the response is "working," the person is marked down as being in the labor force and being employed. If the reply, however, is "looking for work," a second question is asked to determine whether the interviewee worked at all during the survey week.

Unemployed persons comprise all persons who did not work during the survey week, who made specific efforts to find a job within the past four weeks, and who were available for work during the survey week (except for temporary illness). Also included as unemployed are those who did not work at all, were available for work, and (a) were waiting to be called back to a job from which they had been laid off, or (b) were waiting to report to a new wage or salary job within 30 days.

Unemployment Claimants. Presently the household survey is the major source of information about the total labor force as well as about the employed and unemployed. Although the survey method has some weaknesses, the Department of Labor prefers it to the count of unemployment claimants because a large number of persons in the labor force are not eligible for unemployment benefits. In addition, claimants may exhaust their benefits, cease to be claimants, and therefore no longer be listed as unemployed in the state employment office count. According to the Department of Labor, the survey method is 95 percent certain of being correct. Nevertheless, the BES data (Bureau of Employment Security) has certain advantages insofar as the data are prepared every week compared to the monthly data of the BLS-Census method. Furthermore, the data can yield specific information about local labor market areas.

Recent experiences indicate that total unemployment can be estimated by dividing by a factor of .44 the number of unemployment claimants. Thus, average weekly unemployed claimants of 2.8 million in September, 1977, would be adjusted to 6.4 million unemployed of the total civilian labor force. This is still below the actual BLS-Census count of about 6.7 million. This means, of course, that such a method of projecting total unemployment is not as accurate as the survey method. This is especially so since the corrective factor used varies from state to state and changes over time.

Underemployment

Even though for decades the BLS-Census survey has measured the employed and unemployed, it makes no attempt to measure the "underemployed." For this reason, some critics maintain that the survey does not measure the true level of unemployment since it neglects unemployment due to a short work week. So great was this concern that recording of underemployment was started in the mid-1960s.

Labor force time lost is a measure of worker-hours lost to the economy through unemployment and involuntary part-time employment and is expressed as a percentage of potentially available worker-hours. It is computed by assuming: (1) that unemployed persons looking for full-time work lost an average of 37.5 hours, (2) that those looking for part-time work lost the average number of hours actually worked by voluntary part-time workers during the survey week, and (3) that persons on part-time work for economic reasons lost the difference between 37.5 hours and the actual number of hours they worked.

This procedure has some weakness, however. First, it may be questionable whether 37.5 hours or 40 hours should be used as the norm. Second, if we incorporate underemployment in the rate of unemployment, should we adjust the rate downward when we have overtime employment, such as 40.5 average hours of work? Even using a 37.5-hour norm, that would mean hyperemployment of 8.0 percent ($3.0 \div 37.5 = 8.0\%$) from overtime. Overtime then more than offsets the labor force time lost.

Multiple Job Holders

It has sometimes been suggested that the practice of *moonlighting*, the holding down of two or more jobs, should be curtailed in the interest of reducing unemployment. Statistics indicate that in May, 1976, for example, 3.9 million persons in the labor force held two or more jobs. Although most of these multiple job holders, 3.7 million, were in nonagricultural industries, the rate of multiple job holding, multiple job holders as a percentage of all employed persons in the industry, was greater in agriculture. The rate of multiple job holding in nonagricultural industries was 4.5 percent compared to 5.8 percent for agriculture. Eliminating moonlighting would not increase employment proportional to the decrease in multiple job holders, of course, because most of the secondary jobs are part-time. Some of them amount to only a few hours a week, and frequently the rate of pay is less than that for the primary job of the worker. In some cases the secondary job is that of an unpaid family worker. In the case of two thirds of a million persons whose primary jobs were in nonagricultural industries, the secondary jobs were in agriculture. Many of these were farmers working at city jobs.

Job Vacancies

Sometimes it is suggested that jobs are available if the unemployed would just get out and look for them. In many cases, however, the unemployed may not have the skill, aptitude, or mobility to take advantage of existing job vacancies. In other cases the job may be insignificant, vocationally and economically, compared to the usual line of work of the unemployed person.

Job vacancies, as measured by the BLS, are the stock of unfilled job openings for all kinds of positions, both full-time and part-time, permanent and temporary, for which employers are actively seeking workers. The job vacancy rate is computed by dividing the number of current job vacancies by the sum of employment plus vacancies and multiplying by 100.

In 1975 there were an average of 657,000 job vacancies per month reported by state employment services in the United States. About half of these were considered as long-term vacancies, those that remained unfilled for 30 days or more. At that time there were 7.8 million persons jobless. The unemployment rate was 8.5 percent, and the job vacancy rate was .8 percent. If the unemployed had filled the job vacancies at that time the rate of unemployment would have dropped less than one percentage point.

Unemployment Compared to Other Nations

Critics of our economy have called attention to the fact that unemployment in many countries, such as Japan and West Germany, is lower than it is in the United States. After adjusting the rates for comparison purposes, unemployment in the United States and Canada is still considerably higher than in other major nations, as shown in Table 1-8, despite the fact that the economic growth rates of some of these nations have slowed considerably in the 1970s.

Table 1-8
1970 AND 1976 UNEMPLOYMENT RATES
(Adjusted to United States Definition)

Country	1970	1976
United States	4.9%	7.7%
Australia	1.4	4.4
Canada	5.7	7.1
France	2.7	4.6
West Germany	0.5	3.8
Great Britain	3.0	6.4
Italy	3.5	4.0
Japan	1.2	2.1
Sweden	1.5	1.6

SOURCE: *Statistical Abstract of the United States*, 1970 and 1977.

Criticism of the Survey Method

Although there is general agreement that the BLS-Census survey count of employment is very good, numerous criticisms have been leveled at its method of counting unemployment. Some feel that we should not count secondary wage earners among the unemployed, others suggest that students should not be included in the ranks of the unemployed, and many critics object to the listing of pensioners as unemployed. Others go so far as to say that we should not count anyone as unemployed who does not need a job. This does, however, set up a normative qualification which could be very difficult to measure. Furthermore, if people not working who do not need a job are not counted as unemployed, should the people who are working but do not need a job be excluded from the count of the employed and perhaps removed from the labor force? In still other cases, it has been suggested that the degree of unemployment may be influenced by the enthusiasm of the census takers; the harder they look to find unemployment, the more they will find. On the other hand, some critics suggest that the unemployment figure is too low for a number of reasons. Among these they cite the fact that many job seekers may become discouraged and withdraw from the labor market. Then there are those who feel that we put too much economic, social, and political emphasis on the measure of unemployment. They contend that the important measure is that of total employment rather than that of unemployment.

Over the years the Department of Labor has admitted that many complexities exist in the measurement of the unemployed. It has staunchly defended the BLS-Census method, however, explaining the purpose and reasoning behind many of the statistical calculations. The Department has stated many times that what is needed is not a rejection of the statistics, but provision for more detail and more meaningful breakdowns so that the data would be more useful for public policy decisions.

Evaluation of Data

The United States generally receives high praise from statisticians throughout the world for the methods, techniques, frequency, thoroughness, and integrity of its statistical data on such matters as employment, production, and prices. Nevertheless, in recognition of the many questions about the collection and measurement of employment and unemployment data, the President and Congress in 1976 established a National Commission on Employment and Unemployment Statistics to evaluate our present system of collecting, calculating, and disseminating employment and unemployment statistics and to make recommendations on methods of improvement. The Commission was directed to report its findings within 18 months after the appointment of its first five members.[2]

WHAT IS BEING DONE ABOUT UNEMPLOYMENT

Under the Employment Act of 1946, the Administration in office has an obligation toward preventing, reducing, or eliminating unemployment. Section Two of the Act declares:

> The Congress hereby declares that it is the continuing policy and responsibility of the Federal Government to use all practicable means consistent

[2]Although a similar commission, known as the Gordon Committee, submitted its report in 1962, it was decided that substantial changes in the nature and structure of the labor force had occurred in the 1960s and the 1970s to warrant another study.

with its needs and obligations and other essential considerations of national policy with the assistance and cooperation of industry, agriculture, labor, and state and local governments, to coordinate and utilize all its plans, functions, and resources for the purpose of creating and maintaining, in a manner calculated to foster and promote free competitive enterprise and the general welfare, conditions under which there will be afforded useful employment opportunities, including self-employment, for those able, willing, and seeking work, and to promote maximum employment, production and purchasing power.

This Act, furthermore, requires the President to make an *Economic Report* in January of each year. The report, delivered to a Joint Congressional Committee, reviews economic conditions of the previous year, gives a preview of the current year, and makes recommendations for bringing about maximum or full employment. The Act likewise provides for a President's Council of Economic Advisers to aid and assist him in making the report and making recommendations for implementing the Act.

Measures to Alleviate Cyclical Unemployment

Attempts have been made to eliminate and/or alleviate unemployment in many ways. The various measures attempted or suggested fit in two broad categories: those that endeavor to reduce cyclical unemployment, and those that seek to correct structural unemployment. In the first category are the several Congressional acts and executive actions that aim at raising the total effective demand in the economy by encouraging higher consumption, greater business investment, or higher government spending. Liberal monetary policies by the Treasury and the Federal Reserve have worked in this direction. Government deficits up to $66.5 billion in the past several years have been used in an attempt either to increase employment or prevent unemployment.

During the period 1960–1978 many measures and programs were implemented to alleviate cyclical unemployment. In the period of nagging unemployment of the early 1960s, for example, personal and corporate taxes were reduced, an emergency public works program was implemented, a program was inaugurated to reduce poverty, tax credits were used to stimulate investment, unemployment compensation was extended for an additional 13 weeks, and excise taxes were reduced. In the recession of 1974–1975 and subsequently taxes were again reduced, unemployment compensation extended, large federal deficits tolerated, the money supply increased, interest rates lowered, tax credits increased, public employment programs expanded, and other measures were taken to bolster the level of economic activity and to reduce unemployment.

Measures to Alleviate Structural and Technological Unemployment

In measures like tax credits to stimulate new investment, reduced income and excise taxes to encourage a higher rate of consumption, emergency spending on public works, and deficit budgets we see attempts to increase overall effective demand through increases in investment, consumption, and government spending. On the other hand, some endeavor has been made to eliminate or alleviate structural unemployment, a condition in which unemployed workers' skills do not fit available job opportunities.

Area Redevelopment Act. The Area Redevelopment Act of 1961, for example, endeavored to bring industry to depressed areas and jobs to displaced workers. The main features of this Act were the financial aids provided for distressed areas or areas with labor surpluses. These aids took the form of loans and grants for the construction of community projects and loans for private industrial undertakings of various types that would help to lessen unemployment in the area. Included in the program was training to prepare workers for jobs in new and expanded local industries. During the life of the Act, over 1,000 projects involving 65,000 trainees in 250 redevelopment areas were approved.

Manpower Development and Training Act. Congress enacted the Manpower Development and Training Act in 1962. The primary purpose of this Act was to provide training for the unemployed and underemployed to qualify them for reemployment or full employment. The MDTA allocated funds among states on the basis of each states' proportion of the total labor force, its total unemployment, and its average weekly unemployment payment.

The Act established training courses in those skills or occupations where there was a demand for workers, and the trainees had a reasonable chance of securing employment upon completion of the training program. Such programs were set up through the local state employment service utilizing state and local vocational education institutions, although private schools and other training institutions could be used. By 1976 over 2 million enrollees had received training under MDTA programs.

Economic Opportunity Act. In August, 1964, the Economic Opportunity Act was passed for the purpose of establishing several programs in an effort to eliminate poverty. Included in the war on poverty were numerous programs sponsored under the cooperation of several federal, state, and local agencies. Among other things, the Act provided for the establishment of youth conservation camps, work-training programs for unemployed youths, and work-study programs for high school and college students of low-income families. Included also in the poverty package were provisions for special programs to combat poverty in rural areas, loans to business to increase investment and raise employment, urban job centers for youth, literacy programs for adults, and a VISTA Corps (Volunteers in Service to America).

The Office of Economic Opportunity (OEO) was established for the implementation of the Act. Most programs were coordinated at the local level through Community Action Commissions set up in metropolitan centers.

Appalachian Regional Development Act. As a result of the findings of President Kennedy's Appalachian Commission, Congress in 1965 voted to enact the Appalachia Bill, which provided for various types of aid for a 13-state area extending along the Appalachian Mountains from New York State to eastern Mississippi. The program for this depressed area was aimed at developing an economic base to encourage subsequent private investment as a means of improving its economic level.

In the early stages major emphasis was placed on road construction, health facilities, land improvement and erosion control, timber development, mining restoration, and water resource surveys. The Act provided nearly $1 billion to improve the economic condition of the area in the hope of raising production, employment, and income of its inhabitants.

The JOBS Program. Since the return of unemployment in the 1970s, continued emphasis has been placed upon worker development and training. Recent programs involving more creative collaboration between private industry and the federal government have been attacking the problem of hard-core unemployment and poverty. The President's Manpower message of 1968 for example, called for the establishment of Job Opportunities in the Business Sector (JOBS).

The program was built on a commitment by groups of business people in 50 metropolitan areas to hire thousands of seriously disadvantaged people and give them on-the-job training, counseling, health care, and other supportive services needed to make these individuals productive workers. The program was built on the premise that immediate placement on a job at regular wages, followed by training and supportive services, rather than training first in an effort to qualify for the job, would provide superior motivation for these disadvantaged workers. By 1976 more than 425,000 disadvantaged workers had been given jobs by individual company efforts and through Department of Labor contracts. Six of every eight workers hired on federally financed programs were blacks and one in eight was Spanish American. About half of the hires were under 22 years old.

Public Employment Program (PEP). The Emergency Employment Act of 1971 authorized the establishment of a Public Employment Program (PEP). For this purpose Congress appropriated $2.25 billion for a 2-year period to finance transitional public service jobs at state and local government levels. Funds were to be allocated when national unemployment equaled or exceeded 4.5 percent for 3 consecutive months. Special additional funds were made available for areas with 6 percent or higher unemployment for 3 consecutive months. Between August, 1971, and June, 1973, PEP employed 404,000 persons. Approximately 113,000 were summer jobs for youngsters. Of the other regular jobs, 47 percent of the participants were veterans of Vietnam or previous wars. Three quarters of the participants were men. Forty-three percent were minority group members: blacks, 23 percent; Spanish speaking, 16 percent; American Indians, 3 percent; and Orientals and others, 1 percent. Nearly one fifth of the participants were disadvantaged or poor, and 14 percent were former welfare recipients. The average age of the PEP employee was 32 and the average duration of unemployment prior to entering the PEP program was 12 months. Although the Emergency Employment Act has now expired, many concepts of public employment service have been continued and are now incorporated in the new Comprehensive Employment and Training Program.

Comprehensive Employment and Training Act (CETA). A major step toward the decentralization and decategorization of manpower programs was taken a few days before 1974 began when the President signed into law, on December 28, 1973, the Comprehensive Employment and Training Act. A prime purpose of the Act was to transfer the responsibility and resources for many manpower programs from the federal government to states and localities with minimal federal control over the programs. In doing so an effort was made to reduce the fragmented efforts of nearly 10,000 programs throughout the nation independently aimed at similar problems. The new law makes governors and chief, elected officials of major cities and counties responsible for the planning and operation of comprehensive manpower programs. In addition to regular funds for such things as public employment programs, the Act provides special funds for areas where unemployment is 6.5 percent or higher for 3 consecutive months. Eighty percent of the available funds are directed to state and local governments. The other 20 percent is available to the Secretary of Labor to administer certain national programs such as the Job Corps. Many existing programs, such as those of Opportunities Industrial Centers, Jobs for Progress, Service Employment and Redevelopment, Community Action Commissions, JOBS, MDTA, and PEP are now under the jurisdiction of CETA. Since the Act was passed, several states have implemented Comprehensive Manpower Programs (CMPs).

CETA was subsequently amended by the Emergency Jobs and Unemployment Assistance Act of 1974 and by the Emergency Jobs Program Extension Act of 1976. The purpose of CETA is to provide training, employment, and other services leading to unsubsidized employment for economically disadvantaged, unemployed, and underemployed persons. The several titles of CETA authorize a variety of activities.

Title I, for example, established a nationwide program of comprehensive employment and training services administered by prime sponsors which, for the most part, are states and local government units. Titles II and VI provide programs of temporary public service employment during periods of high unemployment. Title III provides funds for supervised training and job placement programs for special groups such as youth, offenders, older workers, persons of limited English-speaking ability, Indians, and migrant and seasonal workers. Title IV authorizes a program of intensive education and training, known as the Job Corps, for disadvantaged youths, primarily in a residential setting. In 1976 Congress appropriated $5.3 billion for various CETA programs, including $1.2 billion to continue the support of 260,000 temporary workers in public service employment (PSE) jobs.

Experience shows that in the past few years CETA has had approximately 60–70 percent "positive terminations" of participants in its programs.

Positive terminations are defined as individuals who are placed either directly or indirectly in unsubsidized employment, who found jobs through their own efforts, or who engaged in other activities that increased their employability.

In fiscal 1976, for example, 67.5 percent of the CETA participants received positive terminations. Twenty-nine percent were placed on jobs either directly or indirectly or through self effort. Thirty-nine percent were considered positive terminations since they left CETA programs to enroll full time in an academic or vocational school, to enter the Armed Services, to enroll in a manpower program not funded by CETA, or to engage in any other activity that increased their employability. Thirty-two percent of the participants were non-positive terminations who refused to continue their participation in CETA programs or left for reasons unrelated to jobs or activities that increased their employability. These figures are shown in Table 1-9.

Table 1-9

CUMULATIVE TERMINATIONS FROM CETA PROGRAMS, FISCAL 1976

Type			Total
All Terminations			100%
Positive			67.5
Placements		28.9	
Direct	6.9		
Indirect	15.5		
Self	6.5		
Other		38.6	
Non-Positive			32.4

SOURCE: *Employment and Training Report of the President, 1977.*

Summer Youth Employment Program. In addition to several special programs for Indians, migrant workers, offenders, and older workers, CETA provides funds for a summer employment program for economically disadvantaged youth aged 16–21. In 1976, $582.4 million was distributed to help provide short-term jobs for 888,100 youths aged 16–21. Participants worked in such places as schools, libraries, community service organizations, hospitals, and private nonprofit agencies. Typical positions included nurse's aide, typist, school maintenance aide, cashier, library aide, clerk, and nutrition and day care aide.

The Job Corps. The Job Corps, established by the Economic Opportunity Act of 1964, continues under Title IV of CETA. It is designed to assist disadvantaged youths aged 16–21 to become more responsible, employable, and productive. All participants are out of work and out of school and in need of additional education, vocational training, and counseling. A total of 43,406 new enrollees entered the Job Corps in 1976. Most of these, about 75 percent, were from low-income families of less than $5,000 annually. Fifty-five percent were black youths and 11 percent of Hispanic origin. Eighty-seven percent had less than a high school education. In fiscal 1976 the Job Corps had an overall placement rate of 92 percent. Of nearly 29,000 placements about 20,000 were placed on jobs and the other 9,000 returned to school. Since its inception in 1964, 567,195 youngsters have enrolled in the Job Corps.

Work Incentive Program (WIN). Another major program established in the 1960s and now under the auspices of CETA is the Work Incentive Program (WIN). All applicants for and recipients of Aid to Families with Dependent Children (AFDC) who are 16 years of age or older are required to register for WIN unless legally exempt. In the early years of WIN emphasis was placed upon increasing job readiness through counseling, training, and supportive measures. More recently emphasis has been shifted to immediate job placement with training and other assistance provided only when placement is not feasible.

In fiscal 1976 there were more than two million current WIN registrants. About one fifth of these were volunteers who had been legally exempt from registering. Three fourths of the registrants were women and more than one half of the registrants were white. Sixty percent of the WIN registrants had not completed high school, and 10 percent had not finished the 8th grade. In 1976, 231,000, or about 10 percent, of the WIN participants entered employment. Most of them were employed in entry level jobs at rates of pay equal to or somewhat above the minimum wage level.

The Carter Program. Upon taking office in January, 1977, when unemployment was 7.3 percent, President Carter pledged to reach full employment, balance the federal budget, and restore price stability to the American economy by 1980–1981. During 1977 the President continued most of the existing programs. In November, 1977, the President publicly endorsed a revised version of the Humphrey-Hawkins bill. Instead of a 3 percent adult unemployment target by 1981, the modified version of the bill established an unemployment target of 4 percent by 1983. Moreover, the bill contained no specific annual unemployment targets, no specific steps that had to be undertaken, no specific jobs program, and the requirement that the government would serve as an "employer of last resort" was deleted.

The revised bill contained a stronger anti-inflationary stand, but it gave no reference to wage-price guideposts or price controls as a means of obtaining price stability. In its revised form the bill appeared to be more of a planning document rather than a call for specific action.

Toward the end of 1977 the President indicated that he would like to create 725,000 public service jobs, that he was planning on a $25 billion tax cut in 1978 to stimulate the economy, and that he hoped unemployment could be reduced to 4.75 percent by 1981. Unemployment for 1977 averaged 7.0 percent, but by the end of the year it had declined to 6.4 percent. In January,

1978, the Secretary of Labor predicted that unemployment for 1978 would decline to 6.5 percent and that it would be down to 6.0–5.5 percent by the end of 1978. It was 6.2 percent in March, 1978.

CONCLUSION

The labor force is destined to grow in the future. There will be more jobs, higher wages, shorter hours, and better working conditions. With this growth and development, however, will come new problems, especially in the absorption of young workers into the employed sector of the labor force and the reabsorption of workers displaced by rapid technological development and automation. In addition, the reoccurrence of cyclical unemployment, such as that which accompanied the 1974–1975 recession, aggravates the problem of unemployment.

It is expected that the total labor force will grow to 111 million by 1985. This will be a 12 million increase over the 99 million labor force of 1977. At the present time we are adding 2 million workers to the labor force annually. During the next 10 years the number of workers in the 25–34 age group will increase 30 percent. The challenge to maintain full employment is highlighted by the fact that many of the new entrants to the labor force are high school dropouts and lack training or a skill. In total, nearly one third of them have not completed high school. Unfortunately the demand for industrial, unskilled workers will not increase in proportion to the number of youths coming into the labor force. The largest increase in demand will be for professional, clerical, and skilled workers, and those occupations which generally require some degree of training, skill, or higher level of education.

Fortunately there will be a decline in the number and percentage of 16 to 19-year-old workers entering the labor force. This should help reduce unemployment among the youth of the nation which, on the average, is more than double the adult unemployment rate. But there will continue to be a rapid increase in the number of young blacks entering the labor force. Unemployment rates among young blacks are usually at least double what they are among white teenagers.

The proportion of women entering and reentering the labor force will continue to rise with married women accounting for the major share of the increase. Especially noticeable will be the re-entry of many homemakers into the labor force once their family responsibilities have been reduced with the maturing of their children.

At the same time that the labor force is growing at its fastest rate in history, we are experiencing a rapid rate of worker displacement because of technological development and automation. At present there are more than 2 million workers displaced each year because of various economic and technological changes taking place.

Another area of difficulty is arising as a consequence of increasing life expectancy and having a growing number of elderly persons in the labor force. Many of these persons want to continue in active employment rather than retire completely from the labor force. Probably the area of greatest difficulty is with the nonwhite worker, since the occupations in which many of them frequently seek employment will not be expanding substantially in the coming years.

Farm workers likewise present a problem, since the actual number required by 1985 will be less than the number required today. Rapid technological development and automation will aggravate the unemployment problem as old skills and occupations disappear and new ones arise in their places. Occupational and geographic mobility will become more essential in maintaining a high level of employment. Training and retraining will become more important in the solution to the problem of persistent unemployment.

MAJOR ISSUES

1. Is 5 percent unemployment a reasonable goal for a full employment economy? Why or why not?
2. Should formal retraining programs, such as those in MDTA, PEP, and JOBS, be continued as a solution to the problem of unemployment?
3. Should the federal government make payments to private industry or give them income tax credits for training disadvantaged workers?
4. Should a short work week be promoted as a means of minimizing unemployment?
5. Should Congress enact the Humphrey-Hawkins bill?

SUBISSUES

1. Should the following categories of workers be classified as unemployed: secondary wage earners (especially married women), pensioners, and students?
2. Would it be beneficial to promote more vocational education in our high schools?
3. Do you agree with the objectives of the Comprehensive Employment and Training Act?
4. Should moonlighting be eliminated or regulated as a means of spreading employment?
5. Has President Carter succeeded in his program to reduce unemployment?

SELECTED READINGS

Bregger, John E. "Establishment of a New Employment Statistics Review Commission," *Monthly Labor Review* (March, 1977).

Connolly, Harold X. "Why Not Actual Full Employment?" *America* (May 11, 1974).

"Education of Adult Workers: Projections to 1985." *Monthly Labor Review* (August, 1970).

Employment and Earnings. Washington: U.S. Department of Labor, February, 1978.

Greenwald, Carol S. "The Changing Composition of the Unemployed." *New England Economic Review*, The Federal Reserve Bank of Boston (July–August, 1971).

Manpower Report of the President. Washington: U.S. Department of Labor, 1976 and 1977.

"Multiple Job Holder, May, 1976." U.S. Department of Labor. Special Labor Force Report 194, 1977.

"New Labor Force: Projections to 1990." *Monthly Labor Review* (December, 1976).

Okun, Arthur. "The Great Stagnation Swamp." *The Brookings Bulletin* (Fall, 1977).

Samuelson, Robert. "Humphrey-Hawkins Hypocrisy." *National Journal* (January 7, 1978).

Saulnier, Raymond J. "A Critique of the Humphrey-Hawkins Bill." *Business Horizons* (February, 1977).

Seater, John J. "Coping With Unemployment." *Business Review*, Federal Reserve Bank of Philadelphia (January–February, 1977).

Shiskin, Julius. "When You Look Behind the Figures on U.S. Jobless —." *U.S. News and World Report* (February 3, 1975).

Stein, Herbert. "Full Employment At Last." *Wall Street Journal*, September 14, 1977, p. 18.

"Structural and Induced Unemployment." *Economic Report of the President*, 1977, pp. 136–146.

"Unemployment Rate Gives Only Part of the Picture." *Business Review*, Federal Reserve Bank of Dallas (January, 1975).

U.S. Manpower in the 1970's. Washington: U.S. Department of Labor, 1970.

Weidenbaum, Murray L. "The Case Against the Humphrey-Hawkins Bill." *Challenge* (September/October, 1976).

Ziegler, Martin. "Efforts to Improve Estimates of State and Local Unemployment." *Monthly Labor Review* (November, 1977).

Inflation — 2
How Much and Where
Does It Hurt?

We often hear much about the twin evils of unemployment and inflation and what detriments they are to the economy. There are several measures of the cost of unemployment, such as the loss of worker-hours, the loss of wages, and the production gap between actual and potential GNP, which measures our loss of goods and services. While there seem to be fairly adequate measures of the cost of unemployment, there is much less certainty about the cost, or adverse effects, of inflation in our economy.

It is said that inflation is the silent thief that robs the consumer of current purchasing power and depreciates the value of savings. It is claimed, too, that inflation forces business people to pay higher prices for current assets and higher replacement costs for machinery, equipment, and buildings. Inflation also weakens our international balance of payments position. Moreover, both consumers and investors are forced to pay higher taxes since inflation increases the cost of government services. Seldom, however, do we see a measure of just how much inflation decreases the current purchasing power of the consumer, depreciates the value of savings, adds to the cost of capital, or increases the cost of government.

The Phillips curve, which we shall examine later in the chapter, endeavors to give some estimate of how prices will react to a reduction in unemployment at various levels of unemployment, and certain figures of the Department of Commerce, Department of Labor, and the President's Council of Economic Advisers indicate that the closer we are to full employment the more difficult it is to reduce unemployment further without substantially affecting the price level. But we have no easy or specific measure of the total cost of inflation, whether it is demand-pull, cost-push, structural, or social in nature. Consequently, we have no formula which accurately measures the disadvantages of a certain degree of inflation. Such a guide, of course, would be of great importance in the evaluation of proposed monetary, fiscal, and psychological measures when the economy is on the brink of inflation.

Among other things, this chapter attempts to give some insight, or measurement, to the cost of inflation. It is only a beginning, however, as the authors realize that much more in the nature of collecting, refining, and ana-lyzing of data needs to be done before there can be a sophisticated measure of the cost of inflation or the establishment of a refined trade-off index between unemployment and inflation.

DEFINITION AND TYPES OF INFLATION

There are many definitions of inflation. In the simplest sense, inflation is merely a persistent rise in the price level. Inflation, however, may be one of four types: (1) demand-pull inflation, (2) cost-push inflation, (3) structural in-flation, or (4) social inflation.

Demand-Pull Inflation

The type of inflation that we have heard about most frequently is known as *demand-pull inflation*, which occurs when the total demand for goods and services exceeds the available supply of goods and services in the short run. This demand-pull inflation, sometimes referred to as excess-demand inflation, is much more likely to occur in a fully employed economy because of the difficulty of producing additional goods and services to satisfy the demand. Competitive bidding for the relatively scarce goods and services forces prices upward. The excess demand, or excess spending, may result from several causes. Consumers may dishoard past savings, consumer credit may be too liberal, government deficits may be too large, commercial and bank credit may be excessive, or the money supply otherwise may be increasing too rap-idly. Generally when the money supply or other forms of purchasing power increase faster than the productivity of our economy, demand-pull, or excess-demand, inflation results.

Cost-Push Inflation

The second type of inflation is known as *cost-push inflation*. This may occur in a fully employed or an underemployed economy. Whether it starts with increased wages, higher material costs, or increased prices of consumer goods is difficult to say. If wages or material costs do increase for some rea-son, however, producers are likely to increase the prices of their finished goods and services to protect their profit margins. Rising prices in effect will decrease the purchasing power of wages. As a result, wage earners, especially through their unions, may apply pressure for further wage increases. This in turn may lead to further increases in the price of materials and finished prod-ucts, which in turn leads to further wage increases and develops into what we generally call the *wage-price spiral*.

Cost-push inflation has become more pronounced in the past few decades with the growth and strengthening of labor unions. It also has been aggravated by the use of administered pricing by large and powerful producers. *Adminis-tered pricing* is a situation in which a seller can exert an undue influence on the price charged for a product because of the absence of competition. Although usually referred to as cost-push, price-pull inflation, labor unions prefer to call it price-pull, cost-push inflation to de-emphasize the role of wages.

Structural Inflation

Another type of inflation that may occur with a fully employed or less than fully employed economy is *structural inflation*. This arises when there is a substantial shift in demand to the products of one industry away from other industries. It assumes that there is a certain amount of inflexibility and immobility among the factors of production, and specifically that wages and prices tend to have downward rigidity and upward flexibility due to administered pricing and labor union pressures. If there is a heavy shift in the demand to the products of Industry X and away from the products of Industry Y, for example, it could push production in Industry X to, or near, full capacity. Under such circumstances the increased demand could cause prices to rise in that industry as a result of demand-pull inflation. This will cause the general price level to rise, since it is assumed that prices in Industry Y will not decline because of inflexibility. In addition, because of the immobility of labor and resources, Industry X may have to pay higher wage and material costs as it endeavors to increase production. The situation is aggravated when the inflationary effects spill over into other industries. The increases in wages and prices in Industry X may actually cause wages and prices to rise in Industry Y. The general increase in the price level could instigate wage increases and subsequently price increases in Industry Y. Although production and employment may be lessened as a result of demand shifts away from Industry Y, employers may be forced to pay higher wages to offset the higher living costs in an effort to hold on to experienced and skilled workers. In effect, structural inflation contains elements of both demand-pull and cost-push inflation.

One answer to each of these types of inflation is increased productivity. In demand-pull inflation, if productivity can be increased to provide the additional goods and services demanded, the inflationary pressure will be removed. On the other hand, the demand for goods and services can be reduced by reducing the money supply or by reducing spendable income. Cost-push and structural inflation can be modified if wage increases are kept in line with increases in productivity. Since wage raises would increase in proportion to the increase in productivity, incomes would stay in balance with the amount of goods produced. Goods and services would be available when wage earners spent their higher incomes.

Social Inflation

In recent years we have witnessed the development of a fourth type of inflation known as *social inflation*. It results from the increasing demand for more government services in the form of higher Social Security payments, improved unemployment benefits, the distribution of more welfare, wider health care coverage, better rent subsidies, and a host of other social services. Social inflation is further encouraged by the rising costs to private enterprise resulting from greater fringe benefits, such as longer vacations, more holidays, shorter hours, better pensions, and broader hospital and insurance coverage for employees. Moreover, the cost of helping to preserve the natural environment through the use of expensive antipollution and depollution equipment, either by the government or by private enterprise, exerts increased pressure on the price level. Likewise do the financial requirements of the Occupational Safety and Health Act (OSHA) and the Equal Employment Opportunity Act (EEOC). Social inflation may occur at full employment, adding to demand-pull inflationary pressures, or at other times it may augment cost-push inflationary pressures.

Demand and Supply

Any type of inflation can be aggravated by changes in demand and supply. With a rising demand and/or a shortage of supply, whether real or fabricated, prices will rise. This has been very much in evidence in regard to food, materials, fuel, and energy in the past few years. Whether price increases due to shifts in supply and demand should be labeled inflation is a debatable issue. Some contend that it is merely a reflection of the market's attempt to allocate scarce resources among users. It is suggested also that higher prices for some goods could cause lower prices elsewhere due to shifts in demand. Nevertheless, such changes can supplement rising price levels and certainly dovetail with the concept of structural inflation.

THE RECENT AMERICAN EXPERIENCE: UNEMPLOYMENT AND INFLATION

During the past 15 to 20 years, the economy has moved through several phases of economic activity including recession, nagging unemployment, stable prices, full employment, inflation, and stagflation. During this time various doses of monetary and fiscal measures have been applied in an effort to stabilize the level of economic activity, reduce unemployment, promote a healthy rate of economic growth, and stabilize the price level. A review of past developments will give us a better insight into our current problems.

Wage-Price Guideposts

After several years of relative price stability during the 1950s, some price unrest was becoming apparent in the economy in the latter half of 1961. To help prevent rising prices, President Kennedy, in 1962, established a set of voluntary wage-price guideposts. Based upon the fact that the average productivity per worker in our economy increased about 3 percent annually, the guideposts recommended that wage increases be held to 3 percent each year.

This would allow the increase in wage costs to be absorbed out of increased productivity without necessitating a price increase. The guideposts did have some flexibility insofar as they suggested that any firm whose gain in productivity per worker-hour was more than the guidepost figure should hold its wage increase to 3 percent and give consumers some benefit by reducing its prices. On the other hand, it recommmended that any firm whose increase in productivity was less than the guidepost figure could grant a 3 percent wage increase but offset this with an increase in prices. Subsequently, using a 5-year average, the guidepost figure was raised to 3.2 percent. Some delicate situations and open confrontations developed between the White House and/or the President's Council of Economic Advisers on the one hand and large industries and powerful unions on the other in regard to voluntary acceptance of the guideposts, especially in the 1965–1967 period. Thus, in 1967 the use of a specific guidepost figure was de-emphasized, although the guidepost concept was retained.

Economy in Transition

After seven years of *nagging unemployment* and relatively stable prices following the 1958 recession, in the winter of 1965–1966 the economy entered a transition phase. By the middle of 1965 unemployment had fallen below 5 percent and by the end of the year it had dropped to 4.1 percent, approaching the full-employment level for the first time in seven years or more.

With the high rate of private investment, exuberant consumer spending, continued outlays for Great Society programs, the escalation of the war in Vietnam, and sizable fiscal stimulants, it was obvious to many that there would likely be considerable upward pressure on the price level. It appeared that we were moving from an economy of nagging unemployment and idle capacity, with an emphasis on poverty, to a condition of full employment and high utilization of capacity characterized by shortages of skilled labor, scarcity of certain materials, and inflationary pressures.

Early in December, 1965, the Federal Reserve, by raising the discount rate, took what it considered a protective step against the clouds of inflation it foresaw on the economic horizon. Its action was both praised and criticized. Among its most vociferous critics were key officials in the Administration and members of Congress who considered the Federal Reserve's action unwarranted, untimely, and a deterrent to the Administration's economic program for growth and higher employment. Nevertheless, during most of 1966 the Federal Reserve continued to apply some brake against inflation by tightening the money supply. This action contributed to the "money crunch" of 1966, which had a substantial impact on the construction industry.

By January, 1966, unemployment fell to 4.0 percent and in February it was down to 3.9 percent, the first time the full-employment level had been reached in more than seven years. The Administration, which only a few months earlier had been studying the possibility of declaring a fiscal dividend in the form of an additional tax cut to prevent a fiscal drag on the economy, faced a serious problem of deciding whether it should continue its expansionary fiscal measures or whether it should shift to anti-inflationary measures.

It was concerned, of course, that anti-inflationary devices could slow down the economy. Some contended that the proposed measures might cause the economy to reverse its upward trend of five years and even precipitate a recession.

Inflation: 1966–1968

After much discussion and analysis, the Johnson Administration took only limited precautionary measures against inflation. In large part it rejected the idea of increasing taxes or reducing federal spending. Wage and price controls appeared to be an extreme. It did little to encourage or supplement the Federal Reserve's tighter money policy. On the other hand, the Administration did not sit by idly and do nothing. Early in 1966 it rescinded the excise tax cuts on automobile sales and telephone service. It also provided for an accelerated method of corporate tax collection and other minor measures to help avert inflation. But the Administration put its primary emphasis on jawbone tactics through its get-tougher policy in regard to implementation of the voluntary wage-price guideposts. Sometimes successful and at other times not, it endeavored to hold wage increases to the 3.2 percent guidepost figure, and it used persuasion of various types to influence major industries and labor unions to hold the price and wage line. Not until it became apparent that the price level was increasing at a 4 percent annual rate did the Administration take further action by suspending in September, 1966, the 7 percent tax credit on new investment and the accelerated depreciation measures.

Although the price increases slowed down a bit toward the end of the year, the CPI showed an annual increase of 3.3 percent. In December, 1966, unemployment measured 3.8 percent of the civilian labor force compared to 4.0 percent 12 months earlier.

Mini-Recession — Early 1967. The price level (CPI) stablized in the latter part of 1966 and the first quarter of 1967, increasing by no more than .2 percentage points in any one month. It was evident that the economy was slowing down since the GNP during the first quarter of 1967 showed only a minimal increase compared to each of the two previous quarters. In terms of constant dollars, figures for the GNP in the first quarter of 1967 actually declined by $400 million. This mini-recession of 1967, as it has frequently been labeled, was caused primarily by a decline in the rate of private investment.

Although the President in his 1967 *Economic Report*, issued in January, mentioned the need for a 6 percent surcharge on personal and corporate income taxes to combat the inflationary tendency in the economy, the measure was not pushed to any degree in Congress in the early part of 1967. Many government officials, economists, and others naturally felt that inflation had been beaten and cited the fact that it was accomplished without any sizable tax increase, without any drastic cut in government spending, or without the imposition of wage and price controls. In fact, by the end of 1966 the Federal Reserve had ceased its tight money policy and in the first quarter of 1967 it was again displaying a more liberal attitude toward the creation of credit. The discount rate, for example, was decreased from 4.5 percent to 4 percent in April, 1967. As a stimulant to the sluggish economy, the 7 percent tax credit on new investment was restored in June, 1967, 6 months ahead of schedule.

Inflation Resumes — Mid-1967. The joys of the stable price advocates, however, were short-lived because by the second quarter of 1967 the consumer price index resumed its upward movement. By the end of 1967, the CPI had risen sufficiently to show a 3 percent increase for the year. Although unemployment again averaged 3.8 percent of the civilian labor force for 1967, by the end of the year it was down to 3.5 percent. As a result members of the Administration and others were again talking about the need for restraint. Some government officials were even suggesting that direct controls of various kinds might be needed to cool the economy if management and labor did not hold wages and prices in check. In the latter part of 1967 and early 1968, the Federal Reserve moved toward a tighter money position by raising reserve requirements and moving the discount rate back to 4.5 percent.

The Income Tax Surcharge — 1968. In his *Economic Report* of 1968, President Johnson called for the imposition of a 10 percent surcharge on personal and corporate income taxes as a means of combating inflation. The size of the proposed surcharge was increased from 6 percent to 10 percent because signs of an overheated economy were more in evidence. The proposed bill to effectuate the tax became embroiled in a Congressional hassle as to whether it was better to increase taxes or reduce federal spending. As a result of prolonged hearings and debate in Congress, final action on the tax bill was delayed until June, 1968. At that time Congress imposed a 10 percent surcharge on personal and corporate income, making the tax retroactive to April 1 for individual income and January 1, 1968, on corporate income, effective until June, 1969.

The impact of the surtax fell more heavily on savings than expected, however, as consumers continued their outlays for goods and services, especially for new cars, and the rate of savings fell sharply. Fixed investment for plant equipment, which increased moderately in the first half of 1968, accelerated in the second half. Capital spending was no doubt spurred by the prognostication of investors that the 7 percent investment credit might again be suspended as an anti-inflationary measure.

By mid-1968 a number of hefty national wage negotiations had taken place in the economy, adding to the cost-push inflationary element. The shortage of skilled labor, and even unskilled labor, was evident in the economy. Average hourly wage gains of 7 percent in manufacturing industries during the year plus a reduction in savings, however, offset the impact of the income tax surcharge. Consequently, labor unit costs rose sharply.

All this, of course, caused prices to continue their upward movement through 1968. The cost of services, such as personal care, medical care, home ownership, and auto repair and maintenance, increased rapidly. By the end of 1968, the Consumer Price Index had risen 4.7 percent. Thus, in spite of the addition of a strong fiscal measure to accompany somewhat restrictive monetary measures, little success was achieved in arresting the upward movement of prices in 1968.

The New Economic Policy

With prices and wages continuing to rise in 1969 the Federal Reserve, which had reduced the discount rate in August, 1968, in anticipation of strong anti-inflationary reaction to the tax increase, adopted a more restrictive policy. As a result of various monetary measures, the rate of growth of the money stock declined. The Federal Reserve, through a series of changes, moved the discount rate from 5.5 percent in December, 1968, to 6 percent in April, 1969. By the summer of 1969 the prime rate for commercial loans offered by banks had reached 8.5 percent. Government bonds were yielding between 7 and 8 percent, high grade commercial bonds over 7 percent, and the interest rate on federal funds had approached the 10 percent level.

By the middle of 1969 prices were still rising. The CPI jumped 0.8 percentage points in June. This meant that the CPI in the first half of 1969 rose at an annual rate of 6.3 percent. In 1969 price increases were especially noticeable in food costs, rising at a rate of 9 percent annually, and services, which rose at a 7.5 percent annual rate in the first 6 months of the year.

Gradualism. With the inauguration of the Nixon Administration, inflation was cited as the nation's number one domestic issue. President Nixon adopted a policy of *gradualism* to bring inflation under control. In this regard he wanted to return the economy to stable prices without seriously disrupting the growth in economic activity. Among other measures, he asked Congress to retain the 10 percent tax surcharge that was due to expire in June of 1969. The budget was balanced and, in fact, ran a slight surplus in fiscal 1970. Defense and other government spending was cut and the Fed tightened the money supply. Although there was some discussion about the need for wage and price restrictions of some type, the President shied away from either formal or informal wage price measures. By the end of 1969, it was apparent that the measures employed to "cool off" the economy were effective in slowing down production. But they were not effective in slowing down the rate of inflation. Although the real GNP declined in the fourth quarter of 1969, the price level was increasing at a rate of 6 percent.

With certain reservations the forecasts for 1970 were favorable. Most analysts suggested that there would be some slack in the first half of the year, followed by a rebound in economic activity in the second half. It was the hope of the President's Council of Economic Advisers that the inflationary rate, which had been in the vicinity of 6 percent, would recede to 3.5 percent by the end of the year. Economic measures designed to cool the economy and bring about a reduction in inflation were expected to result in a slightly higher level of unemployment, up from 3.5 percent to, perhaps, 4.5 percent of the civilian labor force.

The economy did cool off in the first half of the year for a number of reasons, including a decline in business investment, a cutback in defense spending, a tightness of money, and a slowdown in housing starts. The two-quarter decline in the real GNP (4th quarter, 1969, and 1st quarter, 1970) was followed by a sidewise movement in the second quarter of 1970. The price level, however, continued to rise at a undesirable rate of more than 5 percent annually. Measures designed primarily to arrest demand-pull inflation failed to contain cost-push price pressures. Unemployment increased more than anticipated and reached a rate of 5.5 percent by midyear. This left the Administration in the position of deciding whether to continue anti-inflationary measures and risk the possibility of higher unemployment or shift to expansionary measures and risk the resurgence of inflationary pressures, an especially delicate decision in an election year.

Unfortunately the economy did not rebound in the second half of the year. Unemployment for the year averaged 4.9 percent and by the end of the year had reached 6 percent. Although 1970 was officially labeled a recession year, the CPI still managed to increase by 5.9 percent.

In the late months of 1970, the Administration shifted its emphasis to expansionary measures. A number of steps were taken to increase effective demand. Earlier in the year, the personal and corporate income tax surcharge was allowed to lapse. Subsequently the Administration encouraged the Federal Reserve to liberalize the money supply and adopt an accelerated depreciation schedule to spur business investment. Discount rates were lowered several times, moving down to 4.75 percent within three months, and the Administration announced that the federal deficit for fiscal 1971 would be in excess of $18 billion and that the projected federal budget for fiscal 1972 showed an $11.6 billion deficit. The Administration was trusting that any resulting increase in effective demand would not evoke demand-pull inflationary pressures, since the economy was in a state of less than full employment. The administration, however, was concerned about cost-push price pressures. Consequently, in early 1971 it began "jawboning" as a means of holding the price line and more was heard about the possibility of wage and price guideposts and an incomes policy.

The Game Plan. Economic forecasts for 1971 were good, but nothing spectacular. It was anticipated that about half of the projected 6 to 7 percent increase in the GNP would be in real production and the other half in higher prices. Furthermore, the Council set year-end goals of 4.5 percent unemployment and a 3.5 percent rate of inflation. The economic "game plan" was to restore full employment and stable prices by mid-1972. Measures designed to attain that growth rate, remove the production gap, and eliminate nagging unemployment could very well add to price pressures and cause the rate of inflation to accelerate. The task of reaching stable prices was aggravated, too, by the fact that wage increases of 30 percent or more spread over a three-year period had been negotiated in the construction, auto, railroad, and tin can industries. Similar wage concessions in the steel industry in the summer of 1971 led to an immediate 8 percent average increase in steel prices. Some members of Congress, who in early 1971 recommended that President Nixon utilize the authority given to him in 1970 to impose wage and price restrictions, renewed their efforts after the steel settlement.

At the midyear Congressional hearings on the state of the economy, an Administrative spokesman indicated that the Administration was not going to reach its year-end goals of disinflation and reduction of unemployment. It was stated that prices were stickier and unemployment more stubborn than anticipated. A month later, in response to an inquiry of what the Administration was going to do about inflation and unemployment, the Secretary of the Treasury stated that the Administration was not going to impose wage and price controls, it was not going to adopt wage-price guideposts, it was not going to increase government spending, and it was not going to reduce taxes.

Wage and Price Controls

Economic pressures regarding prices, wages, and the balance of payments brought about a change of attitude in the White House by mid-1971.

Phase I: The 90-Day Freeze. With the knowledge that progress on his economic game plan was being stifled by substantial wage and price increases, President Nixon in August, 1971, made drastic and sweeping changes of domestic and international economic policies. Among other measures, he declared a 90-day freeze on all prices, wages, and rents, temporarily suspended convertibility of dollars into gold, imposed a 10 percent surcharge on imports, froze a scheduled pay increase for government employees, sought to reinstitute tax credits as a means of stimulating investment and jobs, asked Congress to reduce personal income taxes, and requested Congress to repeal the 7 percent excise tax on automobiles.

The President established a Cost of Living Council to work out details for restoring free markets without inflation during a transition period following the freeze. Congress did oblige the President by repealing the excise tax on automobiles and reducing personal income taxes by advancing the scheduled date for an increase in personal income tax exemptions.

Phase II. The 90-day freeze was followed by a Phase II control period. For the implementation of this phase the President established a Pay Board and a Price Commission. Each was to work out what it considered permissible non-inflationary wage and price increases, respectively. The Commissions were composed of representatives of labor, management, and the general public. The Pay Board subsequently established a 5.5 percent annual wage increase as a maximum. It did allow that certain exceptions could be made to the 5.5 percent figure.

The Price Commission, on the other hand, indicated that it was going to attempt to hold overall price increases in the CPI to 2.5 percent annually. Since the President did not desire to set up an elaborate formal structure of wage and price controls, such as existed during World War II and during the Korean Conflict, much of the stabilization program had to depend on voluntary compliance. The Cost of Living Council exempted most of the business firms and most workers from any reporting requirements. Others, however, were required to report changes in prices and wages. Larger firms, moreover, had to give prenotification of changes to the Price Commission and/or the Pay Board.

The effectiveness of the wage and price controls in combating inflation can be gauged somewhat by the fact that, during the six months prior to the freeze, prices increased at an annual rate of 4.5 percent. In the five months subsequent to the freeze, they increased at an annual rate of 2.2 percent. The price level for 1972, during which price controls existed for the entire year, increased 3.3 percent.

The stability of prices in the first half of the 1960s compared to the inflationary period starting in 1966 can be seen in Table 2-1 and Figure 2-1. From

Table 2-1
EMPLOYMENT, UNEMPLOYMENT, AND PRICES, 1960–1977

Year	Total Employment	Unemployment	Rate of Unemployment	CPI (1967 = 100)	Rate of Inflation[1]	Discomfort Index
1960	65,778	3,852	5.5	88.7	1.5	7.0
1961	65,746	4,714	6.7	89.6	.7	7.4
1962	66,702	3,911	5.5	90.6	1.2	6.7
1963	67,762	4,070	5.7	91.7	1.6	7.3
1964	69,305	3,786	5.2	92.9	1.2	6.4
1965	71,088	3,366	4.5	94.5	1.9	6.4
1966	72,895	2,875	3.8	97.2	3.4	7.2
1967	74,372	2,775	3.8	100.0	3.0	6.8
1968	75,920	2,817	3.6	104.2	4.7	8.3
1969	77,902	2,813	3.5	109.8	6.1	9.6
1970	78,627	4,088	4.9	116.3	5.5	10.4
1971	79,120	4,993	5.9	121.3	3.4	9.3
1972	81,702	4,840	5.6	125.3	3.4	9.0
1973	84,409	4,304	4.9	133.1	8.8	13.7
1974	85,935	5,076	5.6	147.7	12.2	17.8
1975	84,783	7,830	8.5	161.2	7.0	15.5
1976	87,485	7,288	7.7	170.5	4.8	12.5
1977	90,546	6,855	7.0	181.5	6.8	13.8

SOURCE: *Economic Report of the President*, 1978.

[1]Changes are from December to December.

Index 1967=100

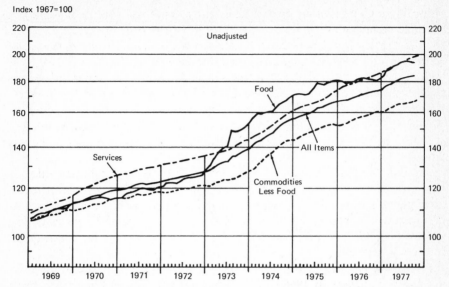

SOURCE: *Economic Indicators* (January, 1978).

Figure 2-1 **CONSUMER PRICES**

1960–1965, for example, prices rose at an average annual rate of 1.3 percent. From 1965 to August, 1971, prices rose at an average annual rate of more than 4.7 percent. Figure 2-2 shows price increases in average annual percentage increments, categorized as creeping, jogging, and galloping inflation.

Although employment increased substantially during this period, the amount and rate of unemployment, after dwindling early in the decade, rose in the next few years. Note the net increase of over 2.0 million in unemployment between 1969 and 1971 in Table 2-1.

Phase III. In January, 1973, after commenting favorably on the results of Phase II in stabilizing prices and wages, the President announced Phase III, which in effect reestablished voluntary guideposts for price and wage increases. The guidepost figures used at that time were 2.5 percent and 5.5 percent annually for prices and wages, respectively.

Phase IV. The removal of compulsory Phase II controls proved to be premature, however, During the first five months after decontrol, the CPI rose at an annual rate of nearly 9 percent. Consequently, on June 13, 1973, President Nixon declared a 60-day freeze on prices. Wages were not affected at this time. Instead of ending the freeze on all goods at the end of the 60-day period, prices were unfrozen selectively, and Phase IV controls were imposed on various categories of goods and services at different times before and after the 60-day period.

Again large firms were required to give a 30-day prenotification of price increases. Unlike Phase II, however, firms did not have to wait for approval

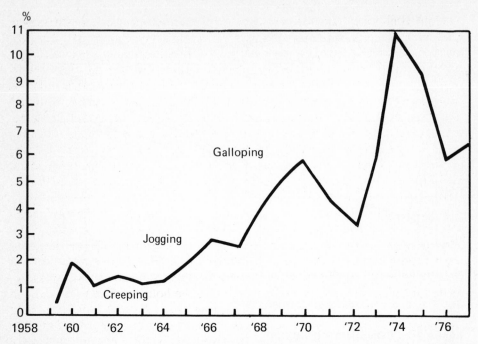

SOURCE: *The Conference Board RECORD* (May, 1969) and *Economic Indicators* (January, 1978).

Figure 2-2   **ANNUAL INFLATION RATE**

by the Cost of Living Council before putting such increases into effect. But the Council had authority to delay any price increases indefinitely, and it reserved the right to reexamine prices at any time. The new base period established was the fiscal quarter prior to January 12, 1973, the date of decontrol of Phase II. Price increases equal to dollar cost increases subsequent to the base period were to be permitted by Phase IV. No allowance was to be made for a profit markup on these cost increases. Controls were imposed on an industry-by-industry basis, thus providing more flexibility than was available under Phase II. At the time of the imposition of Phase IV, several high Administration officials indicated that they hoped controls could be removed by the end of 1973. Most of the controls were removed by early 1974. Unfortunately the CPI rose 8.8 percent in 1973. Inflation was aggravated by higher fuel prices and an increase of 20 percent or more in food prices.

The Recession of 1974–1975

In spite of our hopes and efforts to temper inflationary pressures, the price level continued to rise during 1974, reaching double-digit figures within a few months.

Upon taking office in summer of 1974, President Ford declared inflation, among other things, was to be a prime target of economic policy. He held a summit conference composed of legislators, cabinet members, business people, labor leaders, and both professional and academic economists. The suggestions to combat inflation were many and varied, including a tax surcharge, tighter money, a balanced budget, higher interest rates, wage-price guideposts, reductions in federal spending, and a return to wage-price controls. Before having an opportunity to implement any of these measures, however, the recession of 1974 deepened sufficiently to cause the President to de-emphasize the problem of inflation to concentrate on expansionary measures to offset the adverse effects of the recession. Particularly distressing was the growing rate of unemployment, which reached 7.1 percent in December, 1974, and 8.2 percent in January, 1975. But in spite of the recession, the CPI rose 12.2 percent during 1974.

As the state of the economy deteriorated over the next few months and it became evident to President Ford and his economic advisers that the economy actually was in a recession, the emphasis of economic policy began to shift toward expansionary measures. The real GNP had dropped for a third consecutive quarter, unemployment had reached 6.5 percent and was predicted to reach as high as 8 percent or more, the housing industry was still in the doldrums, inventories of such items as automobiles and appliances were piling up, investment plans were being trimmed, and economic conditions in Europe and Japan were likewise depressed. However, demand-pull price pressure had abated. But with a number of sizable wage settlements and administered prices being set, double-digit inflation still prevailed due to cost-push, structural, and social inflationary pressures in the economy.

It was apparent to all that the state of the economy had slipped downward from *stagflation* to *slumpflation*. Some analysts were talking in terms of a mini-depression. Consequently, President Ford abandoned his plans to reduce federal spending and balance the budget. Early in 1975 he accelerated a public employment program and recommended an extension of unemployment compensation. He presented a $349.4 billion federal budget, including a huge $52 billion deficit. Included in the budget were a $16 billion tax reduction and other measures to offset growing unemployment, which grew to 8.9 percent in May of 1975. By that time the real GNP had declined for its fifth consecutive quarter when it showed a 2½ percent drop in the first three months of 1975. Income taxes were reduced by $23 billion and other expansionary measures were suggested by economists, business people, labor leaders, and Congress.

This slumpflation, of course, threw economists into a new ball game. Previously they had figured they knew what measures to use to expand the economy during a recession and, on the other hand, what measures to recommend to combat inflationary pressures. However, when recession and inflation occurred simultaneously, a condition with which we had very little experience, a real dilemma was presented. Should the Administration, for example, emphasize anti-inflationary measures and risk aggravating unemployment, or should it emphasize expansionary measures and risk higher prices? Not only was there an absence of foolproof economic measures to deal with slumpflation, but also prudent decisions had to be made regarding which was the more serious problem — unemployment or inflation.

THE PROBLEM

This brings us to the heart of the current inflationary problem. It is obvious from an analysis of the previous data that we have had an inflationary trend in the economy since 1966. The initial impact on prices was brought about by demand-pull pressures resulting from exuberant consumer spending, record-level private investment, large government outlays for Great Society programs, the escalation of the war in Vietnam, and large federal deficits during a period of full employment. Since that time, cost-push, structural, and social elements have added to inflationary pressures.

Early measures to combat inflation were rather timid. The primary force was that of Federal Reserve monetary measures. Very little was attempted in the way of fiscal measures to combat inflation in either 1966 or 1967. Furthermore, the mini-recession of 1967 raised false hopes for the restoration of moderate price stability. Although stronger fiscal measures, especially in the form of the 10 percent income tax surcharge and the federal surplus budget of $3.2 billion for fiscal 1969, were employed, along with a continuation of tight money, the upward surge of prices was not arrested until the price freeze of August, 1971.

Perhaps it would be simple enough to arrest the inflation by applying conventional but stringent monetary fiscal measures. But there is always the danger of applying the brakes too strongly and causing the economy to turn downward. Furthermore, any time anti-inflationary measures have an adverse effect on employment, it is frequently the hard core, the poverty level wage earner, the teenager, and the nonwhite workers who are thrown out of work. Consequently, anti-inflationary measures begin to take on political overtones. Thus, the problem or task is to find the proper amount and mixture of monetary, fiscal, and psychological measures to arrest the inflation but not cause unemployment to rise above the 5 percent level consistent with full employment. In this regard it should be remembered that prices are considered to be stable if the CPI does not move more than 2 percent annually.

THE TRADE OFF

Once the economy is at full employment it is difficult to ride the crest of the economy at the point where unemployment is minimized and the price level stabilized. The President's Council of Economic Advisers, the Departments of Labor and Commerce, and others in 1966 thought that we could lower the level of unemployment below the then current goal of 4 percent to 3.5 percent without substantially affecting prices. As the level of unemployment dropped below 4 percent, however, it became evident that maintaining price stability within 2 percentage points was improbable. It became more and more evident that further reductions in the level of unemployment came at the risk of higher prices. Economists then began to explore the trade off between the two values — lower unemployment and stable prices. In fact, when the Nixon Administration took office in 1969, it was stated by several of the newly appointed cabinet members that the major domestic problem was that of inflation. Some of them issued a warning that we might have to tolerate a little more unemployment to restore price stability. From a political point of view, however, none of them would state specifically what level of unemployment they would tolerate in exchange for price stability. Nonpolitical interests, nevertheless, were suggesting that unemployment might rise to 4 to 5 percent if stronger efforts were made to hold the price line.

The debate about the trade off between increased unemployment and an increase in prices renewed interest in the concept known as the *Phillips curve*. This curve was developed by a British economist, A. W. Phillips, who studied the relationship between the level of unemployment and wage increases for the United Kingdom for the years 1861 to 1913. From his studies he found that when unemployment was high, money wage increases were smaller; and when a low level of unemployment existed, wage increases were larger. Phillips concluded that the money wage level would stabilize with a 5 percent unemployment rate.

In the 1960s American economists began to apply the Phillips-type curve to changes in prices in relation to unemployment. This became feasible especially when the level of unemployment began to fall consistently below the 4 percent level. Subsequently a number of Phillips curves have been developed showing the relationship between price changes and the level of unemployment. Any interpretation of these curves must be made cautiously, since they are constructed with various assumptions. There is absolutely no certainty, for example, that because a given relationship occurred in the past it will hold precisely in the future. Many conditions may change in the interim. Furthermore, several curves have been constructed from the same data, each showing a slightly different relationship depending on the time lag actually used. Figure 2-3 on page 44 depicts a Phillips curve developed by Paul Samuelson. It shows price stability at about 5.5 percent unemployment and a 2 percent price rise associated with 4 percent unemployment.

Several other Phillips curves have been developed over the years. One shows a price rise of about 2.5 percent associated with unemployment of 4 percent. Another shows a price increase of around 4 percent associated with a 4 percent unemployment rate. Still others, which have been developed more recently, depict a rightward shifting of the Phillips curve, indicating a higher price level-unemployment relationship in which both the price level and unemployment rates are higher as one is traded off against the other.

The Phillips curve, of course, has some validity when inflation is demand-pull in nature. But the relationship between unemployment and price changes does not hold so well when inflation is of a cost-push or structural variety. A Phillips curve for the years 1970 to 1978 excluding the months of price control, for example, would definitely move the price-unemployment line of best fit far to the right. Particularly out of focus would be the years 1974 and 1975 when double-digit inflation prevailed with unemployment ranging between 5 and 8.9 percent. This has led some analysts to challenge the Phillips curve and its relationship between unemployment and price level changes. It should be

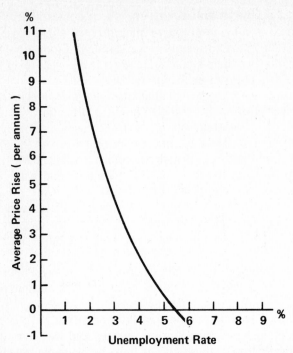

SOURCE: "Analytical Aspects of Anti-Inflation Policy," *The Collected Papers of Paul A. Samuelson-Stiglitz*, Vol. II, MIT Press, 1965.

Figure 2-3 **MODIFIED PHILLIPS CURVE FOR THE UNITED STATES**

remembered, however, that the Phillips curve was originally designed to measure the relationship between demand-pull inflation and unemployment, not cost-push, structural, or other varieties of inflation.

A side effect of unemployment-price change watching has been the development of the *Discomfort Index*, which measures the level of unemployment and the rate of inflation combined. Table 2-1 on page 38 shows the rising level of discomfort as both unemployment and inflation continued to increase in the 1970s.

COST ESTIMATE OF INFLATION

Whether because of normal expansionary forces in the economy, an insufficient tightening of the money supply, the lack of voluntary restraint on the part of consumers and investors, or the failure of the Administration and Congress to adopt more stringent fiscal measures sooner, the price level has risen in each of the past 12 years more than it did in any of the preceding 12 years at a cost to American consumers of several billion dollars. Some idea of the cost of this inflation for one year, such as 1975, may be estimated as shown in the following sections.

Higher Prices for Goods and Services

The CPI was 7.0 percent higher in 1975 than it was in 1974. This means that consumers paid out $64 billion more in 1975 in the form of higher prices for goods and services, as consumer outlay was $980 billion in 1975 ($980 billion ÷ 107 × .07 = $64 billion). The cost of business investment in machinery, equipment, and buildings figures to almost $14 billion more when the 7.0 percent price markup is applied to the $190 billion gross domestic investment in 1975. Government outlays — federal, state, and local — rose by $22 billion due to the higher price tags on the goods and services produced by all levels of government. In short, our cost of production, $1,529 billion GNP, was $100 billion more than it would have been had prices not risen in 1975.[1]

At first glance we may want to conclude that the cost of inflation in 1975 was $100 billion, but it must be kept in mind that we consider prices to be stable when the CPI or the implicit price deflator moves 2 percent or less on an annual basis. Thus, if a 2.0 percent annual increase was considered tolerable, this would mean that excess inflationary pressures in 1975 increased the price level by 5 percent (7.0 − 2.0 = 5.0). In this case it could be considered that the total cost of inflation was only $73 billion, instead of the $100 billion cited above, of which $47 billion was for consumer goods and services.

Depreciation of Savings

There is more to consider, however, since inflation affects not only current income but liquid assets held by individuals, businesses, and the government. For example, in 1975 households held total savings of $787 billion in the form of time and savings deposits.[2] In addition, they held U.S. Government Savings Bonds, other U.S. government securities, state and local government securities, and corporate bonds and notes estimated at a market value of $295 billion. Pension fund reserves amounted to $369 billion. Consequently, the price rise of 7.0 percent for 1975 depreciated the value of these savings by $102 billion ($1,451 × .07 = $102). If only 5.0 percent excess inflationary pressures were applied, the value of these savings still eroded by $73 billion. This adverse effect of inflation on individual savings, however, was offset to some extent by the fact that the $656 billion combined mortgage, installment credit, and other debt burden of individuals was eased somewhat as a result of inflation. The figure would be $46 billion if the 7.0 percent increase in the price index were used, but only $33 billion if the 5.0 percent figure were used.

Loss of Insurance Protection

The effect of inflation on the protection rendered by our life insurance policies must also be considered. At the end of 1975, for example, Americans

[1]If the GNP implicit price deflator of 9.7 percent for 1975 were used, instead of the CPI increase of 7.0 percent, the cost of inflation on the GNP would be $135 billion.
[2]*Statistical Abstract of the United States*, 1976, p. 478.

held $2,140 billion worth of life insurance protection.[3] Thus, the 7.0 percent depreciation in the purchasing power of the dollar lessened the protection of these policies by a total of nearly $150 billion, or $107 billion using the 5.0 percent inflation factor.

Rise in Replacement Cost of Assets

Inflation hits businesses as well as consumers. Not only do higher prices increase the cost of current additional investment, but they also force upward the replacement cost on existing investment.

Whether we consider the increase in replacement cost of $811 billion of corporate manufacturing assets or the cost of replacing the $3.0 trillion in total reproducible tangible assets (a portion of our national wealth) of the economy, it can be observed that inflation of 7.0 percent or 5.0 percent will increase the cost substantially. Replacement of the manufacturing assets alone would cost between $57 billion and $41 billion more using the 7.0 percent and 5.0 percent inflationary factors, respectively.

For those items above, the approximate total cost, in the form of higher prices or loss of value resulting from the 1975 inflation, was somewhere between $409 billion and $294 billion, as indicated in Table 2-2.

Table 2-2
TOTAL COSTS OF INFLATION, 1975

Category	Cost or Loss (In Billions) 7.0 Percent		With Inflation Factor of 5.0 Percent	
Current goods and services		$100.0		$ 73.0
Consumer goods	$64		$47.0	
Private investment	14		10.0	
Government	22		16.0	
Savings		102.0		73.0
Insurance protection		150.0		107.0
Replacement of corporate assets		57.0		41.0
Total cost		$409.0		$294.0

Balance of Trade

Inflation, also, can have an adverse effect on the economy through the balance of international trade. This is especially so when domestic prices are rising faster than are those abroad. In such a case the relatively greater increase in prices in America deters foreigners from purchasing our goods and

[3]*Statistical Abstract of the United States*, 1976.

services, thus causing our exports to decline. On the other hand, the relatively lower price of foreign goods and services encourages Americans to purchase foreign goods, causing imports to increase. Any change in the export-import ratio can affect jobs, profits, and incomes. Any attempt to measure the net effect of such changes is difficult, however. Any disadvantage to particular groups has to be offset by any gains to the total economy through the utilization of the law of comparative advantage. Nevertheless, Table 2-3 gives some indication that the United States compares favorably vis-à-vis other major nations on the matter of inflation.

Table 2-3
CONSUMER PRICE INDEXES — SELECTED COUNTRIES, 1975

Country	Index (1967 = 100) 1975	Average Annual Percentage Change, 1965–1975
United States	161.2	5.5
Canada	160.1	5.6
Japan	204.5	8.4
Austria	157.6	5.3
Belgium	165.6	5.9
Denmark	185.5	7.8
France	178.7	6.5
Germany, F. R. of	144.1	4.3
Italy	186.8	7.1
Netherlands	174.6	6.7
Norway	176.6	6.7
Sweden	164.5	6.2
Switzerland	157.5	5.6
United Kingdom	216.5	8.7

SOURCE: *Statistical Abstract of the United States*, 1976, p. 879.

Comparative Gains in Employment and Wages

Offset against the cost of inflation, of course, must be the gains in the economy obtained as a result of those measures which incidentally brought on the inflationary conditions. First of all, unemployment dropped by 553,000 from 1965 to 1969 and total employment increased by 6.8 million. During this time the rate of unemployment declined from 4.5 to 3.5 percent. Since 1969, however, both the number and percentage of unemployed have been on an upward trend, as shown in Table 2-4. Consequently, inflation in recent years has not been offset by reductions in unemployment. Employment since 1969, however, increased by 12.6 million workers.

Table 2-4

EMPLOYMENT, UNEMPLOYMENT, PRICES, AND WAGES, 1965–1977

Year	Total Employment	Unemployment	Rate of Unemployment	CPI (1967 = 100)	Rate of Inflation[1]	Weekly Money Wage[2]	Real Wage (in 1967 $)	Percentage Increase in Real Wage
1965	71,088	3,366	4.5	94.5	1.7	107.53	113.79	2.7
1966	72,895	2,875	3.8	97.2	2.9	112.34	115.58	1.6
1967	74,372	2,775	3.8	100.0	2.9	114.90	114.90	−0.6
1968	75,920	2,817	3.6	104.2	4.2	122.51	117.57	2.3
1969	77,902	2,813	3.5	109.8	5.4	129.51	117.95	0.1
1970	78,627	4,088	4.9	116.3	5.9	133.73	114.99	−2.5
1971	79,120	4,993	5.9	121.3	4.3	142.44	117.43	2.1
1972	81,702	4,840	5.6	125.3	3.3	154.69	123.46	5.1
1973	84,409	4,304	4.9	133.1	6.2	166.06	124.76	1.0
1974	85,935	5,076	5.6	147.7	11.0	176.40	119.43	−4.3
1975	84,783	7,830	8.5	161.2	9.1	189.51	117.56	−1.3
1976	87,485	7,288	7.7	170.5	5.8	207.60	121.76	3.6
1977	90,546	6,855	7.0	181.5	6.5	226.89	125.01	2.7

SOURCE: *Economic Report of the President*, 1978.

[1]Year to year changes as opposed to December to December changes.
[2]Average weekly earnings in manufacturing industries.

Moreover, it might be said that as a result of some measures contributing toward inflation, such as high level investment, large budget outlays for social programs, spending for the war in Vietnam, and the occurrence of a substantial federal deficit, wages in general were higher and profits greater. In fact, it can be claimed that higher prices have to be offset in large part by higher incomes, since the total cost of production is equal to our national income.

It can be brought out also that inflation made it easier for individuals, banks, government agencies, and insurance companies to meet their fixed obligations. But many of these gains came at the expense of the consumer.

Looking at American consumers only, the inflation of 1975 cost them somewhere between $227 billion and $316 billion, depending on whether one uses a 5.0 percent inflation factor or a 7.0 percent factor. Even if the minimum cost for consumer outlay, depreciation of savings, and loss of protection on life insurance policies is used, higher prices still cost American consumers, directly or indirectly, $227 billion in 1975 compared to what they would have paid if we had stable prices.

It might still be argued that, if prices rise, current incomes have to rise by a similar amount because our total factor cost is equal to our national income. But granting that the 1975 cost of inflation was completely offset by the yearly increase of income, there was still the large loss, $180 billion, resulting from depreciation of our savings and the loss of protection from our life insurance and annuity policies, using the 5.0 percent inflation factor.

Regardless of how the pie is sliced or the cost allocated, American consumers have paid dearly for the excessive inflation of recent years. From most indications, it would have been far better for the economy to have taken more stringent monetary and fiscal measures in the early stages of price pressures in an effort to combat the pending inflation. In the absence of voluntary restraint by consumers and investors or a reduction in spending by the government, an earlier increase in personal and corporate income taxes would have been beneficial and may have been less expensive for consumers in the long run. Our total payout for goods and services would have been less; excessive inflation may have been avoided; and there would have been no long-term loss in the form of depreciated savings, no decline in protection from insurance policies and annuities, and no inflated replacement costs of assets.

Another bit of evidence of how inflation is hitting the pocketbook of the average American can be seen in what is happening to average weekly earnings. In 1967, for example, the wage of the worker in manufacturing increased $2.56 per week, but purchasing power declined by 68 cents. In 1969 the $7.00 per week increase in money wages yielded a net increase of only 38 cents in purchasing power. In 1970 the $4.22 increase received in money wages per week was more than offset by inflation and the worker ended up with a $2.96 decline in purchasing power. In 1974 the money wage rose $10.34 while real wages declined $5.33 per week. In 1975 the $13.11 per week increase in money wages was offset by a $1.87 decline in purchasing power. Fortunately the workers' real wage increased moderately in 1976 and 1977.

In the five-year period prior to our current inflationary binge, 1960–1965, the real wage of the manufacturing worker increased 12.5 percent ($113.79 − $101.15 ÷ 101.15), or 2.5 percent annually. During that period the money wage increased by 20 percent. In the 12-year inflationary period, 1965–1977, the money wage increased by 111 percent but the real wage during this period increased by a mere 9.9 percent, or about .8 percent annually. Moreover, since the higher money wage moved many workers into a higher income tax bracket, their real wage gains were further obliterated by higher income tax payments. Workers in many other categories have had smaller money wage increases than those in manufacturing. Consequently, it becomes obvious that the average worker has made little economic gain during this inflationary period.

Since there is a certain nebulousness about the cost of inflation, and the measures necessary to combat it are seldom politically popular, there is generally a hesitancy to take the vigorous steps necessary to prevent rising prices. It is easy enough to arouse public and political sympathy and support for measures to bolster the economy when an excessive number of people are suffering from unemployment. It is difficult, however, to generate enough public sentiment and political concern to do more to combat inflation, even though the small loss it may involve to each of 216 million consumers may add up to a greater cost than the loss suffered by the excess unemployment of a half million or more workers above the 5 percent unemployment level.

CONCLUSION

It was apparent in early 1978 that we had not been successful in our attempts to arrest inflation. Even though a recession occurred in 1974–1975 and we had a substantial increase in unemployment, there was only a modest slowdown in the rate of inflation. In fact, inflation accelerated in 1974 to a double-digit level and was still 9.1 percent in 1975, the second year of the recession. The inflation rate did slow down to 5.8 percent in 1976 (4.8 percent if a December to December basis is used). But, in spite of the efforts of the Administration, Congress, and the Federal Reserve to combat inflation, prices rose at an annual rate of 6.5 percent in 1977.

During President Carter's first year in office, 1977, it had been suggested that compulsory wage-price controls, or at least voluntary wage-price guideposts should be implemented to deal with inflation. It was recommended by some members of Congress that federal income tax payments be indexed in some manner so the average taxpayer would not be forced to pay higher tax rates when money income increased without a rise in purchasing power. Also, some economists recommended that tax credits be used to reward firms that hold down prices and wages, a recommendation strongly condemned by high level labor union officials.

During the year the Council on Wage and Price Stabilization investigated a number of price increases in major industries. It attempted to determine whether the price increases were inflationary and whether or not they were cost justified. However, it lacked subpoena power to obtain information and had no legal authority to prevent wage and price increases.

In January, 1978, President Carter announced, along with other economic measures, his anti-inflationary program. He denounced the use of compulsory wage and price controls and even the idea of voluntary wage-price guideposts. Instead, the President called for voluntary cooperation on the part of management and labor to hold wage and price increases at or below the average increases of 1976–1977, which were about 7.5 percent for wages and approximately 6 percent annually for prices. He indicated that the Administration would use moral persuasion in an attempt to win cooperation in the fight against inflation. This was to be a softer approach than the so-called "jawboning" of previous Administrations. It called for a one-on-one relationship in working with business firms, industry representatives, and labor groups in an attempt to convince them to hold the wage-price line.

At the same time as he was presenting his anti-inflationary program, the President outlined his program to stimulate the economy. This included a $25 billion personal and corporate tax cut, along with a $500 billion federal budget with a $60 billion deficit. In addition, it was expected that the new Chairman of the Federal Reserve Board, appointed by the President in January, 1978, would advocate a more liberal monetary policy than his predecessor. Increases in Social Security taxes and a three stage rise in the minimum wage also took effect in January, 1978. Although the Administration determined that these programs would not have much impact on demand-pull inflation because of the unemployment, idle productive capacity, and ample supplies of resources in the economy at the time, they do make it a bit more difficult to deal with cost-push, structural, and social inflation.

MAJOR ISSUES

1. Should the Employment Act of 1946 be amended to include price stability as a dual objective, along with full employment, for the U.S. economy?
2. Should wage and price controls be reimposed as a means of stopping inflation?
3. Do higher prices paid by consumers for goods and services represent a real economic cost to the economy, or are they merely a redistribution cost?
4. Are losses from depreciated savings and reduced insurance protection that result from inflation real economic costs or redistribution costs?
5. In your judgment, which is the more serious problem, inflation or unemployment?

SUBISSUES

1. Under the circumstances at the time, do you think the Administration should have taken stronger anti-inflationary measures in the 1966–1971 period? Why or why not?
2. What additional anti-inflationary measures, if any, would you suggest for today's economy?
3. Do you think that a 2 percent rise in the Consumer Price Index is consistent with price stability?
4. Do you think that our unemployment goal today should be 5 percent or something other than that?
5. Do you think that all wage rates should be tied to the CPI, as they are in the auto industry, to protect the purchasing power of workers?

SELECTED READINGS

Ackley, Gardner. "Two-Stage Recession and Inflation, 1973–1975." *Economic Outlook USA*. Survey Research Center, University of Michigan, Winter, 1975.

"A Primer on Inflation: Its Concepts, Its Costs, Its Consequences." *Review*, Federal Reserve Bank of St. Louis (January, 1975).

"Best Ways to Beat Inflation." *U.S. News & World Report* (November 21, 1977).

Bowsher, Norman N. "The Early 1960's: A Guide to the Late 1970's." *Review*, Federal Reserve Bank of St. Louis (October, 1977).

"Carter's Risky Strategy: Gambling on Growth Could Mean More Inflation." *Business Week* (January 23, 1978).

Casson, John J. "Inflation Expectations." *Business Economics* (May, 1977).

The Consumer Price Index Revision — 1978. U.S. Department of Labor, Bureau of Labor Statistics, 1978.

Employment and Earnings (January, 1978).

Fellner, William, Kenneth W. Clarkson, and John H. Moore. *Correcting Taxes for Inflation*. Washington: American Enterprise Institute, 1974.

Francis, Darryl R. "Inflation, Recession — What's a Policymaker To Do?" *Review*, Federal Reserve Bank of St. Louis (November, 1974).

Habeller, Gottfried. *Stagflation: An Analysis of Its Causes and Cures*. Washington: American Enterprise Institute, March, 1977.

"How Inflation Creates Wealth — For the IRS." *Monthly Economic Letter* (September, 1977).

"Inflation." *Economic Report of the President*, 1977, pp. 41–45.

Kosters, Marvin H., and J. Dawson Ahalt. *Controls and Inflation: The Economic Stabilization Program In Retrospect*. Washington: American Enterprise Institute, 1977.

Lawrence, Floyd G. "More Unemployment vs. More Inflation: Dilemma or Myth?" *Industry Week* (January 20,1975).

Lerner, Abba P. "Stagflation — Its Causes and Cure." *Challenge* (September/October, 1977).

Lilly, David M. "The Threat of Inflation." *Review*, Federal Reserve Bank of Dallas (December, 1977).

Miller, Roger L., and Raburn M. Williams. *Unemployment and Inflation*. New York: West Publishing Co., 1974.

Mullineaux, Donald J. "Inflation Expectations in the U.S.: A Brief Anatomy." *Business Review*, Federal Reserve Bank of Philadelphia (July–August, 1977).

"New Man At the Fed Talks About More Jobs With Less Inflation." *U.S. News & World Report* (January 16, 1978).

"Proposed Solutions to Inflation — Effective and Ineffective." *Review*, Federal Reserve Bank of St. Louis (July, 1971).

Selden, Richard T. "Inflation: Are We Winning the Fight?" *The Morgan Guaranty Survey* (October, 1977).

Shanahan, Eileen (Moderator). *Indexing and Inflation*. Washington: American Enterprise Institute, July, 1974.

Tobin, James. "The Economic Impasse: Is There A Way Out?" *Economic Outlook U.S.A.* Survey Research Center, University of Michigan, Autumn, 1977.

Wachtel, Howard M., and Peter D. Adelsheim. "How Recession Feeds Inflation: Price Markups In A Concentrated Economy." *Challenge* (September/October, 1977).

Wachter, Michael L. "Did Wage-Price Controls Reduce Inflation?" *Wharton Quarterly* (Summer/Fall, 1974).

Wallich, Henry. "Why Does This Inflation Hurt So Much?" *Wharton Quarterly* (Summer/Fall, 1974).

Weintraub, Sidney. *Capitalism's Inflation and Unemployment Crisis*. Reading, Mass.: Addison-Wesley Publishing Company, 1978.

Wage 3 and Price Controls — Are They Necessary?

The term "incomes policy" has a variety of meanings. To some people it means strict, compulsory wage-price controls. At the other extreme it is interpreted as mere "jawboning," or moral suasion, which is the attempt on the part of the Administration to induce labor and management to reach noninflationary wage settlements and to persuade businesses to refrain from increasing prices. There are various shades of meaning in between. There are those, too, who think of an incomes policy in a slightly different vein. To them it is a set of economic measures designed to retard cost-push inflation through the reduction of labor bargaining power and the restriction of administered pricing by oligopolies. For our purposes we will consider an incomes policy as a broad set of voluntary, quantitative guidelines that apply to prices, wages, and other forms of income, such as rents and interest, and that may or may not carry some type of economic penalty against nonconformists.

In studying the feasibility of an incomes policy we shall begin with an analysis of our past and current experiences with compulsory wage-price controls which establish specific, allowable increases for wages and prices, and then move on to a review of the voluntary wage-price guidepost periods of the 1960s and 1970s in which general norms were promulgated as guides for wage and price increases.

COMPULSORY WAGE-PRICE CONTROLS

In recent history the United States has imposed wage-price controls on three occasions: (1) during World War II; (2) during the Korean Conflict; and (3) during the period which began in August, 1971, and is somewhat associated with the war in Vietnam. In all three cases controls were initiated with a wage-price freeze, but eventually evolved into a formula of some type to regulate wages and prices. Economists generally agree that economic controls can suppress inflation by preventing overt wage and price increases from taking place. Nevertheless, the overall effectiveness of controls as a means of eliminating the causes of inflation is frequently debated by economists and others.

World War II

During World War II the total endeavor to reduce effective demand and to combat inflation included the use of heavy personal and corporate taxation, voluntary savings, an excess profits tax, rationing, a controlled materials plan, labor restrictions, and credit controls. In addition, wage and price controls were imposed in October, 1942. The consumer price index (1967 = 100), which had increased from 42 in 1939 to 49 by October, 1942, increased only moderately during the war. However, the price level rose 35 percent within 24 months after prices and wages were decontrolled in June, 1946.

Postwar Period

At the end of World War II, firms and individuals had the largest holdings of liquid assets — cash savings, bonds, and other assets easily convertible into cash — in the history of our nation up to that time. Since demand continued to rise, we still had a potentially inflationary situation. As a result, controls were not removed upon the termination of the war in August, 1945. In the early part of 1946, shortages still prevailed, some rationing existed, and people were still standing in queues to buy certain consumer goods.

Decontrol. Finally, in June, 1946, Congress decontrolled prices. This unleashed a flood of spending that pushed total effective demand beyond our ability to produce. Not only were incomes at a record peak, but also individuals and firms had large holdings of liquid assets that they were eager to spend. The effective demand rose quickly due to the pent-up consumer demand from the long war, business demand for expansion of plant and equipment, an inventory build-up, and a large foreign demand for our products. As a result of our fully employed economy, however, the increase in total effective demand resulted mostly in price increases instead of any substantial increase in the output of goods and services.

In addition to the removal of price and wage controls, total tax revenues were decreased and the sale of government bonds declined while bond redemptions increased. We did keep the excess profits tax and rent controls, tightened up on the money supply, and reinstituted credit controls, and the government operated at a surplus in 1947 and 1948. Otherwise the inflationary effects would have been greater.

End of Inflation. Finally, by 1949, total effective demand leveled off and our production capacity caught up with it. Output remained stable, and unemployment reached a postwar high of nearly 4 million. By 1949 we had an ample supply of most types of consumer goods, the demand for business expansion had tapered off, and there was a sizable decrease in foreign demand which mollified inflationary pressures and reduced the CPI for the first time in a decade.

Korean Conflict

In June, 1950, we were enjoying peace and economic prosperity. We were producing at nearly full capacity, and long-awaited consumer goods were readily available. Incomes were at a high level and consumers were spending generously. In addition, many were taking advantage of available credit to increase their purchases of commodities. The price level, which reached a peak in 1948, had stabilized and was beginning to decline slightly — a break for consumers.

With the outbreak of hostilities in Korea on June 25, 1950, the price situation changed quickly. Prices increased more rapidly after the beginning of the Korean Conflict than they had after the beginning of World War II because the former came when we were near the full-employment level. Furthermore, purchases were accelerated as memories of shortages in World War II caused many people to buy and hoard nonperishable goods. With the outbreak in Korea, it was well known that inflationary pressures would increase as our security program expanded. As the total effective demand increased and consumer production gave way to military production, there was a growing gap between the demand for consumer goods and the available supply.

Early Measures to Combat Inflation

To combat the pending inflation, we again increased taxes substantially. We encouraged savings through bond drives, and excess profits taxes were again used to raise funds for the military effort and to combat inflation. We used bank credit controls, reinstituted consumer credit controls, and established controls limiting the purchase of new homes. A controlled materials plan was set up almost immediately. In the early months of the conflict, indirect and voluntary measures were suggested to keep prices down. In an attempt to reduce the level of effective demand, business people, laborers, farmers, and consumers were admonished to exercise restraint. It was hoped that with increased production we could eventually strike a balance which would give adequate support to our military program and still fulfill consumer needs. But in the interim something had to be done to counteract inflation.

Price and Wage Controls

Recognizing the dangers that lay ahead, Congress approved on September 8, 1950, the Defense Production Act, which among other things authorized price and wage controls. The next day President Truman signed an Executive Order establishing the Economic Stabilization Agency (ESA), which was to include an Office of Price Stabilization (OPS), but a Director for OPS was not appointed until November 30, 1950.

In the months immediately following the passage of the Act, the government sought to stabilize prices by general measures and voluntary action. It increased taxes, imposed selective credit restrictions, and established control over the flow of scarce materials. In spite of this, prices continued to increase, especially following the Chinese intervention in Korea in the fall of 1950.

Attempt at Voluntary Pricing Standards. As a result, on December 19, 1950, the Economic Stabilization Agency (ESA) published a set of Voluntary Pricing Standards as a guide to aid sellers who desired to cooperate in a program of voluntary price stabilization. In addition, hundreds of large firms were requested to give advance notice of any intended price increases, and discussions were held among producers of basic commodities to analyze methods of stabilizing prices. By the end of January, 1951, however, the CPI had increased over 7 percent. It became imperative that forceful action be taken. Voluntary, partial, and indirect measures had failed to meet the challenge of inflation.

Compulsory Pricing Regulations. The first major step in the direct fight against inflation was the issuance of the General Ceiling Price Regulation (GCPR) on January 26, 1951. This emergency measure froze prices for all covered commodities and services at the highest level at which they were sold, or offered for sale, during the base period December 19, 1950, to January 25, 1951.

Shortly after GCPR was issued, other ceiling price regulations began to appear. In general, these regulations superseded GCPR. Their purpose was to remove certain commodities and services from pricing under GCPR and bring them under regulations specifically tailored to the market structure of the respective commodity. This proved to be a satisfactory and equitable approach to control.

During a relatively short period, the Office of Price Stabilization (OPS), which had been established upon the creation of the Economic Stabilization Agency, grew from a skeleton crew to a force of more than 12,000 employees. Within six months after a Director of Price Stabilization was appointed, 13 regional and 84 district offices were established. Once started, the OPS did a commendable job of holding prices. During 1951 there was a general leveling off of prices due in large part to price regulations.

In the latter part of 1951 and the first half of 1952, there was considerable softening in our economy. Price declines were in evidence in certain sectors. The defense program was purposely extended over a longer period. However, the heavy inflationary pressures expected in late 1951 and 1952 did not materialize. Shortages predicted did not occur. Strengthening of consumer resistance to high prices, obliteration of scare buying, and accelerated debt repayment mitigated consumer demand. Businesses that had scheduled production of consumer goods at high levels in anticipation of increased demand accumulated large, high-priced inventories. Consequently, curtailment of production and widespread sales pervaded the economy in an attempt to improve inventory positions.

Removal of Controls. Under these conditions it became possible for OPS to begin carrying out its policy of suspending controls where they were no longer required. For emergency purposes, however, each suspension order included a specific "recontrol point." If the price of the suspended commodity reached the recontrol point, the former ceiling again became effective. Fortunately, the inflationary pressures were not too great thereafter, and OPS followed an orderly process of decontrol. Stronger indirect controls, through monetary and fiscal policies, were substituted in many cases for the direct controls. Complete decontrol was accomplished prior to the Korean truce in June, 1953.

Decontrol appeared to be more successful after Korea than it had been after World War II. This may have been due in part to the fact that a more orderly decontrol process on a gradual basis was utilized, but the big factor was the state of the economy at the end of the Korean Conflict compared to World War II. After Korea there was no large pent-up demand for consumer goods since we did not have to resort to rationing under OPS. Second, there was an absence of the large foreign demand since production in other countries of the world had not been interrupted during the Korean Conflict as it had during World War II. Third, businesses generally were not in need of expansion as they were after World War II, since they were able to obtain materials for private investment during the Korean episode. As a result, the price level did not take a jump at the time OPS decontrolled.

Wage-Price Controls, 1971–1974

As we saw in Chapter 2, another bout with inflation commenced in late 1965 and early 1966 and was associated with the war in Vietnam. There was a feeling of confidence on the part of the Administration and many others that we could absorb the increased spending for the escalation of the war, the large outlays for the Great Society programs, the continuation of federal deficits, a record level of private investment, and exuberant consumer demand without having the CPI increase by more than 2 percent annually. Aside from the activities of the Federal Reserve System in tightening the money supply and a few minor measures by the Administration and Congress, very little was done to combat rising prices in the early months of this inflationary period. Subsequent measures, such as removal of the investment tax credit, elimination of accelerated depreciation allowances, imposition of a 10 percent personal and corporate income tax surcharge, balancing of the federal budget, cuts in defense spending, and a tight money supply failed to extinguish the flames of inflation.

Prices rose between 3 and 6 percent annually in the next several years. In the period between 1965 and mid-1971, the CPI rose at an annual rate of 4.9 percent. Eventually unemployment, which had been below 4 percent from late 1965 to 1969, increased to 4.9 percent in 1970, and was at a rate of 6 percent in late 1970 and the first half of 1971.

Phase I

Faced with the dilemma of nagging unemployment on the one hand and inflation on the other, President Nixon, in a dramatic move on August 15, 1971, imposed a 90-day freeze on wages, prices, and rents as part of his New Economic Policy (NEP). The establishment of wage-price controls was a dramatic move, insofar as very few business, labor, or government leaders anticipated such measures. Furthermore, it was a drastic shift in policy by the President and his economic advisers, who on several occasions in the preceding months had indicated that the Administration had no intention of using wage and price controls in its fight against inflation. There were indications, however, that the Administration was moving in that direction. Congress, in April, 1970, had given the President the authority to establish wage and price controls through the passage of the Economic Stabilization Act of 1970. Although the President indicated that he would not use that authority, and did not during the first year of the Act, he encouraged and received a one-year renewal of the Act in April, 1971. On another occasion the President, in an attempt to restrain wage increases and higher prices in the construction industry, appointed a 12-member Construction Industry Stabilization Committee (CISC). Subsequently the President temporarily suspended the Davis-Bacon Act, which requires an employer to pay the prevailing wage as applied to the construction industry on federal construction projects.

The President had also directed his Council of Economic Advisers to prepare and publish quarterly *Inflation Alerts* to "spotlight the significant areas of wage and price increases and objectively analyze their impact on the price level." An interagency Regulation and Purchasing Review Board also was established to determine where federal actions were instrumental in driving up prices and costs. Moreover, a National Commission on Productivity was established to recommend public and private measures that would increase productivity as a means of holding costs and prices down. Also, a few of the President's close advisers, along with an increasing number of business people, labor leaders, economists, and public officials were changing their minds about the use of economic controls. Several who abhorred the idea previously were openly suggesting the implementation of wage and price controls by late 1970 and early 1971. Finally, there was increasing political pressure for the President to do something about the problems of inflation and nagging unemployment. Although a Cost of Living Council was created as a policy-determining body, the wage-price freeze measures were implemented through the existing Office of Emergency Preparedness (OEP), a nationwide organization designed to meet national emergencies or national disasters. The OEP was delegated authority to administer and enforce the freeze. It was assisted in interpreting and enforcing the freeze regulations by the Internal Revenue Service, Department of Justice attorneys, and Agriculture Department field offices.

At the end of 90 days, the freeze, subsequently labeled Phase I of the President's NEP, was replaced by Phase II, which established compulsory wage, price, and rent controls for an indefinite period of time.

Phase II

As a prelude to Phase II, the President announced that a program would be developed to reduce the rate of inflation to a 2–3 percent range by the end of 1972. The Cost of Living Council, composed of high government officials, was delegated the responsibility of establishing broad goals, determining coverage, and directing enforcement of the control program.

The two principal agencies created to develop standards and render decisions on all changes in prices, rents, wages, and other forms of compensation were the Price Commission, composed of seven public members, and a tripartite Pay Board, composed of 15 members divided equally among business, labor, and public representatives. The existing Construction Industry Stabilization Committee was placed under the Pay Board, and the National Commission on Productivity was enlarged and given an advisory role to the Cost of Living Council. Other advisory committees were formed, as shown in Figure 3-1 on page 60. Enforcement of the program was to come through the field offices of the Internal Revenue Service and the field offices of the Department of Agriculture Stabilization and Conservation Service. Existing government agencies and services were used as much as possible in the endeavor to avoid creating a more elaborate and costly type of enforcement and structure such as prevailed with price control programs of World War II and the Korean Conflict.

Members of the Price Commission and the Pay Board assumed their duties in October, 1971, to be ready for action when Phase II took effect at the expiration of the 90-day freeze in mid-November, 1971.

Pricing Standards. With the inauguration of Phase II the Price Commission reiterated the Cost of Living Council's disinflationary policy and announced a goal of holding the rate of average price increases for the economy "to no more than 2.5 percent per year." The Commission set forth the general rule that no price could be increased beyond the ceiling price established by the price freeze, except in accordance with Price Commission regulations. These regulations permitted manufacturers and service organizations to increase prices only to reflect cost increases since their last price increase occuring after January 1, 1971. Moreover, cost increases were to be reduced to reflect any increases in productivity. Such price increases could not have the effect of increasing the firm's profit margin above the margin prevailing in the base period. For purposes of the regulation, the base period was defined as the highest average of two of the firm's three fiscal years ending prior to August 15, 1971. Retailers and wholesalers were permitted to increase prices consistent with (a) maintaining their customary percentage markup equal to or less than that prevailing during the 90-day freeze period or during the firm's last fiscal year ending August 15, 1971, and (b) maintaining the before-tax profit margin of the firm equal to or less than that prevailing in the 3-year base period previously cited.

Landlords were permitted to increase residential rents by 2.5 percent annually above the base rental upon 30-day notice to the tenant. In addition, the

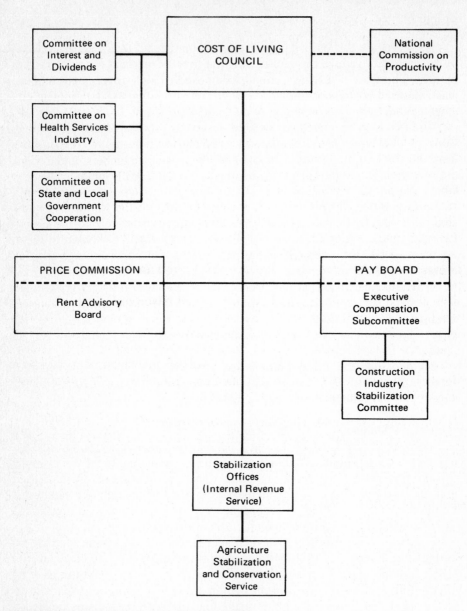

SOURCE: *Economic Report of the President*, 1972.

Figure 3-1 **POST-FREEZE ORGANIZATION**

landlord could increase rent share by the dollar-and-cents amount of the increase in state and local government taxes, along with fees and charges for services allowable to the individual unit. Monthly rents could also be increased by 1.5 percent of the total cost of major capital improvements made after August 15, 1971.

Other price regulations were published for such items as fire and casualty insurance, public utilities, health care services, and fees and charges of federal, state, and local governments. In addition, special regulations were established for firms showing losses or low profits.

Wage Regulations. Early in November, 1971, the Pay Board adopted wage standards to become effective at the beginning of Phase II. These standards were applied to all employees other than those receiving less than the federal minimum wage and federal employees. The guidelines established three provisions: (a) considering the 3 percent annual increase in productivity per worker in the American economy and the likely 2.5 percent increase in the cost of living, the Pay Board initiated a standard of a permissible 5.5 percent annual increase in wages and salary; (b) existing contracts and pay practices established prior to November 14, 1971, would be allowed to operate, subject to challenge by five members of the Pay Board; (c) retroactive payment for wage increments that were scheduled to go into effect, but did not because of the freeze, would be permitted only upon approval of the Board.

In mid-November, however, the Pay Board announced that certain exceptions would be made to the 5.5 percent standard. Exceptions up to 7 percent were permitted primarily where tandem wage relationships existed. Tandem relationships are those in which pay rates for certain employees are based on rates previously received by other groups of workers or firms. This provision allowed a "catch-up" philosophy for those workers involved in a tandem relationship. Exceptions were to be permitted until March 31, 1972, only. Thereafter the 5.5 percent standard would prevail.

Application of the Standards. For enforcement purposes firms were classified according to sales and numbers of employees. Tier I firms, those with sales in excess of $100 million annually or those with 5,000 or more employees, would have to give prenotification of proposed price and wage changes to the Price Commission or the Pay Board, whichever the case may be. Furthermore, these firms were required to submit quarterly information on prices, costs, and profits to the Price Commission. Tier II firms, those with sales of $50 million to $100 million or 1,000 to 5,000 employees, did not have to give prenotification of price and wage changes, but they had to report such changes to the respective board. In addition, Tier II firms, just like Tier I firms, were required to file quarterly reports on prices, costs, and profits to the Price Commission. Tier III firms, those with sales of less than $50 million or those with less than 1,000 employees, were not required to report any actions to the respective board or file quarterly reports with the Price Commission. Tier III firms, however, were admonished to make price and wage changes only in accordance with the regulations and were informed that they would be subject to monitoring and spot checks by the boards. Some prices and wages, such as raw agricultural products and seafoods, postal service, life insurance premiums, tuition fees, and securities were exempted from direct controls. Exemptions were made because the prices of these and certain other commodities and services were either insignificant to the overall problem of inflation or they were subject to other types of controls.

Effectiveness of Phase II. The Economic Stabilization Act was amended and extended for another year in April, 1972. Among the amendments was a provision that permitted pay increases scheduled to take effect after the freeze to be paid unless they were "unreasonably inconsistent" with Pay Board standards. A second important amendment removed employer contributions to group insurance and disability and health plans from the definition of "wages and salaries" for control purposes. Finally, there was to be no limitation to wage increases that could be granted to the working poor and those whose earnings were substandard.

In the early months of Phase II members of the control agencies were confronted with a number of problems and spent much time interpreting and clarifying regulations and processing complaints. Just when things seemed to be operating smoothly, a major difference in policy developed on the Pay Board. This resulted in a permanent walkout by four of the five labor members of the Board. Subsequently the Pay Board purposely reduced the number of business members and operated with a smaller total membership.

By mid-1972 the Cost of Living Council had removed millions of small firms and employers from wage and price controls. Part of the reason for this move was to free some of the 3,000 or more members of the administrative staff of the control program to permit them to devote more time and effort to the problems, issues, and complaints regarding larger firms.

To some degree, the effectiveness of the control program can be ascertained by looking at price level statistics. During the six months prior to the freeze the CPI increased at a rate of 4.5 percent. In the five months after the freeze the CPI rose 2.2 percent, and during the 3-month freeze of Phase I, the CPI rose at an annual rate of 1.6 percent. The price level for 1972, during which price controls existed for the entire year, increased 3.4 percent, as shown in Table 3-1.

On the first anniversary of the freeze, a number of comments and much analysis was generated by the year-old, wage-price control program. By and large, most comments were favorable regarding the effectiveness of the controls. Many high officials within the Administration, business people, and economists, including several who were originally against the use of controls, admitted that the control program had been successful in limiting inflation. Several were concerned, however, about the fact that unemployment was still at a 5.6 percent level. Although there was much speculation about the date when controls would end, no one in authority would hazard a guess.

Discussion centered around what Phase III would bring. Would it be a continuation of Phase II, complete or partial decontrol of compulsory wage and price standards, or the adoption of an official "incomes policy" for the United States?

Phase III

In January, 1973, after commenting favorably on the results of Phase II in stabilizing prices and wages, the President in a surprise move announced the

Table 3-1

CHANGES IN THE CPI AND UNEMPLOYMENT BEFORE AND AFTER THE GUIDEPOSTS AND BEFORE AND AFTER PRICE AND WAGE CONTROLS, 1960–1977

Year	Total Employment	Unemployment	Rate of Unemployment	CPI (1967 = 100)	Rate of Inflation*
1960	65,778	3,852	5.5	88.7	—
1961	65,746	4,714	6.7	89.6	1.0
1962	66.702	3,911	5.5	90.6	1.1
1963	67,762	4,070	5.7	91.7	1.0
1964	69,305	3,786	5.2	92.9	1.3
1965	71,088	3,366	4.5	94.5	1.7
1966	72,895	2,875	3.8	97.2	2.9
1967	74,372	2,775	3.8	100.0	2.9
1968	75,920	2,817	3.6	104.2	4.7
1969	77,902	2,813	3.5	109.8	6.1
1970	78,627	4,088	4.9	116.3	5.5
1971	79,120	4,993	5.9	121.3	3.4
1972	81,702	4,840	5.6	125.3	3.4
1973	84,409	4,304	4.9	133.1	8.8
1974	85,936	5,076	5.6	147.7	12.2
1975	84,783	7,830	8.5	161.2	7.0
1976	87,485	7,288	7.7	170.5	4.8
1977	90,546	6,855	7.0	181.5	6.8

SOURCE: *Economic Report of the President*, 1978, and *Economic Indicators* (January, 1978).

*December to December

immediate termination of compulsory controls and the implementation of Phase III of his New Economic Policy, which in effect reestablished voluntary guideposts for price and wage increases. The guidepost figures used during that time were 2.5 percent and 5.5 percent annually for prices and wages, respectively.

Phase IV

The removal of compulsory Phase II controls proved to be premature, however. During the first five months after decontrol, the CPI rose at an annual rate of nearly 9 percent. Consequently, on June 13, 1973, the President declared a 60-day freeze on prices. Wages were not affected at this time. Instead of ending the freeze on all goods at the end of the 60-day period, prices were unfrozen selectively, and Phase IV controls were imposed on various categories of goods and services at different times before and after the 60-day period.

Again large firms were required to give a 30-day prenotification of price increases. Unlike Phase II, however, firms did not have to wait for approval by the Cost of Living Council before putting such increases into effect. But the Council had authority to delay any price increases indefinitely, and it reserved the right to reexamine prices at any time. The new base period established was the fiscal quarter prior to January 12, 1973, the date of decontrol of Phase II. Price increases equal to dollar cost increases subsequent to the base period were to be permitted by Phase IV. No allowance was to be made for a profit mark-up on these cost increases. Controls were imposed on an industry-by-industry basis, thus providing more flexibility than was available under Phase II. At the time of imposition of Phase IV, several high Administration officials indicated that they hoped controls could be removed by the end of 1973. Most of the controls were removed by early 1974 and the price-wage controls program came to an end. Unfortunately the CPI rose 8.8 percent in 1973. (If the CPI were measured on a year to year average instead of using a December to December basis, the price increase would be 6.2 percent for 1973.)

Toward the end of 1974 the President established a Council on Wage and Price Stability. It served primarily in a watchdog capacity in an effort to moderate inflation, as it could challenge excessive price and wage hikes. The Council's effectiveness, however, was hampered by its lack of authority and its inability to subpoena company records.

Effectiveness of Compulsory Controls

There is little doubt that compulsory wage and price controls are effective in slowing the rate of inflation. This can be seen from the record during World War II, the Korean Conflict, and the 1971–1973 control period. It should be evident, however, that controls tend to suppress inflation rather than cure it. They hold the lid on prices but do not remove the cause or causes of inflation. Other measures are necessary if the causes of inflation are to be eliminated. Moreover, wage-price controls, by aborting the rationing function of the pricing system, may cause distortions in the production and flow of goods and services, resulting in shortages of materials and a scarcity of skilled labor. This is why there may be a rapid acceleration in prices with the removal of controls unless prices are decontrolled selectively.

To those who suggest that compulsory price controls are not worth the cost of implementing them, all one has to do is look again at the record. When the consumer price index rises one percent it costs American consumers more than $12 billion annually. Thus, if the controls can prevent the CPI from rising even fractionally it can cover the budget cost of a control agency. There are, however, other hidden costs in a controls program, such as the restriction on economic freedom and distortions in the marketplace, that are difficult to measure.

INCOMES POLICY

As should be obvious by now, the United States has been flirting with an incomes policy for 15 years or more. During this time the concept has moved from obscurity to the forefront of economic debate. In the interim a number of foreign nations have adopted incomes policies as a means of limiting inflation. As stated at the beginning of this chapter, an incomes policy is a broad set of voluntary, quantitative guidelines that apply to prices, wages, and other forms of income, such as rents and interest, and that may or may not carry some type of economic penalty against nonconformists.

Wage and Price Guideposts

After several years of relative price stability during the 1950s, some price unrest was becoming apparent in our economy in the latter half of 1961. In seeking the continuation of price stability, President Kennedy, in his 1962 *Economic Report*, established a set of voluntary wage and price guideposts. If accepted by the major firms in the economy and in the collective bargaining power centers, it would do much, according to the President, to restrain upward pressures on the price level. As a guide for noninflationary wage behavior, the rate of increase in wage rates (including fringe benefits) in each industry was to be equated with the national trend in overall productivity increase. Although general acceptance of the guideposts would maintain the stability of labor cost per unit of output for the economy as a whole, it would not stabilize labor cost per unit for individual firms or industries. Based upon the fact that the average productivity per worker in our economy increased about 3 percent annually, the guideposts initially recommended that wage increases be held to 3 percent each year. This would allow the increase in wage cost to be absorbed out of rising productivity without necessitating a price increase. The guideposts did have some flexibility insofar as they suggested that any firm whose gain in productivity per worker-hour was more than the guidepost figure should hold its wage increase to 3 percent and give consumers some benefit by reducing prices. On the other hand, it recommended that any firm whose increase in productivity was less than the guidepost figure could grant a 3 percent wage increase but offset this with an increase in prices. Subsequently, using a 5-year average, the guidepost figure was raised to 3.2 percent.

The guideposts, of course, stirred up considerable controversy in both wage and price circles. In many firms and industries where the rate of productivity was less than the national average, the guideposts were used by labor unions as a basis for a wage increase higher than the productivity rate increase within the firm or industry. In other firms or industries where the productivity rate exceeded the national average productivity increase, management often used the guidepost in an effort to limit the amount of a wage increase to 3 percent, even though they might have been able to afford higher wage increases. Another complaint was the fact that the guideposts tended to freeze labor's share of the national income.

Although the concept of price and wage guideposts seemed to be pushed out of the limelight by the emphasis on the tax cut in the 1963 *Economic Report of the President* and by the poverty package in the 1964 *Report*, the guideposts were emphasized again by President Johnson and his Economic Advisers in the spring and summer of 1964. The president's personal representative discussed with industry members the importance of noninflationary wage agreements between labor and management, especially in the automobile and other basic industries. Subsequently, however, the AFL-CIO stated officially and publicly that it did not intend to be limited by the wage guidepost in seeking wage increases during that year, and the president of the United Auto Workers stated that since the productivity increase in the automobile industry was much above the national average, the union was not going to limit its wage demands to the average of 3.2 percent. About the same time, steel companies were talking about the need for a price increase to offset some of their increasing costs. At that time President Johnson publicly warned that any increase in steel prices "would strongly conflict with our national interest in price stability."

With the return of stronger inflationary pressures in 1966, some delicate situations and open confrontations regarding the voluntary acceptance of the guideposts developed between the White House and/or the President's Council of Economic Advisers on the one hand and large industries and powerful unions on the other. Consequently, in 1967 the use of a specific guidepost figure was deemphasized, although the guidepost concept was still retained. By 1968 the guideposts were pretty well shattered as both labor unions and business firms posted wage and price increases that were substantially beyond the guidepost figures.

With continually rising prices, however, there were renewed interest in the guidepost concept during 1969 and 1970. Although President Nixon as late as the spring of 1971 had avoided the use of guideposts, Congress did in 1970 give the President authority to impose wage and price controls. During the period 1970–1971, when the CPI was still rising 5 percent or more annually, several business groups, labor leaders, government officials, and members of Congress were urging the reinstitution of some form of restraint, such as voluntary wage and price guideposts, the implementation of an incomes policy, or the adoption of compulsory wage and price controls. As we have previously seen, the President, in a surprising change of policy in August, 1971, declared a 90-day freeze on all prices and wages.

Effectiveness of the Guideposts

From all indications the voluntary wage-price guideposts of the 1960s were not a great success. Although there was general conformity to the guideposts during the early years, 1962–1964, there was an absence of inflationary pressures during this period of nagging unemployment. How much the price stability of this period was due to the presence of the guideposts and how much was due to the unemployment and competitive conditions of the economy is nearly impossible to ascertain. With the return of full employment and the emergence of excessive demand, conformity to the guideposts diminished considerably. In spite of the jawboning of the Administration with both management and labor, wage and price increases in major industries began to exceed the guidepost limits. In the absence of compulsory measures to command adherence, the Administration was not in a position to hold the line against these wage and price increases. With price increases nearing 3 percent annually in 1966 and 1967, it became more and more difficult to retain acceptance of the 3.2 percent guidepost figure for wage increases. This, in effect, forced the Administration to abandon the numbers in the guideposts in 1968, even though it retained the guidepost concept. Movement in the CPI during the years of the guideposts is shown in Table 3-1 on page 63, along with the rates of unemployment.

Although the evidence does not seem to indicate much success for the guideposts, their existence may have moderated the price and wage increases that would have taken place without them. Furthermore, jawboning efforts of the Administration were successful in preventing some price and wage increases from taking place at all and at times even resulted in partial rollbacks of announced increases.

A Wage-Price Incomes Policy

An incomes policy is generally broader than a wage-price guidepost concept insofar as an incomes policy is not limited to just wages but applies to other forms of income as well, such as interest and profits.

It has often been suggested that we should adopt a formal incomes policy, similar to the wage-price guideposts, and limit wage increases to the rise in productivity per worker. In such a case, however, the limitation would also apply in some manner to other forms of income. Conformity to the incomes policy could be either on a voluntary or a compulsory basis. Since the effectiveness of the former is questionable, especially when strong inflationary pressures exist in the economy, compulsory enforcement is almost a necessity if an incomes policy is going to meet its objectives.

Theoretically the rate of wage increases is limited to the rate of increases in productivity per worker-hour and the cost of the wage increase can be absorbed out of the increased productivity. Consequently, per unit cost will not rise and there will be no need to increase prices. Furthermore, since labor costs are only a portion of total cost, some of the productivity gain would be available for increased profit and/or lower prices. This type of formula appears simple enough, but when figures are attached, the implementation of such as incomes policy can be fraught with difficulties.

First of all, a question arises regarding the calculation of the annual increase in productivity per worker-hour. Under the guideposts of the mid-1960s, initially an increase of 3 percent was used. After a few years, based on a 5-year average, this was adjusted upward to 3.2 percent annually. Subsequently the figure was to be raised to 3.5 percent. But the use of this figure was postponed because of the strong inflationary pressures in the economy at the time and because the Council of Economic Advisers thought the 3.5 percent figure to be a bit beyond the long-run average growth in productivity per worker-hour.

In seeking a proper measure of productivity, data can be found that measures the overall increase in productivity for the economy by comparing the real GNP to total employment. A second productivity figure is that based on the increase in productivity in the private economy only. Still another measures the productivity per production worker. If desired, either changes in productivity per worker-hour in all manufacturing industries or figures for select industries can be used. The average increase in productivity per farm worker also is attainable, as well as an average for nonfarm industries. If a single figure were to be used for the economy as a whole, however, it would be best to use data that measure the overall increase in production for the economy, based on real GNP and total employment.

Even if a single productivity figure were agreed upon, other problems would arise. If wages were permitted to rise at the rate of the national average increase in productivity per worker-hour, what about the firm that has a productivity increase less than the national average? If it granted such an increase in wages, the cost would not be absorbed through increased productivity. Consequently, this could cause prices to rise. If the firm or industry, however, were not in a position to raise prices because of competitive factors or otherwise, the wage increase could put a squeeze on profits. This, in turn, could have harmful effects on output and employment. On the other hand, those firms that had a higher increase in productivity per worker than the national average, but held wage increases to the national average, would experience a substantial increase in profit. This would not be the case if they were to reduce prices to give the consumer some of the benefits of the high increase in productivity in that industry. But what assurance is there that the firm or industry would do this in the absence of compulsory measures?

Some unions and others, too, claim that using a uniform productivity figure, such as 3.5 percent, discriminates against the more efficient firms and their workers, and in effect rewards the inefficient by permitting them to have the same wage increase as more efficient workers. Another concern of unions is that wage increases based on the use of a national average increase in productivity per worker-hour freezes them into a fixed share of the national income. Another objection is that it limits their power of collective bargaining.

As a result of these and other difficulties related to a single or uniform figure for all workers, it has been suggested that multiple productivity figures be used. Even here a question arises as to whether productivity figures should be based on broad industrial categories, such as manufacturing, mining, and transportation; on industries, such as steel, autos, and textiles; or on the performance of individual firms. If either of the two broader categories were used, some of the same problems would arise that are related to the use of a uniform productivity figure. On the other hand, if the productivity of each individual firm were used, it would require a larger and more complex mechanism to implement the system. Furthermore, in some industries, especially service industries, it is difficult to measure productivity increases. Even in some industries where productivity can be measured readily, some firms, especially smaller ones, may have no measure of the average productivity per worker.

In the absence of direct compulsory controls, obtaining general acceptance and conformity to a wage-price incomes policy could very well be difficult. Generally recommended is a National Incomes Board, similar to the Cost of Living Council, through which all requests for wage and price increases would be filed. Upon receipt of an application, the Incomes Board would analyze the request and then make its findings known to the applicants as well as to the general public. In the absence of compulsory regulations, public rebuke may help deter some violations of the guidelines. More commonly, however, tax measures are recommended as a means of obtaining conformity to the guidelines.

A Marketplace Incomes Policy

It has been contended by many economists that inflation, particularly cost-push and structural inflation, results from imperfections in the marketplace. According to this view, instead of having freely competitive wage and price markets, there exists a considerable amount of labor monopoly which can greatly influence wage determination, as well as market conditions of oligopoly and monopoly which can lead to administered pricing. Consequently, commodity prices and wages are not determined completely by supply and demand. The supporters of this theory contend that we should have an incomes policy that would eliminate or prevent market imperfections and promote a more competitive economy. Such a marketplace incomes policy would make the economy less susceptible to cost-push and structural inflation.

The remedy, then, is to take appropriate steps to reduce or eliminate the power of unions to exact from management wage gains that are in excess of those that would be attainable in a competitive market, or at least those wage gains that are in excess of the increase in productivity of the workers. For this purpose it is suggested that, among other measures, any special privileges to labor unions that tilt bargaining power in their favor be reduced, industry-wide bargaining be eliminated, the union shop be restricted, compulsory arbitration be imposed, minimum wage laws be modified, and the right of workers to collect unemployment benefits (as permitted in some states) and welfare benefits while on strike be eliminated.

On the other hand, it is suggested that in the commodities market the oligopolistic and monopolistic powers of business firms be lessened or restricted to prevent them from administering prices that are above what they would be under more competitive conditions. This would involve such measures as more vigorous application of antitrust laws, applying public utility regulations to more industries, placing fewer restrictions on imports, and a general strengthening of competition.

Other measures that would be helpful in improving competition in both the factor and commodities markets include the establishment of national and less restrictive building codes, the suspension or amendment of the Davis-Bacon Act, stimulation of plant and equipment modernization through accelerated depreciation and tax credits, freer admission into skilled worker apprenticeship programs, and broader federally financed worker training and retraining programs.

Many advocates of a marketplace incomes policy contend that a wage-price incomes policy cannot be effective for any substantial period of time unless corollary measures to restrict labor and management monopolistic powers in the market are reduced or eliminated. But the presence of a marketplace incomes policy may avoid the need for a wage-price incomes policy, except in the case of severe demand-pull inflationary pressures.

The primary effectiveness of either a wage-price incomes policy or a marketplace incomes policy would be against cost-push and structural inflation. They would be limited in their effectiveness against demand-pull inflation. Consequently, either type of incomes policy generally envisions accompanying conventional monetary, fiscal, and psychological measures designed to limit demand-pull inflation.

Tax Incentive Incomes Policy (TIP)

Another form of incomes policy that is receiving wide consideration among economists is the tax incentive, or tax-based, incomes policy (TIP). TIP proposals suggest a tie-in between the corporate tax structure and wage rate increases of the firm. A normal wage increase, perhaps in line with the average increase in productivity per worker-hour of 3 percent, would be established for the economy. If a firm increased its wages equal to or less than the established rate, it would have no effect on the firm's income tax rate. A wage increase higher than the established rate, however, would be subject to a surtax. Suppose a firm's income tax for 1979 amounted to $8,000,000 and that a firm's average wage payment, based on the number of its employees and its total wage bill, was $10,000 for 1978. If the firm's average wage payment in 1979 was $10,300, which would equal the national norm of a 3 percent increase, its tax rate would be unaffected. If the firm increased its average wage payment in 1979 to $10,700, a 7 percent increase, however, it would be subject to a surtax of, say, ten percent. In such a case its tax payment would rise to $8,800,000 for 1979.

It is proposed that the surtax penalty be strong and progressive enough to discourage firms from granting wage-salary concessions higher than the established rate. Some plans suggest that a firm holding its wage rate increase below the established norm be eligible for an income tax rebate. Some variations recommend also that in order to prevent a shifting of the surtax to the consumer, and to prevent any national inflationary effect, that a reduction be made in the basic corporate tax scale equal to the total or net tax collected.

Some proponents of TIP suggest a 5 percent annual wage increase as the norm. This would allow for a 3 percent increase in line with the average national increase in productivity per worker-hour plus a 2 percent cost of living allowance (COLA) to offset the effect of a so-called normal increase in the CPI.

TIP has several advantages over compulsory wage-price controls and voluntary wage-price guideposts. It does not saddle the firm with rigid controls. It permits freedom to raise wages as much as desired provided the firm is willing to pay the surtax penalty. In this way it acts much like a tax on pollution. On the other hand, it is more enforceable and certain than voluntary wage-price guideposts. Moreover, TIP can be incorporated within the current tax structure and it does not require much in the way of additional record keeping. It is estimated to be less costly than effective compulsory wage-price controls. One plan placed the cost of implementing and maintaining the plan at one billion dollars annually.

A major weakness of TIP is that most plans provide no direct penalty for price increases. It is conceivable for a firm to limit its wage rate increase but then raise its prices. Although proponents of the various TIP plans claim that it is anti-inflationary and not anti-labor, many national labor leaders object to the concept. They do not like the idea that a firm would be subject to a penalty for raising wages above the norm or eligible for an income tax rebate for limiting its wage and salary increases. Moreover, they have some strong objections to the establishment of a national norm for wage increases.

Incomes Policies Elsewhere

The concept of an incomes policy is not new. It has been tried in a number of other nations during the past few decades. The British experience started shortly after World War II, continuing intermittently since then.

The seriousness of inflation and aggravation of a balance of payment deficit led in 1962 to the publication of a White Paper favoring an incomes policy. Subsequently a National Incomes Commission was established and a target guideline of a 2–2.5 percent annual increase for wages and other incomes was proposed. The Commission was subsequently replaced with a National Board for Prices and Incomes (PIB), the guideline figure was raised to 3.5 percent, prenotification of wage and price increases was recommended, an advanced warning system which afforded the PIB the opportunity to analyze and even temporarily delay wage and price increases was instituted, a wage and price freeze eventually was imposed, and labor and management participation and support was sought. In some years wage increases ran above the guidelines, however. In 1968, for example, following the wage-price freeze, average hourly earnings increased by 8 percent.

The record of the sixties indicated that the British incomes policy met with limited success in its task of stabilizing prices. In the early 1970s the incomes policy in Britain was in a state of suspension. But after discussions were held at high economic and political levels, the incomes policy was reinstituted in November of 1972. British inflationary rates of 9.3 percent in 1973, double-digit inflation in 1974, and a 24 percent increase in prices in 1975, however, indicate the lack of cooperation and ineffectiveness of their incomes policy. In 1976 the trade unions did agree to attempt to hold wage increases to 4.5 percent.

The Canadian experience with an incomes policy was more akin to that of the United States, primarily because of the similiarity of the economies. It, too, began in the 1960s when the Economic Council of Canada commissioned a study of income policies of other nations.

In June, 1969, a Prices and Incomes Commission was established. Instead of arbitrarily setting guidelines, the Commission conducted negotiations with interested groups, such as labor, business, and the professions, in an attempt to establish meaningful guidelines for wages and prices. But its efforts proved to be futile when national labor leaders opted against participating in the Commission's attempt to establish quantitative, yet voluntary, guidelines.

The Commission then shifted to a more atomized approach without specific guidelines. This required considerable jawboning with members of individual industries and firms, but again success was less than desirable. In 1970 the Commission began again to establish a uniform guideline, recommending a 6 percent annual increase for wages and salaries. This figure was arrived at by using a 2.5 percent increase in productivity per worker, plus a 3.5 percent rate of inflation. Actual increases in income during 1970 amounted to 8–9 percent, and resistance to the guidelines from organized labor and the provincial governments became stronger. With the absence of labor participation and support of the guidelines, business also decided to reject the guidelines. By January, 1971, the guidelines concept for all practical purposes was abandoned. Although the inflation rate in Canada was under 5 percent in 1972, it rose 7.6 percent in 1973 and 11 percent in both 1974 and 1975.

A number of other nations have also tried incomes policies. The Netherlands, for example, has had more success than most other nations with its incomes policy because its citizens are more agreeable to economic planning. The Dutch exert considerable direct pressure and control over labor and management regarding price and wage changes. In France an incomes policy has been tied to the economic planning system during the past decade or more. During most of that time, however, wage and price increases generally have exceeded the guideline targets by noticeable amounts. Furthermore, difficulty in obtaining cooperation from labor and mangement regarding wage policies has led to an emphasis on price control measures. In spite of the guideposts, however, the rate of inflation in France averaged 10 percent or more annually during the period 1970–1975. Austria, which has been receiving close cooperation between labor and management in regard to its incomes policy, has experienced an inflation rate in excess of 7 percent over the past few years. Sweden has had a checkered record of implementation and success with an incomes policy over the past two decades. Wage freezes, price stops, guidelines, and jawboning have also been tried in Norway, Iceland, West Germany, and Italy.

INDEXATION

In recent years indexation has been suggested as a means of alleviating the adverse impact of inflation. *Indexation* is a process of linking the amount of money to be paid on a contract to some specific price index. Indexation can be applied individually to specific contracts, to categories of contracts, or to the economy as a whole. The idea of indexation is not new. In fact, it was used on a minor scale in some of the early American colonies. Some of the classical economists of the last century advocated its use in some form. In the early 1940s a number of economists supported indexation of government savings bonds.

In recent history indexation in some form has been utilized in France, China, Israel, Finland, Brazil, and on a limited basis, in Great Britain and the United States. Indexation of bank deposits, for example, was started 25 years ago in China and later adopted in France and Finland. In the United States indexation took a major step after World War II when management and labor in the auto industry negotiated an "escalator clause" linking autoworkers' wages to the Consumer Price Index (CPI). Today nearly 8 million employees are covered by escalator clauses in wage agreements. In addition, the pensions of retired federal employees and military personnel are tied somewhat to the CPI, and since 1975 Social Security payments of 30 million persons have been indexed. The federal food stamp and school lunch programs are currently indexed to the CPI. It is estimated that there are approximately 50 million persons in the U.S. economy who now have some form of income indexed to the price level.

Although several current proponents of indexation admit that it would not stop inflation, they believe that the adoption of widespread indexation would remove a number of the side effects on output and unemployment caused by current measures to combat inflation. By and large, those favoring indexation of some type reason that it would remove the uncertainties relating to the real value of future income by reducing the lag of money wages behind price and cost increases, offsetting the adverse effects of income redistribution caused by inflation, eliminating some of the uncertainties involved in business decision making, and stabilizing the real cost of doing business.

Professor Milton Friedman, an outspoken advocate of indexation, recommends a comprehensive system of indexation for the total economy. He would index wages, interest payments, long-term debt obligations, bank deposits, government bonds, and numerous contracts that have a time dimension. Others have suggested less comprehensive plans. These include indexation for such items as insurance premiums and benefits, mortgages, pensions, and even alimony. A number of advocates, including some members of Congress, recommend the use of indexation for the payment of personal income taxes, since a 10 percent rise in money wages generates on average a 15 percent increase in tax payments.

Just as there are a number of arguments for indexation, so too are there many arguments against tying most contracts to the cost of living index. Most opponents of widespread indexation see it as a built-in, or automatic, inflationary process. In their minds it would establish a continuous cost-price spiral. Price increases would beget wage and cost increases, which would further increase prices. Others look upon indexation as surrendering to inflation. Some critics maintain that it would discourage the fight against inflation. It is also contended that unanticipated inflation encourages workers to view their money wage increases as increases in real income, which induces them to spend. This advantage would be lost through indexation. Critics also suggest that indexation impairs the normal function and operation of the pricing system in allocating labor and resources and rationing goods and services. If all prices and costs change proportionally, it would remove the opportunity for relative changes which bring about shifts in the allocations of labor and resources and the rationing of goods and services. Finally, both proponents and opponents of indexation have some question as to whether the currently structured CPI is an adequate measure for widespread indexation. There is much concern that as presently structured the CPI is too narrow in scope.

CONCLUSION

Based upon our experience in the United States with voluntary wage-price guideposts and the experience of several foreign countries with formal incomes policies, several conclusions can be drawn. First, the probability of success for an incomes policy is better in an economy at less than full employment than it is in a fully employed economy. Second, there is a good probability that an incomes policy, especially one of a voluntary nature, will collapse in a fully employed economy with strong inflationary pressures. Third, an incomes policy is not a substitute for other, more appropriate measures for limiting demand-pull inflation. Fourth, an incomes policy is not likely to be successful unless accompanied by appropriate monetary, fiscal, and psychological measures. Fifth, an incomes policy has more opportunity for success and is more effective when there is a widespread structure of organized labor and management, and both groups are supportive of the objectives of the incomes policy. Sixth, an incomes policy is likely to be more effective if applied to all types of income (wages, rents, interest, and profits), as well as prices. Seventh, the chances for success with an incomes policy are better and the program will likely receive greater support when productivity is increasing sufficiently to provide additional real income in the form of wages and profits. Eighth, the threat of foreign competition, especially through imports, will enhance support and the probable success of an incomes policy. Finally, timing is an essential feature in the success of an incomes policy. It must be implemented at an appropriate time from economic, political, and psychological points of views. Individuals, labor unions, businesses, and public officials must be in a frame of mind to accept and support the incomes policy guidelines. If they are not in such a frame of mind, the program will likely be doomed to failure.

MAJOR ISSUES

1. Do you think the time is appropriate for the adoption of an incomes policy in the United States?
2. Do you think that an incomes policy, if adopted, should be compulsory or voluntary?
3. Evaluate the merits of a wage-price incomes policy versus a marketplace incomes policy.
4. Do you think that wage-price guidepost figures, if established, should be uniform and based on a national average, or should the figures be based on industry averages?
5. Should the United States adopt a policy of indexation?

SUBISSUES

1. Do you prefer direct and compulsory wage-price controls to an incomes policy? Why or why not?
2. Evaluate the success or failure of the wage-price controls of 1971–1974. Do you think they were successful in fulfilling their objectives?
3. What type of economic penalties would you recommend for violations of a voluntary incomes policy?
4. Do you favor a TIP program to combat inflation? Why?

SELECTED READINGS

Cagen, Phillip. *The Hydra-Headed Monster — The Problem of Inflation in the United States*. Washington: The American Enterprise Institute for Public Policy, Domestic Affairs Study No. 26 (October, 1974).

"Dr. McCracken on Price-Wage Controls." *Economic Education Bulletin*, American Institute for Economic Research (January, 1972).

Economic Report of the President. Washington: U.S. Government Printing Office, 1966–1978.

Essays on Inflation and Indexation. Washington: The American Enterprise Institute for Public Policy, 1974.

Ferge, Edgar L., and Douglas K. Pearce. "The Wage-Price Control Experiment — Did It Work?" *Challenge* (July–August, 1973).

Haberler, Gottfried. *Incomes Policy and Inflation: Some Further Reflections*. The American Enterprise Institute, Reprint No. 5 (October, 1972).

Humphrey, Thomas M. "The Concept of Indexation in the History of Economic Thought." *Economic Review*. Federal Reserve Bank of Richmond (November–December, 1974).

"Incomes Policies: What Europe Learned." *Business Week* (November 13, 1971).

Kaplan, Robert S. *Indexing Social Security*. Washington: American Enterprise Institute for Public Policy Research, 1977.

Kohlmeier, Louis. "Wage and Price Surveillance Under Carter." *Financier* (March, 1977).

Lerner, Abba. "Stagflation — Its Cause and Cure." *Challenge* (September/October, 1977).

McCracken, Gardner. "Okun's New Tax-Based Incomes-Policy Proposal." *Economic Outlook U.S.A.* (Winter, 1978).

McCracken, Paul W. "Two Years and Four Phases Later." *The Wall Street Journal*, August 13, 1973.

Mullineaux, Donald J. "Inflation Insurance: An 'Escalator Clause' for Securities." *Business Review*, Federal Reserve Bank of Philadelphia (October, 1972).

"Resolving the Enigma of Inflation." *First Chicago World Report* (November–December, 1977).

Schiff, Eric. *Incomes Policies Abroad*. Washington: The American Enterprise Institute, Special Analysis Number 3 (April, 1971).

——————. *Incomes Policies Abroad: Part II*. Washington: The American Enterprise Institute, Special Analysis Number 27 (September, 1972).

Shanahan, Eileen (Moderator). *Indexation and Inflation*. Washington: The American Enterprise Institute for Public Policy Research (July, 1974).

Stahl, Sheldon W. "Incomes Policies — An Idea Whose Time Has Come." *Monthly Review*, Federal Reserve Bank of Kansas City (September–October, 1971).

Strumpel, Burkhard. "Inflation, Discontent and Distributive Justice." *Economic Outlook U.S.A.* (Summer, 1974).

Tucker, James F., and Warren E. Weber. "Indexation As a Response to Inflation: An Examination." *Economic Review*, Federal Reserve Bank of Richmond (November–December, 1974).

Wachter, Michael L. "Did Wage-Price Controls Reduce Inflation?" *Wharton Quarterly* (Summer–Fall, 1974).

Wallich, H. C., and S. Weintraub. "A Tax-Based Incomes Policy." *Journal of Economic Issues* (June 5, 1971).

Weintraub, Sidney. *Capitalism's Inflation and Unemployment Crisis*. Reading, Mass: Addison-Wesley Publishing Company, 1978. (Particularly Part 3 — Inflation Remedies: Income Gearing.)

Yang, Jai-Hoon. "The Case for and Against Indexation: An Attempt at Perspective." *Review*, Federal Reserve Bank of St. Louis (October, 1974).

Income — 4
Should It Be Guaranteed?

One of the most debatable proposals to arrive on the socioeconomic scene in the past decade is the guaranteed annual income concept. Furthermore, this proposal is sure to be a red-hot political issue in the next few years. The thought of guaranteeing an income regardless of work is repugnant to many Americans, especially those who for years have associated income with work and extol the merits of clean living, hard work, frugality, and savings. Others, however, including some economists, politicians, labor leaders, social workers, and even business people feel that a guaranteed annual income, or income maintenance as it is often called, is an excellent device for eradicating poverty and solving many of the socioeconomic problems of society. Consequently, debate on the subject is often fraught with emotion. Before supporting or rejecting the concept, an economic analysis of what it is, how it would work, and who it would aid should prove helpful.

AID TO THE POOR

An observation of some of our socioeconomic problems, such as unemployment, health care, and poverty, indicates that the common issue in each situation is the lack of, or threatened lack of, income for those affected by the problem. It has often been stated that being poor is simply a matter of inadequate income. Some proponents recommend that we can eliminate most of our poverty and its many related problems simply by maintaining a minimum level of income for everyone.

In spite of our many anti-poverty and work training programs, there are still 25.9 million people in the United States living below the poverty level. Presently many of these people are receiving aid of various types from many different sources. Much aid is distributed through the Aid to Families with Dependent Children (AFDC) Program, especially when the mother, without the husband present, is unable to work to support the family. Aid for the disabled is available through the Federal Old Age, Survivors, Disability, and Health Insurance (OASDHI) Program. Income aid of various types is provided through unemployment compensation, worker's compensation, rent subsidies, food stamps, income maintenance, and other measures.

Since 1950 the income security component of the federal budget has increased from $43 billion to $189 billion. Existing income maintenance programs accounted for a substantial portion of the $189 billion in social welfare payments distributed in 1976, as shown in Table 4-1. The poverty program was designed to give direct and indirect aid to the poor. Training programs under the Manpower Development and Training Act (MDTA) and other acts endeavor to help the poor and others by preparing them to take jobs. Medical aid is available to poor persons through Medicare and Medicaid. Unemployment compensation, of course, gives assistance to workers during layoff periods. Even the poor farmer is given help in maintaining income through various agricultural support programs. Again, the common purpose of most of these programs is to provide funds for the individual or family when in need.

Table 4-1
SELECT FEDERAL AND STATE SOCIAL WELFARE PAYMENTS, 1976 (Millions of Dollars)

Social insurance			$120,809
OASDI	$72,664 ⎫	$90,441	
Medicare	17,777 ⎭		
Railroad retirement		3,500	
Public employee retirement		16,635	
Unemployment insurance		8,491	
Worker's compensation		1,561	
Other		226	
Public aid			$ 33,254
Veterans programs			18,791
Housing			2,428
Other social welfare			4,534
Health and medical programs			9,353
Total			$189,169

SOURCE: Adapted from *Statistical Abstract of the United States*, 1977, page 319.

The GAW and SUB

Over the past few decades a number of firms have adopted some form of a guaranteed annual wage (GAW) plan. Some of these plans are based on the practice of holding in surplus overtime funds and then paying them to the worker during slack employment periods. Others are based on assurance of 48–50 weeks of work per year. Thus, the company by dovetailing production, dovetailing employment, producing for stock, or using some other device gives the worker assurance of stable employment and income.[1] Such plans

---

[1]Three of the best known plans are those of the Hormel Company, Procter & Gamble, and the Nunn-Busch Shoe Company.

have never been widely adopted and are usually unilaterally operated by the management.

Another form of the guaranteed annual income is the SUB (Supplementary Employment Benefits) established in the auto industry in the mid-1950s as a result of union-management bargaining. With SUB, a general reserve fund is accumulated through company contributions of a definite amount per hour per worker. When a worker is unemployed, payments are made out of the reserve fund to supplement regular unemployment compensation benefits. Over 2 million employees are now covered by some form of SUB. In both GAW and SUB plans, the obligation of the firm is limited by a number of factors, such as the length of employment, the size of the reserve fund, and the duration of unemployment. In each of these plans, too, the financial obligation of the firm is limited and the individual has to be employed for a period of time before becoming eligible for coverage by the plan. What happens to an individual, however, when the firm's obligation is terminated? What about the individual who has not worked long enough to qualify? What about the individual who never had the opportunity to be covered by a guaranteed annual wage or employment plan because a job could not be found for one reason or another, such as depression, poor health, physical handicap, or old age?

Aid Through Tax Cuts

At various times, such as in 1954, 1964, 1966, 1971, and 1975, personal income tax reductions and excise tax reductions have been used as a means of bolstering a sagging economy. These do so by raising the disposable income of the income recipient, which permits larger purchases of goods and services. Although this will aid the average wage earner, frequently such measures pass over the low wage earner, the unemployed, and the poor in general. If an individual is not working or the wage is so low that the person pays a zero or a minimal income tax, a personal income tax reduction may be of little or no help. Likewise, an excise tax reduction may be of limited help to the individual who spends very little because of a meager income.

THE ISSUE

With the awareness of a sizable production gap in the GNP in the early 1960s, the existence of nagging unemployment, and the emphasis on the elimination of poverty in America, there emerged in our society various proposals for a guaranteed annual income for all Americans. These proposals were based on social, economic, humanitarian, and perhaps political motives. Moreover, most of the proposed plans would be financed by the federal government, thus reducing employer responsibility in this area. These income maintenance plans to some extent would divorce income from work. Their adoption instead would relate, to some degree, income to need. They would replace the time honored work-income relationship prevalent in our economy for decades.

Some proponents suggest that every American has the right to some minimal amount of goods and services regardless of a job or lack thereof. In 1962, for example, Professor Milton Friedman, a well-known conservative, suggested that a guaranteed annual income be inaugurated and that all current welfare programs be discontinued. In 1963 in his book *Free Men and Free Markets*, Robert Theobald suggested that a guaranteed annual income should be provided to all Americans as an absolute right, that the size of the grant should be determined on the basis of objective criteria, and that the program provide for direct payments to the poor. In 1965 the Office of Economic Opportunity set forth a study indicating the feasibility of a guaranteed annual income plan. Early in 1966 the National Commission on Technology, Automation, and Economic Progress recommended a guaranteed annual income as a means of softening the blow of technological unemployment. In 1967 the President's National Advisory Commission on Food and Fiber recommended an income maintenance plan go into effect during the transition to a market-oriented farm economy.

The concept of income maintenance, or the guaranteed annual income, was mentioned in each of the President's *Economic Reports* from 1966 through 1970. The 1966 *Report* indicated that about half the poor were receiving no public transfer income of any type. The 1967 *Report* stated that "Ideally, an income maintenance system should provide benefits on the basis of need, without degrading means tests, while preserving incentives for self-help." In 1968 President Johnson appointed a Commission on Income Maintenance to study the feasibility of the various guaranteed annual income proposals in existence at that time. In the Commission's report of November, 1969, it recommended a $2,400 income maintenance for a family of four. In the interim, the 1969 *Economic Report of the President* stated that "Americans will soon have to decide how best to help those who cannot earn enough to escape from poverty." In discussing income support, the *Report* indicated that the total shortfall of income below the poverty line amounts to only 1 percent of our gross national product — one fourth of our normal growth in a single year. The 1969 *Report* explained some of the various guaranteed annual income proposals and devoted space to details of the negative income tax plan. The *Report* stated: "A minimum income guarantee would end society's attempts to distinguish between the 'deserving' and the 'undeserving' poor, establishing the principle of social responsibility to aid those in need without questioning whether the fault was individual or social."

Although he definitely opposed the idea of a guaranteed annual income during his 1968 Presidential campaign, President Nixon's first *Economic Report* (1970) contained an income maintenance proposal known as the Family Assistance Plan (FAP). The plan was designed to "supplement the incomes of the poor who have difficulty working, or probably ought not to be working, such as women with low incomes who head families with children."

Although very little was mentioned in the 1971, 1972, or 1973 *Economic Report of the President* about income maintenance, it was much discussed by various federal agencies and mentioned again in the 1975 *Economic Report*.

Both the 1976 and 1977 *Economic Reports* contained sections on income maintenance or government transfer payments, such as unemployment compensation, AFDC, Social Security, and other existing programs without mentioning the guaranteed annual income concept. Moreover, grants have been made by both the Office of Economic Opportunity and the Department of Health, Education, and Welfare to establish experimental guaranteed annual income programs. Consequently, there appears to be very little doubt that in the near future a sharper focus will be applied to the socio-politico-economic issues related to income maintenance. Truly a major decision will have to be made on whether we should adopt some form of a federally financed guaranteed annual income plan.

GUARANTEED ANNUAL INCOME PLANS

In the past several years a number of different proposals have been introduced for the establishment of a guaranteed annual income (GAI) or income maintenance. Most of these were based on the 1964 poverty level income of $3,000 per annum for a four-person family. Today the poverty level exceeds $6,000 per year due primarily to higher prices. Consequently, the figures in most of these plans have been updated to take into account the current poverty level of over $6,000 annually.

Friedman Plan

Professor Milton Friedman suggests that any program to help the poor should operate through the market mechanism, but should not impede or distort the market's functions. Furthermore, he believes that government intervention in the economy should be minimized. Citing the belief that our present collection of welfare programs constitutes a considerable amount of government intervention in the economy, he recommends substituting a guaranteed annual income plan for our present welfare system. This would not only help the poor more directly, but would permit a net reduction of government intervention in the economy. To avoid any work deterrent now contained in many of our welfare plans, especially in those where the workers' welfare payments are reduced by any wage earnings, Professor Friedman built a work incentive component into his plan.

The Friedman plan is based on our present tax structure; therefore, it requires a minimum effort and cost to implement the plan. Based on the fact that an average four-person family has personal exemptions, plus other standard exemptions, Friedman established a break-even income which was close to the poverty level. Today families receiving more than the poverty level income of $6,000 annually would pay income tax as usual. But four-person families with less than a $6,000 income would not only not pay an income tax, they would actually receive a payment in the form of a negative income tax. To preserve some worker incentive, the Friedman plan and those similar to it would not pay the family the full difference between its actual income and the break-even or poverty line income. It would limit the negative tax payment to 50 percent of the difference. Thus, if a family earned $3,000 in income, its poverty gap would be $3,000 ($6,000 − $3,000). The family thus would receive a net allowance or negative tax payment of $1,500 (50% of $3,000), bringing its total income up to $4,500. The minimum income under the plan would be $3,000, as shown in Table 4-2.

It is estimated that the cost of the Friedman Plan would be in excess of $20 billion annually. This cost would be offset in large part, however, by the· elimination of other welfare plans.

Table 4-2
NEGATIVE INCOME TAX PLAN
(Based on a $6,000 Minimum Annual Income)

Family Pretax Income	Poverty Income Gap	Negative Tax Payment	Family Income After Tax
$ 0	$6,000	$3,000	$3,000
$1,000	$5,000	$2,500	$3,500
$2,000	$4,000	$2,000	$4,000
$3,000	$3,000	$1,500	$4,500
$4,000	$2,000	$1,000	$5,000
$5,000	$1,000	$ 500	$5,500
$6,000	$ 0	$ 0	$6,000
Over $6,000	pays regular income tax		

Tax Equity Negative Rates Plan

Another variation of the negative income tax is the tax equity negative rates plan. This plan simply would refund to families a certain portion of their unused personal exemptions and low income allowances (often referred as to as "unused EX + LIA"). Proponents of this plan claim that the low income taxpayer is not getting the full benefit of the allowable exemptions and deductions, nor does such a person benefit from a decrease in rates or an increase in the exemptions. According to supporters of this plan, inequities result especially when families of different sizes, but with the same income, pay the same income tax. In this plan neither a four-person nor a six-person family with an income of $2,000, for example, would pay any income tax. But the larger family would receive a larger negative tax payment than the smaller family. In the case of the six-person family, it would have unused personal exemptions of $3,800. Its personal exemptions would be $4,500 (6 × $750), plus a $1,300 low income allowance. Thus, it has $3,800 of unused EX + LIA ($5,800 − $2,000). The four-person family would have total exemptions and deductions of $4,300 ($3,000 personal exemption plus a $1,300 low income allowance). Its unused EX + LIA would be $2,300. Even at a 14 percent negative tax rate, there would be a considerable difference in the negative tax payment to the two families. Using a 50 percent negative tax rate, as suggested by many, means that the six-person family would receive a negative tax payment of $1,900. This would give it a total after tax income of $3,900 per year. Under the same plan the four-person family earning the same income of $2,000 would receive a negative tax payment of $1,150 (50 percent of its unused EX + LIA of $2,300). This would give it a total income of $3,150 after taxes.

A big advantage of this plan, of course, is its simplicity in that it blends in easily with the present income tax structure. It does have some flexibility. It permits discrimination in favor of large families and against smaller families, as compared to the poverty line plans that would establish a guaranteed annual income around the $6,000 level. It does not, however, contain the worker incentive feature of the Friedman Plan. Furthermore, implementation of such a plan would be complicated by the fact that it is based on the taxpayer and his or her dependents as a unit, whereas the welfare unit is the family. Under present law, some families have several taxpayers. On the other hand, there are many families who currently file no income tax form, but they would be eligible for a negative tax payment if it were in effect. Likewise, a family whose nontaxable income is large enough to put them over the break-even income level would still receive a negative tax payment on the basis of their declared taxable income.

It has been estimated that the cost of the tax equity negative rates plan using the 14 percent rate would have been about $2.8 billion in 1964. With a 50 percent negative tax rate, the cost would have been $10 billion annually.[2] Today it would cost well in excess of $20 billion annually.

Theobald Plan

While both the Friedman and the tax equity negative rates plans provide for a fractional guarantee of poverty level income, the Theobald plan calls for a full poverty level income guarantee. An updated version of his 1960 plan would suggest a minimum income of $6,000 per four-person family with a negative tax payment equal to the difference between actual income and the $6,000 level. Consequently, if a family earned only $3,000 it would receive a negative tax payment of $3,000 compared to a payment of $1,500 under the Friedman plan. The Theobald plan arrives at the $6,000 figure by assuming that about $2,035 is needed by each adult and $965 by each child to ensure their Basic Economic Security (BES).

The Theobald plan incorporates a work incentive feature by adding to BES 10 percent of any private income earned. Thus, a poor person would not be penalized 100 percent for working, as with many existing welfare plans.

[2]Christopher Green and Robert J. Lampman, "Schemes for Transferring Income to the Poor," *Industrial Relations*, Vol. 6 (1966–1967), page 124.

According to the Theobald plan, if a family earned $5,000 it would receive a $1,000 make-up payment to reach its $6,000 BES entitlement, plus an additional payment of $500 as a 10 percent premium or bonus on its private income of $5,000.

Theobald makes a strong point that the link between employment and income should be broken and that a maintenance income from the government should be given to each family or individual as an absolute constitutional right. It has been estimated that the cost of the Theobald plan would run between $42 and $50 billion annually.

On the basis of 1960 data, Theobald estimated that 20 million Americans would be covered by his proposed BES entitlements. Today it would be about 14 million. According to Theobald, BES payments could eventually take the place of many of the existing welfare schemes with the proviso that a full-scale medical care program, especially for the aged, be retained to insure that nobody's savings are wiped out because of unavoidable illness. He suggests, too, that over a period of time the BES level be raised to approach the "modest, but adequate" level of living provided through the Bureau of Labor Statistics' City Worker's Family Budget (CWFB). When Theobald first proposed his BES plan, the intermediate CWFB was in the vicinity of $6,000 for a four-person family. In 1978 it was in excess of $17,000 for the average family.

Tobin Plan

James Tobin, a Yale University economics professor and a former member of the President's Council of Economic Advisers, proposed a slightly different approach to the guaranteed annual income. His plan starts by allowing each family head an allowance of $600 per family member. As income is earned, the government would then take back, or cancel, some of the subsidy. To reduce the disincentive effect of the GAI, the Tobin plan would allow the family to retain two thirds of income earned, applying the other third to reducing the original subsidy.

According to his plan a four-person family would have an allowance of $2,400. If its earnings were zero, it would receive the full $2,400 GAI allowance. If a family earned $1,500, its subsidy would be reduced from $2,400 to $1,900 and its total income after the GAI payment would be $3,400 ($1,500 + $1,900). This process would continue up to the poverty line income, as shown in Table 4-3.

Notice that in the Tobin Plan even families above the poverty level, those earning up to $7,200 per year, would receive some GAI allowance. It has been estimated that the total leakage to the nonpoor would be in excess of $4.0 billion under this plan, which would cost about $18 billion annually.

Schwartz Plan

Professor Edward E. Schwartz of the University of Chicago proposed a guaranteed annual income based on a social work philosophy rather than a tax

Table 4-3
TOBIN PLAN GAI PAYMENTS

Family Income Earned	GAI Allowance	Total Family Income
$ 0	$2,400	$2,400
$ 600	$2,200	$2,800
$ 900	$2,100	$3,000
$1,500	$1,900	$3,400
$2,100	$1,700	$3,800
$2,700	$1,500	$4,200
$3,000	$1,400	$4,400
$3,600	$1,200	$4,800
$4,200	$1,000	$5,200
$4,800	$ 800	$5,600
$5,400	$ 600	$6,000
$6,000	$ 400	$6,400
$6,600	$ 200	$6,800
$7,200	$ 0	$7,200

equity approach. Like Theobald, he feels that the only proper way to eliminate poverty is to have the federal government guarantee to every family and person an income sufficient to maintain a healthful and decent standard of living. The receipt of this income should be a constitutional and civil right. Schwartz stresses the point that the adoption of a GAI plan would get rid of the present means test in determining welfare payments. This, he says, would avoid embarrassment on the part of the poor and free the welfare worker from the distasteful and lengthy task of determining eligibility. Consequently, the social worker could devote more time in giving needed assistance to the poor.

Schwartz's plan calls for an extension of our present tax structure. Presently many of those with incomes above a certain level, especially when it comes from multiple sources, have to pay more taxes than the amount officially withheld. Consequently, they are required to fill out a Declaration of Estimated Income Tax Form. Through this they calculate and pay on a quarterly basis any additional amount of income tax due in excess of withholdings. Schwartz would use a similar form for the poor. Any persons expecting their incomes for the forthcoming year to fall below a federally guaranteed minimum income (FGMI) for themselves and their families would be able to claim a federal security benefit (FSB) for the amount of the difference between the FGMI and anticipated income. The declaration of negative income tax forms, of course, would be checked at the end of the year for validity and accuracy. Any adjustments for overpayment or underpayment would be made as they are now.

The FGMI would be determined initially by a Presidential commission, which would decide also on a schedule of allowances for families of given size and age composition. In addition, the commission would make adjustments in the schedule for regional and urban-rural differences. Provisions would be made in the legislation for periodic adjustments of the FGMI to make it conform to changes in the cost of living. Adjustments in the FSB would be made also, especially among older people, to take into account any financial assets held by families.

Schwartz has less conviction than some others about the necessity of incorporating a work incentive feature into his model. He feels that for reasons of economy and administrative simplicity such a restraint should be dispensed with. He does believe, however, that a work incentive feature may be necessary to meet the test of public debate. In such case he would permit families to keep a portion of their earnings on a graduated scale so that up to a given income bracket they would be better off financially with earnings than without. Moreover, once they reached the current poverty level income through earnings alone, they would remain exempt from a positive income tax until a still higher bracket was attained. Positive taxes would not be applied until income exceeded the poverty level by approximately 50 percent.

Current estimates indicate that the cost of this plan without the work incentive feature would be about $25 billion annually. With the work incentive it could rise to $35 billion.

Lampman Plan

One of the most widely known guaranteed annual income proposals is that devised for the Office of Economic Opportunity by Professor Robert J. Lampman of North Carolina State University. The Lampman plan, containing four models, is probably the most comprehensive of the GAI plans. All of his proposals require tax reform of some type or other. Their relative desirability depends on the importance placed on three different, but not inconsistent, objectives: improving tax equity, narrowing the poverty income gap, and replacing public assistance as a method of providing for the poor. Lampman's plans are of two basic types.

The first type is designed mainly to improve the equity of the tax system while increasing the income of the poor. Lampman feels that since the poor generally do not pay any income taxes, they are unable to take full advantage of the built-in aid to families which permits personal deductions and exemptions for dependents. Furthermore, the poor bear a relatively heavy burden of consumption taxes (sales, food, excise) that are flat rate taxes, as well as absorbing a heavy share of property taxes. These taxes take a heavier bite out of a small income than they do out of a large income. Consequently, Lampman concludes that our tax system discriminates against the poor because it is relatively regressive in regard to incomes.

The first Lampman plan is similar to the tax equity negative rates plan described earlier. His plan would permit those in the lowest income brackets to claim as a payment from the government 14 percent of their unused exemptions and deductions. This plan would cost about $3.5 billion annually and would narrow the income gap by about one sixth.

Lampman has several versions of his second GAI plan which incorporates a negative income tax based on a poverty line income, much like those that have been presented heretofore. The first version of this negative tax, Plan II-A, involves a negative tax rate of a flat 50 percent. The base of the tax would be calculated by subtracting a family's total income from the poverty line income for a family of a given size, composition, and urban or rural residence. Using a poverty line income of $6,000 for a family of four with no income, for example, the plan would guarantee an income of $3,000 per year. The family that earned $4,000 would receive a payment of $1,000, just like the Friedman plan. The cost of this model is estimated to be $14–$15 billion, but this could be offset in part by a reduction of $8–$9 billion in public assistance programs.

Another version of the same plan, Plan II-B, would set the negative tax rate at 75 percent, 50 percent, and 25 percent on successive increments of $1,500 of earned income. An updated version of Plan II-C would call for a zero rate on the first $3,000 of earned income and 50 percent on the second $3,000 of earned income. Plan II-D suggests a 75 percent rate on the first $3,000 and a 33 percent rate on the second $3,000. The sizable initial rates incorporated in Plans II-B and II-D are designed to discourage small amounts of work by the very poor. The lower rates in the higher brackets are designed to encourage incentive among the working poor.

Other Plans

A number of other plans for income maintenance or GAI have been proposed. Many of these are variations of the tax equity and negative income tax plans.

Social Dividend. One plan worthy of mention is the social dividend concept. This plan would provide payments to every citizen in the nation in an amount equal to a poverty income, regardless of other income earned. The transfer cost of such a plan would be enormous. For the U.S. economy it would be $225 billion or more. These funds would be obtained by applying a single tax of 33⅓ percent on all family income. Most of this would go back to the original taxpayers, but about one third of it would be redistributed.

If a four-person family income guarantee of $6,000 were used, it would make the break-even income $18,000 per family. A family with that income would be taxed $6,000 for the plan, but would receive a $6,000 social dividend. A family with an income of $3,000 would pay a tax of $1,000 but would receive a social dividend of $6,000 raising its total income to $8,000 per year. A family with a $21,000 income would likewise receive a social dividend of $6,000 but its tax contribution to the plan would be $7,000. Thus, its total income would be reduced to $20,000 per year. A family with no income, of course, would pay no tax but still receive its social dividend of $6,000 per year. Since poor families would be paying less taxes than higher income families to finance the social dividend, a net redistribution of approximately $100 billion of income would result. Different models of this plan vary the tax rates and change the break-even income to reduce both the gross cost and the transfer cost of the plan.

Family Allowance. Still another popular alternative to income maintenance or GAI is the family allowance system now in effect in 30 or more nations throughout the world, including Canada and several European countries. These plans are based on the premise that our modern day economies or industrial systems, with their emphasis on wage payments, fail to fully take into account the financial needs of large families. Most of the plans provide for a certain payment of money to each family according to the number of children in the family. The amount may vary with numbers and ages of the children. As an income maintenance or antipoverty scheme, the plan suffers from the fact that all families, not only the poor, receive family allowances. It has been estimated that the cost of such a plan for the United States would be about $30 billion. If the payments were limited to poor families, it would cost less than $15 billion to eliminate poverty through a family allowance system. A problem would still remain, however, of finding a way to raise the income of many of the unattached individuals and the poor couples who have no children living at home.

Family Assistance Plan (FAP)

The most talked about income maintenance plan in the early 1970s was the Family Assistance Plan (FAP). It would provide direct payments to poor families whether headed by a female or an unemployed father, or to a working poor family headed by a male. FAP in large part would be a substitute for the current Aid to Families with Dependent Children (AFDC) Program. In its simplest form FAP offers a basic allowance of $500 for each of the first two family members and $300 for each child. Childless families, or those with children over 18 years of age, would not be eligible for FAP. They would receive minimum aid of $110 per person per month under other adult category plans. Under FAP a family of four would have a basic income of $1,600 per year as a result of federal payments. The original plan also provided for a food stamp allowance of $870 per year, which would raise the purchasing power of the family to $2,470 per year.

The FAP contains a dual work incentive. First, to be eligible for benefits the head of the household must register for employment and accept a job or job training if offered. Secondly, the household head could earn as much as $720 per year without suffering any loss of family benefits. Moreover, for any income earned beyond $720 per year the family would lose only 50 cents in benefits for each marginal dollar earned. This is unlike the current AFDC

Program in which the family is penalized 100 percent in benefits for each dollar of earnings. FAP would continue assistance until earnings reached $3,920 per annum, known as the break-even income, as shown in Table 4-4. At that point and beyond, no federal payments would be made under FAP to four-person families. Payments are graduated, however, according to family size. For six-member families, for example, the break-even income is $5,120 per year.

The purpose of the work incentive is to encourage self-sufficiency and to assure that FAP recipients would be economically better off working than not working. Day care assistance would be provided for children of mothers who head households and who choose to work. It is estimated that the cost of the plan would be about $4.5 billion in its initial stages. The number of persons eligible for benefits would be 24 million compared to 12.8 million currently covered under AFDC and other adult category plans. Cost estimates vary with the size of the benefit. If basic incomes were raised from $1,600 to $2,000 per year, federal outlays for FAP would be $5.6 billion. At the $2,400 allowance level recommended by the President's Commission on Income Maintenance, the cost would rise to nearly $8 billion. At a $6,000 figure, it would cost about $75 billion annually. Costs would vary, also, with any change in the size of exempt earnings or with changes in the tax rates applied to nonexempt earned income. Under the original plan, as earned income increased, adjustments would also be made in family benefits for food stamps, public housing, and Medicaid.

Table 4-4

PROPOSED FAP PAYMENT SCHEDULE FOR FAMILY OF FOUR
(Assuming annual payments of $500 each for the first two family members and $300 each for additional members, a $720 income exemption and a 50 percent marginal "tax" on nonexempt earnings.)

Earnings	Nonexempt Earnings (Excess over $720)	"Tax" at 50%	Net FAP Payment ($1,600 Less "Tax")	Net Family Income
$ 0	$ 0	$ 0	$1,600	$1,600
720	0	0	1,600	2,320
1,000	280	140	1,460	2,460
1,500	780	390	1,210	2,710
2,000	1,280	640	960	2,960
2,500	1,780	890	710	3,210
3,000	2,280	1,140	460	3,460
3,500	2,780	1,390	210	3,710
3,920	3,200	1,600	—	3,920

SOURCE: "Welfare Reform Proposals," *Legislative Analysis* (Washington: American Enterprise Institute, May 17, 1971).

THE ARGUMENTS FOR AND AGAINST THE GAI

It is evident that there are many plans and proposals for some form of income maintenance or a guaranteed annual income as a means of eliminating poverty in America, but there are many arguments for and against the concept in addition to numerous arguments for and against each individual plan being proposed.

Arguments for the GAI

Among some of the most popular arguments for a guaranteed annual income are the following.

Direct Aid. It is claimed that being poor or nonpoor is only a matter of money. Proponents of the GAI, therefore, maintain that the quickest, most efficient, and least costly method of eliminating poverty is through direct payments to the poor. The GAI plan would eliminate poverty almost immediately. It would get directly to the heart of poverty by providing funds directly to the poor. Although the various plans would have costs ranging from a few billion up to several billion, commonly in the $18–$25 billion vicinity, GAI proponents point out that this is still a relatively small portion of our GNP or national income. With the GNP at the $2.0 trillion level, most of the plans would involve a transfer cost of less than 1½ percent of the GNP. They also like to compare it with other costs in our economy, such as the cost of the defense program at more than $100 billion annually. Some suggest that it is better to pay the poor and low income groups directly as opposed to the creation of public works and public employment programs that may incidentally give assistance to nonpoor families. Many antipoverty proponents advocate that we should be as willing to spend a proper amount to win the war on poverty as we were to conduct the war in Vietnam, which cost the U.S. $25 billion yearly at the height of the war.

Eliminate the Means Test. Another argument put forth for the GAI is that it would eliminate the need for a means test to determine who should or should not obtain welfare aid. Social workers maintain that the means tests is embarrassing and at times humiliating to the welfare recipient, especially when the social worker is trying to find out whether the applicant is deserving of welfare aid. Inquiries about savings, help from relatives, ability to sell existing assets (such as a home or auto), and how the welfare recipient spent earned income or previous welfare money all dig into matters many families consider private. Attempts also to determine whether the head of the household, whether husband, widow, or unwed mother with dependent children, is capable of holding a job and providing for self-need and those needs of the family is a difficult and time-consuming task. GAI proponents point out that the only test of eligibility for income maintenance would be the status of a person's income. All families and unattached individuals who are poor, whether through their own fault or that of society, would be eligible for income maintenance payments. There would be no restrictions on how they spend their money. It would place the responsibility on each family to take care of its essential needs. In the process they could maintain their dignity without intrusion of an outside agency since neighbors would not know the family was receiving aid through the GAI. Some sociologists and economists suggest that this would give a great psychological boost to the poor and encourage them to work toward further economic improvement. To them it is a means of breaking the poverty syndrome for many families.

Eliminate or Reduce Welfare Programs. At the present time we have a complex mixture of programs to take care of those in need. In addition to the numerous welfare programs, such as aid to the blind, aid to families with dependent children, and aid to the aged, we also have federal old age retirement, disability, and medicare. Currently the Departments of HEW, HUD, and Labor are carrying on numerous programs to help the poor. Moreover, the farm price support program is a means of aiding farmers who in recent decades have been among the lowest income groups in the nation.

Many proponents of income maintenance recommend the GAI as a substitute for all or some of the existing welfare plans. They argue that there would be no need for an unemployment compensation program or an old age retirement program, for example, if everyone was entitled to a guaranteed annual income. Both the unemployed and the retired would obtain benefits through the GAI. Likewise, there would be limited need for welfare agencies, since aid to the indigent would be made through GAI instead of the various welfare programs. Even agricultural price supports could be dropped and crop prices could seek their own level through supply and demand. Although this would lower farm income, it would raise the real income of consumers if prices fell. There would be no need to worry about farm income, however, because it would be adjusted through the GAI program. Some of the GAI proponents, such as Milton Friedman, contend that much of the cost of the GAI could be offset by the reduction in the cost of other welfare and government subsidy programs.

Right to a Decent Livelihood. Certain proponents of income maintenance, such as Theobald and Schwartz, claim that each citizen has a basic right to an amount of goods and services out of our total productive capacity sufficient to maintain a decent livelihood. As Theobald states clearly in his book, this should be an absolute right incorporated into the Constitution of the nation. His position is based on the fact that with the high level of production in our economy, it is possible to provide every citizen with a minimal income for a decent life. Therefore, we have an obligation to do so.

Schwartz and other social dividend advocates have similar feelings. Many think, especially Theobald, that the link between income and employment should be broken and a due-income principle based on social justice be substituted. One proponent suggests that the right to an income, regardless of work, should be taken as much for granted as free public education. Some who look at income maintenance from a social point of view claim that we could ease our national conscience with an income maintenance plan. We would know that we are providing adequately for the poor and that no family would be in need. Professor Friedman, however, looks upon the GAI plan primarily as an economic issue. If we are going to help the poor, one of the least expensive means of doing so is through the guaranteed annual income. Furthermore, Friedman sees the GAI as a means of reducing total government intervention in the economy by substituting income maintenance for other welfare schemes.

Help to Prevent Urban Disturbances. Since a considerable number of the poor are concentrated in urban areas, especially in blighted and ghetto sectors, it can be expected that these areas may be teeming with frustration, disparity, and unrest. Consequently, these people are susceptible to schemes, programs, or activities that might propose to improve their economic lot. This could lead, consequently, to mass demonstrations, picketing, and even riots which could prove disruptive and costly to society. GAI proponents suggest that their plan would help remove some of the conditions that cause frustration, disparity, and unrest. This, in turn, would reduce the probability of urban disturbance.

A strong point is made of the fact that any growing unemployment would add to the precariousness of the urban crisis. In the mid-1960s the economy was in a state of full, or relatively high level, employment. During that time many of the disadvantaged from the urban areas found meaningful employment. When unemployment increases for some reason, as it did in the recessions of 1970 and 1974–1975, the first to be laid off are the workers last hired. Among these are many of the disadvantaged, youths, and unskilled, and ghetto and urban area workers. It is suggested that a guaranteed annual income would ease to some degree the financial plight faced by these so-called marginal workers and that possible social repercussions of their unemployment would be lessened. It is often cited that the cost of a GAI plan may be less than the cost of civil disturbance.

Arguments Against the GAI

Of course, just as many, if not more, arguments have been made against the implementation of a guaranteed annual income or any form of an income maintenance scheme.

Destroys Incentive. Opponents of the guaranteed annual income strongly claim that it would destroy initiative among the lower income and poverty groups. Why should a person work for $6,000 per year when he or she could stay home, go fishing, or engage in other pleasant pursuits and still collect $6,000 through the GAI. Even if the individual could earn more by working, let us say $7,500, the question may arise as to whether it is worth working for the $1,500 of marginal income. Opponents of the GAI, too, maintain that its implementation will perpetuate the poverty syndrome. Although it may bestow some dignity on the poor family if the recipient is entitled to income maintenance as a right, what incentive is there to seek a job, learn a trade, improve skills, or become better educated? Although several of the guaranteed annual income plans have built-in work incentive measures, opponents of GAI generally feel that the gap between the poverty line income and the after-tax income is insufficient. In fact, they point out that in many proposals there is no gap.

Opponents of income maintenance are greatly concerned that the GAI would in large part break down the historic work-income relationship. Traditionally in the free enterprise system the individual has been paid according to economic contribution as measured by employment. The longer and better the work performance the greater the remuneration. Social Security and unemployment compensation still retain this relationship, but with the GAI this would no longer be true. To many it smacks of socialism, which advocates government ownership, control, or direction of the means of production.

Does Not Remove the Basic Cause of Poverty. Although the opponents of the guaranteed annual income would have to admit that it would alleviate, if not eliminate, poverty, they still make a strong point that income maintenance does not eliminate the cause of poverty. A family is poor because it lacks income. To give it money means it is no longer poor. But it may have been poor originally because the head of the household lacked the skill, training, or education to hold a decent job. Perhaps the individual was among the chronically ill or the mentally or physically incapacitated, who have a difficult time holding a job for any extended period of time. The person may be an alcoholic, or simply irresponsible or shiftless. Will the payment of a GAI correct the situation of the unwed mother, or of the mother without husband present, who is now receiving aid for her dependent children? Will the payment of a GAI remove these basic causes of poverty? Many income maintenance opponents think not.

Many of the poor are aged and there is little that can be done to eliminate their cause of poverty even with income maintenance. Furthermore, it is suggested that proponents of the GAI are adding to the problem when they suggest that the GAI be a means of early retirement when a worker becomes technologically unemployed. Opponents of the GAI suggest that the money might be better spent on programs to remove the causes of poverty, such as worker training and retraining programs, basic education for adults, job development, and medical, psychological, and sociological aid to those who are in need.

Will Not Eliminate Other Welfare Programs. Opponents of the various income maintenance proposals will admit that the GAI would remove the necessity for some of the current welfare and social programs. Certainly many of them, such as unemployment compensation and federal old-age, survivors, and disability benefits could be phased out. But since these plans are now working fairly well, a question is raised as to whether it would be wise to make a substitution. Furthermore, the current unemployment compensation and federal OASDHI payments are somewhat related to employment and earnings, which many people favor.

Since income maintenance does not eliminate the cause of poverty, there are many existing federal, state, and local welfare and social programs that still will be needed if we are going to eliminate the basic causes of poverty in America. What about the aged and others who in spite of a GAI still need psychiatric help? What about the potential worker who needs more education or training? Is there still not a need for social workers to discuss noneconomic problems with the poor? And even if many of the current welfare programs could be eliminated, to what extent will the vested interests wage an effort to maintain their programs?

Too Costly. Opponents of the GAI cite that we are already spending billions of dollars for welfare purposes and that the adoption of an income maintenance plan will simply add to the cost of what they consider an overwhelming burden. Although some of the plans would cost only a few billion dollars, opponents of GAI cite this as a foot in the door. They contend that an original plan costing $15–$20 billion would soon lead to cost figures of double or triple that amount. This would result as more individuals were brought under the plan. There is also a strong feeling that once established, the $6,000 guaranteed annual income of 1978 would not be the minimum for very long. Just as the costs of Social Security, union negotiated industrial pensions, and the GAI itself have risen over the past decade or more, so too would the $6,000 minimum GAI. This is evident by the fact that a number of plans already have incorporated a higher level. Once the principle of income maintenance was established, why would its proponents not seek to double the minimum or even raise it to the $17,106 current level (1977) of the intermediate BLS City Worker's Family Budget, which provides for a modest but adequate level of living? Consequently, opponents of the plan can see the cost doubling or trebling within the foreseeable future.

Impractical to Implement. In addition to being too costly, destroying incentive, and being socialistic, some GAI opponents argue that the plan is too impractical. They charge that any plan will be full of inequities. How is eligibility going to be determined? Can the program truly be launched on a family basis or is it going to have to be on an individual basis? What happens in those families where the father is not working, but a teenage son is fully employed? Will the son move out of the house so his family can collect the GAI? If the GAI becomes an extension of our regular income tax procedure, what can be done about those families that have nontaxable incomes that put them over the poverty level, but whose income does not show up on the tax form? To what extent can and should the system adjust the GAI payments in terms of savings and assets held by the family that is about to collect on its GAI?

The proponents of GAI readily admit that there may be some leakage of payments to the nonpoor. In fact, some of the plans have built-in leakages, such as the Tobin plan. Opponents of GAI suggest that these leakages will be magnified once a plan is in operation.

Even tying the GAI to our income tax structure may be unworkable. It is argued that if we wait until the end of the year to make GAI payments they will not have helped the family who needed the money during the year. Another difficulty may arise if the poverty during the year resulted from unemployment. The worker may be back at full-time employment by the time the GAI payment is received. To avoid this, some plans recommend the filing of an estimated income and then having the government pay the wage earner the difference between the estimated income and the guaranteed minimum annual income. But even here this would be done on a quarterly basis and not many of the poor can wait three months between payments. Even if given the money in advance, many of them would have a difficult time budgeting their funds over three-month periods.

CONCLUSION

When the concept of income maintenance or the guaranteed annual income was first introduced on a noticeable scale on the American economic scene in the early 1960s, the reaction by many was one of shock and amazement. Charges of extreme liberalism, if not socialism, were made in regard to the idea. These were reminiscent of the 1930s when the notion of Social Security was first introduced, or of the post-World War II period when industrial pensions were gaining momentum, and even of the late 1950s and early 1960s when the Medicare controversy was rampant. By the mid-1960s the GAI came to be accepted as another dream in the New Frontier-Great Society programs. As various concrete proposals began to appear from such government agencies as the Department of Labor and the Office of Economic Opportunity, more serious consideration was given to the feasibility of a guaranteed annual income.

Support for the idea of a guaranteed annual income has been bolstered by the fact that both the Office of Economic Opportunity and the Department of Health, Education, and Welfare awarded grants for conducting guaranteed annual income plans on an experimental basis. The first OEO experiment with 1,000 families has been going on for several years in six New Jersey cities and in Scranton, Pennsylvania. Another OEO grant went to the University of Wisconsin in 1969 to design a rural income maintenance program for 800 families. Data is being gathered from this program, which is currently in effect in North Carolina. The HEW grant awarded in 1969 provided for the drafting of a GAI plan for Seattle. Experiments with income maintenance plans also were conducted in Gary, Denver, and Seattle.

From still another point of view, an increasing number of highly regarded business executives have supported the need for a guaranteed annual income, although most would probably still reject it. The GAI became an important issue in the 1968 Presidential campaign. Candidate Hubert Humphrey supported income maintenance. Candidate Richard Nixon spoke out against it. Many academicians, labor leaders, business people, and government officials, however, felt that the new welfare program introduced by President Nixon in the summer of 1969 contained what could be classified as a modified form of income maintenance.

Subsequently the FAP was introduced into Congress in 1970 as a part of President Nixon's welfare reform measures. It was debated and analyzed, revised by committees, reported out of committees, one version passed by the House, another changed by the Administration on the advice of the Senate, the food stamp provision dropped, and basic income raised to $2,200. In the early months of 1972, Senator Ribicoff, a strong advocate and champion of income maintenance, backed away from his goal of pushing an income maintenance bill through Congress that year with the recommendation that we needed more research and experimentation before adopting such an awesome measure. The chief of HEW's Division of Income Maintenance Research indicated that it would take five years for income maintenance plans to supply answers to many pertinent questions associated with the GAI.

In the fall of 1974 the Senate Finance Committee approved a bill that would establish an alternative form of the GAI. The bill would provide cash payments to poor working families with incomes under $5,600 per year. The cash payment plan — called a "work bonus" — would reward wage earners who earn less than persons on welfare. Any family with an income of less than $4,000 per year would be eligible for a federal payment equal to 10 percent of its earnings. The money would be paid four times a year. Work bonus payments would diminish as earnings rose above $4,000 a year and would be phased out at $5,600 per year. The cost of the work bonus plan was estimated to be $600 million annually. As late as the fall of 1977, however, no further action had been taken on the work bonus bill.

Certainly the findings of the experiments in New Jersey, Gary, Seattle, Denver, and elsewhere add further enlightenment to the controversial aspects of the guaranteed annual income. Moreover, each new income maintenance proposal brings another round of arguments concerning the pros and cons of the guaranteed annual income. As things progress, it appears to be primarily a matter of time before some form of a GAI bill is passed by Congress.

MAJOR ISSUES

1. Should the United States adopt in principle the concept of income maintenance or guaranteed annual income?

2. If it were decided to adopt a GAI, which of the plans suggested in the chapter should be implemented?

3. If a GAI plan is implemented, should all or some of the current welfare programs be abandoned?

4. If a guaranteed annual income plan were adopted, would it solve the poverty problem in the U.S.?

SUBISSUES

1. Should the traditional relationship between work and income be broken?
2. Do you think the concept of the guaranteed annual income is socialistic?
3. In your opinion what would the adoption of a GAI plan do to incentive?
4. What major difference(s) do you see between Social Security and income maintenance?
5. Even if you do not favor the guaranteed annual income, do you think that it will be adopted in some form in the 1980s?

SELECTED READINGS

An Action Priority Program. White House Conference on Food, Nutrition, and Health. December, 1971.

"Current Status of Income Maintenance Experiments." *American Economic Review* (May, 1971).

Economic Report of the President, 1966 through 1978.

Final Report of the New Jersey Graduated Work Incentives Experiment. Madison, Wisconsin: University of Wisconsin, Institute for Research on Poverty, 1974.

Food and Fiber for the Future. Report of the National Advisory Commission on Food and Fiber. Washington: U.S. Government Printing Office, 1967.

Friedman, Milton. *Capitalism and Freedom.* Chicago: University of Chicago Press, 1973.

"Guaranteed Income and the Will to Work." *Labour Gazette* (May, 1974).

Henderson, R. F. "Relief of Poverty — Negative Income Taxes and Other Measures." *Economic Review* (March, 1971).

Hill, C. R. "Two Income Maintenance Plans. Work Incentives and Closure of the Poverty Gap." *Industrial and Labor Relations Review* (April, 1973).

Hitch, Thomas K. "Appealing As It May Be, the Negative Income Tax Won't Work." *Decisions of the Seventies.* U.S. Chamber of Commerce, March, 4, 1970.

Hushey, R. P. "Work Incentives and the Cost Effectiveness of Income Maintenance Programs." *Quarterly Review of Economics and Business* (Spring, 1973).

Manpower Report of the President, 1970 through 1978.

Moscovitch, Edward. "Income Supplements — How High Should They Be?" *New England Economic Review*, Federal Reserve Bank of Boston (January–February, 1971).

Moynihan, Daniel P. *The Politics of a Guaranteed Annual Income.* New York: Random House, Inc., 1972.

Pechman, Joseph A., and P. Michael Timpane (editors). *Work Incentives and Income Guarantees: The New Jersey Negative Income Tax Experiment.* Washington: The Brookings Institution, 1975.

Preliminary Results of the New Jersey Work Incentive Experiment. Washington: Office of Economic Opportunity, February, 1970.

"Pro's and Con's of Negative Income Tax." OECD *Observer* (June, 1974).

Theobald, Robert. *Free Men and Free Markets.* Garden City, N.Y.: Doubleday and Company, Inc., 1965.

"Unemployment and Income Maintenance Programs." *Economic Report of the President*, 1975.

"Welfare Reform Proposals." *Legislative Analysis.* American Enterprise Institute for Public Policy Research (May 17, 1971).

Social Security — 5
Is It Secure?

After many months of Congressional debate and years of political and public controversy, President Franklin D. Roosevelt, on August 14, 1935, signed into law the Social Security Act, establishing a system of social security for Americans. This event occurred decades after social security was adopted in several European countries. Bismark had inaugurated a social security program in Germany in the 1880s. Austria and Hungary followed shortly thereafter. Great Britain established old-age pension and unemployment programs between 1908 and 1925. The hardships of the Great Depression stimulated interest in the adoption of social security in the United States. As a consequence, President Roosevelt in June, 1934, created the Committee on Economic Security to study the problems relating to economic security and to make recommendations for a program of legislation to deal with unemployment and economic security for the aged. Most of the Committee's recommendations were incorporated one year later in the initial Social Security Act.

THE SOCIAL SECURITY ACT

Contributions were first paid into the Social Security System in 1937. The constitutionality of the System was upheld by the Supreme Court under the "general welfare" clause that same year, and workers began to acquire credit toward old-age insurance benefits in 1937. The first unemployment benefits under the Act were paid by the state of Wisconsin in 1936, and the first monthly payments under old-age and survivors insurance benefits were made in 1940.

Provisions of the Act of 1935

As it was originally passed, the Social Security Act contained three major provisions:

1. A federal system of old-age insurance benefits for workers.[1]
2. A federal-state system of unemployment compensation benefits.
3. A program of federal financial aid to states to help them provide public assistance to the needy aged, the needy blind, and dependent children.

Other programs established by the Act included maternal and child health care services, child welfare services, services for crippled children, vocational rehabilitation, and assistance to states for public health services.

At the time the Act was passed, only 3.5 million workers had any type of old-age retirement benefits, and only four states had any form of unemployment benefits. The Act provided old-age insurance for millions of additional workers. The original Act, however, covered only employees in industry and commerce. Therefore, only 6 out of 10 members of the labor force were included in the federal old-age insurance system, FOAI.

In 1939, a survivorship element was added to the old-age insurance program to provide payments to surviving dependents of insured workers, and the System then became known as FOASI (federal old-age and survivors insurance). In 1956, insurance payments for the permanent and totally disabled was added to the System, and it then became known as FOASDI.

The 1935 Act covered workers in industry and commerce only. Many types of workers were not covered by the new Social Security System because of administrative or other difficulties. These included agricultural workers, domestic service workers, casual laborers, merchant ship crew members, employees of federal, state, and local governments, workers in nonprofit institutions such as schools and hospitals, and all workers over 65 years of age. Railroad workers were also excluded because they had retirement benefits under the federal Railroad Retirement Act.

With subsequent amendments, many of the initially excluded workers were brought under the Act. In 1939, for example, workers in the U.S. merchant marine service, employees of national banks, and workers in savings and loan associations and similar institutions were brought within the scope of the Social Security Act. In 1950, coverage was again broadened to include the non-farm self-employed and the regularly employed agricultural and domestic workers. Voluntary coverage was allowed for employees of nonprofit institutions, and employees of state and local governments who were not already under a retirement system became eligible for coverage. Some civilian workers of the federal government not under an existing retirement program were included also.

Amendments in 1950 extended old-age coverage to nearly 10 million additional workers, most of whom were self-employed. In 1954, coverage was extended to farmers, some professionals, and members of religious orders. In 1956, coverage was expanded to include the 3 million or more members of the armed services currently on active duty. In 1965, self-employed physicians were included under the System. By the mid-1960s the only large group not

[1]This chapter will deal primarily with the federal old-age and survivor's insurance portion of the Social Security Act.

under Social Security coverage was composed of employees of the federal government, who were covered by other federal pension systems. Today the Social Security System provides social insurance protection for old-age, disability, and death benefits for 90 percent of all wage and salary workers and the self-employed.

Federal Old-Age Benefits

The 1935 Act provided for monthly benefit payments, beginning in 1942, to insured workers when they reached retirement age of 65 years or more. Benefits were based upon the employee's earned wages during a qualifying period. The maximum monthly payment was to be $85 per month and the minimum was to be $10 per month. Those reaching age 65 without qualifying for monthly benefits would receive a lump-sum payment equal to 3½ percent of the employee's lifetime earnings. A death benefit of the same amount, less benefits previously received, was provided by the law.

In 1939, the benefit package was amended to start benefit payments in 1940 instead of 1942, benefits were increased, survivor's payments were added, and a new formula for computing benefits was adopted. In 1950, benefit payments were increased again to make it possible to include earnings up to $3,600 per year, instead of the initial $3,000 per year, when computing benefits. In addition, the formula was revised to permit the use of a 1950 starting date to calculate benefits in order to obtain a larger benefit. A major reason for this new starting date was that many of the new groups of workers being brought under the System had no earnings for Social Security credit prior to that time.

In 1955, the maximum earnings taken into account in calculating benefits was raised to $4,200 per year and by the mid-1960s it had reached $6,600 per annum. In addition to increasing the maximum earnings that could be used in calculating the benefits, the formula for determining the benefits was revised several times to also provide for larger benefits.

As originally enacted, the Social Security System provided old-age benefits only for insured workers. But amendments provided for payments to survivors and death benefits in the event the insuree died. Over the life of the Act, these benefits were increased. In 1956, the Act was amended to permit women to receive benefits when they reached age 62. In 1961, this amendment was extended to permit men to draw a reduced benefit at age 62. Disability benefits were added in 1956 and were subsequently liberalized. By the mid-1960s the maximum old-age benefit had increased to $168 per month and the minimum benefit was $44 per month. Average old-age benefits paid had risen from $23 per month in 1940 to $84 per month by 1965.

Eligibility

Initially, according to the 1935 Act, a worker must have had earnings in covered employment over a specified length of time in order to collect benefits. In 1939, amendments provided for two types of insured status. A worker became "fully insured" only when at least $50 was earned in covered employment in each of 40 quarters (10 years). This was later modified because new groups and the self-employed were brought into the System. By 1961, workers were considered fully insured if their quarters of covered employment equaled at least the number of years between 1950 (or age 21, if later) and age 65, or to the date of death if it occurred earlier. This requirement still prevails today.

If a worker were to die today before being fully insured, survivors could benefit if the worker was "currently insured," meaning that the worker had covered employment for at least 1½ years within the 3 years prior to death. The worker's status as fully insured or currently insured has an effect on survivor and death benefits.

Under the initial Act, complete retirement was essential for the receipt of benefits. Amendments followed, however, to permit a worker to earn up to $1,200 per year without losing benefits. This was later boosted to $1,500, then to $3,000, and now to $4,000 per year. If a worker earns over the stipulated amount according to the earnings test, a penalty is imposed with the loss of some benefits. At age 69 and beyond, however, there is no restriction on the earnings of a worker collecting federal old-age benefits.

Hospital and Health Care (Medicare)

In 1965, the Social Security Act was amended to provide insurance protection against the cost of hospital and related health care to covered individuals when they reached 65 years of age or older. The amendments also provided hospital insurance for persons not covered under the Act who reached age 65 before 1968. In addition, the amendments permit all persons 65 years of age and over to purchase protection against the cost of physician's fees with one half of the cost paid by the federal government out of general revenue funds.

The 1965 amendments, moreover, liberalized the earnings test, the definition of disability, and the cash benefits payable for disability. The federal matching ratios for public assistance were increased and federal grants to states for maternal and child health care and welfare services were improved. An addition was made to the Social Security payroll tax to provide financing for the new Medicare package.

Thus, after 30 years there was added to the Social Security program the beginnings of hospital and health care insurance. This was a concept initially recommended back in 1935 by the President's Committee on Economic Security for eventual inclusion under Social Security.

Supplemental Security Income (SSI)

In addition to regular OASDHI benefits, the Social Security program, since 1965, has provided monthly checks to people in financial need who are 65 or older and to people at any age who are blind or disabled. People who have little or no cash income and who do not own much property may get supplementary security income, even if they have never worked or contributed to Social Security taxes. SSI is not the same as Social Security even though the program is run by the Social Security Administration. The money for SSI checks comes from general funds of the U.S. Treasury. Persons who receive Social Security benefits may also obtain SSI checks in some cases. A person, however, does not have to be eligible for Social Security benefits in order to receive supplemental security income.

Financing OASI

According to the 1935 Act, old-age and survivors insurance was to be financed solely through a payroll tax levied on both employers and employees in covered employment. The initial tax rate was set at 1 percent each on the employer and employee on the first $3,000 of yearly earnings. An increase of ½ percentage point was to be made every three years until 1949, when the total contribution by both employer and employee was to become 3 percent. Subsequent amendments by Congress, however, postponed or eliminated these increases until 1950, when the tax rate was increased to 1½ percent and the tax base was raised to $3,600 per year. The tax rate was retained at that level until 1954 when it was raised to 2 percent. It was held there through 1955 and 1956, but the tax base was increased to $4,200 per year. The next year the rate was increased by ¼ percentage point to cover the cost of disability insurance. Increases subsequently raised the rates to 3⅝ percent on $6,600 of earnings by 1966. At that time scheduled increases were to raise the rates to 4.85 percent by 1973. Moreover, additional taxes were to be added to finance hospital insurance, beginning in 1966. That rate, initiated at .35 percent on employer and employee in 1966, was to rise to .80 percent each in 1987.

According to the Act, receipts from payroll taxes were to be deposited in a special reserve account or trust fund with the U.S. Treasury. Future benefits were to be paid from the trust fund without the need to use general revenue funds from the federal government. The law required that the funds in the account be invested in securities of the federal government, and interest from these securities was to be used also for the payment of benefits.

Even though amendments which increased the number of covered workers and raised the size of benefits increased the cost of the Social Security program, the trust fund grew more rapidly than anticipated. This was due to the increase in employment and the payment of higher wages, especially because of World War II. As a result, scheduled increases in the tax rates were eliminated or postponed.

Tax contributions plus earned interest on government securities continued to exceed disbursements for OASI until 1957. In that year disbursements for benefits exceeded net income for the first time in the short history of the Social Security program. Net assets of the trust fund declined thereafter from $22,519 million in 1957 to $18,235 million in 1965.

Increases in the tax rate and in the earnings used as a tax base arrested the diminution of the trust fund and resulted in an increase in its assets. By 1974 total assets in the OASI trust fund had risen to $37,777 million. At the same time the sizes of the disability trust fund and the hospital trust fund had risen to $8,109 million and $9,119 million, respectively.

THE 1972 AMENDMENTS

Prior to 1972 the Social Security law provided that a retiree's initial old-age benefit be based on earnings up to the level of the Social Security wage base existing during a person's working life. Moreover, there were no automatic increases in either the wage base, on which benefit payments were calculated, or in the schedule of benefits. The only way either could be changed was by an act of Congress.

In 1972 the Social Security law was amended, however, to provide automatic increases in the wage base. This would result in a gradual rise in initial old-age benefit payments. In addition, the schedule of future benefits of current workers, along with the current benefits of current beneficiaries, was to be automatically adjusted by tying benefits to the consumer price index. The primary purpose of this measure was to adjust the purchasing power of benefits to offset increases in the cost of living. This resulted in a double cost-of-living adjustment for current workers, however. As prices rose their future benefits were adjusted upward. But higher prices were also in large part responsible for higher earnings, which would yield them greater benefits upon retirement. This double adjustment is commonly referred to as "coupling." This coupling helped cause the "replacement rate," which is the ratio of a worker's retirement benefit to average monthly earnings, to rise substantially, putting an added burden on the Social Security System.

With the highly inflationary conditions of the 1970s, especially the double-digit inflation that occurred during 1973 and 1974, the coupling process resulted in substantial increases in old-age and survivor's benefits payments. Between 1972 and 1976, for example, the average monthly benefit for a retired worker increased by 39 percent in current dollar value.

Table 5-1 on the following page shows changes in federal old-age benefits vis-à-vis changes in the consumer price index. It can be noted that since payments first started in 1940 the average monthly benefit for a retired worker increased from $22.60 to $225.00 in 1976, an increase of 896 percent. In terms of constant or real dollars, the average monthly benefit increased 149 percent, as shown in the final column of Table 5-1. For a more recent period it can be observed that between 1970 and 1976 the average monthly benefit rose from $118.00 to $225.00, a rise of 91 percent in current dollars. During that same period the average monthly benefit in constant dollars rose 30 percent. Observe, too, that after the 1972 amendments the current dollar average monthly benefit had risen 39 percent by 1976. Real benefits in that period, however, remained fairly stable.

STATUS OF THE TRUST FUNDS

By 1976 there were over 33 million persons receiving OASDHI benefits of one kind or another. The average monthly benefit for retired workers was

Table 5-1

AVERAGE MONTHLY BENEFIT FOR A RETIRED WORKER IN CURRENT AND CONSTANT DOLLARS, 1940–1976

Year	Average Monthly Benefit	Cumulative Percentage Increase	CPI — 1967 Base Year	CPI — 1976 Base Year	Average Monthly Benefit In Constant 1976 Dollars	Cumulative Percentage Increase
1940	22.60	—	42.0	25	90.40	—
1945	24.50	8	53.9	32	76.56	−15
1950	43.86	94	72.1	42	104.42	15
1955	61.90	174	80.2	47	131.70	46
1960	74.04	228	88.7	52	142.38	58
1965	83.92	271	94.5	55	152.58	69
1970	118.00	422	116.3	68	173.53	92
1972	162.00	617	125.3	74	218.92	142
1975	207.00	816	161.2	95	217.89	141
1976	225.00	896	170.5	100	225.00	149

SOURCE: *Statistical Abstract of the United States*, 1977, and previous issues.

$225.00, and for a retired worker and spouse the average monthly benefit amounted to $350.00. In 1976, net receipts to the OASI trust fund from tax contributions, transfers from general revenues, and interest income amounted to $66.3 billion. During the same year, expenditures from the trust fund for benefit payments and administrative and related expenses amounted to $66.6 billion. Thus, in 1976 the net assets (reserves) of the OASI fund were decreased to $35.4 billion. The Disability Trust Fund had a $1,500 million net outflow, leaving the fund with assets of $5.7 billion. The Hospital (Medicare) Trust Fund, on the other hand, had a $100 million net addition, raising it to a level of $10.6 billion. These and other data are shown in Table 5-2. From another point of view, in 1976 the OASDI trust funds collected $75.1 billion in funds, but disbursed $76.9 billion. This left $41.1 billion in the combined OASDI trust funds. The $75.1 billion in benefits payments was about 20 percent of the federal budget, an amount equivalent to over 4 percent of the GNP. As late as 1977 OASI was being financed by a payroll tax of 8.75 percent (4.375 percent each paid by the employer and employee) on earnings up to $16,500 per annum. At that time about 90 percent of all wage and salary earners and the self-employed were covered by the Social Security program and subject to its compulsory contributions.

Between 1970 and 1975 total assets (reserves) of the OASDI trust funds fell from 110 percent of annual expenditures to 55 percent of annual expenditures. Moreover, by 1977 reserves equaled only 50 percent of annual expenditures. In addition, in the period 1970–1976, the number of retired workers

Table 5-2

SOCIAL SECURITY (OASDHI) TRUST FUNDS, 1960–1976

(Millions of Dollars)

Type of Trust Fund	1960	1965	1967	1970	1972	1973	1974	1975	1976
Old-age and survivors									
Net contribution income[1]	10,866	16,017	23,138	30,256	37,781	45,975	52,081	56,816	63,362
Transfers from general revenue[2]	(X)	(X)	78	449	475	442	447	425	614
Interest received	516	593	818	1,515	1,794	1,928	2,159	2,364	2,301
Benefit payments	10,677	16,737	19,468	28,796	37,122	45,741	51,618	58,509	65,699
Administrative expenses	203	328	406	471	674	647	865	896	959
Percent of benefit payments	1.9	2.0	2.1	1.6	1.8	1.4	1.7	1.5	1.5
Assets, end of year	20,324	18,235	24,222	32,454	35,318	36,487	37,777	36,987	35,388
Disability									
Net contribution income[1]	1,010	1,188	2,286	4,481	5,107	5,932	6,826	7,444	8,233
Transfers from general revenue[2]	(X)	(X)	16	16	51	52	52	90	103
Interest received	53	59	78	277	414	458	500	502	422
Benefit payments	568	1,573	1,939	3,067	4,473	5,718	6,903[1]	8,414	9,966
Administrative expenses	36	90	109	164	233	190	217	256	285
Percent of benefit payments	6.4	5.7	5.6	5.3	5.2	3.3	3.1	3.0	2.8
Assets, end of year	2,289	1,606	2,029	5,614	7,457	7,927	8,109	7,354	5,745
Hospital									
Net contribution income[1]	(X)	(X)	3,152	4,881	5,731	9,945	10,850	11,509	12,736
Transfers from general revenue[2]	(X)	(X)	312	874	429	499	519	669	141
Interest received	(X)	(X)	51	161	182	281	528	671	753
Benefit payments	(X)	(X)	3,353	5,124	6,319	7,057	9,101	11,318	13,343
Administrative expenses	(X)	(X)	77	157	184	232	271	263	336
Percent of benefit payments	(X)	(X)	2.3	3.1	2.9	3.3	3.0	2.3	2.5
Assets, end of year	(X)	(X)	1,073	3,202	2,935	6,467	9,119	10,517	10,605
Supplementary medical care									
Net contribution income[1]	(X)	(X)	640	1,096	1,382	1,550	1,804	1,918	2,060
Transfers from general revenue[2]	(X)	(X)	933	1,093	1,389	1,705	2,225	2,648	3,810
Interest received	(X)	(X)	24	12	37	57	95	106	106
Benefit payments	(X)	(X)	1,197	1,975	2,325	2,526	3,318	4,273	5,080
Administrative expenses	(X)	(X)	110	238	290	318	410	462	542
Percent of benefit payments	(X)	(X)	9.2	12.0	12.5	12.6	12.4	10.8	10.8
Assets, end of year	(X)	(X)	412	188	643	1,111	1,506	1,444	1,799

SOURCE: U.S. Social Security Administration, *Social Security Bulletin*, May, 1977.

X Not applicable.

[1]Includes deposits by states and deductions for refund of estimated employee-tax over-payment. Supplementary medical insurance represents voluntary premium payments from and in behalf of insured persons.

[2]Transfers for military wage credits and for cost of hospital benefits for persons not insured for OASDHI or railroad retirement cash benefits.

increased 28 percent. It was also projected that in future decades a greater percentage of the population would be in the retirement-age bracket, as shown in Figure 5-1.

With an increasing number of workers retiring with higher initial old-age benefits, the Social Security Administration foresaw the eventual depletion of the OASDI trust funds within 8 years. One projection for the status of the trust funds is shown on the following page.

This depletion of the trust funds and the pending deficit was to occur despite the scheduled increases in the payroll tax wage base and the tax rates, as shown under the old (prior) law, in Tables 5-3 and 5-4, on pages 107 and 108.

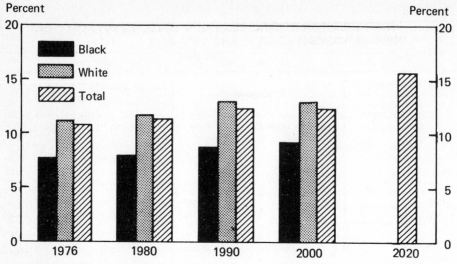

SOURCE: U.S. Bureau of the Census.

Note: Black and White projections to the year 2020 not available.

Figure 5-1 **POPULATION 65 YEARS OF AGE AND OLDER AS A
PERCENTAGE OF ALL AGES, BY RACE
1976 AND PROJECTIONS TO 2020**

A number of factors can be cited to explain the substantial decline in the levels of the OASDI trust funds. First, benefits for persons already retired had been indexed in recent years to the consumer price index. This resulted in a sharp increase in benefit payments with the higher rates of inflation in the 1970s. Secondly, the high levels of unemployment during the 1970s, especially during the 1974–1975 recession, resulted in a slowdown in the growth of payroll tax receipts. Thirdly, the number of beneficiaries receiving disability insurance payments had been higher than anticipated. In fact, the drain on the

Projected Status of Trust Funds

Year	Trust Fund Reserves (Billions)
1977	$41.1
1978	35.5
1979	28.6
1980	20.7
1981	11.6
1982	0.1
1983	−14.8

Table 5-3

TAX RATES FOR SOCIAL SECURITY TRUST FUNDS, OLD AND NEW LAWS, CALENDAR YEARS 1977–2011

[Percent]

Calendar year	Prior law				Social Security Amendments of 1977			
	Total	OASI	DI	HI	Total	OASI	DI	HI
Employer and employee, each								
1977.................	5.85	4.375	0.575	0.900	5.85	4.375	0.575	0.900
1978.................	6.05	4.350	.600	1.100	6.05	4.275	.775	1.000
1979–1980	6.05	4.350	.600	1.100	6.13	4.330	.750	1.050
1981.................	6.30	4.300	.650	1.350	6.65	4.525	.825	1.300
1982–1984	6.30	4.300	.650	1.350	6.70	4.575	.825	1.300
1985.................	6.30	4.300	.650	1.350	7.05	4.750	.950	1.350
1986–1989	6.45	4.250	.700	1.500	7.15	4.750	.950	1.450
1990–2010	6.45	4.250	.700	1.500	7.65	5.100	1.100	1.450
2011 and after......	7.45	5.100	.850	1.500	7.65	5.100	1.100	1.450
Self-employed persons								
1977.................	7.90	6.185	0.815	0.900	7.90	6.185	0.815	0.900
1978.................	8.10	6.150	.850	1.100	8.10	6.010	1.090	1.000
1979–1980	8.10	6.150	.850	1.100	8.10	6.010	1.040	1.050
1981.................	8.35	6.080	.920	1.350	9.30	6.7625	1.2375	1.300
1982–1984	8.35	6.080	.920	1.350	9.35	6.8125	1.2375	1.300
1985.................	8.35	6.080	.920	1.350	9.90	7.125	1.425	1.350
1986–1989	8.50	6.010	.990	1.500	10.00	7.125	1.425	1.450
1990–2010	8.50	6.010	.990	1.500	10.75	7.650	1.650	1.450
2011 and after......	8.50	6.000	1.000	1.500	10.75	7.650	1.650	1.450

SOURCE: *Economic Report of the President*, 1978, p. 235.

disability trust fund was so rapid that it was estimated in 1977 that the fund would be depleted by 1979. Lastly, the unintentional process of coupling benefits to a higher wage base and to the CPI caused initial benefits of retirees to rise more rapidly than wages.

Wage rates were expected to rise because of inflation. Therefore, the wage base for OASI payroll taxes was increased. Since retirees' benefits were based on earnings in their most recent work years (years which, incidentally, had the higher Social Security wage bases compared to earlier years), their initial retirement benefits were higher than they would have been under the older law. Benefits were also tied to the CPI to offset the adverse effects of inflation on the purchasing power of benefits. This meant that benefits would

Table 5-4

SOCIAL SECURITY CONTRIBUTION AND BENEFIT BASE, OLD AND NEW LAWS, CALENDAR YEARS 1977–1983

Calendar year	Contribution and benefit base[1]	
	Prior law	Social Security Amendments of 1977
1977	$16,500	$16,500
1978	17,700	17,700
1979	18,900	22,900
1980	20,400	25,900
1981	21,900	29,700
1982	23,700	32,100
1983	25,800	34,800

SOURCE: *Economic Report of the President*, 1978, p. 236.

[1]After 1978 under the old law and after 1981 under the new law, based on path of wages projected in *The Budget of the United States Government, Fiscal Year 1979*.

increase for two reasons. One, because the wage base increased, and secondly due to the rise in the CPI. But since both the wage base and the CPI increased because of inflation, it was tantamount to giving a double adjustment in benefits for inflation.

Looking at the long run, the OASDI trust funds were in even more serious trouble. Using the wage base, payroll tax, and age and retirement assumptions existing in 1977, it was estimated by the Social Security trustees that average OASDI expenditures over the next 75 years would exceed payroll taxes by an amount equivalent to 8 percent of taxable earnings. To avoid this situation would require a tripling of OASDI tax rates by the year 2050 just to finance the schedule of future benefits provided for in the existing law.

It was calculated that half the projected long-range deficit was due to the technical flaw caused by the double adjustment for inflation resulting from the coupling process. In fact, it was calculated that double indexing would eventually cause benefits to exceed pre-retirement wages for some workers. The other half of the projected deficit was due to a continued increase in disability payments and a sharp rise in the number of retired persons relative to the working population after the year 2000. In 1977, for example, there were 19 persons aged 65 or over for every 100 persons in the 20-64 age bracket. It is estimated that by the year 2030 there will be 34 persons 65 or over for every 100 persons in the 20–64 category. In still other terms, today the ratio of current workers to retirees, their survivors, and their dependents is 3 to 1. In another generation or two the ratio could drop to 2 to 1, putting further stress on the Social Security System.

Based upon the findings of an Advisory Council on Social Security appointed in 1975 and Congressional hearings on the subject, Congress in 1977 struggled hard to find a solution to the Social Security problem.

One major point of controversy revolved around the issue of whether or not OASDHI benefits should be financed solely through payroll taxes or be financed in part from general revenue funds of the federal government. This led to a broader question regarding the nature of the Social Security System. Should it be an actuarially sound system with benefits paid at retirement based strictly on an individual worker's tax contributions (and those of the employer) made during the worker's life? It was evident that the System long ago had moved away from this concept and to a "pay-as-you-go" system in which tax contributions from current workers were used to finance benefit payments to current retirees. Consequently, some analysts suggested the use of general revenue funds to help finance Social Security benefits. Others thought that such a practice would lead to widespread liberalization of benefits and abuses in the System.

It was also pointed out during the hearings that, for a number of reasons, the Social Security System was in large part a huge "transfer payment" mechanism instead of an insurance system. For example, benefits paid to higher-income wage earners were not in proportion to the greater amount of taxes they paid during their work lives. On the other hand, many low-income wage earners were receiving benefits greater than that merited by their tax contributions. This was especially true of those receiving the minimum benefit. In fact, some of the tax funds were used to provide benefits to persons who contributed nothing to the Social Security funds.

A further issue arose along this vein regarding the dual wage-earner family. The husband-wife retirement benefit to a worker and non-working spouse was as good as that going to a family in which both the husband and wife worked prior to retirement. In short, many working wives thought they were being cheated since they would receive the same amount of benefits had they not worked. In effect, the wife's contribution counted for nothing extra in benefit payments for the family.

The question of whether or not the employer-employee tax rates should be indentical also was debated. Some had advocated that the employer ought to pay a larger portion of the total tax. The ratio of the tax rate for the self-employed worker was also given consideration.

Much was discussed, too, regarding the best way to increase contributions to avoid future deficits. Some strongly suggested that tax rates be increased substantially. Others advocated increasing the tax base. Those objecting to an increase in the tax rates did so in large part on the premise that the higher rates would hit hardest on the lower wage-earner groups. Since taxes are paid only on earnings within the tax base, it would mean that some of the earnings by higher wage-earners would not be subject to the tax. On the other hand, practically all of the earnings of the lower and, perhaps, many of the middle income wage-earners would have their entire earnings subject to higher Social Security taxes.

Those advocating an increase in the tax base did so with the notion that the additional funds needed could be raised by increasing the tax base. This would tax those wages in excess of the current base earned by some middle income people and particularly by high-wage earning groups. At the same time it would leave the taxes paid by the lower income group unchanged.

The problems caused by the coupling process came in for much discussion and debate. It was pointed out that coupling had increased the replacement rate, which is the ratio of a worker's Social Security benefit to that worker's final working pay. This replacement rate was 43 percent in 1977 compared to an average of 31 percent between 1950 and 1969. The Advisory Council on Social Security recommended that it be kept between 40 and 45 percent.

Other matters discussed and debated included the feasibility of taxing Social Security benefits, raising the retirement age, incorporating civilian employees of the federal government, along with their existing pension fund, into the Social Security System, and whether or not any future national health insurance program should become a part of the Social Security System.

THE 1977 AMENDMENTS

After much discussion, and faced with a pending deficit in both the short run and the long run, Congress amended the Social Security Act in 1977 to alleviate the System's financial plight. Since Congress has generally operated on the presumption that OASDI benefits should be financed primarily via payroll tax receipts, it was essential to raise OASDI tax rates and/or raise the wage base subject to Social Security taxes if deficits were to be avoided. The major changes brought about by the 1977 amendments include the following.

1. A decoupling of the double adjustment in benefits (wage base increases plus CPI adjustments) for inflation. This was done by stabilizing initial benefit levels for a 65-year-old retiree, who always earned the average wage, at about 42 percent of earnings in the year prior to retirement, regardless of the behavior of wages and prices. This change, it was expected, would cut the pending long-run deficit by one half. In effect, at the time of retirement a beneficiary's past wages will be indexed to a more current level. But no adjustment will be made in benefits for past changes in the CPI. Once the worker retires and begins collecting benefits, however, the benefits will be adjusted periodically for changes in average wage increases.

Under this new method of computation, this formula will be applied:

$$\text{Actual earnings for year being updated} \times \frac{\text{Average annual wage at age 60}}{\text{Average annual wage for year being updated}} = \text{indexed earnings.}$$

If a worker earned $3,000 in 1956 and retired at age 62 in 1979, the $3,000 would be multiplied by the ratio of average annual wages in 1977 ($10,002) to the average annual wage in 1956 ($3,514) as follows:

$$\$3,000 \times \frac{\$10,002}{\$\ 3,514} = \$8,539.$$

Therefore, while the worker's actual earnings for 1956 were $3,000, the relative or indexed earnings, as far as computing Social Security benefits are concerned, would be the indexed annual earnings of $8,539 ($711.58 per month). An average indexed monthly earnings (AIME) is then obtained for the worker's covered employment. Once this is obtained, a worker's monthly benefit will be calculated by taking 90 percent of the first $180 AIME, plus 32 percent of the AIME over $180 through $1,085, plus 15 percent of AIME over $1,085. Once the worker retires, benefits will be adjusted periodically for changes in the average annual wage of Social Security participants.

2. OASDI tax rates for employers and employees would increase above the existing schedule, beginning in 1979. This new schedule can be seen in Table 5-3. According to the new tax schedule, the tax rates for both employers and employees would rise from the current OASDHI rate of 5.85 percent in 1977 to 6.70 percent in 1983 instead of the 6.30 percent scheduled in the old law. By the year 1990, the tax rate will be 7.65 percent for both the employer and employee.

3. The schedule of taxes for the self-employed was likewise increased. Beginning in 1981 the OASDI tax rate for the self-employed will be adjusted to restore its original relationship of one and one half times the OASDI tax rate for employees.

4. To prevent the reserves of the disability insurance fund from being exhausted, the new law provides for a reallocation of current tax rates among the trust funds in 1978.

5. The taxable wage base for employers, employees, and the self-employed was increased, as shown under the 1977 amendments in Table 5-4. The base would rise from the prior maximum of $25,880 in 1983 to $34,800 per annum.

Under the new law, a worker earning the taxable maximum of $34,800 or more annually in 1983 will pay $2,332 ($34,800 × .0670) in Social Security taxes. The employer will match the amount for a total of $4,664 paid on the worker's account. A worker earning the average wage at that time, expected to be in the vicinity of $13,500 per year, will pay $905 in Social Security taxes. The new higher wage base plus the higher tax rates to go into effect in 1979 are expected to yield about $90 billion in additional tax revenues in the five-year period 1979–1983 inclusive. This, too, will prevent any deficit from arising in the various trust funds.

The new law also made a number of changes in the benefit structure. Regarding the retirement or earnings test, for example, under the prior law a retiree between the ages of 65 and 72 could earn up to $3,000 annually without suffering an OASDI benefit penalty. For every $2 in earnings above the $3,000 level, however, the retiree's benefit was reduced by one dollar. There was no restriction for retirees aged 72 or more.

Under the new 1977 law the ceiling on earnings for a retired worker between the ages of 65 and 69 will rise to $4,000 per year in 1978, and then by $500 increments up to a ceiling of $6,000 by 1982. When earnings in any year exceed the ceiling, OASDI benefits are reduced by $1 for every $2 earned in excess of the ceiling.[2] According to the new law, no earnings ceiling is imposed on beneficiaries after they reach 69 years of age.

On the other hand, a bonus is provided for those who postpone retirement beyond age 65. Benefits received will rise from 1 to 3 percent for each year an eligible retiree does not elect to receive benefits between the ages of 65 and 72.

DO WE PAY TWICE FOR SOCIAL SECURITY?

Some critics of Social Security claim that participants are paying twice for their benefits, once when the payroll tax is paid and secondly when they receive their benefits. This happens, they say, because of the way in which Social Security contributions are funneled through the trust funds.

Monies once collected and held in the trust funds by law have to be invested in federal government securities. Thus, the initial payroll tax funds are invested in U.S. government securities and held as assets in the respective trust funds. In short, the Social Security Administration lends its reserves to the U.S. Treasury. Interest collected on these securities adds to the value of the trust funds. When the Social Security Administration needs funds for distribution, however, it must redeem the securities to have money to meet Social Security benefit payments. When the securities are redeemed the Treasury must raise taxes, or borrow funds elsewhere, in order to pay for the securities being redeemed by the Social Security Administration. Thus, say the critics, we pay once again for Social Security when the government taxes us to obtain the money to pay off the securities redeemed by the Social Security Administration for the purpose of paying Social Security benefits.

Even if we were taxed directly to raise money to pay off the government securities, however, it is not a double tax for Social Security. What actually happens is that as a result of the Social Security Administration purchasing government securities, the Treasury can levy fewer taxes. The money borrowed from the Social Security trust funds is used by the Treasury in lieu of tax funds to purchase certain goods and services. Some taxes which should have been collected are thus not collected or the collection postponed. Money borrowed from the Social Security trust funds may have been used, for example, to build a dam or other such project. As a result, no taxes are collected

---

[2]The ceiling is pro-rated and imposed on a monthly basis during the first year of retirement. Thereafter, it is on an annual basis.

for that purpose. When the borrowed funds are paid back at the time the Treasury redeems the securities held by the trust funds, the tax we may pay to give the Treasury the money it needs to pay off the securities is a tax to pay for the dam. In short, the tax we should have paid earlier for the dam was postponed until the time when the borrowed funds had to be repaid. The true purpose of the tax at that time is to pay for the dam, not to again pay for Social Security.

WHO ARE THE DOUBLE-DIPPERS?

Much concern has been expressed in the Social Security controversy regarding the so-called double-dippers. This term refers to a person who is collecting a dual pension from the federal government, one of which is from the OASI program.

Most persons work and pay Social Security taxes on the first dollar earned and on every dollar thereafter, within the Social Security wage base, until retirement. If the person retires or quits early, he or she can collect no pension benefits until age 62. Upon official retirement the participant collects only one federal pension — OASI.

On the other hand, employees of the federal government, excluding military personnel, do not contribute to the Social Security System because most federal employees are covered by their own pension system. The federal employee, however, may get into the Social Security System by holding a second job part-time (moonlighting) that is covered by Social Security. Another way they may attain coverage is by working again after retirement. Many of them do this since they frequently retire at an earlier age than 65. They can collect their federal pension and at the same time be working on a Social Security covered job. The regular worker covered by Social Security is discouraged from working and collecting Social Security benefits simultaneously by the earnings test, which restricts the worker's ability to collect benefits and continue working. Moreover, when the federal employee retires again at age 62, 65, or later, OASI benefits can be collected in addition to the federal pension. Thus, the concept of the double-dipper.

Double-dipping would not be a serious problem except for the fact that Social Security benefits are weighted in favor of those at the low end of the income scale. This is done on the theory that the lower income workers are poor people, who had limited earnings during their work lives, and who need a little more help upon retirement. Social Security benefits are proportionately higher for low income workers. The double-dipper who worked for only a few years, or at part-time work, shows up on the Social Security records as having had limited wage earnings. Consequently, a windfall is received as a result of having minimal Social Security coverage. A post-retirement federal employee who has ten years of coverage under Social Security and has a generous federal pension will show up on the Social Security rolls as poor when in fact that is not true.

It has been estimated that if double-dipping were terminated it would save the Social Security System about $1 billion per year. There are several ways to eliminate this problem, if deemed desirable. One way is to bring all federal employees under the Social Security System. A second method would be to exempt retired federal employees from Social Security coverage whenever they moonlight or take up a second career after retirement. This could be done by exempting them from Social Security taxes on a secondary jobs. Since they pay less in taxes than they receive in Social Security benefits, it would certainly save the Social Security System some money.

CONCLUSION

When the Social Security program was first inaugurated in 1935, it was intended that the program would be self-financing and operated on an actuarially sound basis. Contributions from payroll taxes were expected to exceed benefit payments in the early years and result in an accumulation of assets in the various trust funds.

A retiree's benefits were to be closely related to prior work-life earnings, except for special treatment given to those receiving a minimum benefit. Moreover, it was stated clearly that the purpose of the Social Security System was to provide partial aid for beneficiaries. Social Security was not originally designed or intended to provide complete or full living costs for retirees. Many individuals in the early years thought, too, that their payroll taxes plus their employer's contributions were going into individually numbered accounts, out of which they would receive benefits upon retirement. This was not the case, however, since the payroll taxes of all persons and employers go into general trust funds.

Amendments to the Social Security Act as early as 1939 began to change the characteristics of the Social Security program by providing that some individuals retiring early in the life of the program would receive benefits greater than the actual value of the individual's combined employer-employee contributions, and that dependents of retired workers would receive benefits without any additional payroll taxes required.

In 1950, amendments moved the Social Security System farther away from a fully funded, actuarially sound system toward the type of "pay-as-you-go" system that it is today. Today, those currently working pay for the benefits of those who are retired.

Over the years, additional workers have been brought under the Social Security System and benefits have been increased periodically by Congress. In 1972, amendments provided for adjusting benefit levels with changes in the consumer price index so that benefits would rise automatically with price changes. In addition, the maximum taxable earnings base was indexed roughly to consumer prices. Therefore, it also increased over time. This provided a "coupling effect" or a double adjustment for inflation.

All these changes put a strain in recent years on the trust funds, which had accumulated over the past 30–35 years. Depletion of the trust funds and eventual deficits were projected for the early 1980s by the Social Security trustees. This led Congress in 1977 to make changes designed to strengthen the trust funds and prevent the projected deficits from occurring. The major changes enacted by Congress regarding financing were the increases in the OASDHI tax rates and the increase in the base of covered earnings.

The changes made by Congress in 1977 removed the immediate threat that the cash benefit programs would run out of funds, corrected the obvious flaw in benefit computation, and reduced the projected average deficit over the next 75 years from 8 percent of estimated payroll to 1½ percent.

Some of the long-run issues, however, are still unresolved. The differences in treatment between one- and two-earner households, certain problems between the cash benefit programs and private retirement programs, whether or not government employees, along with their pension reserve fund, ought to be brought under the Social Security System, and the major issue of whether a part or all of the funds for Social Security benefits should come from federal general tax revenues remain as issues to be dealt with.

Moreover, there is concern about the impact from the rise in Social Security payroll taxes on the status of the general economy. At this writing, a movement in Congress has begun to postpone or repeal the increases in tax rate schedules to go into effect in 1979. At the same time, Congress is also scheduled to consider proposals for some form of national health insurance. If adopted, how would it be financed, and what kind of strains might it place on the Social Security System?

MAJOR ISSUES

1. Should OASDHI benefits be financed in whole or in part by general revenue funds?
2. Should civilian employees of the federal government be forced to join the Social Security System?
3. Should the Social Security System revert to a fully funded, actuarially sound basis?
4. If a system of national health insurance is adopted in the United States, should it be incorporated into the Social Security System?
5. Should future Social Security contributions, if needed, be generated through increasing the tax base or the tax rate?

SUBISSUES

1. Should working wives in two-earner households be given their own OASDI benefits?
2. Do you think that Social Security ought to be used as a transfer payment mechanism?
3. Congress, in early 1978, raised the compulsory retirement age from 65 to 70 years. Do you think that Social Security benefits should thus start at age 70 instead of the present 65 or 62 years of age?
4. Do you favor taxing Social Security benefits as regular income?
5. Should double-dipping be eliminated? If so, how?

SELECTED READINGS

Altmeyer, Arthur T. *The Formative Years of Social Security*. University of Wisconsin Press, 1966.

Annual Statistical Supplement, 1975, Social Security Bulletin. 1977 Amendment (Chart Booklet), U.S. Department of Health, Education, and Welfare, Social Security Administration, December, 1977.

Bowen, William G., Frederick H. Harbison, *et al. The American System of Social Insurance*. New York: McGraw-Hill Book Company, 1968.

Campbell, Colin D. *The 1977 Amendments to the Social Security Act*. Washington: American Enterprise Institute for Public Policy Research, 1978.

Daly, John Charles (Moderator). *The Future of the Social Security System*. Washington: American Enterprise Institute for Public Policy Research, AEI Forum No. 13, 1977.

Economic Report of the President, 1978, pages 232–237.

Estimating Your Social Security Retirement Check. HEW Publication No. (SSA) 77-10047.

Kaplan, Robert S. *Indexing Social Security*. Washington: American Enterprise Institute for Public Policy Research, 1977.

Munnell, A. H. "Carter's Proposals For Social Security." *Challenge* (September, 1977).

1977 Amendments Chart Book. U.S. Department of Health, Education, and Welfare, December, 1977.

Schorr, A. L. "Welfare Reform and Social Insurance." *Challenge* (November, 1977).

Social Security Act of 1977: An Analysis for the Business Community. Coopers and Lybrand Newsletter (January, 1978).

Social Security Bulletins, 1977 and 1978 (monthly).

"Social Security's Refinancing Dilemma." *Business Week* (October 4, 1977).

"Social Security — There Is a Better Way." *Monthly Economic Letter* (July, 1977).

Your Social Security. HEW Publication No. (SSA) 77-10035.

The National 6
Debt — Will It Bankrupt Us?

With a number of federal deficits inadvertently and purposely occurring in the past several years and the national debt scheduled to reach $874 billion at the end of 1979 and rapidly rising toward the $1 trillion mark, renewed interest has been generated in the problems of our large national debt. The debt ceiling has been raised substantially in recent years to accommodate large planned federal deficits in connection with major income and excise tax reductions in the economy, outlays for the Great Society programs, accelerated defense spending for the war in Vietnam, and planned deficits to bolster the economy. In a four-year period, 1975–1978, the federal debt increased by more than $300 billion and today it is not uncommon to have an annual federal deficit in excess of $50 billion. How did the debt arise? To whom do we owe it? How long can the debt continue to rise? Can it reach a point where it will bankrupt the nation? Is it fair or possible to pass the debt on to future generations? Why have we not paid it off? Will we ever pay it off? How much interest are we paying on the national debt? What happens when the debt comes due and the government does not have the money to pay? These are but a few of the many questions in the minds of citizens that we will try to answer here.

HISTORY OF THE DEBT

Since our nation first began, the national debt has been a source of heated debate. A brief review of the past will shed some light on the present and reveal that many of the current issues regarding the debt are not new.

The Early Years

Much argument and opposition was expressed in 1789 to Secretary of the Treasury Alexander Hamilton's proposal for the new Union to assume the debts of the various states, as well as the debts of the Confederation. Hamilton's plan divided the public debt outstanding into three major categories: the Confederation domestic debt, the Confederation foreign debt, and the Revolutionary state indebtedness. Most legislators agreed that the foreign debt should be taken care of as soon as possible, especially since the United States would in all probability become a debtor nation in its early years and would want to borrow from foreign nations. There was no such ease of agreement on what to do about the domestic debt, however.

Since some of the original holders of government stock (bonds) had subsequently sold the stock at a market price lower than the original purchase price, a controversy occurred as to whether the government should pay off the current debt holders according to the original value of the stock or at the current market value. Strong objection also was expressed regarding the 6 percent interest charge on the domestic debt; serious debate arose over the suggestion of paying the $13 million in interest that had accumulated on the domestic debt.

An even hotter controversy developed regarding federal assumption of state debts. Since some states, especially in the South, had a limited amount of debt, they stood to gain little from such a measure. It was a compromise move to get support of southern members of Congress on this issue that resulted in the location of our national capital in its present site, a southern location, rather than elsewhere.

Hamilton suggested that the current debts be disposed of by having the new government issue its own bonds in exchange for existing forms of indebtedness. He recommended that the federal government give full service to the national debt so that the government's ability to fulfill its domestic and foreign obligations would never again be questioned. He suggested that interest payments always be met fully at the designated periods, and that the bonds of the federal government be sustained at a premium and not sold at a discount.

Structure of Initial Debt

The entire plan and its funding method according to Hamilton would serve three purposes: it would serve as a common bond to unify the people of the nation and draw the states closer together, it would establish a sound basis for further credit expansion both here and abroad, and the federal instruments of debt would serve as a basis of circulating capital to help alleviate the shortage of currency in the new nation. After winning his point to pay the old debts off at their original price, to pay the interest in arrears, to maintain the 6 percent interest, and to assume the state debts, the new nation began its fiscal career with a total outstanding debt of more than $77 million.

Although in the early years of our nation it was thought that the new federal debt would be gradually retired out of federal surpluses, little effort was made in this direction as government expenditures proved to be larger and revenues smaller than anticipated. In its first decade of operation, the Treasury had difficulty balancing the budget, and the national debt, instead of being reduced, had risen to nearly $80 million by the time the Federalists left office in 1801 and Albert Gallatin became the new Secretary of Treasury under the Jefferson Administration. During the 12 years of the Washington and Adams Administrations, $7.5 million of the original debt had been liquidated, but $10.6 million in new debt had been incurred.

In the next 12 years, in which Gallatin served under Jefferson and Madison, the national debt was reduced by payments of more than $46 million, including repayment of practically all the foreign debt, leaving the unretired amount of debt at $34 million. But the addition of $11 million of new indebtedness for the Louisiana Purchase left a total federal debt of $45 million. Nevertheless, Gallatin was able to show a remarkable 44 percent net reduction in the national debt during the years that he managed our federal finances.

This debt reduction did not continue since the Treasury found its outlays increasing rapidly in the next few years, especially as a result of the War of 1812. Forced to issue bonds at a substantial discount to raise money for the unpopular war and also to issue short-term Treasury notes, expenditures exceeded revenues and the national debt skyrocketed to a new high of $127 million by the end of Madison's Administration in 1816.

Elimination of the National Debt

The next 21 years, 1816–1836, saw a steady and substantial reduction of the national debt. Surpluses experienced in each of these years, some of them quite large, were applied to the retirement of the national debt. Increased trade after the War of 1812 brought about a rise in customs duties, and government revenues increased substantially. Consequently, an act was passed in 1817 to provide $10 million for servicing the national debt, with any surplus after meeting the interest to be applied toward reducing outstanding debt. Increased tariff rates plus large-scale sales of public land further added to federal revenues.

Reduction of the debt was so successful during the ensuing period that during the early 1830s widespread discussion was held about what should be done with budget surpluses when the national debt would be extinguished within a few years. Secretary of the Treasury Roger Brooke Taney in his report of December, 1834, declared that on January 1, 1835, the remaining balance of the federal debt would be paid or provided for, and he stated that "the United States will present that happily, and probably in modern times, unprecedented spectacle of a people substantially free from the smallest portion of the debt."

Not only was the debt completely paid off by January, 1835, but a large surplus had accumulated. The Treasury balance by mid-1836 approached $40 million. After much debate and controversy, a bill was finally signed by President Jackson calling for the Treasury on January 1, 1837, to retain a surplus balance of $5 million and deposit any excess surplus with the states on a pro rata basis according to their representation in Congress. Since the surplus on that date amounted to $42 million, $37 million was available for deposit with the states. Although the distribution of the funds to the states was in the form of non-interest-bearing loans, it was never intended that the federal government would recall these loans. Consequently, they became outright gifts to the states. The distribution among the states was to be made in four installments. After making the first three installments, in 1837 the Treasury found itself in financial difficulty. The fourth installment of $9 million was postponed until 1839 but was never actually paid, and the surplus balance in the Treasury became a thing of the past never to be attained again.

Civil War Debt and Retirement

During the next 15 years, until 1850, the federal government, with the exception of four years, ran into deficits. One big item of expense during this period was the Mexican War that cost approximately $64 million, of which $49 million was financed through the sale of bonds and notes. The maximum federal debt during the period between 1835 and the Civil War occurred in 1851, when it reached a level of $68 million. Thereafter, surplus years and debt repayment brought the national debt down to $28 million by 1857, but it rose to nearly $65 million by the outbreak of the Civil War.

Naturally the financing of the war, which cost an estimated $3.5 billion, necessitated an unprecedented amount of borrowing. Since $2.5 billion, or 70 percent of the war cost, came from loans, the national debt rose to an astronomical $2.77 billion by 1866, the year after the war. This made the per capita burden of the national debt about $80. The war certainly cost more than the $400 million that the President had asked for at the beginning of the conflict so that the war might be "a short and decisive one." Most of the borrowing was financed at interest rates in excess of 6 percent, except for the $450 million non-interest-bearing United States notes, otherwise known as "greenbacks," issued during the period. Unfortunately the large debt and the depreciation of the greenback, which at times was worth as little as 40 or 50 cents, in large part caused prices to rise tremendously.

Expansion of business activity after the war brought about increased tax revenues. In fact, many taxes imposed during the war did not begin to become effective revenue sources until after the war had terminated. In practically every year from 1866 to 1893 government receipts exceeded disbursements, and the government was able to consistently reduce its debt. By the end of this period the national debt was less than $1 billion. Although the debt rose above the $1 billion mark the following year, it remained fairly constant until World War I, fluctuating between $1 billion and $1.4 billion as revenues exceeded disbursements and vice versa. In April, 1917, our net federal debt stood at $1,207,827,886, or $11.59 per capita. This was a reduction of $1.5 billion from the maximum of $2.7 billion of debt existing at the end of the Civil War.

World War I Debt and Retirement

Financing of the First World War resulted in a twentyfold increase in the national debt, which rose to $25.4 billion by 1919. Although Secretary of the Treasury McAdoo originally hoped to finance 50 percent of the war cost through taxation, he was soon convinced that his figure was too high and lowered his estimate to 33.3 percent. With the greater than expected increases in government disbursements and the lag between new tax measures and the collection of revenues therefrom, the need for money was staggering; the only way of obtaining it quickly was through borrowing. An outstanding feature of the war financing was the sale of liberty bonds to the general public in small denominations, with some as little as $50. The success of the first liberty loan campaign led to others. In total, the four liberty loan campaigns plus the postwar victory loan of 1919 netted the federal government $21.5 billion.

After the war, expenditures, which had reached $2 billion per month, dwindled impressively by 1920. The prosperous twenties, which brought sizable surpluses, resulted in a reduction in the debt each year until 1930 when the total national debt was down to $16.2 billion, a reduction of $9.2 billion, or 36 percent, during the decade.

Depression Spending

In the 1930s we witnessed the Great Depression with the gross national product falling from $103 billion in 1929 to $56 billion in 1933, while unemployment increased from 1.6 million to 12.8 million. With one fourth of the labor force unemployed and many more partially employed, with homes being lost through mortgage default, and businesses collapsing through bankruptcy, the federal government began to use the federal budget as a stabilization device. Deficit spending on public works and relief became the order of the day. New Deal deficits ran as high as $4.4 billion in 1936, and during the period 1932 to 1940 totaled more than $26 billion. As a result, the national debt reached a new peak of $43.0 billion in 1940.

World War II Debt

Our entry into World War II in December, 1941, occasioned enormous increases in our national debt. The cost of the war was stupendous. In fact, toward the last few weeks of the war it was estimated that we were spending $1 billion a day on the war effort. The total cost of the war is estimated at $288 billion. Although some of this cost was defrayed through extended and higher taxes, approximately three quarters was financed through borrowed funds. Deficit budgets ran in excess of $45 billion a year in the last 3 years of the war. The national debt surpassed the $100 billion mark in the second year of the war, reached $200 billion during 1944, and by February, 1946, had reached a staggering $280 billion figure. This was a burden of $2,000 per capita. The war financing program was known for its sizable increase in direct taxes, the widespread use of withholding taxes, the levying of excess profit taxes, the advent of war bond campaigns, and a large program of lend-lease to foreign nations. Although the debt was subsequently reduced to $252.2 billion by 1948, no substantial effort has been made to pay off or even to reduce the national debt since the end of the war. In fact, in the more than 30 years that have elapsed since that time, we have had budget surpluses in only 8 years. Deficits incurred during the period of the Korean Conflict, plus the $12.9 billion deficit incurred in connection with the recession of 1958, moved the debt toward the $300 billion mark. Sizable deficits of the next decade, and more especially those of the past few years, as shown in Table 6-1, pushed the current total debt up to well over $700 billion and it is scheduled to reach $874 billion by the end of fiscal year 1979.

Annual deficit budgets ranging as high as $25 billion for fiscal years 1960 to 1972, and recent projected annual deficits of $50–$60 billion, have stirred much controversy over the debt in the past few years. President Kennedy's

Table 6-1

FEDERAL BUDGET RECEIPTS AND OUTLAYS, FISCAL YEARS
1929–1979 (In Millions of Dollars)

Fiscal year	Receipts	Outlays	Surplus or deficit (−)
1929	3,862	3,127	734
1933	1,997	4,598	−2,602
1939	4,979	8,841	−3,862
1940	6,361	9,456	−3,095
1941	8,621	13,634	−5,013
1942	14,350	35,114	−20,764
1943	23,649	78,533	−54,884
1944	44,276	91,280	−47,004
1945	45,216	92,690	−47,474
1946	39,327	55,183	−15,856
1947	38,394	34,532	3,862
1948	41,774	29,773	12,001
1949	39,437	38,834	603
1950	39,485	42,597	−3,112
1951	51,646	45,546	6,100
1952	66,204	67,721	−1,517
1953	69,574	76,107	−6,533
1954	69,719	70,890	−1,170
1955	65,469	68,509	−3,041
1956	74,547	70,460	4,087
1957	79,990	76,741	3,249
1958	79,636	82,575	−2,939
1959	79,249	92,104	−12,855
1960	92,492	92,223	269
1961	94,389	97,795	−3,406
1962	99,676	106,813	−7,137
1963	106,560	111,311	−4,751
1964	112,662	118,584	−5,922

Table 6-1(concluded)
FEDERAL BUDGET RECEIPTS AND OUTLAYS, FISCAL YEARS
1929–1979 (In Millions of Dollars)

Fiscal year	Receipts	Outlays	Surplus or deficit (−)
1965	116,833	118,430	−1,596
1966	130,856	134,652	−3,796
1967	149,552	158,254	−8,702
1968	153,671	178,833	−25,161
1969	187,784	184,548	3,236
1970	193,743	196,588	−2,845
1971	188,392	211,425	−23,033
1972	208,649	232,021	−23,372
1973	232,225	247,074	−14,849
1974	264,932	269,620	−4,688
1975	280,997	326,105	−45,108
1976	300,005	366,466	−66,461
Transition Quarter	81,773	94,746	−12,973
1977	356,900	401,900	−45,000
1978[1]	400,400	462,200	−61,800
1979[1]	439,600	500,200	−60,600

SOURCE: *Economic Report of the President*, 1977, and *Budget Message* (January, 1978).

[1]Estimate.

Note — Data for 1929–1939 are according to the administrative budget and those for 1940–1979 according to the unified budget.
Certain interfund transactions are excluded from receipts and outlays beginning 1932. For years prior to 1932 the amounts of such transactions are not significant.
Refunds of receipts are excluded from receipts and outlays.

budget message for fiscal 1964 calling for a record level of spending, exceeding all previous budget outlays while calling for a decrease in receipts, was received with strongly mixed reaction in Congress, especially since the budget called for a $6 billion reduction in personal and corporate income taxes. The resulting planned deficit of $11.9 billion aimed at bolstering the level of production and employment in the economy would have been the second largest deficit budget in peacetime history, exceeded only by the unplanned $12.9 billion deficit resulting from the recession of 1958. Furthermore, the suggested cut in taxes was only the first stage in a planned reduction of $13.5 billion. Since a revision in the tax structure, primarily designed to plug loopholes, was to increase revenues by $3.5 billion, the net tax reduction was expected to be only $10 billion over a 2-year period.

When the tax reduction bill was finally passed in the spring of 1964, it helped bring about the $5.9 billion and $1.6 billion deficits occuring in 1964 and 1965 respectively. It was suggested by the Kennedy and Johnson Administrations that the deficits accompanying the tax cuts were a down payment on future surpluses, since the rise in business activity occasioned by the deficits would bring about higher tax revenues that would balance the budget and eventually bring about surpluses. Excise tax reductions in 1965, along with higher spending for Great Society domestic programs and the accelerated spending for the war in Vietnam, however, resulted in large deficits. Although the federal deficit fell to $1.6 billion in 1965, it rose to $8.7 billion in 1967 and reached $25.2 billion in 1968. Consequently, renewed interest was elicited on the part of Congress and the public regarding the problems of the national debt. It was hoped that the 10 percent personal and corporate income tax surcharge levied in 1968 would slow down federal deficits and debt accumulation in 1968 and thereafter. Although we had a surplus of $3.2 billion in 1969 and a modest deficit of $2.8 billion in 1970, the federal deficit was $23 billion in 1971 and also $23 billion in 1972. With the use of deficit spending to stimulate the economy during the recession of 1974–1975, the deficit for fiscal year 1975 rose to $45 billion. Deficits of $66 billion and $45 billion for fiscal years 1976 and 1977 added to the federal debt. In addition, deficits of $61.8 billion and $60.6 billion were budgeted for 1978 and 1979, respectively. These would have the effect of raising the total national debt to well over $800 billion.

DEBT CEILING

The statutory limit or ceiling on the national debt was first established in 1917 when Congress passed the Second Liberty Bond Act. This Act authorized the Treasury to issue bonds not exceeding in the aggregate $7,538,945,460 and to issue certificates of indebtedness up to $4 billion. As borrowing to finance World War I continued beyond expectations, Congress merely amended the Second Liberty Bond Act to accommodate new debt authority as needed. After the war the same procedure continued, and it has carried on to the present day. Thus, the rise in the national debt ceiling occasioned by Depression spending of the 1930s, World War II, the Korean Conflict, the war in Vietnam, and intermittent peacetime deficits were permitted through extension of the Second Liberty Bond Act. During World War II, however, there was some change in structure in the debt ceiling. Prior to that time Congress set individual ceilings on the various types of government indebtedness. But in 1941 it did away with the individual debt ceilings and created one ceiling on the total debt outstanding.

This is the type of debt ceiling we have today. Since the debt ceiling has been raised more than 25 times in the past 24 years, increasing from $275 billion in 1954 to $752 billion in fiscal 1978, the statutory limit on the national debt has been a topic of controversy in recent years.

On a number of occasions in the past decade proposals have been made to eliminate the statutory ceiling on the national debt. Arguments for and against the debt ceiling abound. In 1969 the Nixon Administration endeavored to get around the ceiling problem by proposing that certain debts, especially those held by government agencies, be removed from the statutory limitation. This would have eliminated about $80 billion or more from the existing debt subject to the statutory ceiling. This would have left the Treasury with ample flexibility to contract more debt without having to request Congress to raise the debt ceiling. This proposal, however, was not approved by Congress. Subsequently the Treasury asked that the ceiling be eliminated, and in June, 1969, repeal of the ceiling was recommended by a group of 67 leading academic economists, but to no avail.

It is also interesting to note that a federal deficit accompanied by a rise in the debt ceiling will generally provoke more opposition than a deficit that does not involve a hike in the debt ceiling. Much attention, for example, has been given to increases in the national debt in recent years because they involved a need to substantially increase the debt ceiling.

Arguments Against the Debt Ceiling

Many arguments can be marshaled for and against the debt ceiling. Opponents of the ceiling maintain that it may at times limit needed expenditures on important government programs, such as defense or depression spending, whenever tax revenues are not up to expectations or the government has failed to increase taxes sufficiently to take care of its spending obligations. It is claimed also that a debt ceiling results in fiscal subterfuge by the Treasury.

The statutory limit is on a defined portion of the total federal debt that is usually associated with the annual federal budget. The federal government, however, has many nonbudgetary financial obligations. Many federal agencies, such as the Commodity Credit Corporation, the Federal National Mortgage Association, the Postal Fund, and the Rural Electrification Fund, which normally borrow funds from the Treasury, are empowered to borrow from private financial institutions and investors if they desire. Frequently when the Treasury is pinched for funds and is approaching the debt limit, it will request a particular agency to borrow in the financial markets rather than borrow from the Treasury. This, of course, relieves the Treasury of the task of borrowing the funds and avoids raising the national debt to service the agency.

Most of this off-budget financing is done through the Federal Financing Bank, which raises money for other agencies. For 1979 it was estimated that these agencies would borrow $12.5 billion. Had this figure been included in the regular budget for 1979, President Carter would have been presenting a federal budget with a $73.1 billion deficit instead of a $60.6 billion deficit.

Critics of the debt ceiling contend further that it restricts the freedom of the Treasury to manage the debt efficiently, especially when the debt is close to the ceiling. In such circumstances the Treasury may have to wait until old securities mature before issuing new ones for fear of going over the debt ceiling. Critics of the ceiling argue that it would be better for the Treasury to experiment with new issues sometime before the expiration of the old to try out the rate and have time to make any necessary adjustment to obtain the best price. Otherwise the Treasury will be at the mercy of the market if it must wait until the day that old issues expire before issuing new securities to replace them. Frequently they will have to pay a higher interest rate.

Arguments for the Debt Ceiling

Proponents of the statutory limit stress the fact that the debt ceiling is needed to restrain government spending and that it prevents the national debt from getting dangerously high. Although the debt ceiling seems to have been raised liberally by Congress in the past several years, the presence of the debt ceiling does tend to make Congress look a bit closer at the budget and decide whether it really wants to vote for appropriations that will necessitate borrowing and raising the debt ceiling. It is frequently pointed out that, since the interest on the national debt exceeds $40 billion annually, the debt is costly to the American taxpayers. It might also be argued that insofar as the ceiling limits deficits in the annual budget, it makes the taxpayers more conscious of the total cost of government services. Many taxpayers may not balk at a tax bill of $450 billion when expenditures are scheduled to be $500 billion; but if they were taxed $500 billion to cover the total cost of federal spending, they may very well decide to do without some of the government services. In short, deficits and a rising national debt can mislead the taxpayers about the true cost of government services.

INTEREST RATE CEILING ON NATIONAL DEBT

In addition to a statutory limit on the national debt, there is also a ceiling on the interest rate that may be paid on government securities. This interest rate ceiling also was originally established by the Second Liberty Bond Act of 1917, which authorized the Treasury to issue certain amounts and kinds of bonds at interest rates up to 4 percent. Later the Third Liberty Bond Act raised the ceiling to 4.25 percent to assure a successful sale of that issue. From the early 1920s until the 1950s, the cost of federal borrowing was far below the legal interest rate ceiling. With the boom and inflationary conditions of the mid-1950s, however, the interest rate ceiling became a handicap to the Treasury. With high interest rates of 6–9 percent in late 1960s and still higher rates of 10–12 percent in 1973–1974, the problem became more pressing.

Whether the interest rate ceiling is good or bad is a matter of judgment. Proponents of the ceiling maintain that it keeps down the cost of federal borrowing. Opponents of the interest limit claim that it prevents the Treasury from being competitive in the market for funds. Furthermore, since there is no ceiling on short-term government obligations, only on long-term bonds, critics of the ceiling maintain that in a competitive market in which the going rate of interest in the long-term market is higher than the interest rate ceiling, it can force the Treasury into the short-term market where it will have to pay an even higher interest rate than it would in the long-term market.

The elimination of the interest rate ceiling has been an issue for years and again became a debatable issue in Congress in the mid and late 1960s with the general rise in interest rates throughout the economy. In 1969, for example, the federal Treasury was paying interest rates of 8 percent or more for money it borrowed in the short-term market. With the 4.25 percent ceiling, it was almost impossible to compete for funds in the long-term market against high grade corporate securities paying 7–8 percent interest. At that time the Nixon Administration requested that Congress review the 4.25 percent interest ceiling on long-term government bonds. The problem eased somewhat in 1971 when Congress authorized the Treasury to issue as much as $10 billion in bonds at rates of interest exceeding 4.25 percent. But problems with debt financing arose in 1973 when the prime rate peaked at 12 percent and again in 1978 when interest rates generally were rising from the 1974–1975 recession lows.

STRUCTURE OF THE NATIONAL DEBT

The national debt is composed of various types of government obligations and securities, both long term and short term.

Treasury Bills

About 23 percent of the debt is made up of Treasury bills, which are short-term securities with 3 to 12 months maturity dates. Bills issued as frequently as each week are sold to obtain funds to retire portions of the debt that may become due at a given time. These bills, such as the 91-day variety, sell at current interest rates and are sought by banks and financial institutions as a short-term outlet for their reserve cash.

Although Treasury bills have no stated interest rate or par price, they are sold by the Treasury through sealed-bid auctions in which investors are able to submit written bids at prices of their own choosing. Individual bidders may submit multiple prices; that is, they may offer to buy different amounts of an issue for different prices. Once the bids are received they are listed in order of decreasing price and filled accordingly. Beginning with the highest price offered or bid, the Treasury sells to the successively lower bidders until the issues are all sold. Since individual bidders may pay different prices, the yield for each of them will be different with the lowest bidders, of course, obtaining the best yield. Low bidders, however, run the risk of not obtaining any bills from the auction. Some of the bills, however, are reserved to be sold on a noncompetitive basis to small buyers. These bills are sold at the average price of those sold on the competitive bidding basis. Since the price remains rather stable and they can be disposed of readily, they are generally considered as near cash by holders.

Treasury Notes

Investors who desire a higher return but are willing to wait longer for maturity dates can purchase a second form of government obligation,

Treasury notes, which may run as long as 5 years and make up about 34.5 percent of the national debt. At times both of these forms of securities, bills and notes, are sold as tax anticipatory issues. The Treasury will sell them to obtain funds to tide it over until it receives anticipated tax revenues in the immediate future. Businesses frequently will buy such issues with reserves they may be accumulating for tax payments in the immediate future. This gives the taxpayer the opportunity to earn some interest on the money being held in anticipation of tax payments. Furthermore, when the tax payment deadline arrives, the taxpayer's tax obligation may be discharged by turning in the securities to the government.

Treasury Bonds

About 7 percent of the national debt is in the form of long-term obligations known as Treasury bonds. These are marketable bonds payable to the bearer at a particular maturity date. This means that they can be bought and sold by persons other than the original holders. These bonds have maturity periods of 5, 20, and even 40 years. One issue of these bonds paying 4 percent interest matures in 1980; still another paying 3.5 percent does not mature until 1998.

These bonds are sold at a fixed price and a stated interest rate. One disadvantage of this method, compared to the auction technique of selling government securities, is the fact that the Treasury has to set an interest rate or yield on the bond. If for some reason the yield is set too low, the Treasury runs the risk of a financial failure if investors do not purchase the bonds. On the other hand, if the Treasury sets the interest rate too high, it may pay an unnecessarily generous rate of interest to the investors. Holders clip off the coupons attached to the bonds and turn them in to the Treasury, or a designated agent, periodically in exchange for interest payments. Although they are issued and sold at a fixed price and a stated interest rate, the market price of the bonds fluctuates as they are bought and resold in the bond market.

Usually when market interest rates are higher than the coupon rate, these bonds will sell in the market at a discount. This in effect raises the real rate of interest or the yield on the bonds. When market interest rates are lower, the bonds will sell at a premium, which in turn lowers the yield on the bonds. The holder at maturity date, however, is always paid the par or full price of the bond. Consequently, the resale market price of the bond will bear some relationship to the proximity of the maturity date of the bond. As a result of the relatively low interest rate ceiling on these bonds, in recent years their sale has been declining. They now comprise 6.6 percent of the federal debt, compared to one third of the debt in 1965.

Convertible Bonds

Another element of the national debt is in the form of convertible bonds. These bonds, originally offered for sale in 1951, bear an interest rate of 2.75

percent annually, mature in 1975–1980, and can be exchanged at the option of the holder for 1.5 percent, 5-year marketable Treasury notes anytime during the life of the bonds. Although more than $11 billion of these bonds were issued in 1951, most of them have been converted and now only $2.2 billion are outstanding.

Savings Bonds

One of the most popular instruments of national debt is the savings bond, issued in large amounts during and since World War II. They make up 11 percent of the total debt. These are nonmarketable or nonnegotiable securities since they can be cashed only by the person to whom they are issued. The bonds are purchased at a price less than maturity value, and interest accumulates in the form of the higher value on the bond as it approaches maturity. Although savings bonds have maturity dates of 5 years, 10 months, they can be redeemed for cash at any time after 60 days either at the Treasury or through banks.

Government Account Series

Another important part of the debt is in the form of the government account series, issues of which are reserved for government agencies and trust funds. These are issued to federal government investment accounts and comprise about 20 percent of the federal debt. The Federal Old-Age and Survivors Insurance Trust Fund, for example, has certain revenues from the collection of Social Security taxes that it does not need immediately or perhaps for several years to come. These are deposited with the Treasury in exchange for special issue government obligations. When the Social Security Administration needs its funds, the government obligations are redeemed by the Treasury and the cash transmitted to the Trust Fund. This arrangement provides a source of funds for the Treasury and, at the same time, a source of investment for the Trust Fund. Interest receipts on the special issues, of course, help to keep down the cost of Social Security.

Foreign Issues

Foreign issues comprise various nonmarketable certificates of indebtedness, notes and bonds in the Treasury foreign series, and foreign currency. Foreign governments, banks, businesses, and individuals, however, may hold other U.S. government securities as well.

Other Issues

Additional securities of the U.S. Treasury include depository bonds, retirement plan bonds, Rural Electrification Administration bonds, state and local bonds, and special issues held only by U.S. government agencies and trust funds and the Federal Home Loan Banks. In addition, there is another $2.5 billion of non-interest-bearing debt, some of which was not subject to the statutory limit of the debt, excluded from the figures shown in Table 6-2.

Table 6-2

TOTAL DEBT, BY TYPE OF SECURITY, JULY, 1977

		Amount (Billions)	Percentage of National Debt
Total gross debt		$671.4	100.0
Marketable-total		430.3	64.1
Bills	$154.2		23.0
Notes	231.4		34.5
Bonds	44.7		6.6
Nonmarketable-total		241.1	35.9
Convertible bonds	2.2		0.3
Savings bonds and notes	75.2		11.2
Gov't Account Series	132.4		19.7
Foreign Issues	21.5		3.2
Other	9.8		1.5

SOURCE: *Federal Reserve Bulletin* (August, 1977).

Another interesting aspect of the national debt, especially in regard to repayment or refunding, is the maturity dates of the existing debt. As of March, 1978, for example, more than one fourth of the total debt was due within one year. Nearly $100 billion in marketable securities was due in 1–5 years. The remainder was stretched out over a 20-year period. In addition to the marketable securities, there are $72 billion in savings bonds that can be redeemed at the will of the holders. Most of the debt when due is refunded, rather than paid off, either by offering existing debt holders new securities in exchange for the old or by selling securities to new debt holders to pay off the old. To this extent, it means that debt payment and reduction are merely postponed. Many of the new issues offered to replace the old are obligations of one year or less. Consequently, the Treasury is faced with a perennial problem of refunding a large portion of the national debt.

FEDERAL BUDGET AS A STABILIZER

If used properly, debt policy can help to stabilize the economy and modify business cycles. A surplus budget can help prevent inflation during a prosperity period, and a deficit budget can help boost the level of economic activity during a depressionary period. Such use of a budgetary policy is shown in Figure 6-1.

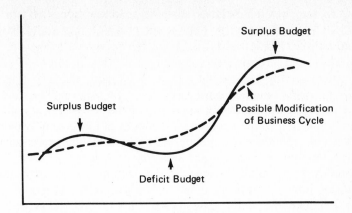

Figure 6-1 **BUDGET USED AS AN ANTICYCLICAL DEVICE**

Balancing the Budget Over the Cycle

When the budget is used as a tool for economic stabilization, it is desirable to balance the budget over the period of the cycle instead of trying to do it on an annual basis. To accomplish this, it would be necessary for the surplus of prosperity to equal the deficit of the recession. However, this would be difficult to accomplish. A question might arise as to whether we should start such a practice by building up a surplus during prosperity and then spending it during the next recession, or whether we should incur the deficit during the recession and then repay the debt with the surplus obtained during the subsequent prosperity.

Assuming that the first method was utilized, a second problem would arise. How much surplus would need to be accumulated during the prosperity period? This would depend not only upon the inflationary pressures of prosperity but also upon the estimated need, or deficit, during the subsequent recession in the economy. It is practically impossible, however, to determine what the duration and the intensity of the prosperity will be, let alone the duration and the intensity of the subsequent recession. Therefore, it is usually suggested that it is more feasible to run the deficit first. This also has its weaknesses. How can we be assured that the subsequent prosperity will be long enough or strong enough to permit an accumulation of a surplus sufficient to pay off the deficit incurred in the previous recessionary period?

Another weakness of this method is that most administrators and legislators are willing to use deficit spending during a recession to help alleviate unemployment, but many of them are reluctant to accumulate the offsetting surplus during prosperity years. From a political point of view, the emphasis is often on tax reduction rather than higher taxes during a prosperity period, especially when there is a surplus in the federal budget. In short, deficit spending insofar as it can be used to bolster the level of economic activity can be very popular with the public during the recession, but increased taxes and budget surpluses to combat inflation during a prosperity period are seldom popular.

It should be remembered also that a surplus acquired during a prosperity period should be held in cash reserves for best results. It can be used to pay off the debt subsequently but not until the level of economic activity begins to decline. If the surplus obtained during prosperity is used immediately to pay off the debt incurred by the deficit spending of the recession, it will merely result in putting back into the economy an amount of money equivalent to the surplus. Thus, the reduction of spendable incomes through taxation will be offset by government expenditures plus debt repayment.

This means that the total spending of the economy will remain the same, provided the recipients of debt repayment spend or invest the money received from the government. In such a case, the surplus budget will have a neutral effect instead of being anti-inflationary. The better practice would be to hold the surplus funds until economic activity begins to decline. Repayment of the debt at such time could give a boost to the economy if the recipients of debt repayment were to spend or invest these funds.

The Full-Employment Budget

In recent years there has been a tendency to look at the so-called *full-employment budget* instead of the actual budget for the purpose of analyzing the fiscal effects of the budget. Regardless of the state of the actual budget, the full-employment budget is a measure of the potential revenue and expenditure that would result in full employment. It is said by some that the actual budget may be misleading. Let us say, for example, that the existing budget showed a deficit (or fiscal stimulus) of $30 billion and that the rate of unemployment was 6 percent. Projection may indicate that if the economy were at full employment (5 percent unemployment or less), the budget would show a surplus of $8 billion. Thus, if the economy expands toward the full-employment level, it will encounter a fiscal drag, which would impede the attainment of a full-employment objective.

Proponents of "functional finance," who look at the budget as a tool of stabilization and growth rather than as something to be balanced annually or even periodically, would contend that the inherent drag of the full-employment surplus should be eliminated if the economy is to attain its goal of full employment. This, of course, could be accomplished by increasing the size of the current fiscal stimulus (deficit) through reducing taxes or by increasing government spending.

Carrying the analysis one step further, proponents of this theory claim that once full employment and a balanced budget have been reached, care must be taken to prevent the development of a subsequent drag on the economy. It is pointed out that with a given tax rate, total revenues will increase by $15 billion or more annually as a result of the normal forces of growth in our economy. To prevent this from occurring, it is suggested that a *fiscal dividend* be declared either in the form of a tax reduction or an increase in federal spending. They place little emphasis on the notion that surpluses should be accumulated during prosperity to offset the deficits of previous periods.

As an example of this type of budgeting policy, President Carter in January, 1978, presented his budget for fiscal 1979 showing a $60.6 billion deficit. His budget message also projected a deficit totaling $37.5 billion for fiscal 1980. The growth of the economy, resulting in part from the two year fiscal stimulus of $98.1 billion, was expected to yield a surplus of $8.6 billion in 1981. Surpluses of $45.2 billion in 1982 and $76.2 billion in 1983 were also projected. This of course assumes everything develops as planned and no substantial changes occur in the economy other than those forecasted.

PROBLEMS OF THE DEBT

Our experience with budgetary policy as a means of stabilizing business activity is rather limited. It is difficult, therefore, to determine whether we can time our deficits and surpluses accurately and have them of proper size to act as stabilizers of the economy. Furthermore, we have not had sufficient experience in the past 40 years to determine whether, in the absence of emergencies, the deficits and the surpluses can offset each other sufficiently to prevent a growing debt. We incurred a sizable debt during the depression of the 1930s as a result of our deficit spending program. Without having had a chance to diminish this debt, we entered World War II, which increased the debt to about $280 billion.

Our opportunity to reduce the debt was further hampered by the outbreak of the Korean Conflict in 1950. Since then we have made very little headway in reducing the debt. In fact, the federal debt, now in excess of $700 billion and rapidly moving toward $1 trillion, has grown to such proportions that it presents several problems. A few of these problems, such as bankruptcy, redistribution of income, debt burden, size of the debt, refunding, and the burden of interest payments are treated in the following paragraphs.

Bankruptcy

The average person often thinks that the debt may become so large that it will bankrupt the nation. It is commonly believed that the government may get into a situation where it will be unable to pay the debt. This misunderstanding arises from the failure to distinguish clearly the true nature of government financing compared to the normal method of business financing. When the government borrows and repays funds, it is more like the financial transactions taking place within a family than the type of financing practiced by private enterprises.

Comparison to Business Debt. From an accounting point of view, whenever a business has total financial liabilities in excess of total assets, it lacks solvency. In short, it does not have sufficient cash to pay its current debts in the immediate future. In such a case, when creditors press for payment, the firm may voluntarily and legally have itself declared bankrupt, or the creditors may force the company into bankruptcy. In either case, the court will decide whether the business should continue under receivership, that is, under a court-appointed manager, or whether the assets of the company should be liquidated to pay off the creditors.

Whenever the firm pays off its debt, it decreases the total assets of the company. Money paid out actually leaves the firm, thereby reducing the assets. A basic difficulty arises in connection with a business debt when debt payments are so large that the company is forced to suspend payment. In such circumstances, the creditors may force liquidation of the firm through bankruptcy proceedings to recover payment on the debt.

Comparison to Family Debt. The national debt is more like an internal family debt than a business debt. Consider the family as a spending unit and suppose that a son borrows $300 from his dad over the period of the school year and that he intends to repay it from the money he earns from summer employment. When he borrows, he does so within the family unit. Likewise, when he repays the $300 in the summer, the money remains within the family.

When the son pays his debt, his individual assets are decreased by $300 but his father's assets are increased by $300. Therefore, the net assets of the family remain the same. Unlike the debt repayment of the firm, in the family situation no money leaves the family as a result of the debt repayment. There is merely a transfer of cash from one member of the family to another, or a transfer of assets from one member of the family to another. There is no net reduction of assets, nor is there any money leaving the family.

The Federal Debt. When the government borrows money, it borrows primarily from individuals, businesses, and banks within the economy. When it makes repayment on the debt, the money stays within the economy. There is no reduction in the total assets of the economy when the government makes repayment on the debt. Furthermore, the government's ability to repay is governed only by the total assets of the economy or, more immediately, by the total income of the economy and the government's ability to tax. For example, the national debt in 1977 was at one time $710 billion. Considering that the gross national product (GNP) for 1977 was $1,890 billion and that the total national income was $1,525 billion, it is easy to see that the total income of the nation was sufficient to take care of debt repayment if the government decided to raise taxes sufficiently to obtain funds required to pay it off. Theoretically, but unrealistically, the government could tax a sufficient amount to pay the debt off in the course of one year. If the government were to do this, it would not in any way reduce the total income or assets of the nation as a whole. The taxation and repayment of the debt would merely cause a redistribution of income, or cash assets, inside the economy. The income given up by individuals and firms in the form of taxes would be offset by payment to those holding the debt. Thus, the total income or assets of the economy would be the same after payment of the debt as before. The major difference is that income and cash assets held by various individuals and firms would be changed. It must be pointed out, however, that foreigners now hold 13 percent of the national debt compared to less than 5 percent as late as 1970.

It is possible, but not probable, that some individuals and firms would have exactly the same holdings of assets after repayment of the debt as they did before. This would occur if an individual or a firm was taxed an amount equal to the amount of debt held. For example, a firm holding $10,000 in government bonds might be taxed $10,000 to help pay off the debt. Since it would receive a payment of $10,000 on its bonds when the debt was repaid, its total assets would remain the same.

Although a tax rate sufficient to pay off the debt in one year would be prohibitive, certainly over a relatively long period, say 30–50 years, the government could operate at a surplus sufficient to pay off the debt. Surpluses obtained during periods of prosperity could be used to pay the debt during periods of contraction in the economy.

Effect of Redistribution of Income

The question naturally arises: Why does the government not take more positive steps to pay off the debt? Reluctance to reduce the debt by sizable amounts stems not only from the fact that the larger tax burden necessary to do so would be politically unpopular, but also from the fact that it would cause disruptive economic repercussions. One important problem involved would be the redistribution of income brought about by repayment of the debt.

If the debt were to be paid off on a large-scale basis, heavy taxes would reduce total effective demand, especially among the lower income groups. Whether such reduction in effective demand would be offset when the government used tax money to pay off the debt would depend on what the recipients of debt repayments would do with the money they received. Since it is quite probable that the total propensity to consume or to invest of the debt holders who receive repayment would be less than that of the taxpayers in total, the net effective demand of the economy could easily be reduced by repayment of the debt. The possibility of this occuring becomes evident when we look at the ownership of the debt. It is generally agreed that the lower income groups do not hold much of the federal debt. It is held primarily by banks, businesses, government agencies, and individuals in the higher income groups. This is shown in Table 6-3 on page 136.

Of course, if the debt holders would spend the income they received at the time the debts were repaid, it would not have an adverse effect on the economy. This would tend to be the case if the debt were repaid during a full-employment period. It would be best, however, to pay off the debt during the periods of less than full employment with money obtained through taxation during a prosperous or inflationary period. In this way, the debt could be used as a tool for economic stabilization.

Table 6-3

**OWNERSHIP OF UNITED STATES GOVERNMENT DEBT,
SEPTEMBER, 1977** (Percentage)

Federal Reserve banks	15.0
Commercial banks	14.4
Mutual savings banks	.8
Insurance companies	2.1
Other corporations	3.4
Individuals	14.9
State and local governments	7.7
United States government agencies and trust funds	22.3
Miscellaneous investors	5.8
Foreign and international	13.6
Total	100.0

SOURCE: *Federal Reserve Bulletin* (December, 1977).

Burden of the Debt

It is often thought that when the debt is not paid during the period in which it is incurred the burden of paying the debt is passed on to future generations. The extent to which this may be true depends upon whether we are considering the effect on the total economy or on individuals and firms, and also on the source of the debt.

Effect on Total Economy. If we are considering the total economy, it is impossible to pass the real cost of the debt on to future generations. The real cost of the debt to the total economy can be measured only by the cost of goods and services that individuals and firms must forego when they give up their purchasing power to buy government bonds. When consumers and investors purchase such bonds, they not only buy fewer goods and services, but they also give the government revenue to make its purchases. For example, during World War II citizens and firms gave up the purchase of automobiles, homes, food, clothing, machinery, raw materials, and the like when they purchased bonds. In the meantime the government, with its borrowed purchasing power, bought tanks, planes, ships, ammunition, and other necessary war materials. The decrease in consumer production was, in effect, the real cost of the debt. The people in the economy at the time the debt was incurred shouldered the real burden of the debt through the loss of goods and services.

For the economy as a whole the debt repayment, whether repaid immediately or postponed until future generations, does not cost anything in terms of goods and services. As a result of the redistribution of income that takes place at the time the debt is repaid, some individuals and firms may suffer a loss of purchasing power; but this will be offset by gains to others, and no net decrease in purchasing power in the economy will take place. For example, if the debt were to be paid even in a period of one year, the total tax necessary to pay off the 1978 debt would be well over $700 billion. This would have a tendency to decrease the purchasing power of taxpayers. It would reduce effective demand and result in decreased production. When the government paid out the $700 billion to debt holders, however, it would tend to offset the adverse effect of the tax. Total purchasing power in the economy would remain the same. The effective demand, and therefore production, would remain the same, provided the propensity of the debt holders to consume and to invest was the same as that of the general taxpayers. There would be no loss of total goods and services at the time the debt was repaid. Thus, since there is no cost or loss for the economy as a whole when the debt is repaid, it is impossible to pass the burden of the debt on to future generations.

Effect on Individuals. Although the burden of the debt cannot be passed on to future generations from the viewpoint of the total economy, the burden for individuals and firms can be passed on to future generations. If the government were to pay off the debt in a relatively short period, say within the generation in which the debt occurred, the particular individuals taxed to pay the debt would have to give up purchasing power. Thus, they would be burdened with individual cost of the debt to the extent that each is taxed. If payment on the debt is postponed for a generation or two, however, the tax will fall to a large extent on the descendants of those individuals and businesses in the economy at the time the debt was incurred. Thus, even though the net cost or burden of the debt cannot be passed on to future generations, the individual burden can be passed on.

For example, during the war in Vietnam we incurred a sizable debt. If the debt were to be paid off within the generation in which it was incurred, Ms. Brown, a taxpayer of the period, might have to pay $2,000 in taxes to give the government the money to pay Mr. White, who, we will assume, is a holder of bonds and therefore an owner of the debt. This payment would decrease the purchasing power of Ms. Brown and it would increase the purchasing power of Mr. White. If debt payment were postponed until 1990, however, Ms. Brown's niece or someone else in the economy would have to pay the taxes, especially if Ms. Brown had died in the meantime. Therefore, the individual burden of the debt would have been passed on from Ms. Brown to someone in a subsequent generation. Mr. White, who made a personal sacrifice to loan the government money for the purchase of bonds, would be deprived of repayment until a later date. In fact, if he passed away, his descendants would receive the individual gain at the time repayment was made instead of Mr. White. In actual practice, however, Mr. White could eliminate this situation by transferring his ownership of the debt to someone else through the sale of his bonds.

Furthermore, even if the debt were passed on to future generations, it can always be argued that, since they receive some benefits as a result of the government incurrence of the debt, they should help repay it. Future generations, for example, reap certain benefits from the use of hospitals, schools, dams, highways, and medical and other research financed through deficit spending.

Effect on the Money Supply. Another problem involved in the repayment of the debt, which tends to strengthen our reluctance to pay it off, is the effect of the repayment on the money supply. We know that when an individual or a business loans the government money, there is no increase in the money supply. For example, if Mr. White buys a bond for $1,000, he generally will pay cash for it. Therefore, there is merely a transfer of cash from the individual to the government with no change in the total money supply. If a bank loans the government money, however, it can pay for the bonds in cash or through the creation of a demand deposit against which the government writes checks. Demand deposits brought about by the creation of credit increase the money supply. Therefore, if a bank were to buy $250,000 worth of bonds and pay for them with a demand deposit, it would increase the money supply accordingly. This process is referred to as *monetizing the debt*.

Changes in the money supply can affect the level of economic activity and/or the price level. When the government goes into debt by borrowing from the banks, therefore, it increases the money supply and thus increases the level of economic activity, or it increases the price level.

Since 1960 the money supply has increased from $144 billion to $333 billion, a large portion of which came into existence as a result of the sale of $200 billion of government bonds to the Federal Reserve and commercial banks. Therefore, the national debt today is supporting a sizable part of the total money supply.

We know that a decrease in the money supply will have a tendency to decrease the level of economic activity and/or decrease the price level, unless offset by some other force such as an increase in the velocity of money. Just as the debt was monetized when the government borrowed from the banks, the money supply will be decreased when the debt is paid off. This is known as *demonetizing the debt*. For example, if the government redeemed the $250,000 in bonds held by the bank, demand deposits would be reduced by that amount and the money supply reduced accordingly. Thus, if the government were to reduce the federal debt by sizable amounts over a relatively short period of time, it could reduce the money supply to such an extent as to have an adverse effect on the level of economic activity. Payment of the debt supported by the bank credit would be beneficial during a period of full employment insofar as it would reduce inflationary pressures. During periods of less than full employment, however, such debt repayment could be inimical to the economy as a whole.

Size of the Debt

The mammoth size of the debt is in itself sufficient to discourage many people regarding its repayment. It might be pointed out, however, that although we have not reduced the debt absolutely, increased productivity and higher income have reduced the size of the debt relative to our annual income. For example, at one time in 1946 the national debt was $280 billion. Our total income (GNP) for that year was $210 billion. Since the debt was considerably larger than our total income, it could not have been paid out of current income within a period of one year even if we chose to do so. As a matter of fact, to pay off at the rate of $20 billion per year would have exerted quite a hardship.

Although the debt was noticeably larger in 1977, the total production of the nation had increased to $1,890 billion. Since the annual income of the nation exceeded the national debt, it was possible to pay off the debt within a period of one year or less. Although possible, of course, it would not be feasible to do so. With a national income exceeding $1,525 billion, however, if we were to decide to pay the debt off at the rate of $20–$25 billion annually, not so much of a hardship would be created on the economy today as it would have been when the gross national product was a substantially lesser amount.

In effect, through our increased productivity and higher price level, the monetary income of the nation increased more than eightfold in the period 1946–1977. Since the absolute amount of the debt increased about 150 percent during this period, the burden of the debt relative to gross national product was reduced by well over two thirds. Actually in 1946 GNP was only 75 percent of the outstanding national debt. Today, however, it is approximately 270 percent of the debt. For this reason, those who were worried about the size of the debt 25–30 years ago have less cause to worry about it today. Another way to state this is to say that the ratio of federal debt to the GNP was 135 percent in 1946 compared to 37 percent in 1977. It should be remembered, however, that decreasing income resulting from either a falling price level or a drop in production or employment would increase the size of the debt relative to income.

The suggestion has occasionally been made that we should postpone payment on the debt since it becomes less burdensome as the years go on. To the extent that we increase income as a result of increased productivity, this suggestion has some merit. But if the higher GNP and therefore the greater income is brought about primarily by higher prices, the suggestion is a poor one, since greater problems than that of debt retirement will result from rising prices. Furthermore, if due to continuous inflation the purchasing power of a $100 Savings Bond at the maturity date is of less value than the $75 price of the bond at the purchase date, the purchase of bonds by individuals and firms could be discouraged when the government needed money in the future.

Refunding the Debt

Since government debt obligations may reach maturity at a time when the United States Treasury does not have the money to pay them, the problem of refunding the debt arises. At such a time, the federal government generally issues and sells new bonds to raise money to pay off the matured obligations. This, however, may not be accomplished easily, especially when billions of dollars worth of bonds may be maturing within a short period of time. Furthermore, the government may be forced to pay a higher interest rate when it borrows funds for this purpose.

For example, billions of dollars worth of long-term bonds paying 4.25 percent interest come due annually. Today, however, it is possible for an investor to buy at discounts many non-matured long-term government bonds that effectively have a higher yield than their coupon rate. In addition, many high-grade corporate bonds are yielding more than 8–10 percent.

Under these circumstances it is difficult for the United States Treasury to sell new bonds at 4.25 percent when existing bonds yielding more than 8–10 percent can be purchased in the open market. It is for this reason that the Treasury Department occasionally requests that the 4.25 percent interest rate ceiling on long-term government bonds be removed to permit the selling of long-term government bonds at a higher interest rate. Because Congress has generally refused to grant this request, the Treasury is forced to sell short-term government obligations on which there is no interest rate ceiling.

Although the Treasury in this manner redeems the matured obligations, the total cost of the debt increases because the interest rate on the new obligations is higher than that on the refunded portion of the debt. Furthermore, it puts itself in a position where it has to pay off or refund again this portion of the debt in another relatively short period. If the Treasury Department were able to issue long-term securities at a competitive interest rate, it would prolong the payment or refunding date for 15, 20, or even 30 years. On the other hand, there could be times when the debt might be refunded at a lower cost. The situation on refunding worsened in the late 1960s and again in the early 1970s, however. In 1973 and again in 1978, for example, the Treasury was paying more than 8 percent to refund billions of the 4.25 percent and under debts coming due at that time.

Burden of Interest Payments

Included each year in our federal budget is $40 billion or more for payment of interest on the national debt. Although taxation for the payment of this interest does not impose a net burden or cost on the economy as a whole, it does cause an annual redistribution of income and, therefore, a specific burden to individuals and firms in the economy. If the government had originally increased taxes instead of going into debt or if the government had paid off the debt shortly after it had been incurred, it would have imposed a smaller total burden on the individuals than it does when the debt repayment is postponed. With postponement of the debt the total redistribution of income necessary to retire the debt is not only in excess of $700 billion, the principal amount, but also $40 billion or more annually for interest on the debt. This interest comes only as a result of postponement of the payment of the debt.

In the last 5 years there has been an interest burden of more than $170 billion because the debt has been outstanding. It is a matter of judgment whether individuals and firms would prefer the hardships of paying off the debt in a relatively short period as opposed to giving up more total income but spreading the hardship or inconvenience in smaller doses over a longer period of time. It brings up the suggestion, also, that some type of interest-free financing for federal borrowing would ease the debt burden.

CONCLUSION

It is unlikely that the national debt will be reduced by any substantial amount in the near future. In fact, in March, 1978, the U.S. Treasury was asking Congress to raise the ceiling on the national debt from the current level of $752 billion to $781 billion by the end of the 1978 fiscal year, which was September 30, 1978, and to $874 billion by the end of fiscal 1979. According to the Treasury, the increases were needed to finance the anticipated deficits in 1978 and 1979. In addition, the Treasury was asking to increase from $27 billion to $37 billion the amount of long-term bonds the Treasury may sell without regard to the statutory 4.25 percent interest rate ceiling. Consequently, the problems of the national debt will continue to be with us. The issues may become more or less pressing, depending on economic measures adopted in the future to alleviate the problems of the debt. Since it does not appear that the debt is going to be repaid any time soon, the most we can hope for is that future increments in the debt will be less than the additions to our national income, thus reducing the relative burden of the debt.

MAJOR ISSUES

1. Will the national debt bankrupt the nation?
2. Should the national debt be paid off either in part or in full?
3. Should the statutory ceiling on the national debt be removed or tightened?
4. Should our national debt be financed through interest-free financing, that is, by sale of non-interest-bearing bonds to the banks?

SUBISSUES

1. Should the interest rate ceiling on the national debt be removed?
2. Do you recommend that the government avoid going into debt by printing more money to cover its expenses?
3. Should the federal budget be used as a device for stabilizing the economy?
4. What do you think of the "full employment" budget concept?
5. Would it be feasible for the government to issue shares of stock in the U.S. economy and declare dividends each year, instead of selling bonds and paying interest on them?

SELECTED READINGS

The Budget in Brief, 1979. Washington: U.S. Government Printing Office, 1979.
The Budget of the United States Government, 1979. Washington: U.S. Government Printing Office, 1979.

Carlson, Keith M. "Economic Goals For 1981: A Monetary Analysis." *Review*, Federal Reserve Bank of St. Louis (November, 1977).

"The Debt Economy." *Business Week* (October 12, 1974).

"Developing An Economic Plan." *National Journal Reports* (January 11, 1975).

"Issues In the 1978 Budget." *The Brookings Bulletin* (Spring/Summer, 1977).

The Proposal to Repeal the Interest Rate Ceiling on Government Bonds. Washington: American Enterprise Institute, Legislative Analysis No. 10, June, 1969.

"Rising Mountain of Federal Debt, and a Sky-Rocketing Interest Burden." *U.S. News and World Report* (January 28, 1974).

Special Analyses of the United States Government, Fiscal Year 1979. Washington: U.S. Government Printing Office, 1979.

"The Treasury Debt and Bond Rate Ceilings." *Monthly Review*, Federal Reserve Bank of Kansas City (April, 1971).

"U.S. Government Securities Reflect No Increase In Uncertainity." *Business Review*, Federal Reserve Bank of Dallas (October, 1976).

Health Insurance — 7
Should Uncle Sam Pay?

One of the most difficult problems facing the American people in the 1970s is that of paying their medical bills. Because of individual and family need for health care and the lack of adequate funds to meet the high cost of medical care, many people are turning to the federal government for a solution to the problem. It is possible that some form of national health insurance will be passed by Congress in the near future. The debate will be a heated one, for national health insurance will be costly. The purpose of this chapter is to present the economic problems relating to the health industry and to evaluate the economic consequences of national health insurance legislation.

SCOPE OF THE PROBLEM

In the broadest view, four out of five people have some form of illness each year. Of those who become ill, one out of seven is incapacitated for more than 90 days. In addition, there are 350,000 citizens who suffer permanent disability each year. Approximately one person out of every three families is hospitalized annually and an estimated 60 percent of these people require surgery. The cost of this care is astounding. Over 500,000 families will have medical bills in excess of their earnings for half a year, while nearly seven million families will have out-of-pocket medical expenses exceeding 15 percent of their annual income. In 1978, 18 million Americans were without medical insurance of any kind, either private or public. During the same year, 40 million Americans with incomes under $10,000 were either uninsured and not eligible for Medicaid or held individual (rather than group) private insurance policies which usually do not include major medical coverage. Keeping these figures in mind, it should not be surprising to discover that close to 50 percent of all personal bankruptcies each year are the result of medical debts.

The essential problem of medical care today is how to pay the bill when costs are soaring. The United States is the only industrialized nation without a universal health insurance program, yet we spend more for health care on a per capita basis than any other country. Table 7-1 presents data on national

143

health expenditures for selected years. In fiscal year 1976, Americans paid approximately $139 billion for medical care. This sum represents a 100 percent increase over what was paid in 1970 and a staggering 1,000 percent increase in health expenditures since 1950. Table 7-1 reveals that hospital care expenditures accounted for $55 billion of the $139 billion expended in 1976. The second most important expenditure was for the services of physicians, which totaled $26 billion. Combined expenditures for hospital care and physicians' services must be viewed in light of the fact that they are the components of medical care that are experiencing the greatest cost pressures.

Figure 7-1 shows that on a per capita basis, America's medical bill has climbed relentlessly during the last 25 years. In 1950 per capita national health expenditures stood at $79. The corresponding figures for 1960 and 1970 were $142 and $328. By 1976 per capita expenditures had reached the lofty magnitude of $638.

Table 7-1

NATIONAL HEALTH EXPENDITURES FOR SELECTED FISCAL YEARS (Millions)

Type of Expenditure	1950	1960	1970	1976
Total	$12,027	$25,856	$68,083	$139,312
Health Services & Supplies	11,181	24,162	63,067	131,022
Personal health care	10,540	22,954	59,525	120,431
Hospital care	3,698	8,499	25,895	55,400
Physicians' services	2,689	5,580	13,450	26,350
Dentists' services	940	1,944	4,233	8,600
Other professional services	384	848	1,386	2,400
Drugs & drug sundries	1,642	3,591	7,111	11,168
Eyeglasses & appliances	475	750	1,814	1,980
Nursing-home care	178	480	2,860	10,600
Other health services	534	1,262	2,776	3,933
Expenses for prepayment & administration	290	807	2,105	7,336
Government public health activities	351	401	1,437	3,255
Research & medical facilities construction	847	1,694	5,015	8,290
Research	110	592	1,846	3,327
Construction	737	1,102	3,169	4,963

SOURCE: Barbara S. Cooper, et al., "National Health Expenditures 1929–1973," Social Security Bulletin (February, 1974), p. 12, and Robert M. Gibson and Marjorie Smith Mueller, "National Health Expenditures, Fiscal Year 1976," Social Security Bulletin (April, 1977), p. 5.

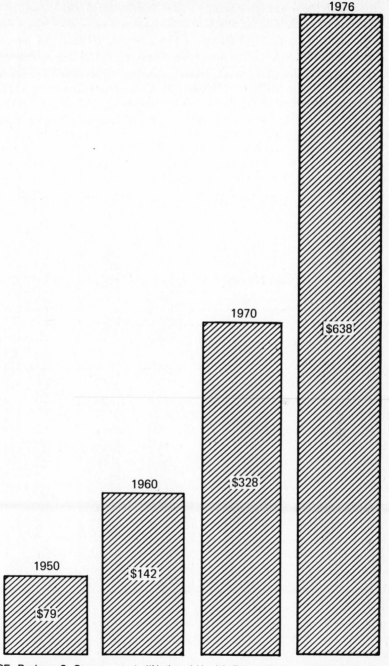

SOURCE: Barbara S. Cooper, *et al.*, "National Health Expenditures, 1929–1973," *Social Security Bulletin* (February, 1974), p. 12, and Robert M. Gibson and Marjorie Smith Mueller, "National Health and Expenditures, Fiscal Year 1976," *Social Security Bulletin* (April, 1977), p. 3.

Figure 7-1 **AVERAGE PER CAPITA MEDICAL COSTS IN THE UNITED STATES**

Figure 7-2 depicts national health expenditures as a percentage of gross national product, again for selected years. The percentage of the GNP attributed to health care has risen from 4.6 percent in 1950 to 8.6 percent in 1976. In fact, in fiscal years 1975 and 1976 health expenditures increased at a significantly greater rate than GNP. Many experts project that by 1981 health care expenditures will account for 10 percent of our gross national product. In many ways the mere size of the health care industry is indicative of the scope of the economic problem, for it has become America's third largest industry, just behind agriculture and construction.

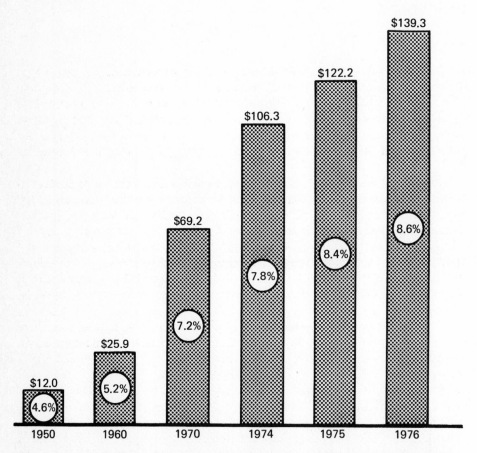

SOURCE: Robert M. Gibson and Marjorie Smith Mueller, "National Health Expenditures, Fiscal Year 1976," *Social Security Bulletin* (April, 1977), p. 4.

Figure 7-2 **NATIONAL HEALTH EXPENDITURES AS A PERCENTAGE OF GROSS NATIONAL PRODUCT FOR SELECTED FISCAL YEARS 1950–1976** (Dollars in Billions)

OUR PRESENT SYSTEM

Americans pay for their medical care in a combination of ways. In addition to direct or out-of-pocket payments to physicians and hospitals, many individuals and families purchase medical insurance, either in the form of individual or group plans. But because of the high cost of medical care, a sufficient level of income is required to make direct payments or to acquire insurance. Unless an individual has employer-paid group insurance, such insurance is unaffordable to many. Therefore, to extend the availability of proper medical attention, the federal government in 1965 passed into law two major health programs — Medicare (for those over 65 years of age) and Medicaid (for the medically poor).

Medicare

The Medicare plan (Title 18 of the Social Security Act), which began paying benefits on July 1,1966, covers almost everyone over 65 years of age. The plan is made up of two kinds of health insurance, namely, hospital insurance and medical insurance. The hospital insurance is obligatory and the medical insurance is voluntary. The hospital insurance is financed by a compulsory payroll tax on all employees in industries covered by the Social Security Act.

Benefits of the hospital insurance are, basically, a maximum of 90 days of hospital and post-hospital care, 100 days of nursing home care, and up to 100 days of home health visits by medical personnel other than doctors. In addition, each person is eligible for a "lifetime reserve" of 60 covered days of hospital and post-hospital insurance to apply to situations in which the number of hospital days during an illness exceeds 90 days. Except for deductible amounts, the cost of room and board in semiprivate accommodations, ordinary nursing services, drugs, and customary service are "free," that is, prepaid by the taxpayer.

The patient had to pay the first $144 of costs in 1978. In addition, there was a patient cost of $36 a day for the sixty-first through the ninetieth days. The patient must pay $72 a day for days ninety-one to one hundred and fifty if the patient must utilize the "lifetime reserve" days.

The other half of Medicare is voluntary medical insurance (Plan B). This plan is financed by monthly premiums of those over 65 years of age. Premiums are deducted from the Social Security checks of those who volunteer to participate. The federal government matches the payments from general revenues. Monthly payments rose from $3 in 1966 to $7.70 in 1978. The medical insurance program pays 80 percent of reasonable charges for covered services, except for the first $60 in a calendar year.

Services covered include physicians' and surgeons' aid, up to 100 home health visits, and diagnostic tests and other health services, regardless of where rendered. In 1976, about 25 million persons were enrolled in the basic

Medicare program and of these over 20 million were also enrolled in the program of supplemental medical insurance.

From the time of its inception in 1966 through fiscal 1976, Medicare has paid out nearly $100 billion in hospital expenses and physicians' fees. On an annual basis, Medicare has grown from a $3.3 billion program in fiscal 1967 to an $18 billion program in fiscal 1976.

Medicaid

Medicaid (Title 19 of the Social Security Act) is a medical assistance program rather than an insurance program. It is a federal-state program administered by the states individually. It is financed out of the general revenue at the federal level along with state and local tax money. Each state determines its eligibility requirements and operating rules under broad federal guidelines. Thus, the number of people eligible or types of benefits received vary considerably from state to state. One state, Arizona, has no Medicaid program.

As previously indicated, Medicaid was passed to help the medically poor pay for medical assistance. But just who are the individuals whom we are classifying as "poor"? According to the Social Security Administration, any household is defined as "poor" if its annual money income is less than three times the cost (in current prices) of a minimal diet for the persons in that household. Hence, a larger family will have a proportionately higher threshold of poverty.

The medical assistance program (Medicaid) was designed to help unify the nation's health care by bringing the medically poor (those with enough money for daily needs but not enough to pay for health care) up to par in terms of benefits with welfare recipients. After some states defined income levels for the medically poor at unrealistically high levels, Congress, in 1969, set income levels for Medicaid at 133 percent of the income level needed to qualify for welfare payments under Aid to Families With Dependent Children (AFDC).

The manner in which Medicaid is implemented has resulted in wide variations in the amount, quality, and types of services provided among the various states. According to federal law, states having Medicaid programs are required to provide care to those individuals and families who are enrolled in the two major programs of federally aided cash welfare assistance — Aid to Families with Dependent Children (AFDC) and Supplementary Security Income (SSI) for the aged, blind, and disabled. Other individuals may or may not be included depending on the type of state program. The major groups that tend to be excluded from Medicaid programs are the non-disabled poor adults under age 65 and adults in intact families with an employed father in the home.

Not only does coverage vary among states, but the quality of service varies as well. All states must provide inpatient hospital services, outpatient hospital services, lab and X-ray services, skilled nursing services, and physicians' services. The law does not require the provision of dental services, prescription drugs, home health care services, private duty nurses, or long-term institutional care in a mental or tuberculosis hospital. However, states may provide the aforementioned services if they so choose. Also, the law does not specify the amount of coverage to be received by various groups. For example, some states use approximately 50 percent of their Medicaid funds for nursing homes while other states spend little for this purpose. Because of these many factors, there has been a growing recognition that the Medicaid program has not been totally successful in providing quality care to all the poor and medically indigent.

In 1976 Medicaid paid medical bills for an estimated 23 million persons eligible under public assistance standards. On a cost basis, total expenditures in fiscal 1976 were approximately $15 billion, of which the federal government paid $8.2 billion.

Private Insurance

About 80 percent of the population has some private health insurance for hospital and surgical expenses, while 70 percent have additional coverage for the more commonplace medical expenses, such as routine doctor bills. Typically the coverage is some sort of group health insurance. Over 80 percent of insurance companies' enrollment is for group plans associated with employment. The same is true of Blue Cross enrollment. Figure 7-3 depicts the percentage of the population under the age of 65 having private medical insurance coverage for hospital care, physicians' services, dental care, and out-of-hospital prescription drug expenses.

Another rapidly growing form of health insurance is catastrophic insurance, often referred to as major medical care. Currently about one half of the

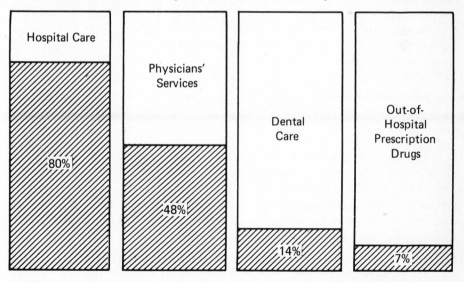

SOURCE: Marjorie S. Mueller, "Private Health Insurance in 1975: Coverage, Enrollment, and Financial Experience," *Social Security Bulletin* (June, 1977), p. 19.

Figure 7-3 **PRIVATE INSURANCE COVERAGE OF PERSONS UNDER 65 YEARS OF AGE (PERCENTAGE HAVING COVERAGE)**

population is covered. Such coverage is typically tied in with other insurance since it pays when Blue Cross stops paying or it pays for certain illnesses not covered by Blue Cross. In addition to having a $100 deductible clause, major medical pays 80 percent of the charges up to a designated maximum (often $25,000).

The most common criticism of private health insurance is that it does not cover a high enough portion of the total bill. A similar charge can be made against Medicare. When one considers the high costs involved, it is probably impossible for any plan to cover 100 percent of personal health expenses.

The plight of the lower segment of the middle-income group highlights the national dilemma. They pay the taxes for Medicare and Medicaid. Their private coverage is not comprehensive and is becoming even smaller in the face of rapidly rising prices. Hence, their out-of-pocket costs for uncovered services is rising. Thus, relative to their needs, total medical care may be less for this group than for the poor. Figure 7-4, which details how health care is paid for, indicates that public insurance payments account for 40 percent of health

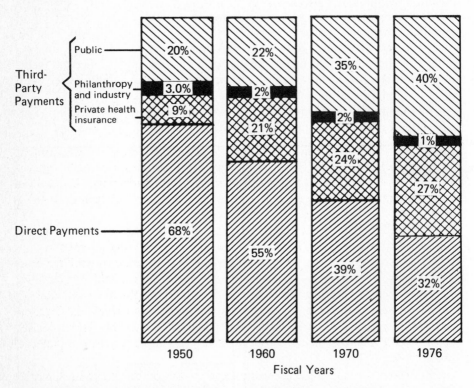

SOURCE: Barbara S. Cooper, *et al.*, "National Health Expenditures, 1929–1973," *Social Security Bulletin* (February, 1974), p. 12, and Robert M. Gibson and Marjorie Smith Mueller, "National Health Expenditures, Fiscal Year 1976, "*Social Security Bulletin* (April, 1977), p. 5.

Figure 7-4 **HOW HEALTH CARE IS PAID FOR (PERCENTAGES)**

care payments, while out-of-pocket payments by health care consumers have declined to a level of 32 percent.

HEALTH MAINTENANCE ORGANIZATIONS

In recent years the Health Maintenance Organization has received wide acceptance as an effective alternative to more traditional private insurance programs. Health Maintenance Organizations (HMOs) consist of groups of voluntarily organized people who band together to receive a wide range of health services. Members prepay for medical service, much like Blue Cross and other insurance programs. The goal of the HMO is to provide satisfactory medical service under one plan at the lowest possible cost.

As members of an HMO, individuals and families have access to an entire team of physicians. In addition to primary-care physicians, such as general practitioners and pediatricians, an HMO typically includes specialists on its staff such as radiologists, surgeons, obstetricians, gynecologists, and neurologists. In large part, the number of specialists included on a given HMO physician team is a function of the size of the HMO. The HMO's team of doctors, nurses, laboratory technicians, and administrators works together in a single building and provides 24-hour medical care, 365 days a year. Many HMOs also have their own pharmacies. If hospitalization is deemed necessary, the patient is admitted and treated at an affiliated hospital at no out-of-pocket expense to the individual. The annual cost of membership in an HMO usually ranges between $1,000 and $1,500, depending on the extent of service provided and the area of the country. Although not inexpensive, HMO membership does provide financial protection against the burdens of catastrophic illness. This protection is usually not included in standard insurance programs and is only acquired at additional expense. Consequently, most if not all of the economic uncertainty resulting from unexpected large medical expenses is precluded.

The Health Maintenance Organization is based on the concept of the efficiency of preventative medicine. By stressing outpatient and preventive care, HMOs hope to reduce economic wastes associated with the overutilization of hospital services. Because members have prepaid for medical service, they are more prone to seek medical care in the early stages of illness, keeping HMO members healthier at reduced costs. Another factor which HMO proponents believe increases its economic efficiency is the fact that HMO doctors are paid on a salary basis, which removes any incentive to perform unnecessary services.

As HMOs grow in number, many experts caution that there are possible disadvantages to this system of health care delivery. The most often mentioned concerns include the limited choice of physicians and hospitals, the impersonality of the system (particularly the doctor-patient relationship), and the possible lack of coverage outside the service area. In many cases these drawbacks are more theoretical than real, but nevertheless they may become more significant as HMOs increase in popularity.

The recent popularity of Health Maintenance Organizations can be attested to by their growth in the last few years. In 1970 there were only 25 HMOs operating in the United States. By 1976 the number of HMOs had increased to several hundred, with more than 7 million persons enrolled. Some experts predict that 25 percent of the population will eventually participate in some form of prepaid medical plan in the future.

MAJOR PROBLEMS IN THE HEALTH CARE INDUSTRY

Despite increased federal participation in the health care field and the rapid development of Health Maintenance Organizations, major problems continue to challenge the health care industry. Two such problems relate to the supply of physicians and the increasing costs of medical services.

Supply of Doctors

One of the major controversies concerning the health industry is whether there is an adequate number of physicians to provide for the medical needs of the population. Patients who have waited for long hours beyond the time of their appointments in doctors' offices are likely to support those who decry the acute shortage of medical personnel. However, many health care experts claim that there is a sufficient number of medical doctors, but what is needed is a more rational medical care system. They point out that the supply of doctors is increasing with the demand for more health services and that each year the number of doctors graduating from our medical schools is growing at a faster rate than the population as a whole. This is happening despite monopolistic factors on the supply side, such as laws on licensed practice and certain restrictive practices of professional associations of doctors.

The underlying basis for such opposing views on the need for additional doctors can be traced to the definitional problems associated with the term "need." If approached according to economic analysis, need is incorporated into consumer demand since it is a measure of the amount of medical care consumers will purchase at various prices. For the most part, however, need is defined in the health industry in a medical or social sense and is related to the standards of the health profession. Needless to say, this approach fosters controversy because of the lack of easy quantification.

Although disagreement exists over the need for increasing the supply of doctors nationally, there is a general consensus that there are distribution problems in the delivery of medical services.

The maldistribution of physicians on a geographical basis has long been recognized. Although the ratio of physicians to population is not a perfect measure of the adequacy of medical service, it is a widely held criterion for designating areas that are underserved. As with most professions, physicians tend to gravitate toward urban areas within more heavily populated states and away from states which are primarily rural. For example, Maryland (253 physicians per 100,000 population) and New York (245 physicians per 100,000 population) have the highest physician-to-population ratios of any of the fifty states. On the other hand, the lowest ratios of physicians to population exist in South Dakota (89 per 100,000) and Mississippi (96 per 100,000).[1]

Certainly the attractiveness of higher incomes and the amenities derived from urban residence are major factors accounting for the lack of geographical balance in the supply of physicians. But there are other important considerations as well. Urban areas offer the undeniable benefits of professional interaction among physicians and a greater opportunity to keep abreast of the constantly changing state of medical science. In addition, urban medical centers provide greater research accommodations and access to the most advanced facilities and equipment. Finally, having spent more than a few years studying medicine, many graduating doctors no longer feel the strong ties to their rural hometowns. These factors undoubtedly loom large in accounting for such a wide range in the physician-to-population ratios among states.

The maldistribution among medical specialties has also hampered the provision of effective health care. While a general shortage exists of physicians providing primary care (general practitioners, pediatricians, and doctors of internal medicine) and of certain specialists (such as radiologists and psychiatrists), there is an oversupply of general surgeons.

The relative decline in primary care physicians can be seen by the sharp decrease in the number of general practitioners as a percentage of the total number of physicians. In 1931, 75 percent of the physicians providing health care primarily outside of hospitals were general practitioners. By 1974 this figure had declined to 22 percent. Even if internal medicine and pediatrics are included with general medicine, they only account for approximately 41 percent of office-based physicians.[2] This trend toward medical specialization is the result of several factors. Perhaps foremost is the fact that, on the average, specialists earn higher incomes than do primary care physicians. In addition, closed hospital staffs encourage specialization. An intern seeking a staff position in a good hospital quickly realizes that the chances for acceptance are enhanced if one is a specialist.

Consequently, medical care delivery not only has become more urban oriented, but more specialized as well. These shifts have altered the structure of both the supply and demand of the services of physicians and have resulted in increased medical costs.

Rising Costs

By 1976 the average citizen was paying about four and one half times the dollar amount for medical services as was paid in 1960. Many factors accounted for such a sharp increase in medical expenditures. Three major causal factors, however, stand out as being most worthy of our attention: price increases as measured by the Consumer Price Index, changes in the composition of medical services and goods provided, and changes in the size

[1]*Statistical Abstract of the United States*, 1976, p. 76.
[2]*Ibid.*, p. 78.

and age distribution of the population. It should be noted that the latter two factors do not represent price increases *per se* but rather increasing expenditures for health care.

Supply and demand analysis serves as a useful framework for analyzing price inflation in the health industry. Although the supply of health care has increased since 1950, increases in demand have been much greater. Figure 7-5 illustrates the result of such supply and demand shifts in the health care industry — a greater quantity of health care service but at a considerably higher price.

On the supply side, monopolistic restrictions such as the overly selective admission practices of medical schools and the power of the American Medical Association in controlling the licensing of physicians, the certifying of medical schools, and the regulating of hospital internship and residency requirements have limited increases in supply. On the demand side, a combination of variables has contributed to rapid increases in demand during the last few decades. Largely responsible have been rising household incomes, the increased availability of private health insurance, and huge outlays on public health service programs, such as Medicare and Medicaid. Thus, the dramatic rise in the price of health care service reflects the inability or unwillingness within the industry to adjust supply to meet increases in demand.

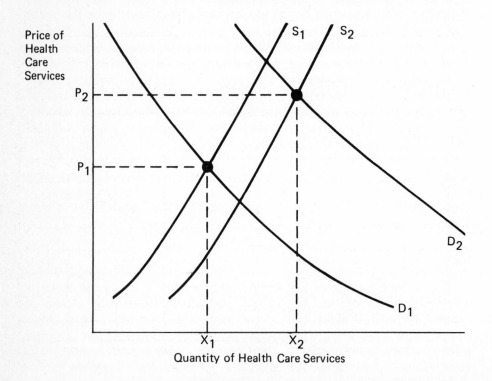

Figure 7-5 **SUPPLY AND DEMAND SHIFTS IN THE HEALTH CARE INDUSTRY**

Price increases for various categories of medical service are compared to changes in the cost of living in Figure 7-6. Using 1967 as the base year, the cost of living as measured by the CPI increased by 69 percent between 1967 and May, 1976. Hospital charges and physicians' fees, however, increased at much faster rates than the overall price index. Figure 7-6 indicates that hospital charges have risen by 163 percent and physicians' fees by 87 percent since 1967. On the other hand, the costs of drugs and prescriptions have increased at a much slower pace.

The effect of changes in the composition of medical services and goods as well as utilization rates are referred to as "changes in the health care system." This category contains a variety of interlocking factors which are difficult to measure independently of each other in terms of their effect on increased health costs. Such factors include changes in technology and

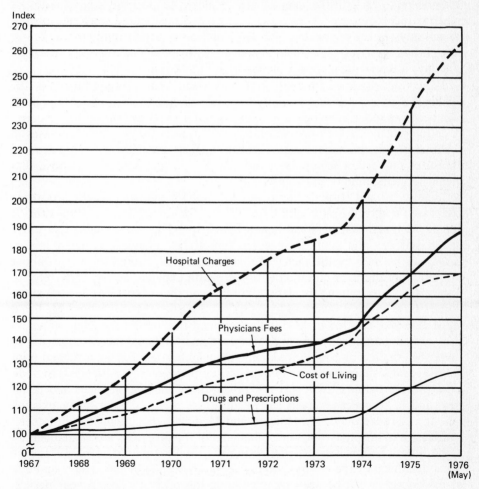

SOURCE: *Statistical Abstract of the United States,* 1976, p. 440.

Figure 7-6 **MEDICAL COST INCREASES (1967 = 100)**

treatment which alter the mix and frequency of services utilized, as well as changes in access to medical care, either by removing financial barriers or by increasing the supply of services, which affects utilization rates. Undoubtedly the quality of health care service in the United States has improved appreciably with the spreading of previously known methods and techniques, coupled with the introduction of new ones. Chemotherapy treatments, dialysis, and open-heart surgery are very expensive and add a significant amount to national health expenditures. However, these examples represent major progress in medical care. In addition, the quantity of health care service utilized has increased with growing demand, increasing aggregate expenditures for health care. One relatively recent phenomenon serving to increase the per capita utilization rates of health services has been the sharp increase in malpractice suits. The fear of malpractice suits has led many physicians to perform as many diagnostic tests as are available to prevent legal charges of medical incompetence. These extra tests are costly and may necessitate longer stays in the hospital, which adds still more to the total cost of health care. It has been estimated that if the average hospital stay were decreased by one day, it would save approximately $2 billion a year.

The third factor contributing to increased health expenditures is the changing size and age distribution of the population. As our nation's population becomes older, it is logical to expect greater expenditures on health care. A counterbalancing factor to an older population is the fact that increases in the total population have declined during the past ten years, reducing demand pressures on certain segments of the health industry, particularly those segments servicing infants and youths.

Figure 7-7 and Table 7-2 on pages 157 and 158 indicate the effect of these factors on personal health care expenditures for selected years 1950–1976. It should be noted that personal health care expenditures are defined as those health services and supplies received directly by individuals. Their importance can be seen by the fact that this category accounted for all but about $19 billion of the $139 billion in national health expenditures in 1976 (refer to Table 7-1). In examining the data it can be seen that from 1965, health expenditures have taken a quantum leap. As cited earlier, Medicare and Medicaid legislation was enacted in 1965 with the result that public spending on health care surged dramatically upward. Medicare and Medicaid increased access to better health care by sharply reducing financial barriers for the aged and poor while creating sharp increases in demand not previously experienced. In addition, these programs led to excess utilization of medical services and facilities, and in some cases even led to an abuse of such. Like many existing private insurance policies, Medicare and Medicaid encouraged the ill to seek admittance to hospitals since many benefits of the programs are available only if the illness is hospital related. During the six-year period, 1965–1971, personal health care expenditures increased by almost $34 billion. The magnitude of this increase can be seen by examining the previous fifteen year period, over which time total costs increased by $23 billion.

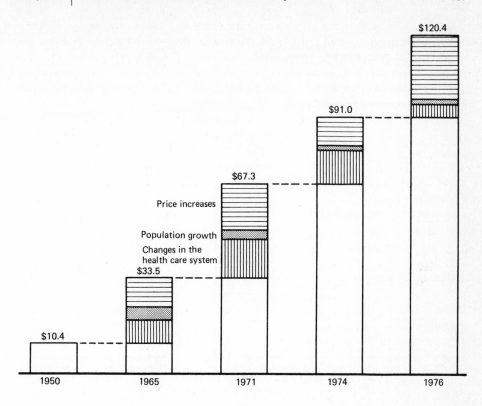

SOURCE: Robert M. Gibson and Marjorie Smith Mueller, "National Health Expenditures, Fiscal Year 1976," *Social Security Bulletin* (April, 1977), p. 16.

Figure 7-7   **FACTORS AFFECTING INCREASES IN PERSONAL HEALTH CARE EXPENDITURES, SELECTED FISCAL YEARS 1950–1976** (Dollars in Billions)

Public policy affected the health industry during the years 1971–1974. In an attempt to beat back the inflationary spiral of price increases, the Nixon Administration applied specific wage and price controls throughout the industry. Health care expenditures continued to climb, however, by a total of $24 billion during the period. With the lifting of economic controls on the health industry in 1974, prices skyrocketed to such heights that price inflation accounted for over 78 percent of the $29 billion increase in expenditures between 1974 and 1976.

It should be clear that rising costs constitute a critical problem in the health industry and there appears to be no relief in sight. As costs continue their upward climb and we as a nation expect greater service from the health care industry, some individuals and institutions have looked to a national health insurance program as a possible solution.

Table 7-2

PRINCIPAL FACTORS CONTRIBUTING TO INCREASED HEALTH EXPENDITURES, 1950–1976

Source of Increase	1950–1965	1965–1971	1971–1974	1974–1976
	Amount of increase (in billions)			
Total..............................	$23.1	$33.7	$24.1	$29.1
Price................................	10.1	16.8	10.4	22.8
Population.........................	4.9	3.0	1.9	1.7
Changes in health care system	8.1	13.9	11.8	4.6
	Percentage distribution			
Total..............................	100.0	100.0	100.0	100.0
Price................................	43.8	49.9	43.1	78.3
Population.........................	21.0	8.9	7.9	5.7
Changes in health care system	35.2	41.2	49.0	15.9

SOURCE: Robert M. Gibson and Marjorie Smith Mueller, "National Health Expenditures, Fiscal Year 1976," *Social Security Bulletin* (April, 1977), p. 14.

MAJOR NATIONAL HEALTH INSURANCE PROPOSALS

Within the past few years, many serious proposals have been brought before Congress in regard to national health insurance. The principal reasons underlying this strong and widespread support for some form of national health insurance, as we have seen, are these:

1. The spiraling cost of health care.
2. The difficulties faced by many private health insurers in maintaining their present levels of benefits.
3. The general popularity of Medicare.
4. The crisis in Medicaid, namely, the failure of the national government to implement uniform proposals, and the federal government's failure to support Medicaid at the level genuinely needed in numerous states.

The large number of bills and the prestige of their sponsors is an indication that Congress is taking national health insurance seriously and that some form of national health insurance will become law in the future. In this section the major health care bills presented to Congress are examined. It is not likely that any one of these proposals will be adopted in its entirety. However, many of the key features of several of the proposals are likely to become incorporated into law.

CHIP

The "Comprehensive Health Insurance Plan" (CHIP) is very similar to a national health insurance bill presented to Congress by the Nixon Administration in 1973. Since then it has been submitted to Congress in only slightly modified forms in subsequent years. Its most recent sponsor is Kentucky Representative Lee Carter.

CHIP would require most employers to provide group health insurance to their employees. These plans would be furnished by private health insurance companies. However, the insurance is not compulsory on the part of the worker, who may choose not to participate in the employer's plan. CHIP has both the employer and the employee participating in the payment for the plan. Initially, the employer would pay 65 percent and the employee 35 percent. Eventually the employer's share would increase to 75 percent.

This package provides institutional health services such as hospital care and skilled nursing facilities for up to 100 days. Expenses associated with diagnosis and treatment are also covered, including physicians' services, laboratory tests, x-rays, prescription drugs, medical supplies and appliances, and up to 100 home health service visits. Other benefits included in CHIP are well-child care, maternity and family planning, dental care, and hearing care for children under the age of 13.

A deductible amount of $150 per year per covered individual is applicable to all covered benefits with a smaller and separate specific deduction for drug expenses. Everyone would be responsible for 25 percent of the remaining expenses in excess of the $150 deductible. An upper limit of $1,500 in family payments for any one year is provided. Beyond $1,500 the catastrophic insurance provisions would relieve the family of any additional payments. Deductible co-insurance and maximum payments are reduced for families with low incomes and for the aged not covered by Social Security.

CHIP entrusts the responsibility of managing national health insurance to private insurance firms and to individual states. Each state would make its own reimbursement policy, deciding how much money doctors and other health providers should receive for services performed. The role of the federal government in regulating national health insurance would be small. In fact, the regulatory and payment aspects of CHIP contain many similarities to the current Medicaid program.

The annual cost of this plan is estimated to be about $12 billion. However, if the entire cost to employers and employees is included, the plan might cost upward of $40 billion a year.

Comprehensive Health Insurance Act

Before Congress is "The Comprehensive Health Insurance Act," sponsored by Representative Richard Fulton of Tennessee, which has the national support of the American Medical Association. This plan relies heavily on the private insurance sector and employer participation with voluntary participation for employees. CHIA requires minimum federal involvement and no added Social Security tax for funding. It is a conservative plan but an expensive one.

Under the plan employers would be required to offer employees a comprehensive health care package from a private insurance company. If the employee desires to join the plan, the employer would pay at least 65 percent of the premium cost with the employee contributing the remainder. Small firm employers whose payroll costs increase by more than 3 percent due to the added insurance costs are eligible for federal tax credits or cash subsidies for the first five years of the plan. The self-employed, non-employed, and elderly would also be covered, but their premiums would be adjusted by federal income-tax credits computed on a sliding scale depending on tax liability. Those individuals having no tax liability would receive health stamps from the government to acquire insurance.

Coverage for institutional care ranges from 365 days of inpatient hospital care to 100 days of skilled nursing facility care. Diagnostic and treatment care for physicians' services, laboratory tests and x-rays, home health services, medical supplies, and equipment are covered, as are physical checkups, well-child care, maternity, family planning, and dental care for persons under 18 years of age.

The plan contains a provision for co-payment but no deductible is applied. A family is responsible for 20 percent of the first $2,000 in medical expenses on all covered items, whereas an individual has a co-insurance ceiling of $1,500. In both cases, whenever the co-insurance ceiling has been exceeded, catastrophic insurance protection would take over.

Claims would be administered by private insurance companies and Medicare would continue intact. A Health Insurance Advisory Board would be created to set standards and regulations. The estimated cost of the Comprehensive Health Insurance Act is in the neighborhood of $20 billion per year.

The Kennedy-Corman Plan

This plan, sponsored by Senator Edward Kennedy of Massachusetts and Representative James Corman of California, has the backing of organized labor. It is a comprehensive and very costly bill. In capsule form, this bill would repeal Medicare and Medicaid and substitute a program of compulsory national health insurance to cover virtually all medical expenses with no co-payments and no deductibles. Private health insurance has no role under this plan.

All necessary hospitalization and physicians' services, including maternity, well-child care, immunizations, physical checkups, family planning, laboratory tests, x-rays, and medical supplies and appliances are fully covered. The costs of prescription drugs are included if required for chronic illnesses. Vision care and eyeglasses and hearing care and hearing aids are also fully covered but dental care is subject to limitations. Orthodontia is excluded from coverage and dental care is initially limited to children under the age of 15, but over a ten-year period coverage will gradually increase to include everyone under the age of 25. Expenses for skilled nursing facility service are covered for up to 120 days, at which time benefits may be extended under certain conditions. Outpatient psychiatric care is covered in full, if provided by a hospital or by a comprehensive health service organization, community mental health center, or other approved institution. Private care is limited to 20 consultations during an illness and inpatient care to 45 days per illness.

The bill would be financed on a tripartite basis from general federal tax revenues, taxes levied on employers, and taxes levied on employees' and other individuals' nonwage income. The proportions coming from the three sources could be as follows: 50 percent from federal revenues, 30 percent from the employers, and 20 percent from the beneficiaries.

The Kennedy-Corman bill sets an additional tax rate of 2.5 percent on employers and 1 percent on employees and the self employed. It also proposes a 1 percent tax on all nonwage income up to $20,000. It is estimated that these taxes would raise 50 percent of the necessary funds. The Medicare tax would be abolished. Funds would be deposited in a special federal fund from which benefit payments would be made. For such a program, the administrative provisions are only sketchily developed. It calls for total operation by the federal government through HEW and its regional units. Private intermediaries are excluded, although the delegation of the payment function is given to a regional medical society or other designated representative of the medical profession.

At the national level the Kennedy-Corman plan calls for a 5-person, full-time Health Security Board, appointed by the President and serving under the Secretary of HEW, to establish policy and regulations, and an executive director appointed by the board. The bill also proposes the establishment of a series of health service areas, which might or might not coincide with state lines.

The Kennedy-Corman bill is a nationwide health care budgeting system wherein each year an advance determination will be made of the total amount to be spent in the various regions of physicians' services, institutional services, and other categories of services provided in local communities. The cost of each kind of service and the overall cost of the Health Security Program will be allowed to increase only on a controlled and predictable basis. The size of the annual Health Security Trust Fund will be determined by the health insurance taxes and the federal government's revenue contributions. Institutional providers, such as hospitals, would be paid exclusively on an approved budget basis. Money for payment of physicians and other practitioners would be distributed to local areas within the region on a per capita basis, with some adjustments.

In general, the program candidly aims to restructure the health care delivery system, and especially to promote comprehensive health service organizations. The bill calls for a massive multimillion dollar planning and grant-in-aid program, aimed both at facilities and personnel training. The estimated cost of the Kennedy-Corman plan may be as high as $100 billion per year.[3] Administrative costs alone are estimated to be about $8 billion per year.

The Long-Ribicoff Proposal

The national health insurance plan submitted to Congress by Senators Russell Long of Louisiana and Abraham Ribicoff of Connecticut contains separate provisions for the poor and the nonpoor. The plan provides both basic and catastrophic insurance for the poor and catastrophic insurance for the nonpoor.

Unlike other proposals, this plan would have no effect on the basic insurance coverage of the great majority of families. Families earning more than $4,800 a year would receive only catastrophic insurance coverage. Families earning less than this amount would be excused from essentially all out-of-pocket payments and thus would be provided with complete insurance coverage, both basic and catastrophic. Benefits for the poor are equivalent to those of Medicare. The Medicaid program would be replaced with a uniform, national program of medical benefits for low-income persons, administered by the Department of Health, Education, and Welfare.

The Long-Ribicoff plan for catastrophic insurance coverage would be financed out of payroll taxes, as is Medicare. According to this plan, employers would pay a 1 percent payroll tax, 50 percent of the amount paid allowed as a federal tax credit. No employee contributions are required under this bill. It should be noted that an employer need not buy insurance from HEW, since the employer has the option of insuring employees through a federally approved plan such as Blue Cross. The self-employed would also be eligible in the same manner. In essence, anyone covered by the Social Security System would be covered by the catastrophic insurance plan. Since state and local governments do not participate in the Social Security System, they would be given the opportunity to buy into the plan for their employees.

Expenditures for health care are subject to a $2,000 deduction for a given year. Any expenses over $2,000 would be covered by catastrophic insurance. Although an individual may continue to opt for private insurance coverage to help meet the first $2,000 in medical expenses, the need for major medical insurance would not be necessary.

For poor people the medical assistance plan would be financed on a state-federal, cost-sharing basis and hospitals and physicians would be required to accept insurance payments as full payment for services rendered. On the other hand, the catastrophic insurance plan for the nonpoor would be funded from special federal payroll taxes with physicians and hospitals permitted to charge more than the sum allowed by Medicare. The annual estimated cost of the Long-Ribicoff plan is approximately $10 billion.

[3]The *net* cost of the Kennedy-Corman plan would be substantially less than $100 billion, however, since other public health programs would be eliminated upon its implementation.

The Ullman Proposal

Representative Al Ullman of Oregon, Chairman of the House Ways and Means Committee, introduced into the 95th Congress a national health insurance bill formally titled the "National Health Care Services Reorganization and Financing Act." The major characteristics of this bill are its cost and its complexity. The Ullman bill has the national support of the American Hospital Association.

The Ullman plan requires employers to provide health insurance for their employees and families. Employers would pay at least 75 percent of premium costs with employees accounting for the remaining share. The federal government would offer health insurance for the elderly, low income, and medically indigent through private insurance companies. The self-employed would enroll voluntarily under group plans. To lessen the financial blow to firms employing less than 10 employees, such firms are eligible for federal subsidies in the form of tax credits. The self-employed would also be eligible for tax credits, whereas individual taxpayers could deduct all insurance premium expenditures from gross income.

Health care benefits under the act are broader than those currently provided by Medicare. All federal health programs would be consolidated within a Department of Health that would make money available. The plan calls for a 5-year gradual phase-in period, after which time full benefits would be accessible. Participants are eligible for up to 90 days hospital care, 30 days skilled nursing facility care, 90 days health-related custodial nursing home care, 10 visits to physicians, 100 days of home health services, and unrestricted laboratory tests and x-ray services. Coverage for prescription drugs is limited to specified conditions, but physical checkups, well-child care, maternity, and medical supplies and appliances are generally covered. Dental care coverage is provided for children under the age of 13. The same age limitation applies for eyeglasses as well.

The Ullman plan requires a 20 percent co-insurance and certain co-payments on many items. Special catastrophic provisions would become effective when a patient's out-of-pocket expenses reach a designated amount. Medicare would be eliminated while federal financing of Medicaid would be limited to services not covered. The estimated cost of the Ullman national health insurance plan is approximately $25 billion a year.

CONCLUSION

The proposals presented in this chapter by no means constitute an exhaustive list of the health insurance plans being examined by Congress. The selection of proposals presented and analyzed is based on the attention they are receiving in Washington and by the prestige of their sponsors. Even in the limited selection presented, however, the reader should appreciate the vast differences in the scope and cost of national health insurance proposals. And like all economic problems, each plan has its appealing benefits and deterring costs. All bills cover the most common medical services, such as hospital, physician, and nursing home expenses, but differ widely in psychiatric care, eye and dental care, emergency transportation, and the like.

All of the proposals appear to provide greater medical coverage for the poor and medically indigent albeit at various costs. Deductibles, co-payments, or co-insurance are incorporated into the Ullman, Carter, Fulton, and Long-Ribicoff plans. The Kennedy-Corman plan, however, contains no cost sharing whatsoever, regardless of income. The general argument in favor of deductible co-insurance and co-payments is that they have some effect in discouraging excessive utilization of medical resources and to some extent serve as a rationing device.

The comprehensive nature of many of the national health insurance plans has also raised serious concern over the likelihood of excessive resource utilization. These plans propose to insure a large number of medical services which many analysts consider discretionary or capable of overuse, such as prescription drugs, physical checkups, well-child care, routine ear, eye, and dental care, and outpatient mental health care.

In regard to catastrophic medical insurance, the question is usually whether such insurance should be automatically encompassed in any national health insurance plan as is the case in the Kennedy-Corman bill. Those who are against mandatory catastrophy insurance base their view on the ability-to-pay principle. If an individual has the necessary financial wherewithal to purchase catastrophy insurance, that individual should be allowed to select the policy believed appropriate for the circumstances. To include everyone in a catastrophic insurance plan is to force this type of insurance on some who do not want it, whereas the nonpoor who want it probably already have it. On the other hand, there are those who feel that catastrophy insurance must be made compulsory because if left optional many individuals may be stricken by a catastrophic illness without adequate coverage. In such cases they may become a burden to taxpayers because they usually will be cared for, financial resources not withstanding.

The Kennedy-Corman plan does not allow supplementary payments to providers. Thus, the plan may not garner support from those who champion the rights of the individual to exercise personal freedoms. The plan also proposes only one type of health package for all individuals, regardless of one's socioeconomic position. This feature is favored by those who take a dim view of the differences in the quality of health care in this country resulting from differences in income. Despite comprehensive coverage, doubts exist regarding the plan's impact on improving health care. These doubts stem from the source of health funds, namely, Congress. Increased demand for doctors, hospitals, and equipment may create short-run shortages. It is possible that to increase the supply of medical personnel and facilities, Congress would have to increase taxes to increase expenditures in the health care field. Since there would be pressures to keep spending down, critics argue that there would be an overall deterioration in the quality of service and increased delays in the delivery of service.

Estimating the potential costs of various health insurance proposals involves assumptions that are difficult to make with accuracy. The approximate costs presented in the chapter of each plan are at best mere "guestimates." But the sheer cost burden involved in expanding the nation's medical-care program is not something that can be taken lightly. Because of chronic deficits in the federal budget and the Carter Administration's desire to keep a lid on spending, the prospects of enacting a national health insurance program are not as promising as a few years ago. Perhaps the most damaging single factor reducing Congressional support for national health insurance has been the financial weakness of the Social Security System and the necessity of increasing payroll taxes dramatically over the next decade. The timing for passage of a national health insurance program is therefore somewhat less than ideal.

Philosophically, however, the climate for passage of some sort of national health insurance is certainly more favorable today than in years past. Rarely are health insurance proposals attacked on the grounds of being "socialized medicine" as nearly all such plans were only a decade ago. The climate has changed to such an extent that even groups representing doctors, dentists, hospitals, and insurance companies have supported.

Whether a national health insurance act will produce more and better health care for the American people is a matter of much discussion. Although many Americans are dissatisfied with the present health care system, it remains to be seen if the benefits and costs derived from terminating the existing system, with its inefficiencies and its spiraling costs, will exceed the benefits and costs of a national health insurance program. If the goal of national health insurance is to increase the quality of health care for all Americans, then more of our nation's resources must be allocated to health care. Any program which seeks to increase the quality of health care in America by a redistribution of medical resources will undoubtedly result in increasing the quality of health care for some people and decreasing it for others.

MAJOR ISSUES

1. Will a national health insurance act necessarily improve health levels in the United States?
2. How important will government controls on supply and demand be under a national health insurance plan? Will it truly be socialized medicine?
3. What are the principal arguments in favor of a full coverage plan such as the Kennedy-Corman plan? What are the arguments against such a plan?
4. List the advantages and disadvantages of a partial coverage plan such as the CHIP plan.

SUBISSUES

1. What will happen to the private health insurance industry if a national health insurance program is initiated?
2. What should be done, if anything, to

remedy the doctor shortage?
3. Should there be federal standards for doctors?

4. Should a license to be a doctor be life-long or should it come up for renewal perhaps every 10 years?

SELECTED READINGS

Altman, Stuart A., and Sanford L. Weiner. "Constraining the Medical Care System: Regulation as a Second Best Strategy." Unpublished paper presented at a conference sponsored by the Federal Trade Commission, *Competition in the Health Care Sector: Past, Present, and Future*, June 1–2, 1977.

Frech, H. E. "Regulatory Reform: The Case of the Medical Care Industry." *Regulatory Reform — Highlights of a Conference on Government Regulation*, ed. W. S. Moore. Washington: American Enterprise Institute, 1976.

Fuchs, Victor R. *Who Shall Live?* New York: Basic Books, Inc., 1974.

Havighurst, Clark C. "Controlling Health Care Costs: Strengthening the Private Sector's Hand." *Journal of Health Politics, Policy and Law*, Vol. 1, No. 4 (Winter, 1977), pp. 471–498.

——————. "Public Utility Regulation for Hospitals." American Enterprise Institute Reprint No. 17. Washington: 1973.

Institute of Medicine. *Controls on Health Care*. Washington: National Academy of Sciences, 1975.

"One-Stop Health Care; How It Works." *U.S. News and World Report* (January 21, 1974), pp. 46–47.

Starr, Paul. "The Undelivered Health System." *Public Interest*, No. 42 (Winter, 1976), pp. 66–86.

U.S. Department of Health, Education, and Welfare. "Hospital Cost Containment Act of 1977: The Bill in Brief." *HEW News* (April 25, 1977).

U.S. Department of Health, Education, and Welfare, Public Health Service. *Trends Affecting U.S. Health Care System*. Health Planning Information Series, Vol. 1. Washington: 1976.

Food — What 8 Happened to the Surplus?

For the past fifty years or more the United States has grappled with a farm problem. The problem has assumed many forms. For a few years in the early 1970s beef and crop shortages, accompanied by strong domestic and foreign demand, caused a dramatic rise in farm prices and farm incomes. At that time the farm problem, to many people, appeared to be one of shortages and scarcities. By 1974 and 1975, however, when surpluses began to appear and farm prices and farm incomes started to decline, it appeared that the problem of shortages was a temporary one. By 1975 indications were that the American farm problem was reverting to what had been, and according to some will continue to be for many years, one of abundance. In fact, by 1977 groups of farmers were demonstrating throughout the country and in Washington, D.C., with tractor parades in protest against low crop prices and high operating and living costs.

The long-range problem of excess supply, low prices, and inadequate farm income has been attacked with a variety of remedies and has been the cause of almost continual controversy at the highest levels of government. But still it remains largely unsolved. Just what is this problem? Is it so complex that it defies clear identification and solution?

THE LONG-RANGE PROBLEM

For decades many authorities stated that the American farm problem was essentially one of abundance. Their position held American agriculture to be so productive that it was capable of supplying the needs of a population vastly larger than our current numbers.

If we were to accept this view of the farm problem, then its cause was to be found primarily in the economics of the situation. The rapid increase in agricultural productivity had simply outstripped the economy's ability to consume farm output. Rising population, new industrial uses, and broadening foreign markets would eventually bring the demand for farm products into balance with supply, farm prices would stabilize at some satisfactory level, the government could withdraw its support, and the problem would solve itself, provided farm productivity ceased growing so rapidly.

167

The continual outpouring of agricultural goods, far in excess of current needs, maintained a constant downward pressure on farm prices and on farm incomes. While farm incomes remained low relative to the incomes earned in other sectors of the economy, the prices paid by farmers for goods and services to meet their production and consumption needs continued to rise. In the face of this problem the federal government intervened in the market for farm products in an effort to raise farm incomes to a level that would enable the agricultural sector to remain a viable part of the American economy.

Subsidies to Agriculture

The one aspect of the farm problem that most disturbed Americans was the continual outpouring of a significant portion of their tax dollars to support a particular segment (and a diminishing segment at that) of the national economy. The thought of paying out tax dollars to farmers for not producing seemed contrary to American values that have traditionally dictated rewards for the producer and penalties for the laggard. If viewed in this light, the solution to our farm problem became obvious. Congress needed only to cancel immediately and finally all programs designed to raise farm incomes. Market forces would dictate farm prices, and only the most efficient producers would manage to survive the shifts in supply and demand caused by such whimsical forces as climatic conditions, changes in consumer tastes, shifts in the rate of population increase, and the changing demand of industry for raw materials. Farm efficiency would continue to rise as farmers sought to lower their costs of production and thus gain larger profits. But again a flaw was encountered in our solution. What of the farmers who could not compete in the free market, for whatever reason? What would become of them?

They would remain a part of the economy; but they would somehow have to be assimilated into other sectors, and this assimilation would be a difficult and time-consuming process. In 1977 the farm population comprised about 8 million people, or about 3.7 percent of the nation's total population. It has been estimated that America could meet its present and foreseeable needs for farm products with a farm population roughly two thirds that size. If the other third, the families now living on marginal farms,[1] were suddenly displaced and forced to relocate in urban areas, the burden of this nonproductive group would probably be more than urban economies could currently bear. Massive financial aid would be necessary to sustain these people until they equipped themselves to compete in an urban industrial society. Considered, too, was the hardship on the displaced farmers and their families. Uprooted from the only way of life many of them have known and placed in a new environment, they would undoubtedly be sorely pressed to conform to urban standards and

---

[1]We shall define *marginal farmers* as farm owners or operators (tenants) who would be unable to support themselves and their families in the absence of government crop support payments or other aids that supplement their income. The causes of their marginal position can be many and varied. The essential characteristic, however, remains their ability to survive, as farmers, in the absence of government intervention in the market for agricultural products.

values. It was easy to foresee antagonisms developing between the original urban dweller and the interloper. It is not necessary to dwell on the consequence of such a move, however, save to state that it would be serious for urban society.

Social Aspects of the Farm Problem

In considering the consequences of final and complete removal of government agricultural subsidies, we were forced to come face to face with the essence of the farm problem. The trouble was found not in the economics of the farm industry, but rather in the social problems that arose therefrom. The American people have long praised the efficacy of a free enterprise competitive economy, but they have never hesitated to interfere with the workings of such an economy when it began to exact social costs detrimental to the welfare of certain groups of citizens. They recognized that competitive pressures placed American farmers in a situation which they could not face unaided. If we, as a people, were willing to accept the displacement of marginal farmers because they could no longer compete with their more efficient counterparts, and if we were willing to accept the fact that a considerable number of these people would be forced to exist in substandard conditions, then we would recognize no farm problem. The humanistic values of the American people, however, were strong enough to prevent such a social calamity, and we lived with what we termed a "farm problem" even though the problem existed because of our efforts to solve a problem of much more serious dimensions.

A Paradox

There have been and are many farm problems and several ramifications to each one. The farm problems in the United States, except for the shortages that occurred in 1973 and 1974, were different from the problems in other parts of the world.

The Real Problem. Since the dawn of recorded history, the human race has struggled with a much more realistic and serious farm problem. A majority of the world's present population still faces this different problem. The problem can be simply stated — not enough food. Historically famine has been coupled with disease and war as one of the most terrible ravagers of the human race. Uncountable millions of people have perished through the centuries because of the lack of an adequate diet. Outright starvation has taken a heavy toll, but far more insidious have been the effects of inadequate diets. The life expectancies of people in countries with sufficient food of the proper types inevitably have been higher than those of peoples existing in countries where food supplies are just sufficient to keep them at the margin of subsistence. This is the real farm problem, and it has been with us for a long, long time. It is only recently, in the last 200 years, that some fortunate countries, including the United States, managed to solve this problem.

Through the application of scientific methods and materials such as fertilizers, insecticides, hybrid seeds, and crop rotation, the countries of North America and Western Europe have managed to provide diets for their people that have been well above subsistence levels. The application of scientific methods to farming, the development of more efficient farm implements, and the substituting of mechanical energy for animal energy in the heavier farm tasks aided in the solution of the farm problem for these fortunate countries. It is now possible to produce, in a given year, a surplus of farm products sufficient to tide the country over in the event of a poor production year. No longer must the peoples of the agriculturally advanced countries live in constant fear of uncontrollable changes of the weather. In short, the peoples of these countries, particularly the United States, need no longer fear the ravages of starvation. For them the real farm problem has been solved. Herein lies the paradox.

The American Problem. In considering the cause of the farm problem in the United States, we learned that it lay in the social costs caused by a rapidly increasing agricultural productivity and the resulting abundance of farm products. We need only consider this particular type of farm problem in light of the real farm problem to see the paradox. We were faced with an embarrassment of agricultural riches because we refused to subject a relatively small portion of our population to inordinate social pressure, while much of the rest of the world did not have enough to eat. When viewed in this context, one begins to wonder whether the United States really had a farm problem.

Having placed our farm problem in its proper dimension vis-à-vis the world food situation, perhaps we can now consider it somewhat more objectively. In the first place, failure to solve the American farm problem would not precipitate starvation conditions for the American people. Thus, a solution predicated over a period of years has become practicable. Second, in seeking a solution we have not been motivated by a lack of economic efficiencies or insufficient resources; rather we have been motivated by a concern for human dignity and values. We very much desire to have our marginal farmers assume an honorable and productive place in our society. This is our ultimate goal. Whatever solutions to our particular farm problem are advanced in the future, they will be conditioned by our experiences and failures of the past. They also will be made with the full realization that our problems are quite different from those existing in most of the rest of the world. To gain a better understanding of the complexities of this American farm problem, we must now turn to a consideration of its historical evolution.

HISTORICAL DEVELOPMENT OF FARM PROBLEMS IN THE UNITED STATES

It is easy to forget, in light of the United States' present prominence as an industrial power, that for the first 100 years of this country's existence agriculture was the most important sector in the total economy. In fact, as late as

1910 the majority of Americans still resided in rural areas. Table 8-1 gives an indication of the dominance of the rural population in the early years of our country. While today only about 18 percent of the population listed as residing in *rural areas* (defined by the Census Bureau as including places of less than 2,500 population) actually live on farms, we can conclude that the vast majority of these people at one time depended on the agricultural sector of the economy for their livelihood.

Early Importance of Agriculture

The root cause of the farm problem can be traced to the dominance of agriculture during the developmental years of our country. The vastly rich, undeveloped areas of the United States were an open invitation to settlement and cultivation during the nineteenth century. The federal government, through a series of public land acts, made available to its rapidly growing population immense tracts of fertile land on a free or nominal cost basis. The

Table 8-1

**POPULATION IN URBAN AND
RURAL AREAS, 1790–1970**
(In Thousands of People)

Year	Rural	Urban
1790	3,727	201
1800	4,986	322
1810	6,714	525
1820	8,945	693
1830	11,738	1,127
1840	15,224	1,845
1850	19,648	3,543
1860	25,226	6,216
1870	28,656	9,902
1880	36,026	14,129
1890	40,841	22,106
1900	45,834	30,159
1910	49,973	41,998
1920	51,552	54,157
1930	53,820	68,954
1940	57,246	74,424
1950	54,230	96,468
1960	54,054	125,269
1970	53,887	149,325

SOURCE: *Historical Statistics of the United States, Colonial Times to 1957*, p. 14; *Statistical Abstract of the United States*, 1978.

great westward shift in population began in earnest in the years immediately after the Civil War, and by 1910 distinct areas of the country were specializing in the production of crops best suited to their soil and climate characteristics. The middle section of the country was characterized by three broad belts, the northern and southern belts raising spring and winter wheat, and the middle belt specializing in corn and hog production. To the west, the vast grasslands of the Great Plains encouraged beef cattle operations on an unprecedented scale. Cotton began a westward movement, and by 1900 Texas was first in cotton production. Tobacco then became the major crop of the deep South.

The net result of the shifting of crop and livestock production to areas best suited to their requirements was a vast increase in farm output, although this fact alone was not sufficient to explain the increase entirely. Not only were the land and climate better suited to the crops raised thereon, but also much larger amounts of land came under cultivation. In short, the major cause of increasing farm output during the latter years of the nineteenth century and early years of the twentieth was extensive in nature. The land itself was not being cultivated with the primary goal of more output per acre, but rather more and better land was being cultivated.

Rising Level of Agricultural Technology

Throughout this period the development of improved farm machinery played a major part. Threshing machines, steel plows, seed drills, mowers, rakes, cultivators, and reapers significantly increased the farmer's efficiency. With these machines the farmer could cultivate much larger acreages than was possible with the primitive hand tools that had historically been available. The mechanization of the American farm was widespread by 1915 and, in addition, the development of the gasoline engine had solved the age-old problem of the limitations imposed by animal power. Some of the steam-operated farm machines of the late nineteenth century had become so large that 40 horses were necessary to move them. The advent of the gasoline-powered farm tractor in the early years of the twentieth century cut the last bond that tied farmers to the relatively puny resources of animal power, and the farmer's capability literally soared.

The period from World War I to the present has witnessed a somewhat different form of improvement in agricultural technology. Prior to World War I, practically all of the increases in farm output could be ascribed to more extensive cultivation of the land. After the war, advances in the pure sciences began to contribute to the increase in output per acre, and intensive cultivation became important. Genetics (the development of improved strains of crops and livestock), soil chemistry, highly efficient fertilizers, and the development of fungicides and insecticides enabled the farmer to raise per acre output to unprecedented levels. Scientific farming, a general term used to describe the application of the latest mechanical, scientific, and methodological improvements to farm operations, became a popular term; and the Department of Agriculture became very active in disseminating the latest of these developments to every portion of the national farm community. The Department has maintained its efforts to increase farm productivity through the years. In addition, the agriculture colleges in various states have played a significant role in the basic research necessary to raising farm productivity.

Increasing Productivity

In summary, we can conclude that the rise in real farm output during the past 100 years has been phenomenal. More recently, the index of farm output compiled by the Department of Agriculture indicates that real output increased 85 percent in the period 1940–1976. But even more important for our purposes, farm output per worker-hour during that period increased sevenfold and the worker-hours of labor required on farms declined by 74 percent. Of course, both of these trends are relatively meaningless unless placed in a wage-price context. That shall be our task in the next section. But both the increase in total farm production in response to population growth and the increase in the farmer's individual productivity because of more extensive and intensive cultivation of the land have been part and parcel of our farm problem. Both trends continue today unabated, and unless they are kept constantly in mind, a meaningful analysis of the future of our agricultural community is improbable.

THE ECONOMIC ASPECTS OF THE FARM PROBLEM

A family farm is a producing unit, and the farmers who operate them have as their goal an income sufficient to cover all costs of production plus a residual amount that will enable them to support their family in a reasonably comfortable manner. This is a basic fact that must be remembered in discussing the farm problem.

During the pioneering years of American agriculture, the family farm was almost a self-sufficient unit. Located far from centers of manufacture and trade, and hampered by a still developing transportation system, American farmers were forced to rely on their own ingenuity for survival. With the construction of regional and national railroad networks and the building of a farm-to-market system of highways, their lot improved. Farmers could begin to specialize in the crop for which their land was best suited, and they could sell this output in ever-broadening national and international markets. The money income that they earned allowed them to purchase the goods of other specialists at prices much lower than the value of their own efforts used in producing similar goods. Thus, American farmers entered the market economy and began to face the rigors of competition.

The Market for Farm Products

The farm economy has always been a prime example of the freely competitive market. The producers of farm products fit well the assumptions of pure competition in that price and output decisions in the market have never resulted from the decisions of one or a small group of producers. American agriculture has historically been characterized by the relative insignificance of the output of the single farm when compared to the entire supply forthcoming from all farms. In addition, farm products, by their nature, are homogeneous so that it is very difficult to distinguish the corn produced on Farm A from that produced on Farm B. As a consequence, it is practically impossible for any farmer to gain any substantial degree of pricing power. Thus, both the larger number of relatively small producers of farm products and the homogeneity of the products themselves tend to negate the chance of monopolistic power developing in the agricultural community. The possibility of controlling the amount of farm goods produced in a given year is likewise largely precluded because of the wide dispersal of farm ownership.

Price Determination

The absence of price power on the supply side of the market for farm products has been one of the most important economic aspects of the farm problem. Since it seems clear that individual farmers are powerless to set the price for their products, they must be considered price-takers. They can only sell their products at the going price. If they choose to charge more than the going price, they can sell little or nothing. If they charge less than this price, they are acting irrationally since the market will take all of their output at a higher price. But if farmers are price-takers, who is the price-maker?

The answer to this question must necessarily involve some discussion of economic principles. Probably the first idea that confronts most beginning students in economics is the interaction of the forces of supply and demand to form a market price. Given a schedule of the units of a good that sellers will sell at various prices, and a similar schedule of what buyers will purchase at various prices, it is possible to determine what the market price will be. Table 8-2 illustrates such a schedule. It is apparent from this table that the market for commodity X will be cleared at a price of $5. Five units of the good will be offered for sale at this price, and all 5 units will be taken off the market. Thus, we state that the forces of supply and demand determine market price and also the number of units of the goods that changes hands.

While this simple example preserves the essentials of supply and demand interaction, at the same time is a heroic oversimplification of reality. It does not tell us why buyers and sellers will exchange 5 units at a price of $5 each, nor does it tell us over what period of time this exchange will take place. To answer these questions, we must probe much deeper into the nature of the supply and demand schedules. We have seen something of the supply side of the market for farm commodities, but until we consider the nature of the demand side we can draw no meaningful conclusions.

Demand Inelasticity. The demand for most farm products is price inelastic. Moreover, the supply is relatively price inelastic. Although economists may

Table 8-2

SCHEDULE OF SUPPLY AND DEMAND FOR COMMODITY X

Price	Number of Units Sellers Will Sell	Number of Units Buyers Will Buy
$10.00	10	0
9.00	9	1
8.00	8	2
7.00	7	3
6.00	6	4
5.00	5	5
4.00	4	6
3.00	3	7
2.00	2	8
1.00	1	9

be familiar with such terms, their meaning may not be immediately evident. When the economist speaks of price inelasticity for a product, this simply means that the buyer's desire for the good is not significantly affected by changes in the price of the good. Conversely, when the economist states that the demand for a product is price elastic, this means that the buyer's desire for the good will be significantly affected by changes in its price. Within this definitional framework we can now discuss the nature of the supply of and demand for farm products.

Probably the most significant limitation faced by the American farm is the size of the human stomach. The consumer can eat just so much food within a defined time span. Whether the price of the food is high or low, it will not significantly affect the amount consumed. The same limitation is true of other farm products that cannot be classified as edibles. Thus, wool and cotton are limited by the population's ability to wear out its clothing, and tobacco growers can hope to sell no more of their output than smokers can possibly smoke. The producers of hides are constrained in the amount of leather they can supply by the ability of people to wear out shoes and other leather goods. What we are really saying is that the demand for farm products is relatively stable over long periods of time, and it is largely determined by population growth and consumption patterns rather than price levels.

We must be careful, however, to keep clearly in mind that we are speaking of the aggregate demand for farm products, not the demand for a particular product. It is entirely possible that falling meat and dairy prices may cause people to shift their demand away from the cheaper products, such as bread and potatoes, and toward the more expensive high protein foods.

Rising incomes may have a similar effect. The overall demand for farm products is income inelastic as well as price inelastic, which simply means that higher incomes will not cause people to consume proportionally more food. Higher incomes, however, will probably cause people to purchase more of the higher priced foods, such as meat and dairy products, and less of the cheaper products.

Supply. If the demand for farm products is stable over long periods of time, then what of supply? Have American farmers been able to regulate their output so that it just meets the stable but growing demand and thus balances farm prices and maintains incomes at some normal level? Unfortunately, no. The variables that determine the level of crop and livestock production are too numerous and unpredictable to submit to the control of humans. Rainfall, days of sunshine, mean temperature, insects, plant diseases, floods, blizzards, and hail all combine to make farming an unpredictable business at best. Even today, after years of intensive research directed toward controlling at least some of these factors, the average farmer can still lose an entire crop because of the vicissitudes of nature. About the only variables that the farmer can meaningfully regulate are the number of acres planted, heads of livestock raised, and the amount of growth that can be induced through the application of scientific farming methods.

The Parity Ratio

What then has been the result of this situation where demand is relatively stable and predictable, and supply is highly variable? The best indicator is the movement of farm prices. In Figure 8-1 this movement is traced for the years 1969 through 1977. In addition, an index of prices paid by farmers is plotted together with a parity ratio. This last measure indicates the change in the purchasing power of farmers. A rise in the parity ratio above 100 shows that the index of prices received by farmers (the numerator) is rising faster than the index of prices they pay (the denominator), and they are enjoying a relative increase in the purchasing power of their income. A drop in the parity ratio indicates that their income is relatively less valuable and its purchasing power is decreasing.

An examination of parity ratios gives a fairly clear indication of the plight of American farmers for the 60 years prior to 1973. In only 15 years (1916–1920 and 1941–1952) did the parity ratio stand in favor of the farmers. Since 1973 it has moved continuously downward.

The record traces a rather dismal picture of the financial plight of the farmer, but it also yields an insight into the nature of the supply of farm products. It indicates that the producers of goods and services sold to farmers — the manufacturer, the retailer, the banker, and the professional person — were better able to match their supply of goods and services to a shifting demand, and the prices they could charge did not vary as much as the prices of farm products. Unfortunately the farmer did not enjoy a similar degree of control over the supply of farm products. Given favorable growing conditions, the farm community would produce a bountiful crop. In the face

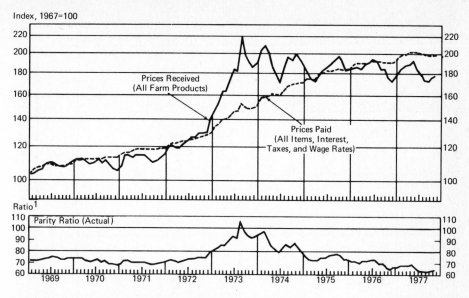

Index, 1967=100

SOURCE: *Economic Indicators* (January, 1978).

[1]Ratio of index of prices received to index of prices paid, interest, taxes, and wage rates, on 1910–1914 = 100 base.

Figure 8-1   **PRICES RECEIVED AND PAID BY FARMERS, 1969–1977**

of stable demand, this increase in supply would cause a fall in farm prices. The farmer, witnessing a drop in income caused by falling prices, could react only by planting more acreage or by raising more livestock the next year to counteract the decline in income. But this additional increase in farm output would only worsen the price situation and cause a further decrease in income. The only way out of this vicious circle was a decline in farm output caused by adverse growing conditions, or an artificial increase in demand stemming from war. Favorable parity years coincide almost exactly with the years of World Wars I and II and a brief postwar era.

The only other solution, voluntary control of supply by the farm community, has never been successfully used. Many attempts at voluntary control of farm output have been made, but all failed, largely because of the independent nature of American farmers. They simply refused to accept the fact that by increasing their output they may well be acting to their own detriment.

Economic Effects of Rising Farm Productivity

The crucial point in this entire discussion centers around the farmer's ability to increase output in an effort to offset falling income. We discussed previously the technological development that has taken place in American agriculture. Figure 8-2 traces the results of this development for the years

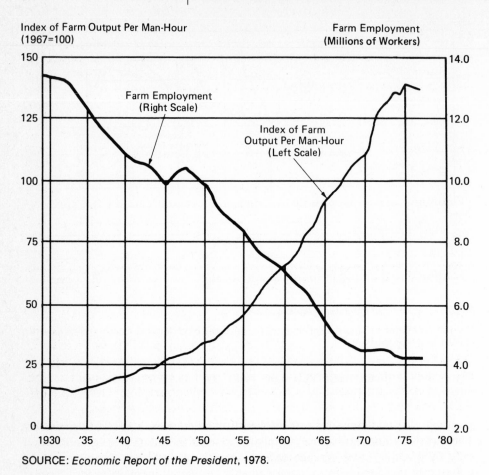

Index of Farm Output Per Man-Hour
(1967=100)

Farm Employment
(Millions of Workers)

SOURCE: *Economic Report of the President*, 1978.

Figure 8-2   **FARM EMPLOYMENT AND WORKER PRODUCTIVITY, 1929–1977**

1929 through 1977, as it has affected the productivity of the farm worker and farm employment. The effects of soaring farm labor productivity are evident. As the farmer added successive increments of capital equipment and fertilizers, the need for farm labor declined, as did the farm labor force. In the 48-year period between 1929 and 1977, the farm labor force was reduced by roughly two thirds, from 12.8 million to 4.3 million. The significant fact about this decline is that it occurred in the face of a growing farm output that more than doubled. Over the same period, 1929–1977, the index of farm production (1967 = 100) rose from 54 to 111.

The revolution in agricultural technology also had a direct effect on the size of the average American farm. As equipment became larger and more specialized, as well as more efficient, farmers were forced to utilize it on larger acreages. The days when the general purpose farm of 100 or so acres would support the farmer and the farmer's family were fast fading. Table 8-3 shows clearly the trend toward the larger farm that seemed to be accelerating

Table 8-3

NUMBER OF FARMS, CLASSIFIED BY ACREAGE, 1940–1969

Size of Farm	1940	1950	1954	1959	1964	1969
Total	6,097	5,388	4,782	3,711	3,158	2,730
Under 10 acres	506	489	484	244	183	162
10 to 49 acres	1,780	1,480	1,213	813	637	473
50 to 99 acres	1,291	1,048	864	658	542	460
100 to 179 acres	1,310	1,103	953	773	633	542
180 to 259 acres	486	487	464	414	355	307
260 to 499 acres	459	478	482	472	451	419
500 to 999 acres	164	182	192	200	210	216
1,000 acres over	101	121	130	136	145	151

SOURCE: *Statistical Abstract of the United States*, 1977.

in the United States. This trend paralleled the surge in farm labor productivity that is traced in Figure 8-2. As the average size of the American farm increased, it took fewer and fewer farm workers to handle it efficiently. As available farm jobs declined, agricultural workers had to find other types of employment or face, at best, a marginal existence on less than marginal farms. Some economists would disagree with the concept of a less than marginal farm because the less than marginal producing unit will not yield sufficient income to maintain the operator at a reasonable level of subsistence. You will recall that earlier in this chapter we stated that estimates by agricultural experts have indicated that the American agricultural sector could meet the country's present and foreseeable needs for farm products with a farm population roughly two thirds its present size. If these estimates are correct, then it follows that the remaining one third of the American farm population is existing on marginal farms. But what sustains them? If their farms are not efficient enough to compete with large, capital-intensive farming operations, in the absence of nonfarm income how do they manage to survive?

COMMODITY PRICE SUPPORTS AND THE CONCEPT OF PARITY

During this century American farmers witnessed a variety of changes in the agricultural sector of the economy in regard to production, employment, and especially income.

The Golden Age

The two decades following the turn of the twentieth century were the golden age for the American farmer. Markets grew apace of industrial production, the work force increased rapidly, and on the farms prices and incomes continued to rise. When war broke out in 1914, the production of agricultural commodities virtually ceased in Europe. The American farm sector rapidly was transformed into the "breadbasket" for the entire allied group.

Farm prices rose sharply and farm output jumped almost 20 percent in the period 1916–1918. Additional acreage was pressed into production to meet the surging demand, much of it originating in Europe. With the end of hostilities, however, the American farmer's golden age came to an abrupt end. European farms began to return to production. Markets became saturated, prices dropped, and farm income fell rapidly under the stimulus of the greatly enlarged farm output flowing from war-enhanced farm capacity. The plight of the American farmer became very serious by 1920 and began to attract government attention.

Farm Legislation of the Twenties

In 1920 and 1921 President Harding signed into law legislation that raised tariffs on those agricultural commodities that were imported into this country. The law worked well with respect to commodities such as wool and sugar where foreign producers were an important element in the market. Unfortunately this action ignored the fact that the United States was almost completely self-sufficient in agriculture. The producers of cotton, tobacco, feed grains, and pork received virtually no help from the tariff since imports of these commodities were limited.

The so-called roaring twenties witnessed good times for most Americans. Industry prospered and the age of mass production and mass consumption arrived. Unfortunately the farmer did not participate in this prosperity. While the cost-price relationship (parity) of farm products was not excessively out of balance, a new factor had been injected. During the war years many farmers had borrowed heavily to finance the cultivation of new acreage, or to bid away available acreage from their counterparts. The high level of farm incomes had been capitalized in farm land values that rose to record heights. With the arrival of depressed farm prices and incomes in the 1920s, the fixed payments for interest and principal repayments on loans contracted during the war became excessively burdensome. As a consequence, farm foreclosures became common, particularly in the Middle West, where many small banks were forced into bankruptcy because of the decline in value of their prime assets, mortgages on farm lands.

The Great Agricultural Depression

By 1929 the situation in agricultural income had reached a stage serious enough to prompt the Hoover Administration to attempt corrective measures. The Agricultural Marketing Act of 1929 created the Federal Farm Board (FFB) and gave the Board power to support farmers' cooperative marketing associations stabilization activities. The Board promptly entered the market for cotton and wheat, and attempted to support their prices at 16 cents a pound for the former and $1.15 a bushel for the latter.

By the summer of 1931, the domestic price of cotton had fallen to 6 cents a pound and that of wheat to 39 cents a bushel, and the Board held some 3.5 million bales of cotton and 257 million bushels of wheat. The failure of this program was highly predictable. It is possible to subsidize farm prices domestically through purchase and storage if sufficient funds are available and where purchased surpluses are to be followed by periods of shortage; but the Board was limited in the funds available to it, and it was trying to deal in farm output that was perennially in surplus. Another feasible solution would have been the introduction of acreage production controls. The Board, however, was forced to plead for voluntary reductions in farm output. Its plea was largely ignored and the program failed.

Parity. With the election of a Democratic Administration in 1932, the philosophy of government support payments to augment agricultural income was made explicit. Stripped of all embellishment, this philosophy was simply "economic equality for agriculture." The Administration was committed to the idea that the purchasing power of farm income was to be the criterion for judging the adequacy of farm policies. The concept of parity was introduced as a standard of the relative well-being of the farm sector. In the first New Deal farm legislation, the Agricultural Act of 1933 redefined support to mean parity; that is, farm prices were to be established and supported at a level which would give farmers an income from agricultural commodities that would result in purchasing power comparable to that of a base period, August, 1909, to July, 1914. Remember that this base period occurred in the middle of the golden age of American agriculture.

Parity is perhaps best understood by means of a simple example. In Table 8-4 the prices of a bushel of wheat (price received) and a shirt (price paid) are listed for the base period (1909–1914) and some assumed year such as 1935. Price indexes of prices paid and received by farmers are calculated with the base period equal to 100. A parity ratio is computed using the index of price paid as the denominator and the index of prices received as the numerator.

Table 8-4

COMPUTATION OF PARITY PRICE

	Good Sold			Good Purchased	
	1909–1914	1935		1909–1914	1935
Wheat, 1 bu.	$1.50	$ .40	Shirt	$2.00	$1.25
Price Index	100	27		100	63

$$\text{Index of Prices Received} = \frac{27}{63} = .43 = \text{Parity Ratio}$$
$$\text{Index of Prices Paid}$$

$$\frac{\text{1935 Price of Wheat}}{\text{Parity Ratio}} = \frac{\$.40}{.43} = \$.93 \text{ Per Bushel of Wheat, Parity Price}$$

The parity ratio of .43 that results shows that while the prices of both goods have fallen, the price of a bushel of wheat had declined much further. The bushel of wheat commanded less than half as much purchasing power, relative to the shirt, as it did in the base period. In the 1909–1914 period the sale of 1.33 bushels of wheat $\left(\dfrac{\$2.00}{\$1.50}\right)$ would have yielded the farmer sufficient income to buy the shirt. In 1935 the farmer had to sell 3.12 bushels of wheat $\left(\dfrac{\$1.25}{\$ .40}\right)$ to purchase the shirt.

To maintain equality of purchasing power for the farmer, the actual price of wheat in 1935, $.40 per bushel, must be adjusted upward by dividing it by the parity ratio. Thus, wheat must be supported at $.93 per bushel, a price that would still allow the farmer to sell 1.33 bushels $\left(\dfrac{\$1.25}{\$ .93}\right)$ and use the proceeds to purchase the shirt.

With the introduction of the parity concept, the farm problem took on explicit social dimensions that had previously been only implicitly present. The federal government committed itself to the philosophy that the farm population should not be subject to an economic situation which placed it in a significantly inequitable position regarding income and purchasing power relative to the rest of the population.

Agricultural Adjustment Act of 1933. The mechanisms for preserving this equity have changed in detail over the years, but they have all been ordered to the same end and have employed essentially the same means. The Agricultural Adjustment Act of 1933 established the Commodity Credit Corporation (CCC). This corporation was similar to the Federal Farm Board under the 1929 Act in that its purpose was to engage in loans, purchases, and storage operations of agricultural commodities. The loans were of the nonrecourse type and stipulated that if the value of crops held as collateral went above the CCC loan, the farmer could repossess the crop, sell it, pay off the loan, and pocket the difference. If prices fell below the loan support price, the farmer would be permitted to default on the loan payment, keep the money loaned, and allow the government to take permanent possession of the crop that was serving as collateral.

The program differed from the 1929 Act in that it did provide for controlled production. The Secretary of Agriculture was empowered to enter into voluntary contracts with farmers who would agree to restrict crop acreage and livestock breeding to a specified percentage of a base period. Another provision of the 1933 Act permitted payments to be made in the form of rentals for acreage taken out of production. The funds to implement this program were to come from a tax on the processors of the supported commodities, such as meat packers, wheat millers, cotton ginners, and canners.

In January of 1936 the Agricultural Adjustment Act of 1933 was held unconstitutional by the Supreme Court. The Court ruled that the tax on processors was being employed in the interest of a particular group (the farmers) rather than in the general welfare. Furthermore, the court stated that the benefit payments it financed were being used to purchase conformity with a program which Congress, under the Constitution, had no power to enact.

The Soil Conservation and Domestic Allotment Act passed in 1936 had as its purpose the conservation and improvement of soils. Direct federal payments were made for planting "soil-conserving" crops in place of "soil-depleting" crops. Since the crops that historically had been supported were defined as *soil depleters*, the result was another method of payment by the federal government for acreage reductions in the prinicpal cash crops.

Agricultural Adjustment Act of 1938. The Agricultural Adjustment Act of 1933 was followed by the Agricultural Adjustment Act of 1938. The new AAA was essentially the same as the Act of 1933 with one significant difference. In the new act Congress specifically directed the Secretary of Agriculture to intervene with nonrecourse loans whenever the prices of basic commodities fell below defined levels, or supplies rose above certain levels. In addition, the loans were to be at rates between 52 and 75 percent of parity. Since that time, Congress has specified support prices at a certain percentage of parity prices.

World War II and After

The war years, with the tremendous increase in demand for farm products caused by America's role as the world's breadbasket, resulted in the use of a substantial part of the pre-World War II agricultural hoard. In 1945 the ratio of farm to nonfarm per capita income, on the 1909–1914 base, stood at 151. Not until 1948 did world agricultural supply catch up with demand. When it did, the consequences for the American farmer were quickly felt. Prices of farm commodities fell drastically and the cry for government supports was quickly taken up by various farm organizations.

New farm legislation was passed in 1948 and 1949, but actually it was new only in sense that its date of passage was somewhat more recent than the acts of the 1930s. There was little appreciable change from past practices. The CCC was placed on a permanent basis, and it began support operations in a manner substantially unchanged from its prewar practices.

Since 1948 there has been no basic or essential change in the government's efforts to support farm incomes. Admittedly new-sounding phrases have been heard, but none involve any real departure from the programs we have discussed. Flexible price supports were simply supports that were not rigidly defined by Congress, but rather limits within which supports could fluctuate depending on potential supply. Parity was redefined in the 1949 Agricultural Act as taking into consideration prices received and prices paid during a fairly recent period (10 years according to this specific act) instead of the relationships existing in the 1909–1914 period.

An innovative plan introduced in 1949 by the Secretary of Agriculture, but never enacted by Congress, would have substituted direct income payments to farmers in place of parity price supports. Food prices to consumers would then be determined by the marketplace. Lower crop prices would have to be offset by higher direct income payments. A soil bank program similar to the soil conservation program of the 1930s, legislated in the 1950s, provided for diversionary payments to farmers who shifted production acreage into a nonproducing soil bank. Flexible price supports were included in the Agricultural Act of 1954 and the Secretary of Agriculture tried to shift farm policy toward a freer market. The Food for Peace program sought to reduce surplus crops through food aid programs to other nations.

The Food and Agriculture Act of 1965 removed many of the mandatory production controls and substituted voluntary acreage limitations, low price supports, and higher direct payments to farmers in an effort to regulate farm supply. The Agricultural Acts of 1970 and 1973 liberalized output restrictions on individual farms and certain crops in an effort to benefit family farms. The Federal Food Stamp program was expanded to give assistance to low income families and help the sale of foodstuffs.

Tremendous stocks of surplus farm commodities continued to pile up throughout the 1950s and early 1960s in the face of government efforts to contract supply. Government outlays to support farm prices continued to mount throughout the period. Table 8-5 gives an indication of the growth in value of price support inventories and loans between 1955 and 1975. This value represents CCC total holdings of loans and crops. Government investment in farm price support activity grew rapidly between 1952 and 1956 and then leveled off around the $7 billion mark. There was a noticeable and substantial decline of surplus stocks in the latter half of the 1960s as a result of

Table 8-5
CCC LOANS AND COMMODITIES OWNED, 1955–1975

Year	Loans Outstanding (In Millions of Dollars)	Commodities Owned (In Millions of Dollars)	Wheat (In Millions of Bushels)	Sorghum (In Millions of Bushels)	Corn (In Millions of Bushels)	Cotton (In 1,000 Bales)
1955	$2,137	$4,572	976	92	581	1,662
1960	1,347	6,021	1,195	570	1,158	5,061
1962	2,255	4,474	1,097	687	659	1,463
1964	2,815	4,338	829	638	735	4,440
1966	2,231	3,113	340	420	280	9,412
1968	2,345	913	102	192	136	659
1970	2,952	1,858	301	163	263	1,978
1972	2,474	1,090	367	46	155	24
1973	1,418	479	144	14	81	2
1974	720	114	19	NA	8	0
1975	334	416	1	NA	Z	Z

SOURCE: *Statistical Abstract of the United States*, 1969 and 1977.

Z = Less than one half the unit indicated.

our greater aid contribution to foreign nations. In the early and mid-1970s there was a dramatic decline in CCC holdings as a result of crop shortages in the U.S. and elsewhere throughout the world.

PROBLEMS OF PRODUCTIVITY

What was the answer to this seeming enigma? What maintained the gigantic government stockpiles of farm commodities in the face of almost constant efforts to contract supply by acreage allotments, soil banks, and land retirement? The answer to this question should, by now, be apparent. Rising farm productivity was the source of the difficulty. As farm acreage was retired through acreage quotas or land retirement, rising production per acre more than offset the yield lost through land taken out of production.

Table 8-6 shows this trend for selected farm commodities and gives some idea of the dimension of the growth rate in output per acre. Such yield increases can only be explained by the tremendous advances in soil chemistry, insecticide chemistry, farm machinery technology, and scientific farming practices, such as crop rotation, contour plowing, and modern farm management. Prior to the 1970s there was thought to be no end in sight to the rising trend in farm productivity. As government price support programs set smaller and smaller acreage allotments in an effort to bring supply into balance with demand, and as the modern farmer obtained more and more production from this shrinking acreage through the application of increasingly sophisticated materials, machinery, and techniques, eventually something had to give. Actually something had been giving all along.

As acreage bases shrunk, more and more marginal farmers found it impossible to support their families through farm work alone, even with price supports supplementing their incomes. Their acreage allotment had become too small to support efficient machinery, and they had turned to outside sources of income, primarily jobs in the city, while residing on a farm. It can

Table 8-6

OUTPUT PER ACRE FOR THE PERIOD 1931–1935 AND FOR THE 1971–1975 PERIOD FOR SELECTED CROPS AND PERCENTAGE INCREASE

Crop	1931–1935 Yield per Acre	1971–1975 Yield per Acre	Percentage Increase
Wheat	13.1 bu.	31.3 bu.	139
Corn	23.3 bu.	86.8 bu.	273
Sorghums	13.3 bu.	53.4 bu.	302
Soybeans	15.4 bu.	26.9 bu.	75
Tobacco	808.0 lbs.	2,031.8 lbs.	151
Cotton	191.0 lbs.	469.4 lbs.	146

SOURCE: *Statistical Abstract of the United States*, 1977.

be seen from Table 8-7, for example, that approximately 60 percent of the income of farm families comes from nonfarm sources.

In increasing numbers many farmers sold their land to larger operators and moved to urban communities. As a result the corporation or commercial farm was rapidly becoming the major source of farm output. This sort of farming operation is usually large enough and well enough financed to take advantage of expensive, but highly efficient, innovations in farming methods. The question then arose that although we still had a significant number of marginal farmers, was it proper to expect the government to subsidize them, while paying the same level of subsidy to the large commercial farming operation that could very well operate without the support? This was a dilemma faced by the federal agricultural policy makers as late as the mid-1970s.

Table 8-7

PERSONAL INCOME RECEIVED BY TOTAL FARM POPULATION, 1970–1977 (Billions of Dollars)

Year	From All Sources	From Farm Sources	From Non-Farm Sources	Net Income Current $	Per Farm 1967 $
1970	27.4	13.0	14.4	$ 4,790	$4,202
1971	28.7	13.4	15.3	5,030	4,263
1972	34.4	16.8	17.6	6,504	5,288
1973	48.6	29.0	19.5	11,727	8,817
1974	44.7	23.1	21.6	9,232	6,114
1975	44.3	21.5	22.8	8,637	5,203
1976	42.0	17.8	24.2	7,203	4,093
1977ᵖ	44.5	18.6	25.9	—	—

SOURCE: *Economic Indicators* (January, 1978).

ᵖ = preliminary.

SUGGESTED SOLUTIONS TO THE LONG-RANGE PROBLEM OF OVERPRODUCTION

In the face of this agricultural problem a number of suggestions were proposed by various experts, committees, organizations, and legislators. A number of sources suggested some form of process of forward pricing in an attempt to balance supply and demand. Several proposals were offered for increasing the demand for agricultural commodities along the lines of Food for Peace and Food for Freedom programs. Other suggestions were made for increasing agricultural exports and for increasing the industrial use of agricultural commodities. The Committee for Economic Development published a document entitled *An Adaptive Program for Agriculture*. The report contained a comprehensive program to gradually move the agricultural sector toward a freer, market-oriented farm sector.

In 1967 the National Advisory Commission on Food and Fiber, established earlier by President Johnson, included in its report some long-run suggestions for a more rational farm policy. The Commission felt that the time was ripe for a major shift in the direction of U.S. food and fiber policy. It recommended unanimously "that the United States adapt its policies to accomplish a market-oriented agriculture." In this regard, they favored aid to farmers in the form of direct payments. It recommended that price supports be set modestly below a survey average of world prices. The Commission rejected the concept of supply management. Lastly, it emphasized the need to channel labor and other resources out of the farm sector into more productive uses and proposed specific measures to accomplish this outflow.

In addition to these many suggestions, a number of recommendations were made to establish some form of guaranteed annual income for farmers, patterned after some of the proposals explained in Chapter 4. In spite of these many suggestions and recommendations, however, very little change was made in U.S. farm policy prior to the early 1970s.

A CHANGING ENVIRONMENT: NEW PROBLEMS

By 1972 a new farm problem had emerged. It was one characterized at times by crop shortages, meat scarcities, and high prices. Whether this was to be a temporary phenomenon or a permanent change in the farm situation was not certain at that time. It is observable, however, that government holdings of agricultural commodities declined dramatically between 1972 and 1974 (see Table 8-5). CCC loans outstanding dropped by more than two thirds, the value of government commodity holdings declined 90 percent, and its holdings of specific crops dropped to its lowest level in decades. All this occurred within a period of just a few years.

Rising Farm Incomes

In the interim, prices of many crops and meats skyrocketed. Wheat rose from $1.33 per bushel in 1971 to more than $5.00 per bushel at times in 1973. Similar increases occurred in the prices of other commodities. Meat prices reached new highs and consumers were worried about the shortage of beef. Farm income from farm sources more than doubled between 1971 and 1973. Although total farm income did taper off somewhat in 1974, it was still 56 percent above the 1971 level. These changes can be seen in Table 8-7.

During this period the retail price of foodstuffs rose by 37 percent in the CPI food category, rising from 118.4 in 1971 to 161.7 in 1974. Did all this spell the end of the perennial farm problem of the past several decades?

Causes of Change

A closer look at the causes of production shortfall, depletion of commodity stockpiles, and rising prices will shed some light on the previous question.

1. In recent years, crop production in the United States was reduced somewhat by poor weather, as crop output suffered its deepest setback in several years.
2. Other major agricultural producing nations, such as Australia and Canada,
   also experienced some very poor crop yields.
3. Domestic food consumption continued to increase in the face of lower production.
4. Foreign demand for U.S. agricultural products accelerated, especially as a
   result of the devaluation of the dollar.
5. We continued our food aid to impoverished areas throughout the world
   stricken by drought, hurricanes, and floods.

As a result of these developments of rising demand and reduced production, U.S. food reserves dwindled markedly and farm prices and farm income
rose sharply. The American farmer and government agricultural officials
found themselves in a new environment. This was certainly a change from the
perennial problem of surplus output, rising stockpiles, lower prices, and lower
farm income. To lighten the burden of the agricultural shortfall and higher
prices for the American consumer, acreage allotments, which restrict farm
output, were liberalized in 1973 and 1974 when 60 million acres were released
from acreage controls.

In spite of the relatively high farm income in 1974, prices in the nonfarm
sector of the economy rose faster than farm prices. As a consequence, real
farm income declined. With rising output, falling crop prices, and a continuous increase in nonfarm prices, farm income dwindled further in 1975 and
1976. By 1977 farm income from farm sources had fallen to about the level of
that in 1972. It was evident by then that the boom in farm income was over
and that farmers were again faced with their perennial problem — surpluses,
rising costs, falling prices, and declining farm incomes.

To bring their plight to the attention of the American public, members of
Congress, and the Administration and the President, groups of farmers
throughout the country, including Plains, Georgia, and Washington, D.C.,
were demonstrating with tractor parades in protest against low crop prices,
higher operating costs, and declining farm income.

Wider Price Fluctuation

According to some agricultural authorities we are experiencing a permanent change in the agricultural environment. It is suggested that four major
developments have substantially reduced the excess productive capacity of
the U.S. agricultural sector. These include: (1) a decline in the growth rate of
productivity from the combined factors — land, labor, and capacity — used
in farm production; (2) a better balance between demand and supply of farm
labor; (3) a substantial decline in estimates of acreage reserves; and (4) a
permanent increase in foreign demand for U.S. farm products.

The diminution of acreage controls and depletion of surplus stockpiles,
unfortunately, will make agricultural prices more susceptible to fluctuations.

A substantial increase in demand, from American or foreign consumers, or a shortfall in production will intensify upward price pressures. On the other hand, bumper crops here or abroad can exert downward pressure on food prices. Government food stockpiles, which formerly helped to stabilize the market price by offsetting year-to-year fluctuations in production, are gone. Excess land reserves have diminished. In addition, increased reliance of foreign nations on U.S. food production now has a more profound effect on prices. Domestic agricultural policies in Japan and the European Economic Community limit adjustments they can make in their agricultural markets. As a result the burden of adjustment to changing demand or supply in the world market is being pushed on the United States and other food exporting countries. Furthermore, the growing involvement of the Soviet Union in world agricultural markets has added a note of instability to commodity prices as a result of Russia's relatively unstable agricultural output. For example, nearly 80 percent of the annual fluctuation in the world wheat trade in the past decade has been accounted for by swings in Soviet wheat trade.

Current Farm Policy

Previous U.S. agricultural policy has been influenced by two somewhat divergent objectives. First was the continuous endeavor to increase agricultural output through agricultural research, dissemination of information, and the use of higher yield seeds, better fertilizers, and new planting techniques. Second, to support crop prices and maintain farm incomes, measures were employed to limit output, particularly through restricting acreage used for cultivation. These measures, of course, resulted in the accumulation of government stockpiles. This provided some stability to commodity markets and prices. It also provided the source of substantial food aid to foreign nations under the U.S. foreign assistance programs.

But in the late 1960s and early 1970s the U.S. experienced a decline in food reserves. The output shortfall, rising demand, devaluation of the dollar, higher crop prices, and higher farm incomes reduced the severity of the farm problem that had prevailed for decades. The U.S. is also now more embroiled in the world food situation. Consequently, it appears that our agricultural environment requires new policies and new developments.

In the past decade U.S. farm policy has been going through a transition. Previously agricultural commodity programs dating back to the 1930s were designed around a system of mandatory acreage controls, marketing quotas, and high support prices for individual crops. These programs provided for artificial benefits or subsidies, resulted in higher domestic prices, required restrictions on imports, made subsidies necessary on exports, conflicted with liberal trade policies, and resulted in huge government stockpiles of various commodities.

A major step away from this prevailing policy was the move to reduce price supports (and market prices) on individual crops and replace them with direct cash payments for diverting land from crop production. The emphasis on controlling individual crops was eventually eliminated and farmers were permitted to plant the crops they desired. Today only a few crops (rice, peanuts, tobacco, and certain types of cotton) still have rigid controls. Consequently, it appears today that U.S. farm policy is based on the following principles: (1) Market prices should not be supported at levels above those required to clear the market. Price supports in years of surplus output should be relatively low; i.e., high enough to cover only the variable cost of production. This will provide some element of stability to farm income. Lower prices will encourage domestic consumption, stimulate exports, and remove the need for export subsidies. (2) Production of individual crops should be free of restrictions and acreage controls. This would permit farmers to make the best use of their resources and maximize the efficiency of the agriculture sector. (3) Direct cash payments are more efficient than high price supports as a method of providing income support to farmers.

The implementation of these principles or measures was accelerated in 1972. Since that time almost all farmland has been released from acreage controls, import restrictions have been relaxed substantially, and many export subsidies have been phased out. Farm prices and incomes increased sufficiently that direct payments were limited to wool and soil conservation. These principles were incorporated into the Consumer Protection Act of 1973.

CONCLUSION

Even though economic circumstances in recent years have resulted in a more market-oriented farm policy in the U.S., they have also brought the return of two basic characteristics of agricultural marketing. These are wide price fluctuations and income uncertainties that result from crop surpluses and shortfalls. In fact, within a few years we went from beef scarcities and high prices to a point where cattle growers were appealing to the government to purchase large quantities of beef to take supplies off the market and maintain prices. Again in 1975, in the face of an expected bumper crop, Congress was deliberating the need for higher support prices on crops to protect farm incomes.

By 1977 it was evident that the shortages, scarcities, rising prices, and high farm incomes of the mid-1970s were a temporary phenomenon providing a brief respite from the perennial problems of crop and livestock surpluses, low market prices, and depressed farm income. Adding to the current problems of overcapacity, surpluses, low prices, high operating costs, and declining farm income is the projection of the Department of Labor that the number of farmers and farm workers will decline by one third, to 2.9 million, by 1985. The question now arises as to whether we can continue moving toward a market-oriented agricultural policy or will the future require a return to restrictions and controls for the agricultural sector of the U.S. economy?

Regardless of the direction farm policy takes in the coming years, the voice of the farmers will still be heard, perhaps in a rising crescendo. Despite their shrinking numbers, farmers are still a significant political force and the prime producers of those goods that Americans need most to sustain life. American farmers will not be ignored in the future just as they have not been ignored in the past. They are human beings existing in a free America, and without them and their products the United States would immediately lose its preeminent position among the nations of the free world.

MAJOR ISSUES

1. Are the social implications of the American farm problem more serious than its economic implications?
2. Is it possible to reconcile the American ideals of free enterprise and individual dignity with federal agricultural support programs as these programs have evolved over the years?
3. Should the U.S. be less generous with food assistance programs now that government stockpiles of excess commodities have been trimmed to minimal levels?
4. Would a forecast of greater or lesser federal involvement in the American agricultural sector seem most likely to you at this time?
5. Do you think that the U.S. should move more toward agribusiness and away from the family farm concept?

SUBISSUES

1. Does the concept of parity seem to be a usable device in the farm price support programs?
2. It is possible that a movement toward a more price or income elastic demand for certain farm products might be a long-run solution to the American farm problem?
3. Is the corporate farm a logical result of current trends in American agriculture, and if so, what are the implications of such a result?
4. Should there be a ceiling imposed on the size of government subsidy that can be paid to any individual farmer or farm corporation?
5. Does there appear to be a conflict between the welfare of the consumer and the desire of the government to improve the income of the farmer?

SELECTED READINGS

A New U.S. Farm Policy For Changing World Food Needs. New York: Committee For Economic Development, October, 1974.

"Agricultural Highlights: 1976." *Business Conditions*, Federal Reserve Bank of Chicago (August, 1976).

Balz, Daniel J. "Farm Income Outlook." *National Journal Reports* (March 29, 1975).

Brandon, G. E. "Agricultural Policy: Different Now?" *Challenge* (March–April, 1974).

Cameron, J. "Golden Chance to Get Uncle Sam off the Farm." *Fortune* (July, 1973).

Cochrane, Willard W., and Mary E. Ryan. *American Farm Policy, 1948–1973*. Minneapolis: University of Minnesota Press, 1976.

Cordaro, J. B. "Providing the World with Enough Food." *American Federationist* (May, 1973).

"Dealing with World Hunger." *Current* (September, 1974).

Duncan, Marvin, and C. Edward Harshbarger. "A Primer on Agricultural Policy." *Monthly Review*, Federal Reserve Bank of Kansas City (September–October, 1977).

——————. "Agricultural Policy: Evolution and Goals." *Monthly Review*, Federal Reserve Bank of Kansas City (November, 1977).

Economic Report of the President, 1977. "Agricultural Developments," pages 94–99.

Employment and Training Report of the President, 1977.

"Farm Credit Concerns Rise." *Economic Prospectives*, Federal Reserve Bank of Chicago (September–October, 1977).

"Farm Prices, Incomes and Policies." *First Chicago World Report*. First National Bank of Chicago (August–September, 1977).

"Farmers on Threshold of New Opportunity." *Business Review*, Federal Reserve Bank of Dallas (May,1974).

Food and Fiber for the Future. Washington: Report of the National Advisory Commission on Food and Fiber, 1967.

"Gloomy Forecast for Grain Hungry Countries." *Business Week* (September 14, 1974).

Harshbarger, C. Edward. "1975 Agricultural Outlook: A Year of Continuing Adjustments." *Monthly Review*, Federal Reserve Bank of Kansas City (December, 1974).

——————, and Sheldon W. Stahl. " A Dispersed or Concentrated Agriculture? The Role of Public Policy." *Monthly Review*, Federal Reserve Bank of Kansas City (March, 1975).

Johnson, D. Gale. "Are High Farm Prices Here to Stay?" *The Morgan Guaranty Survey* (December, 1974).

McLaughlin, M. M. "Feeding the Unfed." *Commonwealth* (July 12, 1974).

"The New Farm Program — What Does It Mean?" *Monthly Review*, Federal Reserve Bank of Kansas City (January, 1974).

"Reaping Bigger Profits Down on the Farm." *Monthly Letter* (October, 1973).

Reubens, Edwin P. "The Food Shortage Is Not Inevitable." *Challenge* (March–April, 1974).

Ross, D. N. "Wanted — World Food Security." *Conference Board Record* (October, 1974).

"The Russian Wheat Deal — Hindsight or Foresight." *Review*, Federal Reserve Bank of St. Louis (October, 1973).

Stevens, Neil A. "The Futures Market for Farm Commodities — What It Can Mean To Farmers." *Review*, Federal Reserve Bank of St. Louis (August, 1974).

Ward, B. "Fat Years and Lean Years." *Economist* (November 2, 1974).

Clean Air — 9
Are We Willing
to Pay the Price?

During the last decade pollution began to attract national attention as one of our most critical problems. Today it is an issue on which we have made a national commitment. Although the goals of public policy in regard to pollution extend far beyond the confines of economic analysis, the problem is not without its economic aspects. Vital discussions concerning the costs and benefits of abating and preventing pollution are well within the province of the economist. Fortunately the economist, as well as experts in other disciplines, is now coming to grips with the pollution problem. Economic data are being provided on pollution, but much more must be forthcoming before economic analysis can be adequately utilized as a basis for rational decision-making in this area.

While recognizing the importance of water, solid waste, noise, and radioactive pollution, this chapter focuses on the problem of air pollution, since that is presently the most widespread and pressing of all pollution problems.

AN ECONOMIC PROBLEM

Air is a resource provided by nature without charge and is available in abundance to anyone willing to utilize it. Being so copious, it is rather difficult to place a price tag on air. For this reason, air has been classified as a "free" good by the economist, and free goods are outside the realm of economic analysis. Public acceptance of this classificatory procedure actually stimulates pollution. As a free good, detrimental social consequences caused by misuse of air are not directly allocated to the costs of producing goods and services.

Air then is underpriced; and because it is underpriced and used without regard to its purification, clean air is becoming increasingly scarce in many urban areas. The contamination of our atmosphere necessitates a change in the economist's concept of air as a free good. To the contrary, clean air must be classified as an "economic" good. The scarcity of clean air is evident by the fact that under certain conditions a price must be paid to acquire it.

The mere presence of air pollution represents a marked departure from the workings of a perfect market economy. If perfect competition were operative, all economic resources would be directly allocated and the welfare of society would be maximized. Prices, insofar as they would reflect the true costs of production, would provide automatic, socially valid guidelines for investment and production.

The existence of air pollution, however, entails a misallocation of resources. Pollution implies that some portion of the total production costs are being externalized and are being borne by other economic units in our society. Externalities arise because the marginal private cost function that dictates the behavior of a profit-seeking firm is less than the marginal cost to society. Unless all costs of production are internalized, a firm's cost structure will not accurately determine the firm's product price and its optimum output level. The firm will underprice its product, overproduce, and reap greater profits as a result. Other firms in the area, however, are forced to account for costs stemming from pollution because of damaged crops and deteriorated materials, structures, and machines. Consumers of products produced by the pollution-causing firm also absorb these costs, for in purchasing these products they forgo the opportunity of acquiring other products that could have been produced with these additional resources. The pricing mechanism is not reflecting the alternative uses to which these resources might be put; thus, there is a misallocation of resources.

However, if all costs of production, including the external cost of pollution, are fully internalized, the firm's product will sell at a higher price and fewer units will be sold. Now the additional resources can be channeled into producing alternative products. The value of these alternative products, which could not have been produced if the cost of pollution were not internalized, represents the external cost of pollution to the consumer.

In addition to actual cost outlays by firms and foreclosure of consumer opportunities, air pollution harms our health, affronts our senses, and lessens our enjoyment of life. In analyzing the imperfections of the real world, however, the economist does not advocate the universal elimination of externalities because in doing so net benefits may be negative. Also in many cases the costs of preventing air pollution may exceed the costs of depollution. Rather, the economist is mainly concerned with a method whereby all costs and benefits from an economic activity are included in the firm's economic decision-making process. Thus, the economist is indeed very much concerned with the problem of air pollution.

POLLUTION-CAUSING FACTORS

Air is a resource necessary for survival. It is a gaseous combination of mainly oxygen, nitrogen, and argon and to a much lesser extent helium, hydrogen, krypton, neon, xenon, and carbon dioxide. These harmless gases constitute the earth's atmosphere, the habitable portion of which is but a relatively thin layer tightly encompassing the earth. Despite the seeming vastness of the earth's total air supply, estimated by scientists to be in the neighborhood of 6 quadrillion tons, people have, in their own inimitable way, managed to crowd, dirty, and deplete this resource to the extent that the air we breathe is injurious to human, plant, and animal life. The crux of the problem is that the total volume of air is much less a concern than is the availability of sufficient quantities of fresh air in a given place on the earth's surface at a given time.

Air is never really pure. Even excluding consideration of people-related pollution activities, some contamination of the air from natural processes occurs all the time. Natural occurrences, such as volcanic eruptions, forest fires, dust storms, and vegetation decay discharge a variety of gases that pollute the air. But the pollution resulting from such natural phenomena rarely looms large in the atmospheric pollution problem. What is a major concern, however, is the pollution of the air stemming from the activities of people, whether they be farming, manufacturing, or simply moving about. In emitting a vast number of gases, fumes, and particles into the sky from these activities, humanity has caused a significant pollution overload, which when combined with certain environmental factors might produce catastrophic ecological consequences.

Industrialization

Air pollution is directly related to a nation's level of output and utilization of economic goods and services. Thus, it is a by-product of affluence. Being the most affluent nation in the world, the United States is therefore confronted with an air pollution problem of great magnitude. Industrial production in the United States increases on the average of about 3–4 percent per year. Extended growth rates of this sort require greater participation in traditional pollution-causing activites. More electric energy results in greater coal consumption; more automobiles result in greater utilization of gasoline; more garbage results in a greater number of public dumps; more homeowners result in a greater burning of leaves and trash; and more materials' processing results in greater industrial waste emissions.

Concommitant with these activities, technological advances are constantly being realized that not only increase the variety and number of goods at our disposal but also load the air with thousands of new pollutants. In areas characterized by a concentration of such industrial activity, there is likely to be an acute air pollution problem.

Urbanization

Air pollution also tends to be directly related to population density. More than ever before, Americans are crowding themselves together on less and less land. At present, over 50 percent of the population is concentrated on

less than 1 percent of the land. Urban areas, which have tripled their populations since 1940, now account for over 70 percent of the nation's population.

This increased urbanization process has inevitably resulted in increased
atmospheric pollution levels in our cities. As more and more of our people
congregate in urban areas, they are being exposed to larger amounts of pollution without a corresponding increase in the available air supply. As a result,
no major American city is without an air pollution problem. The essence of
the problem is that it is becoming increasingly more difficult for us to continue
to crowd together and, at the same time, survive amidst our own wastes.

Weather

Air movement is essential to pollutant dispersion. As a rule, the earth's
atmosphere is capable of cleansing itself of the various pollutants discharged
from heavily populated, industrialized areas as long as either horizontal or
vertical air currents prevail. Should both of these air currents be absent, however, an air pollution disaster may be in the making.

Without horizontal wind movement, the sole means of dispersing pollutants in the atmosphere is by vertical air currents. Ordinarily atmospheric
temperature is inversely related to height. The temperature of air falls by 5.4
degrees Farenheit for every 1,000 feet above the earth's surface. This temperature gradient allows the atmosphere to rid itself of pollutants because the
warm polluted air, being lighter, can rise into the cooler air and disperse.
However, if the temperature decrease is less than 5.4 degrees Farenheit per
1,000 feet, the warm air, unable to rise because of the existence of even
warmer air above it, then hovers over the sources of pollution. Pollutants
concentrated in the lower stratum thus become trapped. This situation is
known as a "thermal inversion."

There are two basic ways in which a thermal inversion can occur. One
type of inversion occurs usually at night when the earth's surface loses the
heat radiated by the sun during the day. As the earth cools, so does the air in
the lower stratum. The upper air, however, remains warm and acts as a ceiling to cooler air rising from below. The lower stratum of air, then, remains
polluted. The inversion will normally persist until the sun's rays of the following day warm the earth's surface, making the lower air once again warmer
than the air above it. Unfortunately, this "radiation" inversion traps pollutants emitted during the peak hours of pollution-causing activities. It begins in
the evening when auto transportation is at a peak and continues long enough
in the morning to overlap the morning rush hours.

The second type of thermal inversion is of a greater latitude and longer
duration. It stems from windless high-pressure systems, which can blanket an
entire section of the country. As such a mass of cold air approaches, it moves
beneath a layer of warmer air, creating an inversion which can last for weeks.
The danger will continue until a moving storm or weather front arrives to
break up the inversion. In the eastern part of the United States, inversions of
this nature often occur in late summer or early autumn, creating the hazy

"Indian summer" weather. United States Weather Bureau studies indicate that these inversions are occurring about 25 percent of the time throughout the United States. The role of inversions in air pollution crises is a major one. They have been present in every air pollution disaster involving death and serious illness.

POLLUTANTS

Until recently, concern over air pollution was centered mainly on discharges of smoke and visible particles. Today, however, it is recognized that in addition to particulate matter, a large variety of gases, emitted by a multiplicity of sources, also cause air pollution. The latter are more diverse and complex than the nefarious black smoke belching from smokestacks. They are also more deadly.

Carbon Monoxide

Carbon monoxide is one of the most abundant pollutants found in the atmosphere. Each year upwards of 94 million tons of carbon monoxide are emitted into the air. It is a colorless, nonirritating, highly poisonous, odorless gas produced by the incomplete combustion of carbon-containing compounds. Although automobile exhaust has been the major source of carbon monoxide, this gas is also the product of various industrial operations, such as electric and blast furnaces, gas plants, and petroleum refineries. If small amounts are absorbed into the human bloodstream, the result may be sickness, dizziness, and pain. Large doses can be fatal.

Sulphur Oxides

Most fuels contain a small amount of sulphur. When the fuel's sulphur content is burned, both sulphur dioxide and sulphur trioxide are created. Sulphur dioxide (one part sulphur plus two parts oxygen) is a colorless gas with a suffocating odor. It is irritating to the eyes, nose, and throat. Sulphur trioxide (one part sulphur plus three parts oxygen) is an invisible gas having much the same effect on humans as sulphur dioxide. When combined with moisture in the air, however, sulphur trioxide gives way to sulphuric acid, which causes corrosion and deterioration of steel and stone structures. It may also cause irreparable heart and lung damage. Our air is contaminated by approximately 31 million tons of sulfur oxides annually.

Hydrocarbons

The term "hydrocarbons" encompasses a vast number of organic compounds which contain only carbon and hydrogen. Acetylene, ethylene, propane, and butane are but a few members of this chemical family. Emitted mainly by automobiles, hydrocarbons by themselves are generally nontoxic and are harmful only in very high concentrations. However, the real danger lies in the fact that when combined with nitrogen oxides in the presence of sunlight, photochemical smog results. With some 30 million tons of hydrocarbons in the atmosphere, smog can be a severe problem in urban areas.

Particulate Matter

Particulate matter, accounting for 20 million tons of pollution, consists of smoke, dust, fumes, and water droplets emitted from industrial, commercial, domestic, and agricultural activities. Particulate matter blackens physical structures, clothes, and furniture, and may severely restrict visibility. Smoke consists of fine particles in a mixture with flue gases and is the result of inefficient fuel combustion. Soot particles contained in smoke are a powdered form of carbon. Also accompanying smoke may be fly ash, the unburned residue in fuel. Other particulates we breathe include arsenic, asbestos, beryllium, fluorides, and lead.

Nitrogen Oxides

Nitrogen in the air combines with additional atoms of oxygen to create various oxides of nitrogen. Nitrogen dioxide is the unpleasant-smelling, brown-colored, poisonous gas formed by the combustion of all types of fuels. Its presence in the atmosphere is greatly accelerated by the same conditions which lead to the formation of photochemical smog. Chemical reaction may also result in ozone. This gas has a sharp smell and is light blue in color. It cracks rubber, causes eyes to tear, and severely damages vegetation. Nitrogen oxides account for about 23 million tons of atmospheric pollution.

SOURCES OF POLLUTION

The sources of pollution are many. Transportation, industry, fuel combustion (stationary sources), and solid waste are the major contributors to atmospheric pollution. The source distribution for previously mentioned pollutants is presented in Table 9-1.

Transportation

Included as major components of the transportation category are jet aircraft, trucks, buses, and autos. Air travel is a severe problem when pollution overloads result adjacent to airport facilities. Much has been done in recent years to drastically reduce emissions from jet aircraft. Pollution from land transportation vehicles, however, especially automobiles, is a more general and pressing problem.

Today there are over 133 million registered motor vehicles in the United States and virtually every one of them pollutes the air. Although diesel exhaust emitted from trucks and buses is usually more obvious to the senses,

Table 9-1

NATIONWIDE EMISSIONS OF MAJOR POLLUTANTS IN 1974[1]

(Millions of Tons per Year)

	Carbon Monoxide	Sulphur Oxides	Hydro-carbons	Particulate Matter	Nitrogen Oxides
Transportation	73.5	0.8	12.8	1.2	10.7
Industrial processes	12.7	6.2	3.1	11.0	0.6
Fuel combustion (In stationary sources)	0.9	24.3	1.7	5.9	11.0
Solid waste	2.4	0.1	0.6	0.5	0.1
Miscellaneous[2]	5.1	0.1	12.2	0.8	0.1

SOURCE: Environmental Protection Agency.

[1]Figures for 1974 are not comparable to those of earlier years because of changed methods of calculation.

[2]The table does not include data on photochemical oxidants because they are secondary pollutants formed by the action of sunlight on nitrogen oxides and hydrocarbons and thus are not emitted from sources on the ground.

pollutants stemming from automobiles are of greater significance. Automobiles are important sources of carbon monoxide and smog-forming hydrocarbons. These emissions are the result of incomplete fuel combustion. Theoretically this need not happen. If automobile engines functioned perfectly, the gasoline's hydrogen and carbonation content would mix completely with oxygen, discharging only carbon dioxide and water vapor. But the theoretical case of perfect combustibility differs sharply with what exists in reality. Automobile engines are not perfect. Fuel escapes from the engine mainly by way of the exhaust pipe and the crankcase, although small amounts do evaporate from the gas tank and carburetor. Carbon monoxide and roughly 65 percent of the hydrocarbon emission, either in unburned or partially burned form, escape from the exhaust pipe. In addition, ingredients that have been added to improve fuel performance, such as anti-knock, anti-rust, and anti-icing additives, also spew from the exhaust pipe unburned.

Despite significant progress in pollution control, transportation continues to be the major source of pollution emissions. As a group, transportation activities annually discharge 73.5 million tons of carbon monoxide and 12.8 million tons of hydrocarbons into the atmosphere.

Industrial Processes

Industries of varying sorts and sizes contribute a major share of both the gases and particulate matter found in our atmosphere. There are over 300,000 manufacturing establishments across the United States. Of these, iron and steel mills, petroleum refineries, chemical plants, smelters, and rubber manufacturers are among our worst offenders.

Iron and steel mills, which consume enormous quantities of coal and coke, pollute our skies with substantial amounts of particulate matter and sulphur dioxide. The petrochemical industry is responsible for the emission of hydrocarbons, sulphur dioxide, carbon monoxide, and fluorides into our atmosphere. The metal industry, including primary smelters and the producers of metal products, emits such contaminants as carbon monoxide, metallic oxides, and fumes of arsenic lead. Rubber manufacturers release vapors from solvents used in the bonding, coating, and drying of lead. Each year industries discharge some 33.5 million tons of pollutants into the atmosphere.

Fuel Combustion (Stationary Sources)

Approximately 70 percent of the nation's electric generating stations utilize coal and oil as fuel. These fuels, particularly coal, contain sulphur as an impurity. In 1974 fuel combustion alone emitted 24.3 million tons of sulphur oxides. The development of larger and more efficient combustion units has worsened the pollution problem. Technological advances of this sort not only result in the consumption of larger coal tonnages each year, but also permit the utilization of coal with higher sulphur content.

Particulate matter is also discharged in large quantities by power plants. Smoke, soot, and fly ash from generating stations can pollute the air across a large area. In fact, electric power plants are likely to be the largest single source of air pollutants in their communities.

In addition to the fuel used by electric generating stations, the fuel we consume each year to heat our homes, apartments, and offices also contaminates our air. The problem is particularly acute during winter months when furnaces and boilers burn large quantities of coal, flooding the air with sulphur oxides, particulate matter, and other pollutants.

Solid Waste

This nation produces roughly 360 million tons of solid wastes each year. This means that the average American discards about 1.7 tons of such things as paper, grass, garbage, ashes, metal, and glass. Unfortunately, there are but two ways of disposing of solid wastes: they can be burned or buried. Space for land fill is scarce so more refuse is being burned each year. Solid wastes are not good fuels. They are not meant to be burned. Consequently, only partial combustion occurs, and the atmosphere is poisoned by a plethora of gases and particulate matter.

THE POLLUTED

Initially the process of comparing communities on the basis of their air pollution levels may appear to be a relatively easy task. However, this is far from being the case. The problems involved in an undertaking of this type are so complex that the existing ratings serve as but a rough measure of the relative intensity of air pollution found in communities throughout the nation.

First of all, the nature of air pollution differs from place to place. The pollution problem in New York, for example, is much different from the pollution problem in Los Angeles. In New York, sulphur oxides stemming from the consumption of sulphur-bearing fuels for generating electricity and heating buildings comprise a major share of the pollutants in the atmosphere. But in Los Angeles, the problem is primarily one of photochemical smog, produced by the combination of weather stagnations, radiant sunshine, and heavy automobile traffic. These two pollution problems are chemically different and have different effects.

Secondly, the mere measurement of pollution levels in various communities does not in itself reflect the magnitude of air pollution problems. The presence of some pollutants in the atmosphere will influence the effects of others. The effects of sulphur oxides, for example, are worsened by the presence of particulate matter. In addition, some pollutants may react with others to form new substances. The extent of these reactions can be influenced by other factors, such as temperature, relative humidity, sunlight, and the concentration of pollutants. The level of pollutants in the atmosphere is also a function of time. Patterns of daily pollution levels show a direct correlation with traffic flow, operation of heating units, and the degree of business activity. Meteorological and topographical factors are also determinants of pollution levels. Faced with these problems, comparative measures of air pollution problems are not easily made. At present, a means of systematically reporting and quantifying all of these effects is not available.

Air pollution is a problem in every urban area in America. The problem tends to be most acute within the inner city. It is estimated that 50 million people in the United States live in areas having major air pollution problems. In effect, it has become increasingly difficult for Americans to escape air pollution and its harmful effects.

EFFECTS OF AIR POLLUTION

Air pollution is costly. The economic consequences of a comparatively do-nothing policy in regard to air pollution has resulted in untold costs to life and property throughout urban America. Government, private enterprise, and households have failed to recognize air pollution for the hazard that it is. Persistent air pollution too often has been accepted as a necessary cost of progress. At last, however, certain segments of our society are having second thoughts about our passive acceptance of pollution and its effects. Unfortunately, it has required air pollution episodes of a calamitous nature to reverse this trend of thought.

The first recorded air pollution catastrophe in modern times occurred in the Meuse River Valley in Belgium from December 1 to December 5, 1930. Heavy industry characterized the economic structure of the valley, and substantial amounts of sulphur dioxide and particulate matter were being regularly discharged into the air. During the first week of December, a static air mass hung over the valley. This stationary air mass was accompanied by heavy fog. The result was a thermal inversion. Trapped by the ceiling of warmer air, industrial wastes became concentrated in the motionless air, causing a serious pollution overload. By the time that the inversion lifted — four days later — 63 persons had died and approximately 5,000 had become seriously ill.

A similar episode occurred in Donora, Pennsylvania, during October, 1948. Donora is a small industrialized town situated on the banks of the Monongahela River, some thirty miles south of Pittsburgh. The daily radiation inversion, which normally cleared around noon, did not lift on October 26. A windless high-pressure system had blanketed the entire eastern section of the country, and in Donora a recent rainfall added fog to the inversion. Particulate matter and large amounts of sulphur dioxide, discharged by industrial plants, river boats, and trains, saturated the atmosphere. This low-hanging air mass continued for four days. During that time, 20 persons died and nearly 6,000 of the 16,000 residents became ill. Like the incident in the Meuse River Valley, this disaster was caused by the combination of pollutants and thermal inversion accompanied by fog.

On December 5, 1952, a killer smog settled over London, England. Pea-soup fog and coal smoke combined together in the inverted atmosphere. Occurring during December, the situation was immeasurably aggravated by the widespread utilization of soft, smoky coal in household furnances. As the black smoke belched from chimneys throughout London, the city's air became inundated with pollutants. This disaster lasted a full four days, killing approximately 4,000 people and resulting in numerous respiratory illnesses. But unlike the Meuse Valley and Donora episodes, household coal burning, rather than industrial wastes, was the most probable source of the pollution.

Some areas in the United States experience pollution overloads all too frequently. In November, 1971, Birmingham, Alabama, a steel producing center, was severely affected by a thermal inversion lasting three days. It was not the first air pollution crisis for the city. In fact, there had been a similar crisis only eight months before. The November crisis, however, was more severe. On the second day of the inversion, the pollution count had climbed to 771 micrograms of particulate matter per cubic meter of air. This is three times the level at which negative health effects are produced. Particularly affected were the elderly, the young, and those people suffering from cardiovascular or respiratory ailments. It was the sixty-sixth time in 1971 that the danger level in Birmingham had been passed.

Emissions declined in the following days as industrial plants curtailed operations and a westerly wind broke up the inversion. During the inversion, 5,000 workers were laid off with a loss of $400,000 in wages. The costs to human health have not been ascertained, but they undoubtedly were large.

These major air pollution episodes are relatively unique. But as deadly as they are, persistent air pollution may be more harmful in the long run. Persistent pollution involves the daily low-grade contamination of our atmosphere. Its effects are insidious. Its costs are extremely high.

Health

Air pollution is linked with a number of respiratory ailments. These ailments include lung cancer, emphysema, asthma, and chronic bronchitis, among others. A conservative estimate of the economic cost of air pollution to human mortality and morbidity is $6 billion annually.[1] This figure relates, however, only to medical care and work loss. If the costs of discomfort, frustration, and anxiety were included, these estimates would be much higher.

Lung Cancer. The exact cause or causes of lung cancer remain unknown, but certain empirical relationships are evident. The lung cancer rate in large urban areas is twice that of rural areas, even when allowing for differences in smoking habits. Thus, lung cancer and air pollution rates are both directly related to city size. One basis for associating lung cancer with air pollution is due to our exposure to large amounts of poisonous hydrocarbons found in urban air. Benzopyrene, a by-product of coal burning activities and cigarette smoking, is one such hydrocarbon. Cancer researchers have produced cancer in the laboratory simply by smearing benzopyrene on susceptible animals. Because benzopyrene is produced by both smoking and fuel burning activities, there exists much controversy within the medical profession as to which activity may be the primary cause of lung cancer. A growing body of evidence, however, seems to indicate that the poisons in the air are as deadly as the poisons in a cigarette.

Emphysema. This disease involves a progressive functional deterioration and eventual loss of vital lung tissue. In recent years the United States has experienced a rapid rise in the number of emphysema cases. Records maintained by the Social Security Administration indicate that emphysema is the second leading cause of disability. Only arteriosclerotic heart disease, including coronary disease, exceeds emphysema.

Emphysema may be brought about through exposure to polluted air. Certain relevant relationships relegate air pollution to a position of suspect. Emphysema's incidence is greater in cities than in rural areas. It also has been shown that emphysema patients improve when they are removed from a polluted environment.

Bronchial Asthma. Bronchial asthma is a chronic respiratory illness characterized by wheezing, coughing, difficulty breathing, and a suffocating feeling. Polluted air is one factor among many which is capable of initiating acute asthmatic attacks. Of the pollutants, sulphur dioxide and hydrocarbons are known to serve as allergenic agents.

There have been several instances in which asthmatic attacks have been associated with air pollution levels. In New Orleans, for example, outbreaks

---

[1]*Second Annual Report of the President's Council on Environmental Quality* (Washington: U.S. Government Printing Office), p. 106.

of asthmatic attacks have been stimulated by specific wind patterns. One day in November, 1960, 1,500 asthmatic cases requiring medical attention were reported in New Orleans. In October of 1963, two persons died following another outbreak. In both cases, air pollution was considered a major factor.

Chronic Bronchitis. Chronic bronchitis victims suffer from an inflammation of the mucous lining of the bronchial tubes. People with advanced cases of chronic bronchitis experience difficulty in breathing, constant coughing, and become susceptible to additional infections. This disease has been shown to be positively connected to air pollutants, especially nitrogen dioxide, sulphur dioxide, and particulate matter. In the United States the condition of chronic bronchitis has been treated as a general rather than specific diagnostic term. Seldom has it been listed as a cause of death. Instead, the practice has been to associate the death of a patient with one of the other diseases which stem from chronic bronchitis. Thus, the reported death rate from chronic bronchitis has been artificially low in the United States.

Property

The true extent of property damage resulting from air pollution is unknown. One frequently used estimate sets the annual property damage from air pollution at $10 billion. However, this sum does not include the indirect economic loss of declining property values. It is estimated that the nationwide values of property are diminished by an additional $5.2 billion annually from air pollution.[2] Most experts believe this to be a very conservative estimate.

Air pollution is responsible for abrasion, corrosion, tarnish, soil, cracks, and the weakening of materials, structures, and machines. Sulphur compounds in the atmosphere are particularly damaging. They are known to attack and destroy even the most durable of materials. Sulphur dioxide attacks iron and steel, rots leather, destroys cotton, wool and nylon fabrics, and harms upholstery. Sulphuric acid in the air causes sulphates to form on the surface of stone. These sulphates dissolve in water, wearing away buildings and statues. Limestone, marble, roofing slate, and mortar are especially vulnerable to attacks of sulphuric acid. Hydrogen sulphur, another sulphur compound, reacts with lead compounds and blackens homes painted with lead-based paints. It also tarnishes both copper and silver.

Ozone, a product of photochemical smog, cracks rubber rapidly. Ozone produces heavy costs to car owners and the telephone and electrical industries. Particulate matter soils cars, homes, clothing, and buildings. This necessitates the steam cleaning of buildings, additional cleaning expenses in the home, and more frequent cleaning of cars. In addition, it has a negative effect on real estate values. Studies conducted in St. Louis, Kansas City, and Washington, D.C., indicate that houses located in areas of greatest air pollution

[2]*Ibid.*, p. 107.

generally bring $300 to $500 less than comparable dwellings in cleaner communities.[3] These are but a few of the many types of property damages resulting from air pollution.

Agriculture

Every metropolitan area in the country now experiences some damage to vegetation from air pollution. The true extent of plant damage caused by air pollution has not been ascertained. Livestock and vegetation losses stemming from currently known pollutants probably amount to hundreds of millions of dollars each year. Trees, shrubs, flowers, vegetables, fruits, and grain are all being damaged by air pollution. Sulphur dioxide, ozone, and fluorides are known to be major destroyers of plant life.

Sulphur dioxide unites with water contained in leaf cells to form sulphate, which, in turn, kills off plant cells. Cotton, wheat, barley, and oat crops are especially susceptible to sulphur dioxide poisoning. Ozone enters into the underside pores of a leaf and begins destroying cells under the leaf's surface. Grapes, tobacco, and spinach are examples of the dozens of crops injured by ozone. Fluorides destroy plant life by accumulating on the tips of leaves, causing them to wither. With increased accumulations of fluoride, the entire plant may die. Corn, peach, and flower plants of many varieties are severely damaged by fluorides.

Farm losses directly attributable to air pollution are estimated to be about $500 million per year. Because of their proximity to heavy concentrations of smog in the southern part of the state, California farmers and ranchers, for example, experience losses of over $130 million annually.[4]

These examples serve to indicate the costly damage of air pollution to vegetation. It has become evident, however, that much additional study is required before the extent of the total damage to nature can be ascertained.

Safety

Air pollution represents a definite safety hazard to land and air transportation because it reduces visibility. When combined with fog, pollutants from industry and smoldering refuse can present extremely dangerous driving conditions. A motorist entering a cloud bank of smoke and dust is inclined to swiftly apply the brakes for lack of visibility. As other automobiles enter the cloud bank, a chain collision results. Several major accidents of this sort have occurred along the New Jersey Turnpike in recent years, as well as on other major thoroughfares throughout the country.

Air pollution also can be hazardous and costly to air transportation. Air pollution mixed with normal fog conditions can result in costly delays to both

---

[3]"Pollution Price Tag: 71 Billion Dollars," *U.S. News & World Report* (August 17, 1970), pp. 38, 40.
[4]*Ibid.*, p. 38.

travelers and airlines. Worse yet, this combination may also be responsible for tragic airplane crashes. On the basis of a sample study of airplane accidents in the United States in 1962, the Civil Aeronautics Board stated that 15 to 20 plane crashes in that year could be attributed to smoke, haze, sand, or dust. How many were attributed to weather conditions but were also aggravated by air pollution remains a matter of conjecture.

Total Loss

The annual toll of air pollution on health, vegetation, materials, and property values has been estimated by the Environmental Protection Agency at more than $16 billion annually. On a per capita basis, this results in a charge of around $73 per person.[5] These estimates would be higher if the impact on esthetic and other values were able to be calculated, if the cost of discomfort from illness were considered, and if damages could be more precisely traced to pollutants.

COMBATING POLLUTION

The nation's fight against air pollution is largely based on federal legislation. However, it was not until 1955, seven years after the Donora episode, that the first federal law regarding air pollution was passed.

Federal Programs

The federal government's fight against air pollution was launched in 1955 with the passage of the Air Pollution Act. In retrospect, the Act was but a modest beginning toward cleansing our nation's air. The Act primarily dealt with research into the nature and extent of the nation's air pollution problem. The Public Health Service was authorized to prepare or recommend research activities, conduct studies, disseminate information, and provide limited funding to private and public agencies for surveys, research training, and demonstration projects.

Although not of great importance in itself, the Air Pollution Act of 1955 provided the basis for a series of landmark amendments to the Act in subsequent years. The Clean Air Act of 1963 authorized the Public Health Service to take corrective action in areas in which air pollution was an interstate problem and to grant money to local agencies to initiate or expand their control programs. Local areas initiating or expanding control programs were eligible to receive a two-thirds subsidy from the federal government toward the cost of a program. In 1965 amendments to the Clean Air Act gave the federal program authority to curb motor vehicle emissions. Federal standards were first applied to 1968 motor vehicles.

[5]*Second Annual Report of the President's Council on Environmental Quality* (Washington: U.S. Government Printing Office), p. 107.

Current federal government activity in air pollution abatement and research stems from the Air Quality Act of 1967 and the Clean Air Act of 1970. The Air Quality Act of 1967 represented a systematic effort to deal with air pollution problems on a regional basis. It called for states to set air pollution standards on a regional basis and for regional standards to be enforced, locally if possible. It also substantially strengthened the powers of local, state, and federal authorities in matters of pollution. The work accomplished under the 1967 legislation paved the way for enactment of the Clean Air Act of 1970.

The Clean Air Act of 1970 is undoubtedly the most controversial and comprehensive federal pollution control program. The 1970 Act was the first law to call for national, uniform air quality standards based on geographic regions. The Environmental Protection Agency has the authority to enforce two sets of standards, primary and secondary. Primary air quality standards concern the minimum level of air quality that is necessary to keep people from becoming ill. These levels are based on the proven harmful effects of individual pollutants. Secondary standards are aimed at the promotion of public welfare and the prevention of damage to animals, plant life, and property in general. Within each geographic region, state governments may determine how national air pollution objectives are to be reached.

Automobile emissions received particular attention in the 1970 Act. The sale of new cars must meet EPA emission standards, which are applicable to vehicles and engines for their useful life, five years, or 50,000 miles, whichever comes first. The Act called for 1975 automobiles to emit 90 percent less carbon monoxide and hydrocarbons than the 1970 car, and for 1976 automobiles to emit 90 percent less nitrogen oxide than the 1971 car. The effect of these amendments was to require a virtually emission-free automobile by 1976. Since leaded gasoline has been shown to impede the effectiveness of pollution control devices and is a danger to human health, the EPA required that nonleaded gasoline be made available for all 1975 automobiles.

The Act required the EPA to set standards of performance for new and modified stationary sources of pollution. This has resulted in direct emission limitations on all major pollutants from specified types of sources. For all existing unmodified sources in specific categories the states are required to set state performance standards.

The Clean Air Act of 1970 was amended again in 1977. These amendments include an extension of the auto emission abatement schedule and imposed requirements for use of the best available control technologies for new sources of the dirtiest pollution.

Faced with the possibility that no new 1978 model cars could be produced because of the inability to comply with pollution control laws, Congress substantially relaxed the schedule for abatement of auto emissions. Automobile manufacturers were given until 1981 to achieve the standards that were initially required by 1975 for hydrocarbon and carbon monoxide pollutants. Also, the 1977 amendments increased the amount of nitrogen oxides that will be legally permissible in 1981 and thereafter. The law now allows nitrogen oxide emissions to remain at 2½ times the levels permitted under the original standards of the 1970 Act.

In addition, the 1977 amendments provided that stationary sources of pollution would be given an extension until 1979 to meet clean air requirements, after which time stationary sources would become liable for penalties calculated to remove the economic incentive for noncompliance. In any area where air quality standards have not been fully attained, no new industrial plant can be built after July 1, 1979, unless the state has adopted an acceptable air pollution control plan that will assure compliance by the end of 1982. Any new source of pollution would be required to install the best available control technology as defined by the federal government.

Under the Act, citizens are specially authorized to take civil court action against the private or governmental officials who fail to carry out the provisions of the law. Public hearings are required at various steps in the standards-setting, enforcement, and regulatory procedures to enable all interested persons to make their feelings known.

State and Local Programs

To be effective, national programs to prevent and abate air pollution must function at all levels of government. Many states have tightened pollution control standards or expanded their coverage to new pollutants or activities. State governments possess regulatory authority to combat air pollution and often set a precedent for federal action. California's automobile emission laws, stemming from air pollution problems in the Los Angeles basin, are an example. Air pollution laws in California set the stage for national legislation in this area. The federal government has traditionally looked to the states for effective control over pollution in order to encourage comprehensive regional programs.

With the new federal Act the costs of state control programs can be expected to rise even more steeply than the costs of local programs, since the Act places the primary control responsibilities on the states. However, it should be noted that dollars expended by states do not fully depict the adequacy of state efforts. In determining the extent of such efforts, factors such as population, pollution sources, past accomplishments, and organizational efficiency must be weighed heavily.

At the local level early efforts to combat air pollution centered on only one aspect of air pollution — smoke emissions from fossil fuels, primarily coal. Chicago and Cincinnati led the way with smoke control laws in 1881. By 1912 most of our largest cities had similar laws. Although a few states involved themselves directly in control programs, regulation for the most part remained a local concern until the mid 1950s. But even on the local level, air pollution control continued to be primarily a matter of controlling smoke through local ordinances. With increased knowledge of gaseous pollutants, coupled with the realization that the problem should no longer be thought of as essentially local in character, much of the authority for setting air quality standards and for translating them into emission limitations and compliance schedules is still largely delegated to the local level.

The success of both state and local efforts is mixed, but there is a marked trend toward improvement. Although state government expenditures for air quality control totaled nearly $223 million for fiscal years 1970 through 1974, only with continued federal funding is it likely that states and localities can sustain and increase their pollution control activities.[6]

Progress with Automobile Pollution

Largely because of the previously described federal programs. substantial progress has been made in reducing automobile emissions in recent years. Beginning in 1965, the automobile industry initiated steps to drastically reduce the outpouring of hydrocarbons and carbon monoxide into the air. Following the installation of several pollution-controlling devices, auto manufacturers have nearly eliminated crankcase emissions, sharply reduced evaporation losses from the carburetor and fuel tank, and reduced tailpipe emissions. On most 1975 model cars, catalytic converters were installed to reduce emissions further. A catalytic converter is a muffler-like device containing a special chemical "catalyst" which speeds up the conversion of exhaust emissions to harmless gases.

However, compounding the automobile producer's problems is the legal necessity to improve the average fuel economy of new automobiles to 27.5 miles per gallon by 1985. Manufacturers contend that unless pollution control standards are delayed or relaxed, there is little hope of meeting these standards while continuing work on new engines or trying to improve fuel economy. Thus, they argue that the Wankel rotary engine, the stratified charge engine, the lean burn engine, the turbine diesel engine, or the electric car will not materialize during the next few years.

Automobile manufacturers defend their plea for relaxation of standards on the basis that they are unnecessarily stringent. Although it is true that the automobile accounts for approximately 40 percent of people-oriented air pollution on a weight basis, automobile interests claim that the car's contribution to total air pollution should be based on its relative effects on human health and plant life. Carbon monoxide, for example is the largest of the automobile's emissions; yet, carbon monoxide is generally considered one of the least harmful of the common pollutants. It is much less hazardous to health than sulfur oxides, which are produced mainly by industrial sources. Carbon monoxide can be a health concern in dense-traffic areas where it cannot be dissipated rapidly enough. Even when hydrocarbons and oxides of nitrogen are included, the automobile is responsible for only about 10 percent of manufactured air pollution measured on a health concern basis.

Notwithstanding such arguments, the Environmental Protection Agency has broadened its attack on automobile pollution by extending its enforcement

[6]*Statistical Abstract of the United States*, 1976, p. 186.

powers to automobile owners as well as producers. The EPA requires mandatory periodic inspection and maintenance of individual automobiles' smog controls in designated areas having harmful levels of air pollution. In Cincinnati, the EPA attempted to enforce compliance by having the Ohio Department of Highway Safety withhold license plates for Cincinnati cars which do not pass the emissions test. The issue was turned over to the courts for a decision which could have affected automobile owners in many major cities. However, the EPA's request was denied.

The issue of emission standards is still not resolved. But critics of the automobile industry seriously question whether a genuine effort is being made by manufacturers to meet the standards. Undoubtedly Detroit will continue to present its case at EPA hearings. Because of the apparent conflict between energy and environment, compromises may be necessary.

Industry

Industry in general has been slow in developing and utilizing pollution control techniques. In fact, it is doubtful whether many of the current control facilities would have been brought to fruition were it not for government regulations. In recent years, however, industry has been spending massive sums of money to control pollution emissions. In 1975, industry planned on capital expenditures of $3.7 billion for this purpose. Manufacturing industries making the largest expenditures were primary metals ($648 million), petroleum ($580 million), chemicals ($215 million), and paper ($262 million). Of the nonmanufacturing producers, electric utilities anticipated spending a staggering $1.2 billion for pollution abatement.[7]

Significant decreases in the levels of the most serious pollutants will require an effective and sustained effort by industry. Industry accounts for roughly one third of total air pollution from major pollutants. However, and perhaps more importantly, industry sources account for about three fourths of stationary source emissions, which include the most damaging air pollutants.

A key element in any discussion of the industrial sector's role in combating air pollution is technology. It is a widely accepted fact that without advanced technology some of the more stubborn pollutants cannot be effectively reduced. A number of technological innovations have already contributed dramatically to pollution control. For example, the electrostatic precipitator, developed years ago, made possible the external elimination of all fly ash and dust emissions from fuel burning activities. A more recent example is that of the Monsanto Company, which has developed a process of removing sulphur oxides from gases emitted from smoke stacks.

But despite the need for new technology, many pollutants could be curbed with the utilization of existing technology. For example, if existing technology were utilized on all sources of particulate emissions, the Environmental Protection Agency estimates that particulate emissions would decrease by 95 percent.

[7]*Statistical Abstract of the United States*, 1976.

If industry is to effectively control pollution, management must not only commit itself to the task, but must reorganize as well. Many firms have set up separate corporate units or assigned environmental enhancement activities to specific parts of the organization. General Motors, for example, has a vice-president for environmental activities.

OPTIMIZING AND CONTROLLING POLLUTION

Two very difficult problems faced by environmental policymakers concern the amount of pollution that is acceptable to society and the methods by which predetermined pollution limits may be achieved.

Optimal Pollution Levels

Recognizing that a pollution-free environment is not a rational objective, government must set standards which allow for the existence of tolerable amounts of pollution. Not unexpectedly, the lack of an "all-or-nothing" standard has generated heated controversy over the levels of pollution which should be permitted. As pointed out in this chapter, polluted air and pollution control are both costly choices for society. The objective, therefore, is to minimize the sum of both costs and in so doing determine the optimum amount of pollution.

Figure 9-1 graphically presents the economic approach to arriving at the optimum level of pollution. The curve labeled *PC* represents the increased cost to society of additional amounts of pollution and is read from left to right. The *CPC* curve refers to the increased cost to society of controlling additional pollution emissions and is read from right to left on the graph. By adding the cost of pollution to the cost of pollution control, a total cost curve (*TC*) can be constructed. The minimum point of the *TC* curve indicates that the optimum level of pollution occurs at point *A*. To reduce the pollution level below point *A* would be noneconomic since the extra cost of pollution control would exceed the extra cost to society of the additional pollution. On the other hand, at pollution levels greater than point *A*, the social cost of the additional pollution is greater than the additional cost of preventing pollution. In both cases, the total cost function would be higher than the mimimum cost at point *A*.

The major drawback in using this analysis in the making of public policy lies in the measurement of costs. Although it is relatively easy to measure the control costs of preventing pollution, it is far more difficult to calculate the costs resulting from additional levels of pollution.

Controlling Pollution

Although our current approach to controlling air pollution is by means of regulation, there are other proposals calling for different approaches. In addition to regulation, two often mentioned schemes are those of direct payments and effluent fees. At this point, it may be helpful to compare and contrast regulation with other possible approaches.

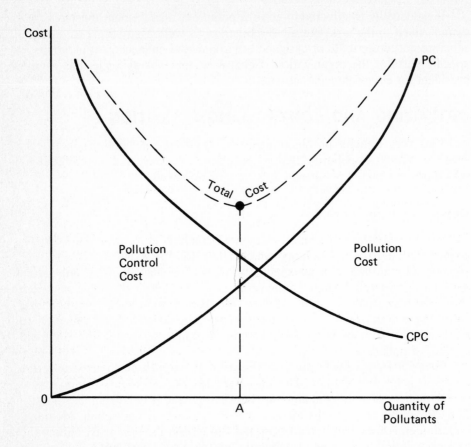

Figure 9-1 **OPTIMIZING POLLUTION LEVELS**

Direct Regulation. Of the suggested approaches, direct regulation is most often used. Usually minimum acceptable levels of air pollution are established and firms are then required to meet these standards. One advantage of direct regulation is the ease with which it is administered. This results mainly from the fact that noncompliance is easily detected. A second advantage is that of low cost. Finally, the direct regulation method is considered equitable, since all firms in an industry face the same standards.

Opponents of direct regulation point to its disadvantages. As they see it, little incentive exists for improving air standards once the minimum standards are satisfied. Also, the system may not be as equitable as it seems. Firms may face the same standards, but each firm is, in fact, different. Individual firms have different cost structures and impose various amounts of costs on society. The application of general standards can result in too much control in some cases and insufficient control in others.

Another drawback to the direct regulation approach is the heavy burden it places on government in both the investigating and decision-making areas. To place these responsibilities in the hands of government is to encourage strong political lobbying for "proper" regulation.

Direct Payments. This approach entails the granting of tax reductions and subsidies for the acquisition of pollution control equipment. Direct payments may take the form of local property tax exemptions on pollution control equipment, accelerated depreciation of control equipment, or tax credits for investments in control devices. The primary purpose of the direct payment approach is to lessen the financial burden involved in acquiring control equipment. In this manner, it serves as an incentive to invest. The biggest advantage of the direct payments plan is its ability to gain legislative approval, since firms and industries see this plan as the least painful alternative.

There are several disadvantages associated with the direct payments approach. For one thing, there is little incentive to acquire pollution control equipment, even with a subsidy of one sort or another. Pollution control equipment is inherently unprofitable because it adds nothing to revenue and does not serve to reduce the costs of production. Critics also see great difficulty in determining the amount of subsidy which firms should receive. Once acquired, they argue, there is no incentive to use effectively or maintain the recently acquired pollution control equipment. Another disadvantage is that a direct payments approach ignores the possibility of other adjustments in the production process, or the product itself, which may prove more beneficial to society. In essence, the direct payments plan is one in which society pays the producer, thus reducing the indirect costs that the producer imposes upon society.

Effluent Fees. The third approach to pollution control involves the use of effluent fees or taxes. Some estimate of the indirect costs of pollution must be made prior to calculating and levying the appropriate fee. When implemented, the fee is adjusted to reflect the marginal cost to society of pollution-causing activities. Thus, if the fee equals the marginal social cost, the external costs of production will be internalized. In this way, the producer is paying society for the indirect costs imposed upon it.

If effluent fees result in higher prices, they are passed on to those for whom the product is produced. This differs markedly from the direct payments plan in which the cost of pollution control is passed along to society as a whole.

Advocates of the effluent fees approach claim that the obvious difficulty of measuring indirect costs is outweighed by several major advantages. First, this approach provides the incentive not only to reduce emissions at a cost less than the effluent fee, but also to develop less costly control equipment. The effluent fees approach is also a decentralized approach insofar as it places the burden of investigation and decision making on management and not government. This approach also has the advantage of providing revenue to control agencies. Finally, the effluent fees method is flexible in that fees could be altered according to such things as weather, time of day, and time of year.

THE IMPACT OF CLEANER AIR

The process of cleaning the atmosphere entails major adjustments. Some firms and individuals are making the necessary adjustments with relative ease, while others are finding the transition difficult or even impossible. The following section discusses the impacts of air pollution control costs on economic growth, business and industry, firms, employment, and consumers and taxpayers.

Economic Growth

Economic growth is one of the primary goals of our national economy. The economy must grow to prevent increased unemployment resulting from annual increases in productivity and annual increases in the civilian labor force. Hence, concern over the possible negative effects of air pollution control on economic growth is justifiable.

Most economists, however, believe that the nation's aggregate output and employment are not likely to experience significant changes as a result of pollution control. But pollution control will undoubtedly bring about noticeable changes in both the composition of output and the allocation of resources. The effects of such shifts will likely balance out, however, so that in final analysis aggregate economic growth will not be detrimentally affected.

Business and Industry

Most industries have found the increased burdens of pollution abatement costly but manageable. All but a few industries expect only a relatively brief period in which antipollution spending accounts for a large share of total investment. Once industry converts its existing facilities to meet environmental regulations, antipollution investment expenditures should decline, both on an absolute and relative basis of measurement.

But this is not to deny that industries facing large pollution control costs are detrimentally affected by antipollution requirements. Of particular concern is the extent to which capital investment aimed at pollution investment is squeezing out investment needed to modernize and expand industry's capital stock. Many economists believe that unless our nation's key industries invest in modern plants in the near future, our industries will neither be able to compete with suppliers from abroad nor will there be enough capacity to meet the normal growth in domestic demand.

For example, it has been estimated that the steel industry must allocate at least $8.2 billion to install pollution control equipment on existing production facilities alone between 1974 and 1983 to comply with federal standards.[8] But the steel industry is in dire need of modernization, and profit in the industry is not sufficient to satisfy both ends. Consequently, the size of the domestic

[8]American Iron and Steel Institute.

steel industry appears to be shrinking as investment capital is being channeled elsewhere. As the industry approaches the 1980s, this shift in resource allocation has resulted in plant closings, unemployment, and protective tariffs and quotas on imported steel products.

The electric utility industry is also beset by a number of pressing problems, not the least of which is pollution control. Because of stringent regulations on burning coal of high sulfur content, electric utilities are seeking efficient ways to convert "dirty" coal into "clean" coal. One such way is to install smokestack scrubbers. Between 1980 and 1990, this would require expenditures of $127 billion or, in other terms, 16 percent of the industry's total capital investment.[9]

The multifaceted problems of the automobile industry are well known. As the industry enters the decade of the 1980s, it faces difficult challenges in satisfying tougher federal standards in the areas of safety, fuel consumption, and pollution control. Chrysler Corporation alone anticipates capital expenditures of more than $700 million a year so it can produce cars that meet 1985 emissions and mileage standards.[10]

Antipollution efforts have been costly for American industry. Future efforts will also be costly, particularly if the federal government strengthens environmental restrictions beyond present standards.

Firms

Individual firms also face adjustments, with some faring better than others. Universal control requirements will have a different impact on firms comprising an industry. In large part, the extent of the impact is related to the individual firm's market position. If the demand for the firm's product is inelastic, it may be able to pass along increased costs in the form of higher prices. On the other hand, if many substitutes are available, the firm may have to diminish production while reaping less profit. Over a longer period, the harmfully affected firm will experience greater difficulty in acquiring capital for expansion purposes and hence, its position in the industry will decline. Small firms operating single plants are most vulnerable and a good number may leave the industry. For the most part, these firms are already inefficient and obsolete and are thus considered marginal enterprises. In some cases a plant owned by a multiplant company may be closed because it also was inefficient and the expense associated with control equipment provided as good an excuse as any for the company to eliminate one of its inefficient or obsolete segments.

In general, however, major air polluters tend to be concentrated in industries characterized by large firms, such as chemicals, iron and steel, and automobiles. Thus, small enterprises may not be quite as vulnerable as it may at first appear.

[9]*The Wall Street Journal* (June 14, 1977), p. 1.
[10]"Auto Makers Play an Expensive New Game," *Business Week* (October 24, 1977), p. 83.

Employment

It was previously pointed out that aggregate employment will likely change very little as a result of pollution control. But even individual hardships may be minimized. Pollution control primarily affects manufacturing industries. Manufacturing accounts for about 20 percent of the total civilian labor force of approximately 95 million people. Those manufacturing industries experiencing the greatest pollution problems account for about 28 percent of total manufacturing employment or about 6 percent of the total work force. Of this number, only a small percentage are employed in plants that will be so hard pressed by control requirements that layoffs will result. Despite this evidence, of course, the individuals who do lose their jobs may undergo severe economic hardships.

Consumers and Taxpayers

Higher prices on consumer goods tend to penalize lower income families more so than higher income families. And the latter tend to allocate a larger share of their income for services, which by and large are not affected by pollution control costs. Hence, lower income families may well be penalized more severely by higher prices caused by increasing pollution control costs than will higher income families.

Public financing of pollution control will likely result in increased taxes. The impact of such taxes on the family unit is mixed. Federal appropriations for pollution control are largely financed by the personal income tax, which is progressive. As such, federal taxes have a greater impact on higher income groups. State and local appropriations, however, are financed by means of regressive taxes and place a greater burden on lower income families.

Although lower income groups may bear the brunt of state and local taxation, they may also experience greater benefits from cleaner air. In large part this is due to the fact that lower income families are heavily concentrated in the city core and in older manufacturing districts, which are the areas of greatest pollution.

CONCLUSION

Prospects for the future are mixed. With increasing population, urbanization, and industrialization, the pollution crisis will worsen unless the goal of preventing and abating air pollution receives the utmost priority during the 1980s. It is the responsibility of government, industry, and the general public to meet the challenge.

Despite what has been accomplished in abating air pollution on the part of all levels of government, much more needs to be done. Research programs need to be expanded, air quality criteria for selecting air standards must be refined, federal grants must be increased, and greater emphasis must be placed upon multijurisdictional control programs..

Consideration should also be given to tools other than regulation. Many experts have proposed various systems of subsidies and charges. Subsidies could be given to firms combating pollution by means of tax credits on investments for control devices, reductions in local income or property taxes, or direct payments for the purchase of pollution control equipment. On the other hand, charges could be levied on firms that continue to pollute the air. These and other schemes deserve close attention in the future.

Industry must be called upon to internalize the external costs of air pollution and view them as part of the true costs of production. The result can only be a more efficient allocation of resources. Several major industries are already moving in this direction.

Public understanding and support will also be necessary, since the battle against air pollution will entail painful adjustments in our economy. The costs of many items, such as cars, gasoline, chemicals, paper, electrical bills, and taxes are already increasing as their prices continue to reflect the costs of pollution abatement. More jobs may also be eliminated as marginal producers find it impossible to justify expensive control equipment and close their doors.

The fight against air pollution is proving to be costly, but in the long run it will be cheaper than the costs associated with a policy of limited action. In the final analysis, it all depends upon the price we are willing to pay.

MAJOR ISSUES

1. In compliance with the Clean Air Act of 1970, automobile manufacturers have made substantial reductions in air pollution emitted by new automobiles. What costs have been associated with these improvements?
2. If need be, should economic growth be sacrificed for pollution control?
3. Of the three major approaches to pollution control — regulation, direct payments, and effluent fees — which do you believe will be the most workable in the long run?
4. From an economic point of view, do you believe we overestimate our country's productive capacity when we ignore air pollution in calculating gross national product? Give specific reasons for your answer.
5. How have rapid advances in technology influenced the air pollution problem?

SUBISSUES

1. What can the public do to help EPA carry out its research and monitoring activities?
2. What advantages do you see in regional control of air pollution?
3. Does your community suffer from an air pollution problem, and if so, what is the nature and cause of such pollution?
4. Why has it taken so long for our nation to recognize air pollution for the hazard that it is?
5. Must our nation control population to control pollution?

SELECTED READINGS

Barkley, Paul W., and David W. Seckler. *Economic Growth and Environmental Decay*. New York: Harcourt Brace Jovanovich, Inc., 1972.

Department of Health, Education, and Welfare. "Sources of Pollution." *Man's Impact on Environment*, edited by Thomas R. Detwyler. New York: McGraw-Hill Book Company, 1971.

Dorfman, Robert, and Nancy Dorfman. *Economics of the Environment — Selected Readings*, 2nd. ed. New York: W. W. Norton & Company, 1977.

Edel, Matthew. *Economics and the Environment*. Englewood Cliffs, New Jersey: Prentice-Hall, Inc., 1973.

Hagevick, George H. *Decision-Making in Air Pollution Control*. New York: Praeger Publishers, Inc., 1970.

Hirst, E. "Energy Cost of Pollution Control." *Environment* (October, 1973), pp. 37–44.

Navarra, John Gabriel. *The World You Inherit: A Story of Pollution*. Garden City, New York: Natural History Press, 1970.

Newell, R. E. "Global Circulation of Atmospheric Pollutants." *Scientific American* (January, 1971), pp. 32–42.

Perkins, Henry Crawford. *Air Pollution*. New York: McGraw-Hill Book Company, 1974.

Schachter, Esther Roditti. *Enforcing Air Pollution Controls*. New York: Praeger Publishers, 1974.

Stern, A. C., *et al. Fundamentals of Air Pollution*. New York: Academic Press, 1973.

Thompson, Donald N. *The Economics of Environmental Protection*. Cambridge, Massachusetts: Winthrop Publishers, Inc., 1973.

Crime — 10
Does It Pay?

In recent years crime has surfaced as one of our nation's greatest concerns. Only the chronic problems of economic stabilization and energy utilization take greater precedence. This is not to imply that the problem of crime is new, for crime is as old as humanity itself. What is disconcerting to the American public is the dramatic rise in the frequency and severity of criminal activity since the early 1960s. But despite the gravity of the crime problem, only recently have economists applied their analytical and empirical skills to the development of an analysis of criminal activity. Traditionally, crime and criminal behavior have been largely the subject matter of sociologists and criminologists, and since the economist's treatment of the topic differs markedly from the dominant, traditional views espoused by sociologists and criminologists, a lively and healthy controversy has been generated among the professionals of several disciplines.

It should be clear in view of the multifaceted nature of the crime problem that economic analysis alone cannot pretend to provide all of the solutions relating to the causes, prevention, and control of crime. But there is no doubt that an understanding of economics does provide greater insight of the determinants of criminal behavior as well as the steps that might be taken to efficiently allocate our nation's resources to the control of crime. Thus, the major contribution of economic analysis should lie in the development of broad policy guidelines which have the effect of reducing criminal activity.

CRIMINAL ACTIVITY

The most straightforward definition of crime is that it is any act in violation of the law. Thus, in a legislative sense there can be no crime without criminal law, and since criminal law reflects the fundamental values of a society, the definition of what constitutes a criminal act varies between places and over time. Although crime is prevalent in varying degrees in all modern societies, especially in those which are urban and industrialized, particular forms of crime relate to the manner in which a society is organized. As a democratic and market-oriented nation, the United States protects individual political and economic freedoms, emphasizes the value of materialism, and rewards individual economic incentive. At the same time, these values not only serve to increase the motivation for criminal activity, but also permit the freedom to engage in an illegal act before being confronted with punitive measures.[1]

CRIMINAL vs. NONCRIMINAL

Although crime can be defined rather easily, the distinction between criminals and noncriminals is more complex. If we simplistically conclude that a criminal is one who has violated the law, then one would reasonably assume that nearly everyone reading this book, as well as its authors, can be classified as criminals. If this seems somewhat farfetched, the reader might ask if there has not been an occasion when he or she has driven in excess of posted speed limits, parked illegally, or been guilty of jaywalking. Although in the preponderance of cases we escape detection and citations from police officers, the point becomes clear: they constitute examples of acts which violate the law and thus are criminal. Yet we do not think of ourselves as criminals and, more importantly, neither does society. According to a national survey conducted by the President's Crime Commission, 91 percent of all adult Americans admitted they had committed acts for which they might have received jail sentences.[2] But the labeling of a person as a criminal only occurs when an individual violates a set of social norms which are backed up by strict sanctions. A criminal, therefore, is one who negatively evaluates the serious costs of an act on what society deems to be its best interests. Crime against people, property, and society as a whole constitutes acts which our society does not accept as being part of our conduct norm.

EXTENT OF SERIOUS CRIME

Since our laws are so pervasive, crime can be classified in numerous ways. The most often referred to source for crime statistics is the FBI Uniform Crime Reports (UCR). These annual reports present data on seven major crimes, classified into two major groups: violent crime (murder, forcible rape, robbery, and aggravated assault), and property crime (burglary, larceny-theft, and motor vehicle theft). Table 10-1 presents statistics indicating the number and type of serious crimes for the years 1967–1976. The significance of the economic motivations underlying most serious criminal offenses is seen by the fact that of the 11.3 million serious crimes recorded in 1976, property crimes accounted for 10.3 million, or 91 percent of the total. But even this approach tends to underestimate the economic aspects of serious criminal activity, since the commission of recorded violent crimes against people were in many instances incidental to obtaining money, property, or both.

---

[1]In a dictatorial society, individuals may be incarcerated on the grounds of being likely to commit a crime.
[2]President's Commission on Law Enforcement and Administration of Justice, *The Challenge of Crime in a Free Society*, U.S. Government Printing Office, Washington, 1967.

Table 10-1

CRIMES AND CRIME RATES, BY TYPE: 1967–1976

Item and Year	Total	Violent Crime					Property Crime			
		Total	Mur-der[1]	Forc-ible rape	Rob-bery	Aggra-vated assault	Total	Bur-glary	Lar-ceny-theft	Motor vehicle theft
Number of offenses:										
1967.....1,000..........................	5,903	500	12.2	27.6	203	257	5,404	1,632	3,112	660
1968.....1,000..........................	6,720	595	13.8	31.7	263	287	6,125	1,859	3,483	784
1969.....1,000..........................	7,410	662	14.8	37.2	299	311	6,749	1,982	3,889	879
1970.....1,000..........................	8,098	739	16.0	38.0	350	335	7,359	2,205	4,226	928
1971.....1,000..........................	8,588	817	17.8	42.3	388	369	7,772	2,399	4,424	948
1972.....1,000..........................	8,249	835	18.7	46.9	376	393	7,414	2,376	4,151	887
1973.....1,000..........................	8,718	876	19.6	51.4	384	421	7,842	2,566	4,348	929
1974.....1,000..........................	10,253	975	20.7	55.4	442	456	9,279	3,039	5,263	977
1975.....1,000..........................	11,257	1,026	20.5	56.1	465	485	10,230	3,252	5,978	1,001
1976.....1,000..........................	11,305	987	18.8	56.7	420	491	10,318	3,090	6,271	958
Rate per 100,000 inhabitants:										
1967..................................	2,990	253	6.2	14.0	103	130	2,737	827	1,576	334
1968..................................	3,370	298	6.9	15.9	132	144	3,072	932	1,747	393
1969..................................	3,680	329	7.3	18.5	148	155	3,351	984	1,931	436
1970..................................	3,985	364	7.9	18.7	172	165	3,621	1,085	2,079	457
1971..................................	4,165	396	8.6	20.5	188	179	3,769	1,164	2,146	460
1972..................................	3,961	401	9.0	22.5	181	189	3,560	1,141	1,994	426
1973..................................	4,154	417	9.4	24.5	183	201	3,737	1,223	2,072	443
1974..................................	4,850	461	9.8	26.2	209	216	4,389	1,438	2,490	462
1975..................................	5,282	482	9.6	26.3	218	227	4,800	1,526	2,805	469
1976..................................	5,266	460	8.8	26.4	196	229	4,807	1,439	2,921	446

SOURCE: Adapted from *Statistical Abstract of the United States*, 1977, p. 168.

[1]Includes non-negligent manslaughter.

Note: Data refer to offenses known to the police. Rates are based on the Census popula-tion data, excluding Armed Forces abroad.

Is crime increasing at epidemic rates as some suggest? Calculations made from Table 10-1 indicate the seven indexed crimes increased in number by 92 percent between the years 1967 and 1976. However, despite the magnitude of increasing crime, caution should be exercised prior to drawing conclusions based upon crime statistics.

In the first place, a truer picture of the changing crime rate is one which relates changes in the number of crimes to changes in population over a given time period. Table 10-1 data show that on the basis of indexed crime per 100,000 population, crime increased by 76 percent between 1967 and 1976. By using the crime rate approach, the extent to which crime has increased is somewhat lessened, but the figure is a formidable one nonetheless.

Secondly, the validity of the statistics depends upon victims reporting crimes to local police departments and local police departments reporting these crimes to the FBI. In 1968 the number of agencies reporting crimes to the FBI totaled 6,187, but by 1976 a total of 9,512 agencies submitted crime reports. Consequently, some of the increase in indexed crime is the result of a more extensive reporting base and not solely due to an increase in criminal activity. In any event, the FBI does not vouch for the reliability of its crime statistics.

Thirdly, it should be noted that the statistics are presented only for the seven indexed crimes and should not be taken as a yardstick for total criminal activity. Excluded from the Uniform Crime Reports of the FBI are crimes which are much more numerous and in some cases just as serious as the seven indexed crimes. Considered serious but excluded from the index are such offenses as vandalism, assaults against family and children, fraud and embezzlement, as well as many others. However, most of the nonindexed crimes are usually classified as *victimless* crimes, since such crimes generally involve some form of illegal behavior rather than crime against people or property. Examples of victimless crimes include prostitution, drunkenness, gambling, pornography, disorderly conduct, and drug-related offenses. It is estimated that victimless crimes account for approximately 40 percent of all arrests, and of the victimless crimes, drunkenness and disorderly conduct are by far the most prevalent.

A final consideration in drawing conclusions about changing crime rates stems from the fact that the definition of criminal behavior changes with the passage of time. A criminal act undertaken in one year may not be judged criminal in another, or vice versa. The recent relaxation of marijuana laws in many states is a case in point. Nevertheless, despite the aforementioned reservations relating to statistical interpretations, the general consensus is that crime is definitely on the rise across the country.

COSTS OF CRIME

The economic costs of crime are not easily measured but estimates run well into the billions of dollars. A major problem in developing cost data is the uncertainty of what should be included in the cost of crime and how to arrive at dollar estimates. It is evident that different measurement approaches are required for the various types of crime. For 1965, the President's Crime Commission estimated the cost of all crime at $20.9 billion. More recent cost data are unavailable, but cost estimates would be appreciably greater than those for 1965 because not only has the number of crimes increased, but the economic loss involved in each crime has risen due to chronic inflation.

The economic costs of crimes perpetrated against persons are difficult to measure because opportunity cost estimates are necessary. The costs resulting from crimes against persons would correctly include the present value of future income losses in the case of death or permanent disability which prevents future employment, loss of earnings if disability is temporary, medical expenses, and the costs of pain and suffering to victims and their families. It is because of such measurement problems that the costs of such crimes as murder and rape are so difficult to grasp. The Commission calculated the cost of crimes against persons to be $815 million for the year 1965. However, this figure excluded dollar estimates for the costs of pain and suffering.

The measurement of economic loss in cases of crimes against property is somewhat less difficult since the costs of such crimes can be measured by the value of the lost or destroyed property. This is particularly true in cases of vandalism, sabotage, and arson where there is physical destruction of property and a reduction of national wealth. From the standpoint of society, however, a complication arises in the case of theft since the value of stolen property does not change, only its ownership does. Although costly to the victim, theft essentially involves a redistribution of income from the victim to the thief, resulting in a net economic loss to society of zero. The Commission listed the economic loss of crimes against property as $3.9 billion for 1965.

But the real economic cost of crimes against property is much greater than the value of diminished or destroyed property. With rising crime rates, there has been an increase in self-imposed costs to society for protection and deterrence of crime. To avoid being victimized by crime, billions of dollars are expended for such things as burglar alarms, property insurance, legal expenses, security personnel, and avoidance of high crime areas. Crimes against property also impose hidden costs on nonvictims in the form of higher prices for goods and services resulting from such activities as shoplifting, hijacking, robbery, and burglary.

Finally, the costs of crime imposed upon society include expenditures associated with public law enforcement and criminal justice. Some of these services would be required even if crime could be eliminated. Police services such as traffic control, crowd control, and the tracing of lost persons would continue without crime. But the bulk of the costs of law enforcement, justice, and corrections are linked to crime. The governmental costs of crime prevention and control is borne primarily by local governments. Table 10-2 provides cost data of public expenditures for police, courts, prosecution and defense counsel, and corrections for all levels of government for recent years.

OPTIMIZING CRIME LEVELS

As a starting point, it is safe to say that in a civilized society people prefer less crime to more crime and that the amount of crime is inversely related to the amount of resources allocated to crime control. Because crime control is costly, society must compare the economic loss resulting from criminal activity to the cost of providing better crime prevention and control. Theoretically, it would be possible to achieve a zero level of crime by devoting nearly all of our resources to law enforcement agencies. However, the opportunity costs of foregone goods and services would be so overwhelming that it would be irrational to seek a crime-free society, for beyond some point the cost associated with crime reduction exceeds the benefits. Instead, society prefers to opt for a tolerable level of criminal activity which optimizes resource allocation. In this sense, the annual budget appropriations of federal, state, and local law enforcement agencies reflect the amount of crime society will accept

Table 10-2

**CRIMINAL JUSTICE SYSTEM — PUBLIC EXPENDITURES,
1965–1975, BY LEVEL OF GOVERNMENT**

Level of Govern- ment & Activity	Expenditures (mil. dol.)					
	1965	1970	1972	1973	1974	1975
All governments	4,573	8,571	11,725	13,051	14,954	17,249
Police	2,792	5,080	6,903	7,624	8,512	9,786
Judicial	748	1,190	1,491	1,579	1,798	2,068
Legal services[1]		442	580	664	771	933
Public defense[1]		102	168	207	245	280
Corrections	1,033	1,706	2,422	2,740	3,240	3,843
Federal government	377	978	1,496	1,695	1,961	2,189
Police	243	589	962	1,080	1,222	1,461
Judicial	75	129	179	118	136	165
Legal services[1]		102	107	123	118	177
Public defense[1]		56	80	90	92	87
Corrections	59	83	133	171	215	217
State governments	1,135	2,134	2,948	3,304	3,900	4,612
Police	348	689	993	1,132	1,308	1,512
Judicial	155	282	346	386	439	498
Legal services[1]		83	125	143	178	216
Public defense[1]		9	24	37	52	65
Corrections	632	1,051	1,378	1,534	1,813	2,193
Local governments	3,062	5,454	7,281	8,052	9,092	10,449
Police	2,201	3,803	4,948	5,403	5,982	6,813
Judicial	518	779	965	1,075	1,223	1,405
Legal services[1]		257	348	397	475	540
Public defense[1]		37	63	79	101	128
Corrections	343	572	911	1,035	1,213	1,434

Source: 1965, U.S. Bureau of the Census, *Governmental Finances and Public Employment.*
Beginning 1970, U.S. Law Enforcement Assistance Administration and U.S. Bureau
of the Census, *Expenditure and Employment Data for the Criminal Justice System.*

[1]Not included prior to 1970.

in a given year, as well as the number of crimes it is willing to control. The
optimal amount of resources can be examined by means of a cost-benefit analysis as presented in Figure 10-1.

The economic damage resulting from additional acts of crime is measured
along the marginal cost of crime curve, whereas the increased costs of crime
control is measured along the marginal cost of crime control curve. The horizontal axis in Figure 10-1 represents both the amount of crime committed in a

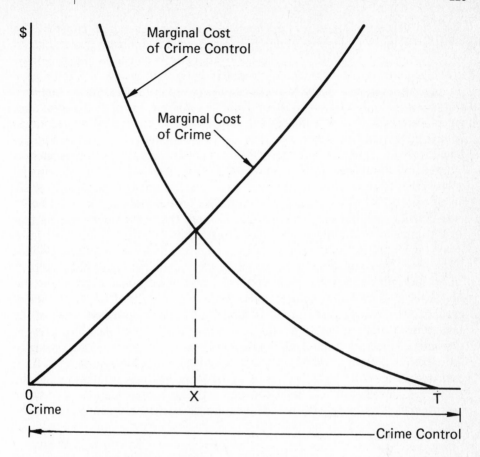

Figure 10-1 **OPTIMIZING CRIME EXPENDITURES**

community (read from left to right) and the amount of crime control (read from right to left). The marginal cost of additional crime begins at the origin, for at this point crime control is at a maximum and no crimes are committed. The marginal cost of crime control begins at point T, which reflects the maximum number of crimes committed with no control expenditures. At first this curve increases slowly, since in the early stages small increases in control expenditures can significantly reduce criminal activity. However, beyond some point the marginal cost of controlling additional crime is likely to increase more rapidly, indicating the extremely high extra cost in reducing crime as the number of crimes approaches zero.

The socially optimal level of crime is determined by the intersection of the two marginal functions and occurs at point X. At this point, a dollar expended to prevent an additional act of crime is equal to a reduction in crime costs of one dollar. At crime levels greater than OX, the marginal benefits from crime reduction exceed the marginal costs of crime control. The result is that for every dollar society spends on law enforcement, society will save more than a dollar in damages. Thus, it is economically efficient to reduce crime by the amount TX and to tolerate OX number of crimes. To eliminate criminal activity beyond point X, however, is to act irrationally because the marginal cost of crime control exceeds the marginal dollar amount of damage due to crime.

But deciding how many resources to devote to crime prevention and control is not the only major allocative decision required, for once the total budget is determined, law enforcement officials must then allocate resources among the various departments. Again cost-benefit analysis serves as a guideline. If, for example, an increase of $1.00 spent on controlling crimes such as murder and homicide yields a return of $3.00 in the form of reduced social cost while the same $1.00 channelled into the vice squad benefits society by an amount of $1.50, then the dollar should be properly allocated to the homicide division for that purpose. It follows, then, that police departments that seek to maximize the total number of arrests, particularly in the easier cases involving victimless crimes, in order to present the image of an efficient police force are guilty of inefficiently allocating scarce economic resources. The public position taken by some police officials, that since police departments do not enact laws but only enforce those which are legislated, is not sufficient grounds for employing resources as though all criminal offenses were of the same approximate severity. As long as economic resources for crime prevention and control are limited, then priorities must be established according to the costs of certain criminal acts and the benefits accruing to society from their reduction. Although the use of cost-benefit analysis in determining the social costs and social benefits associated with the various amounts and types of criminal offenses is difficult, in most cases reasonable estimates can be made.

CRIME PATTERNS

A general profile of crime across the country indicates that it is mainly an urban phenomenon, while criminals are likely to be young, male, and non-white. FBI statistics showing crime rates for violent and property crimes according to city size are presented in Table 10-3. Crime statistics presented in the table refer to offenses known to the police per 100,000 population. In all categories, the direct relationship between the crime rate and city size is evident. Data presented for selected cities indicate that on the basis of the seven indexed crimes, San Francisco, Detroit, and Dallas are the cities with the most crime per 100,000 population. Detroit is the leader in crimes against persons while San Francisco leads in crimes against property.

Urban areas contain large numbers of people at both extremes of the income scale — the very rich and the very poor. The obvious wealth of affluent families makes criminal activity appear very lucrative to the large number of poor concentrated in our larger cities and suffering from slum conditions and economic deprivation. Several studies cited by the President's Commission support the view that most of the serious crime in the city is committed by individuals at the lower end of the income ladder. Research conducted in

Table 10-3　　**CRIME RATES, BY TYPE — POPULATION GROUPS AND SELECTED CITIES: 1976**
[Offenses known to the police per 100,000 population]

	Crime index total	Violent Crime					Property Crime			
		Total	Murder	Forcible rape	Robbery	Aggravated assault	Total	Burglary—breaking & enter.	Larceny—theft	Motor vehicle theft
Total, 9,512 agencies	5,525	488	9.1	28	213	238	5,037	1,502	3,064	472
Total, 7,361 cities	6,366	580	9.9	31	276	264	5,786	1,652	3,561	572
59 cities, 250,000 or more	8,263	1,095	19.3	54	626	396	7,167	2,287	3,886	994
110 cities, 100,000–249,999	7,558	573	10.0	35	238	290	6,985	2,000	4,376	610
265 cities, 50,000–99,999	6,243	416	6.4	26	161	223	5,827	1,606	3,731	490
604 cities, 25,000–49,999	5,537	338	5.4	19	115	199	5,199	1,327	3,486	386
1,398 cities, 10,000–24,999	4,676	254	4.0	14	69	167	4,422	1,112	3,029	281
4,925 cities, less than 10,000	3,988	216	3.6	11	38	163	3,772	929	2,644	199
Suburbs, 4,022 agencies	4,627	292	5.1	20	85	182	4,334	1,253	2,757	325
Rural areas, 1,677 agencies	2,215	174	5.5	15	21	132	2,041	826	1,103	112
Selected cities:										
New York, N.Y.	8,740	1,781	21.5	45	1,144	570	6,958	2,593	3,082	1,284
Chicago, Ill.	6,829	978	26.0	38	561	353	5,852	1,233	3,583	1,036
Los Angeles, Calif.	8,057	1,167	18.3	75	519	554	6,890	2,403	3,341	1,146
Philadelphia, Pa.	4,018	684	17.5	40	406	220	3,334	1,046	1,578	710
Detroit, Mich.	11,512	2,226	49.7	92	1,590	494	9,286	3,347	3,847	2,093
Houston, Tex.	7,196	545	21.7	47	374	102	6,651	2,052	3,781	819
Baltimore, Md.	7,847	1,648	23.2	53	901	671	6,199	1,779	3,736	684
Dallas, Tex.	10,274	815	25.9	67	350	373	9,459	2,581	6,300	578
Washington, D.C.	7,083	1,481	26.8	72	1,003	379	5,602	1,691	3,491	421
Cleveland, Ohio	8,274	1,323	36.7	78	849	359	6,951	2,047	2,940	1,964
Indianapolis, Ind.	7,877	838	13.7	70	478	276	7,040	2,093	4,135	811
Milwaukee, Wis.	5,671	413	8.7	26	248	130	5,259	1,095	3,533	631
San Francisco, Calif.	11,622	1,618	19.7	93	997	508	10,004	3,307	5,165	1,532
San Diego, Calif.	8,092	532	7.6	30	294	201	7,559	2,049	4,706	804
San Antonio, Tex.	8,172	436	15.8	35	168	218	7,736	2,759	4,484	493

SOURCE: U.S. Federal Bureau of Investigation, *Uniform Crime Reports for the United States.*

Philadelphia found that 90 percent or more of the criminal homicide offenders, rape offenders, and robbery offenders were persons ranging on the economic scale from the unemployed to skilled laborers.[3] A separate study in which a comparison was made of the crime rates of male youths from both high income and low income areas of Philadelphia also supports the economic scale approach to crime.

Age and sex are also important factors in violent crimes. Table 10-4 depicts the number of arrests by age and sex for 1976. Approximately 42 percent of all individuals arrested for serious offenses committed in 1976 were "juveniles" — youngsters under 18 years old. Of the youths arrested for serious crimes, 80 percent were male. Many of those arrested were not yet teenagers. The total number of juveniles arrested in 1976 for serious crimes was over 1.4 million. Young people under 18 accounted for 9 percent of all arrests for killings, 31 percent of those for armed robbery, 17 percent of those for forcible rapes, 52 percent of those for burglaries, 54 percent of those for auto thefts, and 43 percent of those for larceny thefts. Of all the aspects of crime today,

Table 10-4

ARRESTS — NUMBER, BY SEX AND AGE: 1976

[In thousands, except percent. Represents persons arrested, not charges.]

Offense Charged	Male		Female		Percent under 18 yr. old	
	Total	Under 18 yr.	Total	Under 18 yr.	Male	Female
Total persons arrested	5,077.4	1,218.1	975.9	335.2	24.0	34.3
Serious Crimes	1,117.7	478.5	286.3	108.3	42.8	37.8
Murder*	10.0	1.0	1.8	.1	9.5	6.9
Manslaughter by negligence	2.0	.2	.2	(Z)	10.5	12.3
Forcible rape	17.1	2.9	(X)	(X)	17.3	(X)
Robbery	73.8	22.6	5.8	1.8	30.6	31.0
Aggravated assault	124.8	20.4	19.3	4.0	16.3	20.5
Burglary — breaking or entering	299.6	156.7	17.1	8.8	52.3	51.3
Larceny — theft	512.4	232.7	236.1	90.1	45.4	38.2
Motor vehicle theft	77.9	42.0	6.1	3.6	53.8	58.4

SOURCE: U.S. Federal Bureau of Investigation, *Uniform Crime Reports for the United States.*

(Z) Less than 500 or .05 percent.
*Includes non-negligent manslaughter.

[3]*Final Report of the National Commission on the Causes and Prevention of Violence*, U.S. Government Printing Office, Washington, 1969, p. 22.

what alarms Americans most is the soaring rate of criminality among the nation's youth.

There is also a much higher crime rate for nonwhites than for whites.[4] But these differences are thought to be primarily the result of living conditions in the urban core. Since the central cities of most major urban areas are becoming increasingly nonwhite, and since crime tends to be urban oriented, the higher rate of crime among nonwhites is largely a function of environment.

CRIMINAL BEHAVIOR

Prior to considering possible public policy approaches for reducing the extent of criminal activity, economic analysis can provide insight on several motivating factors that determine criminal behavior. It is this particular facet of crime analysis that has triggered the greatest controversy.

Rational Behavior

Economics is concerned with choices and assumes that as individuals we possess the freedom to exercise our choices in the marketplace. Faced with numerous constraints which limit our freedoms, we nevertheless choose the best option, given the many choices available. To consistently act in such a way as to maximize the returns available is to behave rationally in the economic sense. This principle of behavior serves as a motivating factor for both consumers and producers. Criminal activity may simply be another example of rational behavior, since engaging in criminal acts is a matter of choice. Because an individual violates the law and risks a monetary fine or prison term does not necessarily imply irrational behavior, for every choice involves some costly risks. If costs associated with risk-taking constituted irrational behavior, then many financial investors, entrepreneurs, and laborers such as steeplejacks, high-rise window-washers, and Hollywood stunt performers would fail the rationality test. However, we usually do not think of their actions as being irrational since it is assumed that they individually arrived at their decision to engage in such activity after having examined the costs and benefits entailed in their next best choices. The fact that some criminals are apprehended and punished is not proof of irrationality any more than the fact that some steeplejacks fall off the Golden Gate Bridge. It only indicates that rationality need not assume perfect knowledge of future events. The implementation of a rational decision can entail mistakes, but unlike the steeplejack, the criminal usually has the opportunity of increasing professionalism by eliminating such mistakes in the future.

Benefit-Cost Approach

If rational behavior can be assumed, then economically motivated crime can be examined within the framework of benefits and costs. Consider first

[4]The crime rate measures the number of arrests per 100,000 whites vs. nonwhites.

the expected benefits from a criminal act. Although in some cases nonmonetary returns in the form of prestige or thrilling experiences serve as motivating forces, the gains from crime are usually of a monetary nature. Thus, for most participants crime is an activity which is income producing and it is anticipated income that constitutes the major benefit to the criminal.

But, as in other occupations, a person considering criminal activity must include the costs of attaining the expected benefits, for it is net income, not gross income, which is important. One major cost to be considered is the opportunity cost of using one's skills and abilities in legal employment. Foregone income from legitimate sources serves as the appropriate measure of income loss for the criminal. However, since most criminals are lacking in skills and education, their foregone income from legal employment opportunities can be quite low. This has the effect of reducing the cost of criminal activity, since crime may be viewed as the best available alternative.

In addition to foregone earnings from legal endeavors, the criminal must also weigh the costs of being arrested, convicted, and imprisoned. These are considered the "occupational" costs associated with crime. In essence, these are the probabilities and costs of failure.

The probability of being arrested for the crime is largely a function of the type of crime involved, the skills of the criminal, and a certain element of luck, whereas the probability of being convicted depends upon the evidence presented and the skills of the defense attorney. A third probability estimate must be made for the likelihood of receiving a prison sentence if convicted, as well as the length of time to be served. Factors affecting the outcome include the severity of the crime, the criminal's past record, and the judge's view of appropriate punishment.

The cost of failure varies greatly among individuals. The nonmonetary cost of arrest, conviction, and imprisonment is the social stigma of having a criminal record and having "served time." For repeaters, however, these costs may be relatively low, for their criminal records have been well established, and if incarcerated previously they are more easily able to adjust to prison life. But for many, the cost of imprisonment is largely the loss of income which results. Obviously the opportunity cost of imprisonment will be greater for highly educated and skilled people, while the uneducated and unskilled may experience little income loss, particularly when free room and board are provided at public expense. The significant nonmonetary cost is the individual's loss of freedom, but again this cost is nonmeasurable and differs widely for those removed from society.

A hypothetical example of the rational decision-making process is illustrated in Table 10-5. Assume two individuals, A and B, are independently considering a robbery and the target is a local retail store that is open for business until 10 p.m. Routine surveillance plus inside information indicate that on Friday nights the store holds an estimated $15,000 in cash at closing time. Thus, the sum of $15,000 constitutes the marginal private benefit resulting from the robbery. Note that this sum represents only the anticipated value since the individuals cannot be positive that on a given Friday night the store won't be light on cash. Having reasonably estimated the marginal private

Table 10-5

EXPECTED BENEFITS AND COSTS OF ROBBERY

	A	B
Private Benefits		
Cash from retail store	$15,000	$15,000
Private Costs		
Probability of being arrested	0.4	0.4
Probability of being convicted	0.5	0.5
Expected length of sentence	10 years	10 years
Annual income loss from legal employment	$ 3,000	$10,000
Expected Private Costs	$ 6,000	$20,000
Net Benefits	+$ 9,000	−$ 5,000

benefits from the robbery, each individual must calculate marginal private costs, for in order to perpetrate the robbery, anticipated benefits must exceed anticipated costs.

Cost calculations on the part of individuals A and B would require the multiplying of expected costs associated with the crime by the probability of arrest, conviction, and imprisonment. For the sake of simplicity, assume that both A and B estimate the probability of being arrested at 0.4 and the probability of conviction at 0.5. By multiplying the two probability figures, the combined probability of arrest and conviction is 0.2. If A and B expect a prison sentence of 10 years if arrested and convicted, then the expected sentence term is reduced to only 2 years (0.2 × 10) since there is only a 0.2 probability of arrest and conviction.

The next step is to approximate the foregone earnings from legitimate employment and then multiply the estimated income loss by the probability of arrest and conviction. If A calculates possible income loss of $3,000 per year, then A's total foregone earnings would be $6,000 ($3,000 × 2). Assuming B estimates foregone annual earnings at $10,000, B's total income loss becomes $20,000 ($10,000 × 2).

To arrive at net private benefits, costs must be deducted from benefits. The net gain from committing the robbery is $9,000 for A ($15,000 less $6,000) but is a negative $5,000 for B ($15,000 less $20,000). Therefore, A has a positive economic incentive to carry out the crime, while for B the act would be economically irrational. The deciding factor influencing the result is the greater opportunity costs of B's legitimate earnings loss, since both individuals maintained identical anticipated benefits and anticipated risks of arrest and conviction. On an annual income basis, B's income loss was over three times that of A.[5] In general it can be concluded that since anticipated future income

[5]Readers familiar with the process of discounting future values to arrive at present worth recognize that the net benefits presented in Table 10-5 are undiscounted figures. Since A's stock of human capital is lower than B's, the discount rate applied to A's loss of future income would be higher, making the crime even more profitable to A than to B.

is a function of human capital value, individuals possessing higher stocks of human capital from investment in education or job skills are less likely to commit economically motivated crimes. Those with little in the way of acquired investment in human capital would expect a smaller flow of future income and would have far less to lose from committing acts of crime.

Thus, the motivating factors contributing to criminal behavior are much the same as those which serve to guide decision-making in everyday life. As long as individual behavior is the result of subjectively weighing benefits and costs and acting accordingly, economists consider such behavior rational. But since the calculated benefits and costs of criminal activity vary among individuals, depending upon their attitudinal make-up and perceived income opportunities, different crime levels are to be expected from different types of people. The point is that for many individuals crime is rational because it may be the best available economic opportunity.

ECONOMIC POLICY

The preceding theoretical approach to explaining criminal activity is not meant to imply that all criminals behave rationally in the economic sense of the word. It is true that some criminals are irrational or "sick" in that they do not consider the costs of their actions. But the economic approach appears applicable for any crime for which it can be presumed that the individual is not wholly irrational and is therefore responsive to changes in the costs and benefits of crime. It follows that in order to be effective, public policy must make crime less attractive by increasing its costs.

Increasing Legitimate Opportunities

A positive approach to deterring crime is to create more legitimate income opportunities, particularly for minority youth. Sufficient evidence exists that indicates a direct relationship between unemployment and crime. As long as the unemployment rate for urban youths consistently ranges between 15 to 20 percent, the opportunity cost of crime will remain quite low. By making legal activity more attractive through an upgrading of economic opportunities, the cost of crime will increase and the quantity of crime should fall. Law enforcement officials repeatedly claim that in periods of prosperity, with the economy nearing full employment, crime rates decline. But nagging unemployment and reduced economic growth rates have characterized the American economy in recent years. A fully employed economy is difficult to achieve and impossible to sustain as long as the private market sector is subject to the workings of the business cycle. Thus, even if the economy were fully employed with many urban youths on private payrolls, cyclical prosperity may only serve as a short-term palliative, for with the downturn, those without job skills or education are the first to be released from employment and will be the last hired back when prosperity returns. Thus, legal opportunities for employment may be viewed by many as only temporary and lacking a steady long-term income flow. Crime may seem a more rewarding activity to those individuals.

An expanding economy is an important factor in reducing crime but, in addition, a greater investment in human capital is required. Increasing an individual's stock of human capital by means of education and vocational training is a form of investment since it increases the economic value of human services and results in a greater flow of future income. The beneficial long-lasting effects of increasing economic opportunities have long been recognized by the public sector, as evidenced by the various federal training programs.

Unfortunately, upgrading economic opportunities is easier said than done. Thus far, training programs have been expensive failures. But continued experimentation, albeit on a smaller scale, with programs aiming to increase the value of human capital may yet prove successful. If and when that occurs, the cost of crime will increase for large numbers of the poor. But even with greater economic opportunities and income stability, there will always be wage earners along any point on the income scale who are at the threshold of viewing crime as a more rewarding alternative to legitimate employment, or perhaps an attractive source of supplementary income. This is true for very high income individuals as well, for no matter how high the costs of crime there will always be some individuals at the margin. However, the greater the costs of crime, the greater is the rationing effect and consequently the fewer the number of crimes.

Increasing the Cost of Punishment

Because of the dismal experiences with programs geared to increasing economic opportunities, most economists place greater emphasis on the role of punishment in deterring criminal behavior. Unlike the former approach, which is generally supported by sociologists, urbanologists, and criminologists, the punitive approach to crime reduction is met with stiff opposition from members of these groups. The root of the controversy lies in the economist's assumption of rational criminal behavior.

Traditional View. The traditional view held by many sociologists and criminologists is that criminals are sick or abnormal individuals who are totally unresponsive to the costs of crime, or they are socioeconomically deprived because of environmental factors. According to this view, the criminal mind is not rational. It functions irrespective of the expected costs and benefits of its actions. Individual behavior is assumed to be independent of past experiences and the experiences of others. Increased costs of punishment are not only ineffective but also reflect a cold and somewhat cruel attitude toward the sick and environmentally deprived. The function of criminal justice, according to this view, is to detain criminals until such time as they are rehabilitated and ready to resume their proper place in society.

Economist's View. The economist's view of criminal behavior rests on the assumption of rational behavior, as developed earlier in this chapter. Acceptance of rational criminal behavior logically leads to a policy recommendation of increased punishment as a deterrent to crime. But it must be emphasized that many crimes may not be prevented by increasing the costs of punishment. Included in this category are such crimes as drunkenness and narcotic addiction, which are really illnesses rather than crimes, as well as crimes of passion and crimes committed by the criminally insane. Many of these people are better treated by means of social programs which include education and physical and mental health care.

But for the majority, economists maintain that punishment deters crime. Rehabilitation of prisoners is not likely to be successful in changing behavior if the crime was a rational act in the first place. Behavioral modification rests on the assumption that the criminal was socially deviant and in need of reform. However, economists agree that prisoner rehabilitation is likely to be successful if it increases the chances of employment upon release from prison, for it will increase the individual's opportunity cost of committing future crimes. Unfortunately, however, relatively few rehabilitation programs are successful.

If one places any merit to the saying that "a person can be judged by the company he keeps," it is not likely that a person sent to prison for a serious crime will come out any better than when initially imprisoned. Consequently, many people convicted and imprisoned for criminal offenses return to the life of crime almost immediately upon release from confinement. To these people, crime still pays. Many repeaters were considered model prisoners and parolled for good behavior. But good behavior within the confines of prison walls does not necessarily result in good behavior in a free society where economic choices concerning income must be made. Ex-convicts must face the same decisions concerning legal vs. criminal income opportunities as they did prior to imprisonment. In a good number of cases, the costs of criminal activity have changed little despite imprisonment. This is particularly true where judges are lenient in sentencing criminals and parole boards are lenient in releasing them.

Economists hold that crime can be reduced by increasing the probabilities of arrest, conviction, and imprisonment as well as increasing the length of time served in prison. Increasing the probabilities of being apprehended and punished deters crime because, unlike the traditional view, economists maintain that criminal behavior is affected by past experiences and the experiences of others. Stiffer punishments also serve to reduce crime but care must be exercised in relating punishment to the severity of the crime. For example, if the crime of armed robbery carries with it the death penalty, then the armed robber faces no additional costs in committing crimes of murder, kidnapping, hijacking, or treason. To be effective, penalties must be gradationally implemented to ensure marginal deterrence. In practice, this has become increasingly difficult as the number and types of illegal activities increase.

Supply and Demand Analysis. The deterrent effect of punishment on criminal activity is shown graphically in Figure 10-2 by the use of market supply and demand curves. Assume the crime is auto theft and participants in the market include the buyers of "hot" cars as well as the car thieves. Thus, the demanders of stolen cars and the suppliers of stolen cars are assumed to be

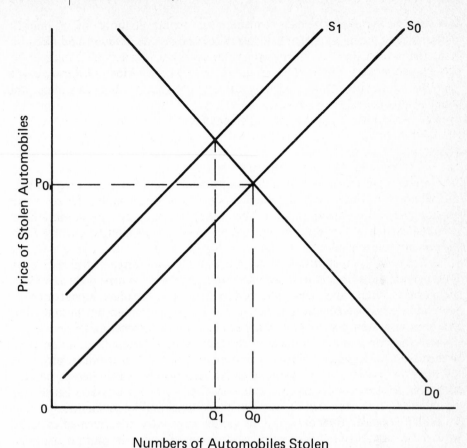

Figure 10-2   **SUPPLY AND DEMAND FOR STOLEN AUTOMOBILES**

two different groups of people. Since most stolen cars are quickly sold by the thief, this represents a realistic view of the marketplace.

The price of stolen cars is measured on the vertical axis and the quantity of stolen cars is measured on the horizontal axis. The demand curve for stolen cars slopes downward and to the right as does the demand curve for any normal and legal commodity. Buyers of illegal goods are willing to purchase a greater quantity at a lower price than at a higher price. As usual, demand at any given price is determined by such factors as tastes, income, price expectations, and the prices of related goods. The supply curve, on the other hand, slopes upward and to the right, indicating that the quantity of automobiles that thieves are willing to steal and offer to demanders is directly related to the price received in the market. At any given price, the supply of illegal goods is a function of the costs of production (special tools, labor, etc.), available technology, distribution costs, and the costs of punishment.

Given the supply and demand functions (S_0 and D_0) in Figure 10-2, market equilibrium is reached at a price of P_0 and quantity of Q_0. If a lower level of market equilibrium is desired by society, this can be achieved by increasing the costs to suppliers. Society can increase supply costs by increasing the probability of being apprehended and punished for the crime. The effect of higher supply costs is to shift the market supply to the left (S_1), resulting in fewer automobiles stolen (Q_1). If, however, criminals are "irrational" and therefore insensitive to changes in the expected costs of punishment, the number of cars stolen would not diminish but would remain at Q_0 despite the greater likelihood of arrest and punishment.[6]

Policy Toward Victims

In recent years, many states have introduced compensation programs for the victims of crime. Although such programs are new and their economic impact is uncertain at this time, it does reflect a policy change in the area of criminal justice. Compensatory programs give recognition to the fact that crimes of violence involve victims and for every victim there is a personal loss. Essentially, compensation programs involve some type of public insurance against the personal costs of victimization. Premiums are collected in the form of tax dollars, and claims are paid to those subjected to criminal attack.

Public pressure for compensatory programs is founded on the view that our present system has ignored the victims of crime. The criminal chooses to commit the criminal act and selects the person to be victimized. Even if apprehended and sentenced, there are cases in which the criminal is left better off than the victim. From the time of arrest, the criminal receives medical attention, an attorney if the criminal cannot afford one, room and board and, if sentenced, opportunities to increase educational and vocational skills — all at public expense. By contrast, the victim may have to pay medical bills, replace property losses, miss work, and absorb the cost of trial proceedings. In addition, the victim may be dissatisfied with the results of the trial and live in fear of retaliation.

Although Congress has not passed a national compensation program for the victims of crime, it is currently studying the various state programs to determine its feasibility. The State of New York, for one, has had a compensation program for several years. In 1977, New York provided for maximum awards of $20,000 to cover loss of earnings, while providing full payment of medical expenses. To be eligible, victims must prove serious financial hardship. During the state fiscal year 1976–1977, over 1,500 awards were granted totaling $2.3 million.

Ohio initiated its program in late 1976 and during the six-month period between March and October, 1977, a total of 261 Ohioans received awards resulting in a pay-out of approximately $289,000. Under Ohio law, innocent victims of crime are eligible for awards to compensate for lost earnings due to absence from work and any expenses incurred as a result of the crime for which the victim is not reimbursed. The victim may receive up to $50,000 as

[6]Supply curve S_0 is assumed to contain some expected costs of punishment. If the market were comprised of irrational criminals, the market equilibrium would lie to the right of Q_0 and not change with higher punishment costs.

compensation. Financing for the program is collected by means of a $3 surcharge on all criminal court costs throughout the state.

Should a national program to compensate crime victims be implemented, it will more than likely be one in which the federal government shares the funding costs with the states. It is also likely that any federal program will include some type of "means test" whereby victims must show financial hardship. The prevailing opinion is that there is little justification for providing public insurance against crime to those who have the financial means to acquire private insurance. Thus, federal support will probably be limited to the poor, and it is the poor who face the highest probability of criminal injury.

Policy toward Victimless Crimes

One area of criminal activity that is becoming an increasingly controversial policy issue is that of victimless crime. Various estimates indicate that victimless crimes account for approximately 40 percent of all arrests and nearly 50 percent of the total economic costs of crime. The latter figure is based on the revenue received by the criminal sector from the sale of illegal goods and services. Although the list of laws prohibiting certain types of behavior is extensive and differs among communities according to citizen attitudes, activities presently commanding the greatest attention are those of prostitution, gambling, narcotics, and pornography. There appears to be growing support in this country for legalizing or decriminalizing a number of victimless crimes.

The first argument for legalizing victimless crimes is based on economic costs. The relevant factor is not whether such activities entail large costs, but whether the costs are borne by willing participants. The direct costs of purchasing drugs, acquiring the services of prostitutes, absorbing gambling losses, and buying pornographic books and magazines and admission to pornographic movies constitute a large share of the private costs to the participant. Total private costs would also include the possibility of experiencing deteriorating physical and mental health from venereal disease, drug addiction, gambling addiction, or sexual deviance. Although private costs can be substantial, the economic approach to victimless crimes is based on whether negative externalities or social costs result from such activities, for if the costs of victimless crimes spill over to nonparticipants, then legal prohibitions or restrictions can be justified. Unless social costs result, making such activities illegal directly interferes with the rights of individuals to exercise their consumer freedoms.

But it appears that most laws pertaining to victimless crimes are based on moral and not economic principles. Although members of the community may feel morally victimized by "sinful" activities, this does not constitute grounds for making them illegal. Such laws are the expression of value judgments based on personal beliefs as to what is right and wrong. Nor is the fact that participants may be engaging in self-destructing activity a justification to protect individuals from the consequences of their own behavior. The deleterious mental and physical effects that can result are the costs stemming from the lack of complete information. Rather than interfere with consumer sovereignty, a more suitable alternative in some cases may be regulation or public information concerning possible costs to potential demanders.

A second argument concerns the role of organized crime in monopolizing markets for illegal goods and services. The greater the number of goods and services made illegal, the greater the incentive for organized crime to assume the role of supplier. Outlawing supply does not make the demand for an illegal good or service disappear. It merely makes its acquisition more expensive and channels business away from the legitimate private sector to the criminal sector. Thus, many crime experts argue that since people are going to gamble, buy drugs, and hire prostitutes anyway, why force them to patronize organized crime. Legalization of these activities could provide two benefits: a reduction in organized crime activity, and an increase in tax revenues which could be used to provide sorely needed public services.

In recent years there has been a dramatic shift in public policy toward gambling. Many states have instituted legalized gambling in the form of lotteries, numbers games, and off-track betting. Only Nevada and Atlantic City have legalized casino gambling. Although considered successful in some quarters, it is still questionable whether revenue raising and the undercutting of organized crime is compatible. Some experts doubt if legalized gambling can effectively compete with the gambling odds and tax-free status of syndicate games.

A third argument in support of legalizing victimless crimes is that it will permit police, prosecutors, and courts to devote greater resources to preventing and controlling serious crime. The extent to which this is true depends on the amount of resources individual communities allocate to enforcing victimless crime. Overall, however, the benefits of relieving an over-burdened criminal justice system by progressively decriminalizing victimless crime could be worth literally billions of dollars in crime-control funds and bring about a substantial reduction in the number of serious offenses.

CONCLUSION

The information presented in this chapter should leave no doubt that the crime problem is a very serious one. However, crime can be reduced to a more tolerable level by a redirection of public policy aimed at making the pay-off from crime less attractive. Crime cannot be totally eliminated any more than pollution can be eliminated, regardless of public policy. Economists believe that the public must realize that the traditional approaches emphasizing environmental factors and irrational behavior as causes of crime and prisoner-rehabilitation as the cure have been largely unsuccessful in achieving reduced crime levels. Public policy would be more effective in emphasizing the rational behavior of many criminals and the deterrent effect of punishment on many crimes.

In many states it appears that such a change in public policy is taking place. In at least twelve states, discretionary sentences have been replaced by fixed-term, mandatory sentences for various offenses, such as committing a crime with a gun, kidnapping, and arson. Thirty-five states have passed new death-penalty provisions since 1972. Prison sentences also appear to be lengthening and there is a growing movement to apply stiffer penalties to juveniles committing serious crimes. Gun control legislation continues to be a controversial issue in many state legislatures.

Whether taxpayers are willing to bear the increased costs of a criminal justice system that emphasizes deterrence remains to be seen. Nearly all observers agree that the public will have to commit substantial additional resources for prisons, courts, and prosecutors to reduce crime levels. Increased crime prevention and control is going to be costly, but less costly than crime itself.

MAJOR ISSUES

1. Most serious crimes are committed by young males living in urban areas. What factors account for this?
2. In your opinion, which kinds of crime are likely to be rational in the economic sense and which are likely to be irrational?
3. Should public policy be geared more to increased punishment as a means of deterring crime? If so, is the certainty of punishment or the severity of punishment more important?

4. What should the role of public policy be in so-called victimless crimes such as prostitution, pornography, drugs, and gambling? Consider as possibilities complete prohibition, decriminalization, and legalization, with and without regulation.
5. What are the benefits and costs of programs which offer to compensate the victims of crime for their losses?

SUBISSUES

1. What role should the death penalty play in the area of criminal justice?
2. White collar crimes are usually committed by individuals with relatively high stocks of human capital. How can cost-benefit analysis explain such criminal behavior?
3. A public policy emphasizing the deterrent effects of punishment will require

substantially more resources than are presently allocated to the criminal justice system. What costs and benefits would be entailed for your own community?
4. Do you believe that prison rehabilitation programs can succeed? What changes would you propose in present rehabilitation programs?

SELECTED READINGS

McKenzie, Richard B., and Gordon, Tullock. "Crime and Dishonesty." *The New World of Economics*, 2nd ed. Homewood, Ill.: Richard D. Irwin, Inc., 1975.

North, Douglas C., and Roger L. Miller. "The Economics of Crime Prevention." *The Economics of Public Issues*, 2nd ed. New York: Harper and Row, 1977.

Phillips, Llad, Harold L. Votey, and Darold Maxwell. "Crime, Youth, and the Labor Market." *Journal of Political Economy*, Vol. 80, No. 3 (May/June, 1972).

Reynolds, Morgan O. *The Economics of Criminal Activity*. Andover, Mass.: Warner Publications, Module 12, 1973.

Rogers, A. T. III. *The Economics of Crime*. Hinsdale, Illinois: The Dryden Press, 1973.

Rottenberg, Simon, ed. *The Economics of Crime and Punishment*. Washington: American Enterprise Institute, 1973.

Stigler, George. "The Optimum Enforcement of Laws." *Journal of Political Economy* (May, 1970).

Mass 11 Transit — Will It Get Us There?

Within the framework of urban economics, one problem area of great significance is that of urban transportation. It is not a new problem, but because of our failure to exercise control over the forces that have exerted change in our cities, the problem has reached the crisis stage in many metropolitan areas throughout the nation.

The urban transportation problem involves the movement of people within a metropolitan area. Cities depend upon such movement, but today in all major and many middle- and small-sized cities, a breakdown in our complex transportation network has occurred. Consequently it has become time-consuming, costly, and dangerous to move about in urban areas. The nature and degree of the urban transportation problem differ widely from city to city. The problems of large cities differ not only from those of small cities, but also among themselves. In essence, there is no single urban transportation problem; there are many, depending upon the size, age, location, topography, and wealth of the city in question.

Despite actions on the part of cities to manage their particular transportation problems, they have been frustrated in their attempts to do so, and each year their problems become more severe. Efforts to alleviate traffic congestion by constructing multilaned, high-speed expressways obviously have solved little. On the other hand, efforts to promote the use of mass transit facilities also have fallen short of the mark because for many people mass transit is not a viable substitute for the automobile. For others in areas without mass transit, there is no choice at all. The purpose of this chapter is to examine the transportation problems of our cities in light of the fantastic use of the automobile and steady decline in mass transportation.

HISTORY OF URBAN TRANSPORTATION

The growth and development of urban areas has greatly influenced and, in turn, been influenced by changing modes of transportation. A brief review of the historical modes of urban transportation and their part in the expansion of our cities should shed some light on our current transportation problems.

In the early days of our country, cities were closely tied to water transportation. By being situated along bodies of water, cities could actively partake in commercial trade with other communities, the hinterland, and foreign nations as well. Major cities emerged, not only on coastal sites, but also along inland navigable rivers, such as the Ohio and Mississippi. With water transportation as the dominant form of transportation between cities, the city was quite compact as the business and residential districts were in such proximity to the water and to one another that the perimeter of the city seldom exceeded two miles.

The advent of the trunkline railroad considerably weakened and, in some cases, altogether severed these close ties with water transportation. The city, however, remained compact. Moving about in the city was a matter of walking or riding in a horse-drawn carriage. In large cities this meant that people in various neighborhoods had little, if any, contact with people in other neighborhoods throughout the city. Thus, reliance on horse-drawn and ambulatory means of travel constrained outward expansion while at the same time, because of the compactness of the city, these methods of moving about sufficed for early transportation needs. But some traffic congestion became commonplace as industrialization and increased population density developed in our cities, creating the demand for a more efficient transportation system.

Mass Transit

The beginnings of public urban transit in the United States date back to the omnibus. First introduced in New York City in the 1830s, the omnibus soon became a major mode of transportation in that city. The omnibus was a horse-drawn vehicle with a seating capacity of usually eight persons. Although the omnibus offered passengers a slow and somewhat uncomfortable ride, these disadvantages were lessened substantially because most journeys were of short distances near the hub of economic activity. In fact, omnibus traffic served to develop the beginnings of a core area in the city, even though it did little in the way of expanding cities outward.

The omnibus reached its zenith of popularity in approximately 1870. Its popularity began to wane about that time due to the appearance of the horsecar. This vehicle was actually a modification of the omnibus. The horsecar, instead of running over rough cobblestone streets, had flanged wheels which ran on steel tracks. Thus, the horsecar provided a relatively fast and more comfortable ride. Its popularity quickly spread to many of the larger cities. But several major disadvantages characterized the horsecar. It was expensive to operate because it was slow and small and required a substantial investment in horses to make the many trips necessitated by a large number of passengers. Also, its source of energy, the horses themselves, were particularly vulnerable to inclement weather and disease epidemics. These disadvantages eventually led to the demise of the horsecar. But like the omnibus, it contributed to the formation of a city core and, in addition, to a small extent, extended the boundaries of city life.

The first instance in which a mechanized method of transit was substituted for the horse-drawn vehicle came about with the introduction of the cable car. The cable car was first operated in San Francisco in 1873. One advantageous feature of the cable car was its ability to ascend steep grades, an obvious asset in cities such as San Francisco. The cable car flourished for about two decades, but heavy fixed cost requirements and relatively slow speeds soon led to its decline. In fact, only San Francisco has a cable car system in operation today. It survives, however, primarily as a tourist attraction rather than as an efficient transportation system.

At about the same time the cable car was gaining acceptance, the electric streetcar or trolley car was introduced. This new mode of transportation was to have a much greater impact on city life. Cheaper installation costs and higher speeds meant that the transportation system could provide efficient service, not only in the core of the city, where a high density of traffic already existed, but also to the outskirts of the city as well. Consequently cities began losing their compactness. The streetcar pushed the city outward along the major arteries it served, creating a starfish-like pattern of urban development and inflating property values along the way. Land between these arterial lines lacked streetcar service and usually continued in agricultural use. Today the electric streetcar exists in only a few cities, including Boston, Pittsburgh, New Orleans, San Francisco, and Cleveland.

While the electric streetcar grew in popularity, new developments occurred in the transportation industry. One such development was the motor bus, first used by the Fifth Avenue Coach Company of New York City soon after the turn of the century. Early versions of the motor bus were quite crude compared to the streamlined models of today, and they did not win general public favor for years to come.

Several years after the introduction of the motor bus, the trolley bus became a part of the urban transportation scene. The trolley bus, like the motor bus, did not run on tracks but rather on rubber tires. The trolley, however, was not powered by a gasoline engine (as was the motor bus) but by electricity supplied by overhead wires to which the trolley made contact. Together the motor and trolley buses made little impact until the depression years of the 1930s. Unlike the motor bus, however, the trolley's life span was cut short. Trolleys grew in use until 1952 when transit companies, seeking to standardize service and rid themselves of maintenance costs associated with the trolley's overhead power system, began to phase them out.

Of course, improvements in the quality of service partially accounted for the growing acceptance of bus transportation, but it was the effects of the depression years that shifted the emphasis away from streetcars and toward buses. Transit companies found themselves in dire financial straits. Faced with falling patronage, obsolete equipment, high maintenance costs, and increased competition from the automobile, transit companies decided in favor of buses, which required less investment and offered higher rates of return.

Buses were so widely substituted for streetcars that by 1950 streetcars had all but disappeared from city streets. In many cities only their tracks remained.

Concurrent with the previously mentioned modes of urban transportation, several of the nation's largest cities sought additional transportation through the use of rapid transit. Elevated rapid transit originated in this country in 1868 in New York City. In later decades elevated lines were constructed in Chicago, Boston, and Philadelphia. Because of their obvious lack of esthetic qualities and their corresponding depreciatory effect on property values, the elevated form of rapid transit was generally scorned by the communities through which they were built. Instead, preference was indicated for the subway, an underground rapid transit system. Rapid transit serves to lessen congestion in already heavily crowded urban streets, but the requirements of heavy population density and extremely large sums of money to finance construction restrict its use to all but the largest metropolitan areas.

Although technically not included within the scope of mass transit, large metropolitan areas also rely on commuter railroads to whisk people from the suburbs to the city and home again. In cities such as Boston, New York, Philadelphia, San Francisco, and Chicago the commuter railroad provides a much needed balance to their transportation systems.

Mass transportation has certainly improved a great deal since the days of the omnibus. This evolutionary progress has brought us to the point where rapid transit and buses now comprise, with but few exceptions, the transit industry. For all but the largest cities, however, mass transit is synonymous with bus transportation.

Regardless of the type of transportation services offered in the cities, they generally have one unfortunate thing in common — they are experiencing serious financial difficulties. Prior to examining the current plight of the mass transit industry, one must peer outside the industry itself to the use of the automobile, for the automobile more than anything else has restructured the American way of life and, in so doing, has dealt mass transit a major blow.

The Automobile

Although the automobile was first introduced in 1896, its general acceptance was delayed until Henry Ford utilized mass production techniques in manufacturing the 1908 Model T Ford. Mass production resulted not only in less expensive and better quality automobiles, but it also stimulated improvements in complementary items such as gasoline, tires, and roads. As automobile usage increased, the federal government responded in 1916 by providing funds for the financing of highway construction. These funds were in addition to those allocated by state and local governments to meet the demand for new and improved roads. In essence, this was the prelude to the massive expenditures of more recent years.

Spurred on by continued entrepreneurial ingenuity, the automobile's popularity was such that it soon began to transform urban living. The automobile gave a family flexibility and independence, things which mass transit did not offer. Capitalizing on this newly discovered mobility, families began leaving the central city in large numbers in favor of taking up residence in the suburbs. This rapid spillover across traditional city boundaries slowed appreciably during the depression and war years, only to resume with a tremendous resurgence thereafter.

As the automobile opened up the suburbs and promoted the exodus of middle and high income families from the city, the structure of the urban area underwent a marked change. Decentralization began taking place in a hodge-podge fashion, first developing the areas between the starlike arteries forged by mass transit, and then sprawling outward in all directions, creating the so-called "metropolitan area." Urban sprawl cut the close ties between mass transit and many of its former patrons because transit companies were not equipped to provide adequate service to such a decentralized population. Confronted with diminished revenues stemming from falling patronage, transit lines sought to recoup losses by increasing fares and cutting service. Remaining service rapidly deteriorated as companies lacked the financial wherewithal to compete aggressively with and overcome some of the inherent advantages of the automobile. The result has led to an overwhelming dependence on the automobile by urban dwellers. This radical shift in transportation modes has brought about traffic congestion of a magnitude never encountered in simpler days. The basic truth of the matter is that many existing city streets were, for the most part, built to accommodate horse-drawn vehicles, not automobile traffic. The inability to move traffic efficiently because of traffic congestion constitutes the problem to which we shall now direct our attention.

HIGHWAY CONGESTION

The American public's relationship with the automobile has resulted in transportation difficulties of unprecedented magnitude. In some respects these difficulties are directly related to urban growth and development, while others are more inherent in the actual use of the automobile. In essence, the problem is one of congestion. Some of the more important factors contributing to congestion are diverse traffic patterns, obsolete and inadequate facilities, new construction, and peak-hour traffic.

Diverse Traffic Patterns

The dependence upon private transportation is linked to the extension of suburbs into what was formerly the hinterland. As the density of metropolitan areas declines, families are faced with greater traveling distances. The greater the distance from the employment core, the greater the propensity for automobile ownership. But as business enterprises, shopping facilities, and recreational areas expand to outlying areas, a complex traffic pattern emerges. In addition to those people who live and work in either the city or the suburbs, many now live in the suburbs and work in the city, while others live in the city and work in the suburbs. In many cities chaotic congestion is created by this heavy concentration of downtown, crosstown, and suburban-oriented traffic, particularly during rush hours. And the congestion caused by such diverse traffic patterns is likely to worsen as urban sprawl continues.

Inadequate Facilities

Congestion also stems from the inadequacy of existing streets and parking areas to handle automobiles. Most street patterns were not designed for the automobile, but for facilitating the subdivision of land and providing a transportation network for horse-drawn vehicles. Although there have been new roads built to replace old ones, the problem still remains. Traffic becomes stymied where several roads converge into a single lane. Congestion also occurs at crowded intersections where all four roads meet at one point instead of being diverted from one another. Finally, the narrow streets of the core area, particularly in older cities, challenge both the skills and patience of the driver at practically any time of day.

Upon arriving in the downtown area, the motorist experiences difficulties in acquiring a parking space. Although off-street parking is on the rise in many cities, on-street parking still prevails. On-street parking produces congestion because it takes up valuable road space and considerably reduces traffic speed. Viewed from the air, many urban areas appear as giant parking lots. As in the case of street improvement, increasing the supply of parking spaces does not tend to alleviate congestion, but to worsen it, for it entices even more autos to enter the city each day.

New Construction

Closely connected with the problem of inadequate facilities is the problem resulting from the construction of new buildings in downtown areas. Urban redevelopment programs generally have shown little concern for traffic congestion. Older structures are replaced by newer ones of greater capacity in areas where congestion is already staggering. But while the central city suffers from the pains of new construction generated by inadequate planning, the suburbs, too, are undergoing the same dilemma. The failure to preserve open space and to balance new growth has led to congestion in the suburbs, a situation which suburbanites were seeking to avoid in the first place.

Peak-Hour Traffic

Although the sheer number of automobiles in the United States is indicative of the nature of the urban transportation problem, the full dimensions of the problem cannot be appreciated unless peak-hour traffic is examined. "Peak hours" refer to those hours in which the traffic flow is heaviest due to commutation between residence and employment. Normally in most major cities peak hours extend from 7 to 9 a.m. and from 4 to 6 p.m. The automobile is the major mode of commuting to and from work and thus the most severe traffic problems occur during these hours.

Statistics indicate that 82 percent of commuting workers use automobiles as a means of transport and that 56 percent of the commuting workers drive alone. Only 26 percent of the commuters travel in cars containing more than one person.[1] Thus, it is the peak-hour traffic that places heavy demands on our urban highway transportation system.

The problem of traffic congestion is a costly one, both to individuals and society. Yet, despite increasing costs of congestion, more and more automobiles stream in, out, and around our major cities each year. At the same time, however, mass transit systems continue to deteriorate. To appreciate why households are willing to absorb the high costs of automobile transportation, the economic state of mass transit must be examined.

THE FINANCIAL PLIGHT OF MASS TRANSIT

The continued decline of the mass transit industry has brought tremendous financial pressure to bear on individual transit companies. At this point, the major factors accounting for such financial difficulties must be analyzed.

Ridership

Figures indicating the trend of total passengers carried on transit lines are presented in Table 11-1. Except for the years 1974–1976, statistics show a

Table 11-1

TREND OF TOTAL PASSENGERS CARRIED ON TRANSIT LINES

Calendar Year	Railway			Trolley Coach	Motor Bus	Total Passengers
	Light Rail	Heavy Rail	Total Rail			
	(Millions)	(Millions)	(Millions)	(Millions)	(Millions)	(Millions)
1940	5,943	2,382	8,325	534	4,239	13,098
1945	9,426	2,698	12,124	1,244	9,886	23,254
1950	3,904	2,264	6,168	1,658	9,420	17,246
1955	1,207	1,870	3,077	1,202	7,250	11,529
1960	463	1,850	2,313	657	6,425	9,395
1965	276	1,858	2,134	305	5,814	8,253
1970	235	1,881	2,116	182	5,034	7,332
1973	207	1,714	1,921	97	4,642	6,660
1974	150	1,726	1,876	83	4,976	6,935
1975	124	1,673	1,810	78	5,084	6,972
1976p	112	1,632	1,759	75	5,247	7,081

SOURCE: American Public Transit Association, *Transit Fact Book 1976–1977*, p. 26.

p = preliminary.

[1]Automobile Manufacturers Association.

steady decline in transit passengers since 1945. The sharpest declines are evident for both surface railways and trolley coaches, for these modes of transportation have experienced large-scale service elimination as well as declining patronage. The recent reversal of the general declining trend in transit ridership is the result of increased motor bus patronage since 1974 which has outweighed continued declines in other forms of service.

Profit — Loss

Concomitant with falling patronage, the financial position of transit companies has been characterized by deficit. Although operating revenue has increased over 2.5 times since 1940, operating expenses have increased even faster, to the point that in recent years they have exceeded operating revenues. On the basis of net operating revenue, losses have been recorded by the industry in every year since 1968. When taxes are included, the financial record of transit lines indicates that 1962 was the last year in which overall transit operations were profitable. Since that time, deficits have become chronic. Financial data for urban mass transit systems are presented in Table 11-2. A

Table 11-2
TREND OF TRANSIT OPERATIONS

Calendar Year	Operating Revenue	Operating Expense Including Depreciation[a]	Net Operating Revenue (Loss)	Operating Licenses and Taxes	Operating Income (Deficit)[b]
	(Millions)	(Millions)	(Millions)	(Millions)	(Millions)
1940	$ 737	$ 598	$ 138	$ 62	$ 76
1945	1,380	1,067	313	164	149
1950	1,452	1,297	155	89	66
1955	1,426	1,277	149	93	56
1960	1,407	1,290	117	86	31
1965	1,443	1,373	70	80	(10)
1970	1,707	1,891	(184)	104	(288)
1973	1,797	2,419	(622)	116	(738)
1974	1,938	3,102	(1,162)	137	(1,300)
1975	2,002	3,535	(1,535)	171	(1,704)
1976[p]	2,101	3,839	(1,678)	182	(1,860)

SOURCE: American Public Transit Association, *Transit Fact Book 1976–1977*, pp. 22–23.

p = preliminary.
a = Excludes operating licenses and taxes.
b = Excludes government subsidies for operating assistance. Operating assistance from the federal government totaled $301 million in 1975 and $423 million in 1976. State and local government subsidies for 1975 were $1.1 billion and $1.2 billion for 1976. Data not available prior to 1975.

graphic portrayal of operating revenues and losses from 1940–1976 is also presented in Figure 11-1.

A quick inspection of both the table and the graph reveals that operating losses have increased dramatically since 1968 to the extent that in 1976 losses totaled in excess of $1.6 billion.

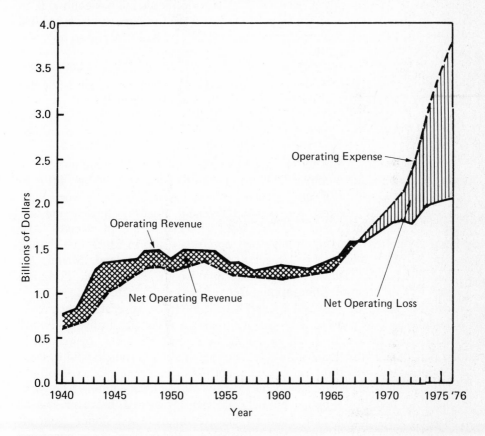

SOURCE: American Public Transit Association, *Transit Fact Book 1976–1977*, pp. 22–23.

Figure 11-1   **RESULTS OF TRANSIT OPERATIONS, 1940–1976 (NET OPERATING REVENUE OR LOSS)**

Fares and Costs

To compensate for increased costs, the average fare for all modes of transit has risen from 10 cents in 1950 to 35 cents in 1976.[2] These increases in the cost of ridership have caused a further drop in the number of passengers carried. The impact of rising fares may not be immediately evident because of the lack of suitable alternatives, but over longer periods of time, a policy of

[2]American Public Transit Association, *Transit Fact Book 1976–1977*, p. 32.

rising fares tends to encourage increased automobile usage. Rising fares have fostered intense indignation among transit riders who find the incongruity between rising fares and deteriorating service too much to bear.

In response to large deficits, transit companies have attempted to cut costs. But this has not proved to be an easy task. Despite the fact that fewer employees are on the payroll than in 1950, the total wage bill has continued to climb. In 1950 transit companies paid out over $837 million to some 240,000 workers. In 1976, although the number of employees had dropped to approximately 163,000, the total wage bill was over $3 billion.[3]

To cut costs, transit lines have also curtailed maintenance. Companies have been forced to allow buses, subways, and other facilities to get older and older. This in turn has caused many people to abandon mass transit.

Ownership

Because of the failure to improve their financial status, a large number of transit companies have converted from private to public ownership. Prior to 1958 public ownership of mass transit systems existed in only seven major U.S. cities: Seattle, Detroit, New York, Cleveland, Boston, Chicago, and San Francisco. Since that time, there has been a virtual parade of changes from private to public ownership in large metropolises. Cities in which this change has taken place include Los Angeles, San Antonio, Oakland, Miami, St. Louis, Pittsburgh, Dallas, Philadelphia, San Diego, Providence, Portland, Kansas City, Baltimore, Minneapolis, Denver, and Cincinnati.

Of the remaining privately owned transit systems, several are presently contemplating public ownership and are likely to make this transition in the relatively near future. It should be noted, however, that public ownership is not a panacea for the financial problems of the industry. Deficits still characterize publicly owned transit companies, but instead of total reliance upon the fare box to meet expenses, companies receive subsidies stemming from government tax receipts. Whether publicly or privately owned, however, transit companies are seeking and receiving greater financial assistance from all levels of government. In 1976 total operating assistance from government exceeded $1.6 billion, comprised of $857 million in local funds, $367 million in state funds, and $423 million in federal funds.

COLLECTION, DELIVERY, AND PEAK HOURS

The factors accounting for the distressed state of mass transit are essentially the same as those which have stimulated automobile use; namely, the problems of collection, delivery, and peak-hour traffic.

As urban sprawl has diminished population density, it has become extremely difficult for mass transit companies to collect riders over a widely dispersed area. Faced with a dispersed residential and employment pattern

[3]*Ibid.*

and unable to collect people on a door-to-door basis, transit companies have increased the number of stops to increase payloads. This practice has led to higher operating costs for the firm and less utility for passengers. Thus, to overcome the difficulties brought about by low collection densities, companies have had to reduce the efficiency of their service, driving even more customers away.

The delivery problem has become significant because of changes in the scale and distribution of economic activities. The increased diversity of travel patterns has reduced the effectiveness of highly centralized, radial transit systems. Dispersal of places of work and of central points of attraction even within the downtown area has greatly lengthened that portion of the trip between arrival at the terminal and arrival at the final destination. This may necessitate a walk of some distance or additional expenses for taxi fare subsequent to disembarking from mass transit. The inadequacies of mass transit in collecting and delivering passengers are major obstacles in providing point-to-point transportation service.

The basic problem of peak demand is the inability of transit companies to achieve the economies associated with the intensive utilization of capital and labor. Demand for urban transportation is imbalanced insofar as it is not spread evenly throughout the day. It is estimated that nearly 80 percent of the volume of traffic handled by mass transit occurs during 20 hours of the week. This results in a need for transportation equipment and personnel for rush-hour traffic far in excess of what is needed throughout the day. As such, the amount of physical equipment is determined by the extent of peak demand, leaving idle capacity during the remainder of the day. Because sharp peaks in demand inevitably lead to higher operating costs, the average cost of all rides tends to be higher than if demand were evenly distributed.

COMPARATIVE PRICES AND COSTS

An insight into the urban transportation problem necessitates an examination of the relative prices and costs of transport modes. In fact, the elements of price and cost play a decisive role in selecting one mode of transportation at the expense of another.

Price Elasticity

A basic proposition in the study of economics can provide assistance in analyzing the price-ridership relationship for mass transit service, namely, the law of demand. The law of demand states that if all other factors which affect the demand for a good or a service are held constant, an inverse relationship exists between price and quantity demanded. Thus, the higher the price, the lower the quantity demanded, and vice versa.

Although the demand for a good or a service is simultaneously affected by many variables, empirical evidence indicates that in the mass transit industry higher prices do result in less patronage. Figure 11-2 depicts the inverse

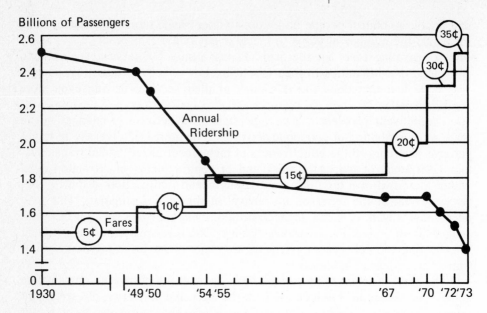

SOURCE: New York City Transit Authority.

Figure 11-2 **RISING FARES AND DECLINING PATRONAGE ON THE NEW YORK CITY TRANSIT SYSTEM, 1930–1973**

relationship between New York City transit fares and ridership for the year 1930 through 1973. The extent to which decreasing ridership can be attributed to the effect of higher prices alone is difficult to ascertain but no doubt the pricing policy of transit companies has played a major role.

Mass transit officials realize that a policy of increasing prices to meet rising expenses may result in financial calamity in the long run, but increased prices do achieve stopgap results in the short run because of the inelastic nature of the demand for transit service. By elasticity, the economist refers to the degree of responsiveness or sensitivity on the part of the consumer to changes in price. If the change in quantity demanded is more than proportionate to the change in price, the demand is said to be elastic. If quantity changes are less than proportionate to the price change, the demand is inelastic, while proportionate changes in price and quantity result in unitary elasticity.

The fact that the demand for mass transit service is inelastic is looked upon with mixed feelings. On the positive side it means that although patronage will decline following a price increase, percentage-wise the drop in ridership will be less than the increase in price. Studies in transit fares in New York City bear this out. It is interesting to note that the elasticity coefficient is estimated to be somewhere in the neighborhood of .33, according to transit industry estimates. This means that a given percentage increase in fares will result in a diminution of traffic by roughly 33 percent of the percentage increase in price.

Thus, the ability to increase prices without fear of an immediate collapse in patronage can be construed as an advantage of having an inelastic demand in the short run. But inelasticity is a "two-edged sword." It carries with it disadvantages as well as advantages. The major drawback is that attempts to increase patronage by lowering prices are largely unsuccessful because of the relatively low degree of sensitivity to price changes. More people will ride the transit at lower prices (law of demand), but the increase in patronage is insufficient to compensate for the loss of revenue stemming from the lower prices.

Over longer periods of time, the demand for mass transit service becomes more elastic as households make adjustments in their transportation purchases. For those lacking the necessary financial resources, higher prices ration their use of mass transit and sharply curtail their mobility. For others more affluent, substitute methods of transportation may be utilized.

Income Elasticity

What is the relationship between income and transit ridership? Again, elasticity proves to be a helpful tool for analysis. However, instead of measuring the consumer's response to changes in the price of ridership, let us substitute the consumer's response to changes in income. If ridership is directly related to income changes, demand is said to be positively elastic. If an inverse relationship exists between ridership and income changes, demand is said to be negatively elastic, meaning that less ridership would be demanded as incomes increase as compared to a greater demand for ridership at lower levels of income. It has been emphasized that as households acquire auto ownership, they tend to abandon mass transit. Thus, an inverse relationship exists between income and transit ridership. Therefore, as an economic good that possesses the qualities of negative income elasticity, mass transit suffers as the urban population prospers.

Declining patronage resulting from rising prices of transit service concurrent with rising household incomes may culminate in a gradual decline and, in some cases, complete abandonment of service. Despite pleas from both transit and city officials alike, households continue increasing their usage of the automobile.

Costs

Although speed of travel and convenience are usually deemed the most decisive factors in preferring the automobile over mass transit, cost considerations play a major role. The general consensus of those who drive is that it is more economical to travel by car than by transit. The extent to which this is true depends upon the manner in which costs are calculated. To maximize society's welfare, economists hold that any decision based upon benefits and costs should be made only after being sure that all benefits and costs are fully allocated. Herein lies the problem, for in calculating the costs of automobile travel, motorists include only a portion of total costs. Many costs are ignored altogether.

Private Costs. When individuals travel by mass transit, they are confronted with a user charge. This cost to the rider is obvious and is associated with the journey. But if the individual decides to drive, the costs of automobile usage are largely hidden.

In the process of cost examination, the economist classifies cost elements to facilitate analysis. One such classification involves the concepts of private and social costs. *Private costs* are those which are borne by the motorist personally. Private costs can be subdivided into direct and indirect costs. *Direct costs* vary with the use of the automobile, such as gasoline, oil, wear and tear, and excise taxes. *Indirect costs* associated with the automobile are costs which do not vary with usage. Examples of the latter include such items as insurance premiums, property taxes, fees, and model obsolescence. Since the motorist is faced with indirect costs regardless of how often and for what purpose the auto is utilized, these costs usually do not influence the choice of transportation mode. The only exception to the rule occurs when an individual is considering the purchase of an automobile. At this point all costs are direct and must be included in the total cost of commutation.

After having purchased the automobile, however, the motorist seldom includes all private costs in the decision-making process. In many cases only the price of gasoline is considered. But when all private costs (direct plus indirect) are properly allocated by the motorist, travel by automobile is much more expensive than it would at first appear.

Social Costs. Social costs exist as well as private costs. *Social costs* are costs which are borne by society as a whole and not directly by the user. The largest social cost stemming from automobile usage is congestion, which results when too many vehicles attempt to use a limited amount of space at the same time. Congestion is a fact of life in our cities today. Every auto in a congested area adds to congestion, increasing the cost to others. When caught in a traffic jam, the individual motorist may claim that all other motorists should be charged something for the cost of the lost time they are imposing on him or her. On the other hand, the motorist will be included in the cost claims of other motorists since he or she too is adding to congestion. Examples of the social costs resulting from congestion might include fatigue, lost leisure time, accidents and loss of life, lost productivity, air and noise pollution, increased costs of police and fire protection, increased transportation costs of goods and services and resulting higher prices, and the costs of constructing new highway facilities to decongest city streets.

Social costs are recognizable, but since they are not priced in the marketplace they are extremely difficult to measure. If they could be assigned pecuniary values, the motorist would readily see that the cost of traveling by car is understated, particularly during peak-hour traffic. One possible method of internalizing peak-hour congestion costs is by means of toll charges. Figure 11-3 indicates how peak-hour congestion affects the marginal cost of driving.

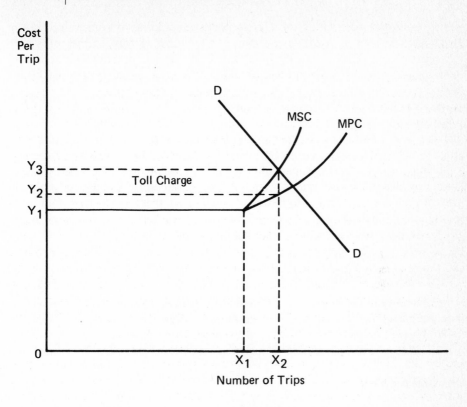

Figure 11-3 **USE OF TOLL CHARGE AT PEAK HOURS**

The number of automobile trips is measured along the horizontal axis, whereas the cost per automobile trip is measured along the vertical axis. As long as the number of automobiles on the highway does not exceed Ox_1, all costs are private costs to the motorists, assuming that the marginal private cost (*MPS*) is constant and identical for all motorists if the highway is used during the off-peak hours and that the traffic flow is evenly maintained on the highway. Beyond Ox_1, however, each motorist that comes onto the highway experiences increasing marginal private costs because congestion has reduced the motorist's effective rate of speed. But the entry of an additional motorist has the effect of diminishing the speed of all motorists on the highway as well. Thus, in addition to shouldering increased marginal private costs, each additional motorist also indirectly increases the cost to all other motorists on the highway since that motorist is reducing the speed of each car. As seen in Figure 11-3, the marginal social cost (*MSC*, which all drivers must bear as a result of each additional motorist entering the highway beyond Ox_1) now exceeds the increasing marginal private cost of the entering motorist.

If *D-D* represents peak-hour demand for the highway, then the social costs of congestion can be partially internalized by means of toll charges. Given demand as *D-D*, the vertical distance between the *MSC* and *MPC* curves is the toll charge that should be imposed on each motorist. Thus, the actual total cost to each of the Ox_2 motorists of adding to congestion during peak-hour periods is equal to the sum of Oy_1 (cost of travel time) plus y_1y_2 (increased cost of travel time) plus y_2y_3 (toll charge for congestion), all of which sums to Oy_3. With the use of tolls, peak-hour congestion could be reduced as users make their journeys by driving different routes, forming commuter car-pools, or by riding mass transit.

But even after being confronted with a cost structure which reflects both private and social costs, the motorist's decision to drive may still be a rational one. The motorist may continue to drive because the advantages of time and convenience more than compensate for the previously mentioned cost factors. To many drivers, mass transit is a very poor substitute for the automobile, regardless of cost. Thus, toll receipts collected from peak-hour motorists could be utilized for socially beneficial transportation purposes, such as financing transit operations or improving highways.

FEDERAL LEGISLATION

The role of the federal government in our nation's transportation system has been a controversial one. A treatment of both the pros and cons of the federal government's role will be presented after examining several major pieces of legislation pertaining to highway and mass transit transportation.

Federal Aid For Highways

The federal government first involved itself in highway legislation in 1916. Since that time, most expenditures have been funneled into highway construction. The 1916 Act appropriated some $75 million over a 5-year period to state governments for the purpose of improving their rural post roads. To be eligible, states had to create their own highway departments and agree to maintain the roads upon completion of construction work. In 1921 highway legislation was enacted limiting aid to a designated system of interstate highways. As in the 1916 Act, states had to match the federal monies they received. The Federal Highway Act of 1944 provided for the designation of a national system of interstate highways. Limited to 40,000 miles, this highway network was to be comprised of main routes linking cities throughout the country.

But the most significant and controversial federal legislation relating to highway development was the Federal Aid Highway Act of 1956. This Act constituted a major departure from previous legislation insofar as it established a highway trust fund out of which all federal highway expenditures were to be distributed. Under this provision federal gasoline taxes, taxes on vehicles and tires, and taxes on heavy trucks and buses were channeled into the trust fund. No disbursements could be made from sources other than the fund. A nationwide interstate and defense highway system of some 41,000 miles (since expanded to 42,500 miles) at a projected cost of over $46 billion (now estimated in excess of $90 billion) was authorized. Target date for completion was 1970, although by 1978 completion of the original project still had not been realized. The federal government would provide 90 percent of the funds, with the states contributing the remaining 10 percent. Also contained within the Act was the provision that the federal government would contribute half the cost of constructing primary, secondary, and urban highways. In 1970 the federal government increased its share of costs of constructing primary and secondary highways from 50 to 70 percent and committed itself to financing up to 95 percent of the cost of "economic development" highways as a means of fostering economic growth in depressed rural areas.

As the federal interstate highway system neared completion, mounting pressures were exerted to divert funds from the highway trust fund to urban mass transit systems. In 1973 the Federal Aid Highway Act was amended to permit a part (about 20 percent) of the regularly allocated highway trust fund monies to be used for either urban highways or mass transit capital projects, depending on local choice.

Mass Transit Legislation

Unlike highway legislation, federal legislation pertaining to mass transit is relatively recent. In fact, despite the long-existing traffic problems in our major cities, federal legislation was not enacted until 1964.

Urban Mass Transportation Act of 1964. Under this Act the federal government declared its willingness to finance two thirds of the net project costs of approved capital expenditures in the mass transit industry. These funds could be utilized for a variety of purposes, including land acquisition, rights-of-way, parking facilities, buses, rail cars, and stations. If transit operations are in private hands or in those of public agencies lacking taxing powers, state and local governments are to contribute the necessary funds to meet the remaining expenditures. If a transit situation is deemed to be in a state of crisis and loss of transit service appears imminent, the federal government will supply 50 percent of the needed funds with the state and local governments providing the rest.

To finance the federal government's share of the project expenditures, $375 million was made available over a three-year period. To be eligible, communities had to organize regional, coordinated planning programs. Consequently a lag of several years existed prior to the implementation of a project of any major significance.

Urban Mass Transportation Act of 1970. Although the Nixon Administration favored a $10 billion mass transit program over a span of 12 years, Congress appropriated only $3.1 billion under the Urban Mass Transportation Act of 1970. Authority was given to the Secretary of Transportation to distribute loans and grants of $3.1 billion and to request additional sums for the fiscal years of 1976–1982.

The Act sets limitations of 12.5 percent of the federal appropriation for any one state, although densely urban states can compete for up to 15 percent

of the total federal allocation in a given year. The federal share of capital
investments is limited to 66.6 percent.

Federal Aid Highway Act of 1973. Although previously referred to as highway legislation, this Act must also be considered as major mass transit legislation since a part of the highway trust fund was earmarked for mass transit
use. In fiscal 1975 this portion was funded at $200 million and cities could opt
for either the construction of highways or the purchase of buses. In fiscal
1976, cities received an amount equal to $800 million which could be used for
highways, buses, or rail systems. An important feature of the Act is that cities
and states are able to return to the trust fund monies designated for urban
segments of the interstate highway system which state and local governments
no longer wish to build. The Treasury will then reimburse the state and local
governments out of general revenues and the returned funds may then be used
for transit projects. In an attempt to provide greater equity in the funding of
transportation projects, the Federal Aid Highway Act of 1973 raised the maximum federal capital grants ratio for mass transit from 2:1 to 4:1.

National Mass Transportation Assistance Act of 1974. This Act changes the
basic concept of federal support for mass transit. The Act provides contract
authority of $11.8 billion to be available through 1980. Of this total, $7.8 billion is earmarked for existing federal assistance programs. The remaining $4.0
billion will be distributed by formula among state and local governments to
divide as they see fit between capital expenditures and operating subsidies.
The formula is based on each urbanized area's relative population and density. Funds can be used to cover up to 80 percent of project construction
costs. When used for transit operating subsidies, federal funds must be
matched by equal subsidies from recipient governments.

CONTROVERSIAL ASPECTS OF THE FEDERAL ROLE

Controversy revolving around the federal government's role in urban
transportation stems from its lack of a balanced program of federal aid. Over
the years massive sums of money have been funneled into the highway program with but meager amounts made available to mass transit. Critics of the
highway program point to the fact that in fiscal 1975 more than $4.6 billion of
federal money was spent on highways throughout the land. The corresponding
figures for mass transit, however, indicate that only $420 million was appro-
priated in fiscal 1975. Critics of the present federal role assert that it will be
impossible to achieve a balanced transportation network without a balanced
federal program of assistance.

Transit Interests

A more equitable treatment in the manner in which highway and transit
operations receive financing is often suggested as a first step in achieving balance. The highway system is financed by means of the highway trust fund,

which from the point of view of highway interests has been highly successful. Mass transit, however, is without a separate trust fund and until recently had to rely solely upon appropriations from Congress. Lacking the greater degree of automaticity which the trust fund technique provides, mass transit has been vulnerable not only to political considerations but also to changing economic conditions. It was not unusual to witness appropriations slashed to meager amounts in Congress because of the need to reduce domestic spending in times of inflation. Communities have been understandably reluctant to spend large sums of money in the planning and early development stages of a mass transit system only to learn that expected federal funding will not be forthcoming either because of appropriation cuts or possibly because of a reluctance on the part of the President to release appropriated funds.

With the 1973 amendment of the Federal Aid Highway Act, mass transit has arrived at a crossroads in federal funding. Mass transit now has a source of funds which is less vulnerable to the vagaries of Congressional appropriation procedures but is still without a separate trust fund. Undoubtedly the inclusion of mass transit in the highway trust fund reduces the inflexibility of the urban highway funding process. It also places mass transit on a healthier financial basis than ever before. But mass transit interests maintain that its 20 percent share of the highway trust fund monies is insufficient. Without substantially greater financial support, federal funding will only provide stop-gap results in reversing the general transit decline. Hence, it is argued that either a much larger share of trust funds should be diverted to mass transit, or a separate trust fund to provide for both capital and operating expenses must be initiated if mass transit is to receive sufficient funding.

Transit proponents also fear that new highway "requirements" will be created to absorb recent surpluses in the highway trust fund. Should this occur, it would mean that the amount of money spent on highways is not a function of our national transportation needs, but instead is one of the revenue produced by the trust fund. To mass transit interests this is unacceptable.

In fact, from their viewpoint the federal government's role has heretofore been a negative one since it has served to substantially exacerbate the problem of resource allocation. By subsidizing the automobile, expensive parking and congestion problems have resulted. Also, freeway construction has blighted our cities and has occupied very costly land space, resulting in a drop in municipal tax bases. Subsidizing the automobile is also indirectly discriminatory, for it discriminates against the poor, the young, the old, and the physically incapacitated. All of this, according to transit advocates, adds up to a severe misallocation of resources.

Highway Interests

Highway interests contend that they too are very much interested in a balanced transportation system. Increasing the federal government's role in mass transit, however, should not mean fewer funds for highways. It is not a transit versus automobile issue. The goal, they claim, is to increase the funding of both mass transit and highways to provide a more efficient system.

Rather than spreading anti-highway propaganda, transit proponents should see the need for continued highway spending.

To attack the highway program, they argue, is to ignore the facts. An efficient highway network is critical in meeting the bulk of our urban transportation needs. The argument that there are too many cars in our cities is fallacious. Congestion in our cities is caused, not by too many cars, but by insufficient highway and parking facilities. In regard to the accusation that freeway construction has blighted cities, highway interests retort that, to the contrary, freeways have made significant contributions to their renewal and in so doing have served to increase municipal tax revenues. Finally, highway proponents point to the fact that people prefer the automobile to other modes of travel and increasingly demonstrate this preference. This, along with increased population, is justification enough for an expanding highway program.

BART — THE BEGINNING OR THE END?

When the Bay Area Rapid Transit System (BART) was first conceived, it was looked upon as a model of rail rapid transit that would set a standard for future systems in other metropolitan areas. The project began in 1962 when three California counties — San Francisco, Alameda, and Contra Costra — passed a $792 million bond issue for BART's construction, the largest bond issue ever undertaken for an urban transportation system. In addition to the bond issue, funds were received from the state of California and the federal government. BART was expected to cover operating expenses and additional capital costs from operating revenues. Consisting of 71 miles of track, 16 miles of subway tunnels, and a 4-mile tube under San Francisco Bay, the system was designed to handle 260,000 passengers a day at an average speed of 50 miles per hour. When fully operational, BART was to relieve automobile congestion and to integrate the Bay area by providing a regional transit system that could handle the projected large increase in commuters.

BART was completed in 1974 at a cost of $1.6 billion. But rather than leading rapid transit into an era of sleek, silent, and computerized rail service, it appears to be leading some cities toward an increased emphasis on improved bus service and other cities to a revival of trolley service. BART, in the eyes of many transit critics, has been an enormously expensive failure.

Operating costs for the system have skyrocketed, largely because of unexpected high payroll and power costs. Maintenance costs per car in the initial years of service were approximately double what was anticipated as many of the computerized trains had to be taken out of service because of brake and door malfunctions, erratic speed control, and loss of automatic power. In its first year of service, BART's operational deficit was approximately $40 million, despite enacting a .5 percent increase in the sales tax within the three counties. At present BART pays for only about 33 percent of its operating costs out of the fare box, far short of the 100 percent predicted at the outset. The remainder of its revenue is from taxpayers in the form of federal subsidies and local tax collections.

In addition to its failure to become self-supporting, BART has not met ridership expectations. Although the system was designed to accommodate 260,000 passengers a day, BART has been carrying approximately 135,000 per day and at an average speed of 38 miles per hour, not the 50 miles per hour projected. Although difficult to calculate with precision, several estimates indicate that as much as 50 percent of BART's ridership can be attributed to individuals who formerly traveled by bus to and from San Francisco. As a result, BART has not significantly reduced traffic congestion but has replaced bus service at very high costs.

Because of BART's problems, transit experts seriously doubt the wisdom of constructing limited-access rail lines in the foreseeable future. BART, critics contend, reinforces what was already known in the transit industry — heavy fixed rail systems are too costly and lack sufficient ease of accessibility to commuters. As long as commuters must use the automobile to drive to rail stations, many find it faster and less troublesome to drive directly to the city. If a system such as BART were to construct a large number of outlying routes and stations, train speeds would be reduced and construction costs increased to prohibitive levels. It would, in effect, create more problems than it would solve.

If BART is a multi-billion dollar mistake, it may be joined by others. Both Washington, D.C., and Atlanta are constructing rail transit systems with sizable federal aid. Recent estimates of Washington's completed subway system hover around $5 billion, while Atlanta's combination rail-bus system approaches the $3 billion figure. In New York, a two-block extension of an existing subway line will cost at least $155 million, or about $126,000 per foot. Cities such as Baltimore, Miami, Honolulu, and Detroit are either planning new rail systems or presently constructing them. Unlike BART, however, these rail lines are short and some are light rail. Other cities, including Seattle, St. Louis, and Los Angeles, have dropped their plans for rail transit systems altogether.

Cities now appear to be allocating their resources to more flexible modes of transit, such as buses and trolley lines. With new and better buses, expanded service, and reduced fares, many transit systems are experiencing steady increases in bus ridership. Also, for the first time since 1952, trolley cars are being manufactured in the United States. New cars have been put into service on existing lines in Boston and San Francisco, while Pittsburgh is planning to revamp its existing trolley system and Buffalo plans to construct an entirely new trolley line. The new light rail lines, or trolley lines, will operate on their own right-of-way instead of sharing the streets with automobiles and trucks.

Recent transit gains in ridership and those expected in the future entail increased costs, not only to the rider of transit but even more so to the taxpayer. The view that transit should be self-sufficient from revenues collected from the fare box is now held only by the minority. Today the attitude appears to be that mass transit should be considered a public utility that requires public financing.

CONCLUSION

It has become apparent that mass transit is a very costly public good for nearly all cities. Recognizing that economic costs may well exceed benefits from the construction of new and flamboyant heavy rail systems, most communities are scaling down their transit plans and are looking to simpler, less expensive, and probably more efficient forms of transit, such as buses and light rail trolleys. Whether the transit aspirations of many of our cities ever get off the drawing board will depend in large part on financing from the federal government.

For cities to implement their plans, the federal government has to provide massive sums of money in a manner in which uncertainty is eliminated. The unpredictability of funding by the appropriation method does not provide assurance at the local level that federal funds will continue flowing in the future. A better balance must be struck between mass transit funding and highway funding if cities are to provide their citizens with balanced transportation systems. The Carter Administration is on record as supporting increased federal assistance for mass transit, including options for local authorities to use federal funds either for capital improvements or for operating expenses, depending on need. Should such funding materialize, communities should have greater flexibility in utilizing federal aid.

Most experts believe that since urban transportation is a local problem, transit systems should, whenever possible, utilize local funds for the construction and operation of their systems. If local funding is inadequate, then federal funds should be sought to guarantee completion of worthwhile projects or to help cover operating costs of those already completed.

In the meantime, automobiles will continue to congest our city streets in increasing numbers. As costly as such traffic is to urban residents, it remains to be seen whether improved mass transit will diminish to any great extent America's love for the automobile.

MAJOR ISSUES

1. Should automobiles be penalized for entering and leaving major cities during peak hours?
2. Do you believe the public can be best served by privately owned or publicly owned mass transit systems?
3. In the case of those cities which have publicly owned transit systems, should transit fares be subsidized through increased taxes to lower fares and increase ridership?
4. Do you believe the federal government will eventually own or control mass transit systems throughout the U.S.?

SUBISSUES

1. Do you believe that continued urban sprawl will undermine the attempts to rejuvenate mass transit?
2. Should the federal government set up a mass transit trust fund similar to the highway trust fund?
3. Do you think that efficient mass transit systems would lessen the demand on

the part of households for a second or third car?

4. What is the present state of mass transit in your community?

SELECTED READINGS

Bendixson, Terence. *Without Wheels: Alternatives to the Private Car*. Bloomington: Indiana University Press, 1975.

Catanese, Anthony. *Urban Transportation Policy: New Perspectives*. Lexington, Massachusetts: Lexington Books, 1976.

Hilton, George Woodman. *Federal Transit Subsidies*. Washington: American Enterprise Institute, 1974.

Lansing, John B. *Urban Transportation*. U.S. Department of Transportation, Bureau of Public Roads. Ann Arbor: Survey Research Center, University of Michigan, 1970.

Owen, Wilfred. *Transportation For Cities: The Role of Federal Policy*. Washington: Brookings Institute, 1976.

——————. *Urban Transportation*. Washington: Brookings Institution, 1972.

Pikarsky, Milton, and Daphne Christensen. *Urban Transportation Policy and Management*. Lexington, Massachusetts: Lexington Books, 1976.

Reische, Diana L. *Local Transit*. H. W. Wilson, 1970.

Smerk, George M. *Urban Transportation: A Dozen Years of Federal Policy*. Bloomington: Indiana University Press, 1976.

Williams, Ernest W., Jr. *Future of American Transportation*. Englewood Cliffs, New Jersey: Prentice-Hall, Inc., 1971.

Revenue Sharing — An 12 Alternative To Going Broke?

Federal revenue sharing with states and localities came into being with the passage of the controversial State and Local Fiscal Assistance Act of 1972, popularly known as the Revenue Sharing Act. What is revenue sharing? How does revenue sharing work? Why is there a need for revenue sharing? How does it differ from other federal grant programs? How does revenue sharing affect the budgets of federal, state, and local governments? What are the purported advantages and disadvantages of revenue sharing? These aspects of federal revenue sharing, as well as others, will be examined in the course of the discussion. But prior to analyzing revenue sharing, a basic understanding of the present fiscal problems of state and local governments must be presented, as well as the role of the federal government in helping to alleviate these problems. Then, hopefully, the discussion of revenue sharing will take on deeper significance to the reader.

STATE AND LOCAL FINANCIAL PROBLEMS

Many state and local governments are presently so hard pressed to pay expenses that in recent years some have been unable to meet their debt obligations and have approached bankruptcy. In 1975, for example, New York City had to increase taxes, reduce employment on city payrolls, and appeal to both the state and federal governments for additional financial assistance to reduce a staggering $641 million deficit for 1975–1976. The causes of such severe financial pressures are many. Basically, however, the unifying element accounting for this financial dilemma is the fact that the demand for city and state public services has been growing more rapidly than the financial ability of these governments to supply them.

Expenditures

Prior to the Great Depression, the greatest percentage of federal government expenditures was related to national defense, the care of war veterans, and the payment of interest on the debts of World War I. Relatively little was expended on domestic public services. Today a large share of the federal budget is still used for purposes of defense, but large allocations are now also made for human and physical resources throughout the nation.

The state government's functional role increased significantly with the rapid growth of automobile usage after 1900. This new mode of transportation meant that an entire system of roads and highways had to be constructed and maintained between cities. It was the state governments that assumed the bulk of these tasks. Thus, in addition to maintaining courts, a small executive force, and a legislative body, states began to collect revenues to finance their expanded functions. The present functions of state governments include providing for and maintaining educational institutions, hospitals, prisons, courts, highways, and other services of this sort.

Local governments, including cities, towns, counties, and various other districts, have had as their primary functions the construction and maintenance of streets, public schools, police and fire departments, and health and welfare facilities, as well as a host of other services. As late as 1932, local government expenses exceeded those of the federal government. Today, however, federal expenditures are nearly twice as great as expenditures of local governments.

In recent decades, expenditures at all levels of government have increased markedly. Except for national defense and social welfare payments of the federal government, the big increases have occurred at the state and local levels. Table 12-1 presents the expenditures of federal, state, and local governments for selected years between 1950 and 1975. State expenditures have increased some 845 percent while local expenditures have risen by 847 percent during the period. The corresponding figure for the federal government is 593 percent. State and local government expenditures in 1975 were recorded at $265 billion. The dramatic rise in government spending is also evident when the figures are examined on a per capita basis.

Table 12-1

EXPENDITURES OF FEDERAL, STATE, AND LOCAL GOVERNMENTS, 1950–1975 (In Billions of Dollars)

	All Governments	Federal	State and Local			Per Capita (Dollars)		
			Total	State	Local	Total	Federal	State and Local
1950	70	42	28	11	17	400	250	150
1955	111	70	40	14	26	592	388	204
1960	151	90	61	22	39	714	426	288
1965	206	119	86	31	55	896	511	385
1970	333	185	148	56	92	1,353	707	646
1975	556	291	265	104	161	2,610	1,366	1,244

SOURCE: *Statistical Abstract of the United States*, 1977, p. 276.

Increases in state and local expenditures over the past few decades can be traced to several major factors. One of the main reasons for increased government expenditures is population. It is not merely a problem of sheer numbers; it is also related to the changing characteristics of the nation's population. Age and mobility factors, for example, have exerted great fiscal pressure on community budgets.

Throughout much of the period, the age groups requiring costly public services increased the fastest. Although the total population increased some 41 percent between 1950 and 1976, school-aged population increased 62 percent and the number of persons 65 years of age and over increased by 85 percent. A youthful population creates pressures for more schools and teachers, while the aged require additional costly services, many of which would be classified under the heading of welfare. Because of declining birth rates, the demand pressures caused by the public service needs of the young have eased appreciably in more recent years. However, since the number of elderly persons is expected to increase, both in absolute terms and as a percentage of total population, the costs of providing needed specialized services for this group will continue to climb.

In addition to the age factor, our nation's population has become more and more mobile. A general migration of families from the farm to the city has been taking place for generations, resulting in increased demands for public services. The problem has been compounded in recent decades by urban sprawl. As new communities develop outside the boundaries of older cities, many public services have to be duplicated, often at a very high cost per capita. Since it is the more affluent families that are leaving the city, the poor and aged are left behind in need of costly services. But suburbanites continue to rely on costly services from the city since they generally maintain employment within the city. Thus, during the daylight hours suburbanites demand police protection, parking facilities, efficient traffic flow, and other services, but often contribute little if any tax revenues to support such services.

A second factor accounting for increased spending is affluence itself. There tends to be a direct relationship between personal income and the scope and number of government activities. As average wealth increases, there is a greater ability and inclination on the part of the population to finance better schools, better equipped hospitals, better police and fire departments, and better roads. Thus, in addition to providing more services, the quality of government services has generally been on the rise.

Another major factor causing increased public expenditures is inflation. Governments, because such a large share of their income is spent on services, are more susceptible to inflation's confiscatory nature than many of our nation's manufacturers. Service industries are hit in aggravated form by inflation since productivity increases in those industries have generally lagged far behind wage hikes. The growing militancy among government employees, along with increased unionization, has also pushed wages up at a faster rate. Historically the pay of municipal workers tended to lag in periods of rapid wage increases in industry. But this lag has diminished and, in some cases, has all but disappeared. In addition to expenditures for services, governments are faced with inflationary prices on purchases of materials and supplies as well.

A final factor deserving mention is the continued funding of outdated programs. Many municipal governments are particularly guilty of this. While they continue to finance programs that should be discarded on a cost-benefit basis, new public services also continue to be provided annually. Attempts to terminate an outdated service are usually met with strong resistance by those few who benefit from it, despite an overwhelming cost to the community as a whole.

Revenues

The failure of state and local revenues to keep pace with the increased demands for public service is linked to the state and local governments' sources of revenue. The federal government relies on a progressive income tax to the extent that about 43 percent of federal budget receipts are derived from this source. Based on the ability-to-pay principle of taxation, the progressive personal income tax is thought to be the most equitable and efficient source of personal taxation. State and local governments are restricted in their use of this tax, however, because it has been largely preempted by the federal government since 1913. Today the federal government collects about 83 percent of the personal income taxes paid in this country. From a budgetary point of view the progressive personal income tax of the federal government produces tax revenues at a faster rate than the growth of the economy. For every 1 percent increase in GNP, federal revenues tend to increase by 1.5 percent.[1] Since increases in federal expenditures tend to be directly related to the economic growth (during peacetime), they can be financed largely from the increased revenues stemming from the progressivity of present taxes without resorting to higher tax rates or additional taxes.

State and local governments are not as fortunate. They rely heavily on sales, gross receipts, customs, and property taxes for the dominant share of their revenues. Sales, gross receipts, and customs taxes account for about 53 percent of state tax revenues, whereas property taxes account for nearly 81 percent of all local tax funds. These taxes are regressive and respond more sluggishly to economic growth. At constant rates, state and local tax revenues rise little in proportion to GNP, while the rate of growth in state and local expenditures is approximately 1.3 times greater than the GNP growth rate. Table 12-2 depicts revenues of federal, state, and local governments for selected years from 1950 to 1975. Revenues flowing to state governments totaled $117 billion in 1975, an increase of over 963 percent since 1950, while the revenues for local governments had risen to $98 billion, a 717 percent increase over the period. Federal revenues totaled $304 billion in 1975 and comprised almost 59 percent of all government revenues. On a percentage basis, federal receipts have increased over 591 percent since 1950.

[1]"Revenue Sharing: What It Might Mean," *Monthly Revenue* (Atlanta: Federal Reserve Bank of Atlanta, 1970), p. 50.

Table 12-2

REVENUE OF FEDERAL, STATE, AND LOCAL GOVERNMENTS, 1950–1975 (In Billions of Dollars)

| | All Governments | Federal | State and Local | | | Per Capita (Dollars) | | |
			Total	State	Local	Total	Federal	State and Local
1950	67	44	23	11	12	386	264	121
1955	106	72	34	17	18	564	395	169
1960	153	100	53	26	27	726	484	242
1965	203	126	77	39	38	876	551	325
1970	334	206	128	69	60	1.341	805	536
1975	519	304	215	117	98	2,427	1,426	1,001

SOURCE: *Statistical Abstract of the United States*, 1977, p. 276.

Debt

In recent years many states have adopted new taxes and increased rates on old taxes. Several large cities have adopted municipal income and sales taxes. But as the figures contained in Table 12-3 indicate, the gap is widening between expenditures and receipts, despite increased taxes. Since 1950, state debt has increased 1,340 percent, local debt 684 percent, and federal debt 112 percent. On a per capita basis, state and local government debt alone stood at $1,038 in 1975.

Table 12-3

OUTSTANDING DEBT OF FEDERAL, STATE, AND LOCAL GOVERNMENTS, 1950–1975 (In Billions of Dollars)

| | All Governments | Federal | State and Local | | | Per Capita (Dollars) | | |
			Total	State	Local	Total	Federal	State and Local
1950	281	257	24	5	19	1,856	1,697	159
1955	319	274	44	11	33	1,928	1,660	268
1960	356	286	70	19	51	1,979	1,591	389
1965	417	317	99	27	72	2,150	1,637	513
1970	514	371	144	42	102	2,531	1,825	706
1975	765	544	221	72	149	3,591	2,553	1,038

SOURCE: *Statistical Abstract of the United States*, 1977, p. 276.

The burden of higher taxes to finance the debt has become a heavy one. The regressive nature of state and local taxes exacts a stiff penalty on taxpayers of middle and lower incomes. A loud cry for tax relief is being heard throughout the country. Yet the demand for costly public services continues upward. Thus, leaders of state and local governments are faced with a dilemma. On the one hand, they must raise taxes or cut services to avoid bankruptcy. On the other, taxpayers are demanding expanded public services at lower cost. To at least narrow the gap between expenditures and receipts, state and local governments have turned to the federal government. But before examining the nature of present federal assistance, a short digression into the historical aspects of federal assistance to state and local governments may prove fruitful.

HISTORY OF FEDERAL AID TO STATES

State and local governments have received financial assistance from the federal government since the beginning of the nineteenth century. The first recorded instance in which federal revenue was shared with the states dates back to 1802. In that year Congress passed a law providing that 5 percent of the proceeds derived from the sale of public lands in the new state of Ohio were to be allocated to the construction of roads in that state. Later, Congress applied this 5 percent principle to all states in which public lands were sold. There were no reporting requirements by states receiving such funds, but usually some informal understanding existed as to their use.

In 1836 Congress endorsed a type of revenue sharing in the form of general purpose grants when it voted to distribute surplus funds to the states. Although authorization was given for the distribution of $37.5 million, only $28 million was granted. The states utilized these funds for a variety of purposes, including repayment of local debt, capitalizing state banks, and financing public works. However, this program met with only limited success. With the onset of the 1838 recession, both the surplus and the grants disappeared.

With the Civil War, Congress once again became favorably disposed to distribute federal grants to the states. In 1862 Congress passed the Morrill Act. This act provided for the allocation of public lands to states for the purpose of establishing land-grant, agricultural colleges. Funds stemming from the Morrill Act were not only specific in nature but conditional as well. The conditions spelled out by the federal government were few but noteworthy. Land-grant colleges were required to submit annual reports to Congress, and state governors were obligated to inform Congress as to how the funds were being distributed. Later, in 1890, a second Morrill Act was passed authorizing annual cash payments for land-grant colleges. These funds could be used to pay instructors once the states had constructed the colleges. In this sense, these grants were the forerunners of latter-day matching grants.

In 1887 the Hatch Act authorized $15,000 a year for each state to operate an agricultural research station, and in 1911 the Weeks Act provided grants for forest fire protection. The Weeks Act is significant, however, because it imposed tighter restrictions on the use of grant funds. To receive grant funds, state plans had to be approved in advance by the federal government and once underway, projects were to be under close federal supervision.

Federal assistance totaled about one percent of state and local general revenues at the time the Weeks Act was passed. In retrospect, federal grants were relatively modest until the 1930s, when the financial conditions of states and localities became desperate. In 1932 a new and much stronger involvement began. At that time the New Deal Policy of President Roosevelt began employing the federal budget as a countercyclical device to combat the serious depression already underway. For this purpose money was turned over to states and municipalities on an emergency basis to construct physical facilities, such as schools, parks, and stadiums. These funds were only available on a temporary basis, however, for once prosperity was restored, these emergency funds were withdrawn. The peak year for this federal aid was 1939, when nearly $3 billion flowed from the federal treasury to lower governments. With the outbreak of World War II, these grants diminished markedly.

The nature and extent of these grants was unprecedented. But in addition to emergency grants, the Roosevelt Administration laid the foundation for the vast number of federal grant programs that were to follow when the Social Security Act of 1935 was passed. Amended many times over, the Social Security Act was joined by a host of new specific grant programs after World War II. In subsequent years specific grant programs were initiated in such areas as health and welfare, commerce and transportation, education and manpower, and housing and community development.

CURRENT FEDERAL GRANTS TO STATES AND LOCALITIES

The extent to which federal grant expenditures provide financial assistance to state and local governments can be ascertained from the information presented in Table 12-4. In 1977, federal grant funds to state and local governments approximated $70 billion.

Table 12-4 indicates that the four largest functional categories of federal grant expenditures to state and local governments account for 70 percent of the federal allocations. Education, employment, training and social services grants constitute the largest category, followed by income security, health, and revenue sharing and general assistance grants.

Because of the multiplicity and resulting overlap of federal aid programs, it is difficult to calculate the exact number of these programs. Not withstanding statistical variances, however, one thing has become quite clear — what began as several relatively inexpensive and clearly defined programs has generated a bureaucratic Goliath. This unintended result has engendered strong dissatisfaction on the part of the recipients of federal grant funds. Such dissatisfaction is based on functional and philosophical grounds.

One major source of unrest lies in the manner in which specific grant funds are distributed. Concern is expressed over the long and costly delays in receiving federal approval of various state and local projects, along with the costly administrative requirements that must be satisfied as part of routine procedure. Once approved, the danger persists that anticipated funds might

Table 12-4

FEDERAL AID TO STATE AND LOCAL GOVERNMENTS, BY FUNCTION, 1977 (estimated)

Function	Amount (Millions of Dollars)	Share (%)
Agriculture	349	0.2
Commerce and Transportation	8,362	11.9
Community and Regional Development	5,846	8.3
Education, Employment, Training and Social Services	15,485	22.0
Health	12,402	17.6
Income Security	12,804	18.2
Law Enforcement and Justice	716	1.0
Natural Resources, Environment and Energy	5,222	7.4
Revenue Sharing and General Assistance	8,938	12.7
Other[1]	850	0.4
Total	70,974	100.0[2]

SOURCE: *Statistical Abstract of the United States*, 1977, p. 284.

[1]Includes national defense, international affairs, general government, and veterans' benefits and services.
[2]May not add to 100.0 due to rounding.

be withdrawn at any time by Congress. Also, to guarantee their fair share, state and local governments have spent substantial sums of money on "grantsmanship" to insure that they are not only kept abreast of programs for which they might be eligible, but also to insure that they maintain a competitive edge over other state and local governments in attaining grants.

Another source of dissatisfaction is the belief on the part of state and local leaders that the federal government has rapidly expanded its powers into problem areas which are essentially regional and local in character. Although recognizing the need for federal assistance, states and localities resent their lack of control over grant funds due to the standards, regulations, and guidelines imposed by the federal government. This is particularly irritating to state and local governments because in many instances federal funds are too narrowly restricted to benefit their needs. In some cases, no federal funds are available for high priority purposes. Because states and localities lack the freedom and flexibility to utilize federal funds effectively, critics contend that lower levels of government are merely becoming the administrative instruments of the federal government in local affairs.

Thus, there has been a growing feeling that state and local governments are in need of federal assistance but of a different sort. As a result, federal, state, and local governments have been seeking viable alternatives to the existing system. From the various schemes suggested as possible solutions, a program of revenue sharing was implemented in fiscal 1973.

REVENUE SHARING

Revenue sharing is a program which promises far-reaching reforms in the area of intergovernmental finance. General revenue sharing involves two essential characteristics. First, a specified portion of federal revenues is distributed to lower levels of government. Second, these revenues flow from the federal government to state and local governments with little or no restrictions on their use. The most obvious difference between revenue sharing and a system of specific federal grants is that the former is unrestricted while the latter has been earmarked for particular projects or purposes.

As envisioned, revenue sharing is an important national policy innovation for two reasons. First, it serves as a fiscal tool for dealing with the fundamental imbalance between needs and resources among the various levels of government; and second, it serves as a political instrument for decentralizing the intergovernmental fiscal policies of the federal government and delegating more administrative control to lower levels of government. Revenue sharing, then, is a program which constitutes a marked change from traditional fiscal policy.

An ongoing interest in revenue sharing has been prevalent for the past 20 years. Although primarily discussed in academic circles in the early 1950s, revenue sharing was first introduced in Congress by former Congressman Melvin Laird in 1958. But the person who is credited with bringing the concept of revenue sharing to the public's attention is the former Chairman of the President's Council of Economic Advisers, Walter Heller. His proposal was prompted not only by the desire to alleviate the financial distress of state and local governments but also to utilize most effectively the projected fiscal dividend accruing to the federal government in subsequent years. Heller, looking beyond the rising costs of Vietnam and large budget deficits, visualized budget surpluses due to the increased revenues produced by a growing economy at existing federal tax rates. Unless the federal government injected these surplus funds back into the economy, a fiscal drag might result. Hence, Heller proposed that revenue sharing be adopted as a propitious use for these excess funds.

Heller's revenue sharing proposal did not receive serious attention until the spring of 1964, but because of chronic deficits in the federal budget and the historic tax cuts enacted at that time, revenue sharing was temporarily shelved. Soon thereafter, revenue sharing was given added impetus when it was embraced by both Presidental candidates in the 1964 election. Shortly after the election, President Johnson, at the urging of Heller, appointed a task force comprised of individuals from government and business to study alternatives to the prevailing system. Although the recommendations made in the task force's formal report were never publicly disclosed by the Johnson Administration, the basic elements of the report were later published by the press.

The task force, after considering various alternatives, came out in favor of revenue sharing. The revenue sharing plan of the committee was a modified version of Heller's original thoughts on the matter. The plan contained the following features:

1. Automatic allocation of funds. Shared funds would be allocated on the basis of a percentage of personal taxable income and distributed automatically to states and localities without need for annual Congressional appropriations.
2. Unrestricted nature of grants. No restrictions would be made as to how these funds could be used, except that they could not be used for highway expenditures.
3. Balanced distribution formula. Allocated funds would be distributed according to population, tax revenues, and need.
4. Pass-through to local governments. Funds would pass from state governments down to local governments.

The task force proposed that a federal revenue sharing program along the lines of their proposal be instituted in addition to already existing federal conditional grant programs. Despite its lack of public endorsement by the Johnson Administration, the plan served to stimulate additional interest in the subject. Shortly thereafter, the nation's Republican governors published a policy paper calling for enactment of the plan. By 1968 both presidential party platforms contained revenue sharing proposals.

Soon after his inauguration, President Nixon called for action on federal revenue sharing with the states. A committee was designated under the leadership of Arthur F. Burns, who at that time was serving as Counselor to the President. The committee recommended that the Administration proceed with a plan for revenue sharing. The Nixon Administration's proposal for revenue sharing was sent to Congress in 1969, where the Nixon Plan, along with several other major revenue sharing plans, received careful scrutiny.

THE ARGUMENTS FOR AND AGAINST REVENUE SHARING

The concept of revenue sharing did not receive universal acceptance in Congress. Many members of Congress believed that revenue sharing would fall far short of its objectives. The controversy presented here is concerned with the concept of revenue sharing in general and not with the particulars of the State and Local Fiscal Assistance Act of 1972. Controversy pertaining to the Act itself is presented in a subsequent section of this chapter.

State and Local Finances

Proponents of revenue sharing maintained that federal assistance was needed to relieve the financial hardships of state and local governments. It is the major, heavily populated, and highly urbanized states that are affected most. Because the pressures on these areas call for increasing expenditures in costly governmental services, new sources of revenue will be required. But future state and local revenues will not be adequate to close their respective fiscal gaps. Advocates of revenue sharing cited the inability of growth revenues derived from sales, gross receipts, and property taxes to keep pace with expenses, as well as the apparent resolute stand on the part of taxpayers throughout the nation to resist higher taxes. Elected officials are very sensitive to this attitude on the part of taxpayers and, because of political realities, are not prone to stump their territory justifying the need for tax increases. In addition, these leaders fear that higher taxes may cause existing industry to leave the area and discourage new industry from entering.

Critics, however, claimed that the assumption that state and local governments were in dire financial straits was an exaggerated one. Admittedly, a number of state and local governments were experiencing serious financial difficulties, but it was likely that fiscal pressure on states and localities would be growing somewhat more slowly in the near future than had been the case in the recent past. Critics projected a decline in overall expenditure growth by noting several factors. Highway expenditures were not likely to rise at the rate they did in the last 20 years. A declining birth rate would lead to a much slower expansion in school expenditures on the part of state and local governments. Finally, the tremendous stockpile of general needs stemming from both the Great Depression and World War II had been largely fulfilled.

On the revenue side, critics asserted that the projected growth of state and local income was underestimated. Not enough emphasis was given to the point that state and local taxes were capable of producing rapidly rising revenues. In fact, revenues are likely to increase faster than expenditures during the current decade.

Opponents of revenue sharing argued, too, that emphasis on the inability of state and local governments to finance increased public services was somewhat misleading. Opponents contended that in many states and communities voters were unwilling to support a level of service determined by external standards or by a small segment of the population. If the residents of a particular area in fact want more or better public services, however, they should be willing to pay a price reflecting the cost of the scarce resources needed to provide such services. In this sense, the demand for public goods should be measured on the same basis as the demand for private goods.

Fiscal Drag

Advocates of revenue sharing pointed to the possibility that surpluses would accrue in the federal budget as revenues rose faster than expenditures. A growth dividend of some $15 to $17 billion per year was likely to result from the progressivity of the personal income tax. The contention was made, therefore, that the effect of the growth dividend would act as a fiscal drag on the economy and would bring about deflation unless these surplus funds were meaningfully distributed throughout the economy. The most sensible solution, it was argued, was to share at least a portion of these funds with the states. In this manner, revenue sharing would serve to eliminate the fiscal drag, while at the same time lessening the financial burdens of state and local governments.

Opponents took issue with the position that a surplus budget automatically results in a fiscal drag on the economy. This would be true, of course, if the government allowed these surpluses to remain idle, causing a net decrease in aggregate demand. But the use of the budget as an economic stabilizer indicates that surpluses should be used to retire the national debt. If the economy is in a recession, repayment of the debt could give the economy a boost by lowering interest rates and promoting capital investment. Depending upon the marginal propensity to consume of bondholders, it also could stimulate consumer spending. But the point being made is that budget surpluses do not necessarily imply a fiscal drag.

An even more basic argument concerned the assumption that budget surpluses were likely to occur in the near future. Since deficits had been recorded in all but 13 of the past 45 years, opponents contended that only the naive would propose federal programs on the basis of federal surpluses. It would be difficult, indeed, to share in the extra revenue when there was none.

Decentralization

Another asserted advantage of revenue sharing was that it would diminish the ever-growing expansion of federal influence into what are essentially state and local problems. Existing federal grant programs were created because of the financial inability of state and local governments to solve these problems. Hence, the federal government has become involved in problems which are far from national in scope, such as mass transit, housing, education, and urban renewal. With revenue sharing, state and local problems can be handled at the appropriate governmental level without constantly depending upon help from Washington.

But opponents felt that revenue sharing would not lighten the heavy hand of Washington in state and local matters. It was very difficult to accept the notion that federal control would somehow disappear. Congress might be in an even more controlling position. By threatening to enact changes in the revenue sharing program, Congress could effectively coerce state and local governments to see things as Washington does. Soon, they argued, states and localities could realize that this steady stream of unrestricted funds was in danger of no longer being either steady or unrestricted.

Efficiency

An often mentioned claim of revenue sharing was that it would allow for an efficient utilization of resources. States and localities would be free to spend federal funds according to what they deemed to be important priorities. With specific grant programs, federal funds are spent on things that Washington wants and in the way Washington orders. Consequently, states and localities undertake programs which for them might be of very low priority. Since funds may not be available for programs of great importance to particular state and local governments, obtaining funds for low priority purposes is considered better than no funds at all. Moreover, because the categories for which federal grant money is given are often very narrow, the result is a very rigid funding policy. The restricted nature of individual grant programs has led to a proliferation of such programs with little concern as to how new programs coordinate with existing ones.

Also, the critical element of uncertainty associated with federal funding is eliminated by revenue sharing. Each year state and local government units must concern themselves with Congressional appropriations that can drastically alter already existing plans. Revenue sharing, with a fund increasing steadily and predictably, makes for more intelligent long-range planning.

Critics were not at all convinced that revenue sharing would lead to a more efficient allocation of resources. Nothing in revenue sharing guaranteed that state and local governments, given a free hand, would allocate funds more wisely. Doubts stemmed largely from the fact that the collection authority (the federal government) and the spending authority (state and local governments) were separate entities under revenue sharing. Since states and localities were not directly responsible to taxpayers for the collection of federal taxes, they would be less likely to exercise prudence in spending the shared revenue. When one considers the fact that state and local governments have not been models of efficiency to begin with, this fact is noteworthy.

Equity

Under a system of specific federal grants to states and localities, great inequalities exist in terms of the amounts collected from states via the federal personal income tax and the amounts returned to states in the form of federal grants. Thus, the system of federal grants has unfortunate redistribution effects. Supporters of revenue sharing argued that many heavily populated states contribute on a per capita basis far more to the federal government in personal income tax than sparsely populated states, yet in return receive lower per capita grant funds. Revenue sharing diminishes these inequities by allowing proportionately more federal money to those states whose citizens shoulder a heavier tax load. This argument, advocates believed, was even stronger when a "need" factor was included. (In the State and Local Fiscal Assistance Act of 1972, relative income was a basis for recognizing needs.)

Opponents held that revenue sharing was not an equitable method of redistributing income. Distributing revenue on the basis of need merely involves a transfer of funds from a state with a high per capita income to a state with a low per capita income. A system based upon tax effort redistributes funds from states with a low tax effort to states with a high tax effort. But states aren't rich or poor; people are, and both rich and poor people live in states having both high and low per capita income.

THE STATE AND LOCAL FISCAL ASSISTANCE ACT OF 1972

After examining the merits and drawbacks of the various revenue sharing proposals, as well as alternatives to revenue sharing, Congress made revenue sharing a reality with the passage of the State and Local Fiscal Assistance Act of 1972. The Act allocated over $30.1 billion to some 38,000 state and local government units for a 5-year period, retroactive to January 1, 1972. During calendar year 1972, $5.3 billion was expended under this program. State governments received one third of the total and local governments (cities, counties, villages, and townships) received a two-thirds share. Revenue sharing funds are received by state and local governments in addition to those federal funds received for specific purposes or projects.

Use of Funds

State governments were free to utilize their portion of the shared revenue as they so choose with no strings attached. Local governments, however, were somewhat restricted in their use of shared revenue. Funds received by units of local governments could be used only for "priority" expenditures. Included under priority expenditures were:

1. Ordinary and necessary maintenance and operating expenses for (a) public safety, including law enforcement, fire protection, and building code enforcement; (b) environmental protection, including sewage disposal, sanitation, and pollution abatement; (c) public transportation, including mass transit systems, and streets and roads; (d) health; (e) recreation; (f) libraries; (g) social services for both the poor and aged; and (h) financial administration.
2. Ordinary and necessary capital expenditures authorized by law.

Revenue sharing funds could not be used for education and welfare by local governments because they already received billions of dollars from the federal government for these purposes. Also, no state or local governmental unit could use, either directly or indirectly, any part of the revenue sharing funds it received as matching funds in obtaining financial support from the federal government.

Distribution of Revenue Sharing Funds

The means whereby funds are allocated to states and localities is a somewhat complicated process. A given local government's share is calculated by multiplying the population of the local government by the general tax effort of the local government, which is then multiplied by a relative income factor. The resulting product is then compared to the sum of the products for all other local governments within that state and funds are then allocated accordingly. It should be noted that the relative income factor contained in the formula is intended to be utilized as a method of meeting "needs" within the localities.

The state's portion of revenue sharing funds can be determined by either of two methods, depending on which method produces the most revenue. The first method is similar to the one utilized for determining a local government's share. This method multiplies the population of the state by its general tax effort, then multiplies this product by the relative income factor for the state (which measures the "needs" of the individual states), and then compares the resulting product with the sums of the products of other states. Funds are then allocated accordingly.

The second method includes five factors. For example, in 1972 the amount allocated to a state was the amount to which that state would be entitled when:

1. One third of $3.5 billion was allocated among states solely on the basis of population.
2. One third of $3.5 billion was allocated among states on the basis of urbanized population.
3. One third of $3.5 billion was allocated among states on the basis of population inversely weighted for per capita income.
4. One half of $1.8 billion was allocated among states on the basis of income tax collections.
5. One half of $1.8 billion was allocated among states on the basis of general tax effort.

Administration

Revenue sharing funds are administered by means of newly created trust funds at all levels of government. Each state and local government established a trust fund for deposit of revenue sharing funds received, and they must account for this money apart from other funds. The federal government's revenue sharing trust fund is administered by the Office of Revenue Sharing within the United States Department of the Treasury. State and local governments must file annual reports with the Secretary of the Treasury. These reports must indicate anticipated expenditures, as well as funds already disbursed or earmarked.

STATE AND LOCAL FISCAL ASSISTANCE ACT OF 1976

To the surprise of no one, the general revenue sharing program was extended beyond the 1976 termination date by the State and Local Fiscal Assistance Act of 1976. With the strong backing of state and local government officials, the program was continued until September 30, 1980. The new funding level was set at $25.5 billion for the period. On an annual basis, this sum provides shared revenue of some $6.375 billion per year, which amounts to an annual increase of $350 million over the 1972 allotment. It is this aspect of the new law which state and local officials found most disappointing. The slight increase over the funding provided by the 1972 Act is not sufficient to keep pace with rising cost pressures experienced by the public sector. If inflation is considered, the new funding levels result in reduced fiscal support since the rising cost of public service programs has eroded the buying power of a nearly constant annual sum of shared revenue. One study estimates that by 1980, the real value of revenue sharing dollars will have declined by as much as 17 percent since the program's inception in 1972.[2]

Less controversial aspects of the Act were the continuance of the basic "no strings" nature of the revenue sharing program as well as the formula utilized to distribute funds. Two minor changes served to increase the flexibility in using revenue sharing funds. The original restriction prohibiting the use of revenue sharing funds for the purpose of matching federal categorical grants was eliminated. Also dropped was the rule which prevented local governments from using revenue sharing funds for non-priority expenditures.

ALLOCATION AMONG STATES

The passage of the State and Local Fiscal Assistance Act of 1976 guarantees the continued flow of shared revenue to state and local governments. Between January 1, 1972, and October 7, 1977, a total of $35.1 billion had been distributed. Table 12-5 on the following page presents the allocation of state and local revenue sharing funds among the fifty states. For the country as a whole, the federal government allocated a per capita average share of $164 over the period. Southern states and sparsely populated states, because of their relatively low income, did surprisingly well in receiving shared revenue. Six states received combined state and local shares of over $200 per capita. These states are Mississippi, South Dakota, New York, Vermont, Louisiana, and Maine. Of these states, only New York can be considered a heavily populated, industrialized state. On the other hand, Ohio ranks 48th in per capita shares and Florida 50th.

USES OF REVENUE SHARING

During the initial five-year program, revenue sharing funds were spent by state and local governments in a variety of ways.[3] Many state and local governments have used revenue sharing funds to reduce the pressure to increase taxes to balance their budgets. For others, revenue sharing has meant maintaining present tax rates while enabling them to bolster existing public services and initiating new ones. Of the recipients, 5 percent of the state and local governments report that they have been able to reduce taxes and 34 percent report that general revenue sharing has enabled them to prevent tax increases.

State and local governments that have opted to utilize revenue sharing funds to increase the quantity and quality of public services have found a large number of programs deserving additional or new financial support. The largest portion of the federal revenue sharing dollar has been used to bolster

[2]Richard P. Nathan and Charles F. Adams, Jr. *Revenue Sharing: The Second Round* (Washington: The Brookings Institution, 1977), p. 171.
[3]Uses of revenue sharing funds presented in *The Budget of the United States Government, Fiscal Year 1978* (Washington: U.S. Government Printing Office, 1978), p. 193.

Table 12-5

FEDERAL REVENUE SHARING FUNDS DISTRIBUTED FROM JANUARY 1, 1972, TO OCTOBER, 1977

	Total (millions)	Per Person[1]		Total (millions)	Per Person[1]
Alabama	$ 582	$159	Montana	$ 135	$179
Alaska	53	139	Nebraska	241	155
Arizona	351	154	Nevada	80	131
Arkansas	366	160	New Hampshire	113	137
California	3,725	173	New Jersey	1,101	150
Colorado	376	145	New Mexico	223	191
Connecticut	451	145	New York	3,935	218
Delaware	107	183	North Carolina	887	162
District of			North Dakota	122	190
Columbia	218	310	Ohio	1,410	132
Florida	1,053	125	Oklahoma	391	141
Georgia	739	148	Oregon	359	154
Hawaii	158	178	Pennsylvania	1,849	156
Idaho	139	167	Rhode Island	155	167
Illinois	1,792	160	South Carolina	486	171
Indiana	738	139	South Dakota	143	208
Iowa	473	165	Tennessee	661	157
Kansas	329	142	Texas	1,693	136
Kentucky	575	168	Utah	204	166
Louisiana	789	205	Vermont	101	212
Maine	217	202	Virginia	718	143
Maryland	697	168	Washington	512	142
Massachusetts	1,115	192	West Virginia	335	184
Michigan	1,476	162	Wisconsin	877	190
Minnesota	705	178	Wyoming	61	156
Mississippi	566	240	*United*		
Missouri	662	139	*States*	35,164[2]	164

SOURCE: Department of the Treasury, Office of Revenue Sharing.

 [1]Per person amounts were calculated from Bureau of Census provisional population estimates for 1976.
 [2]The sum of individual state allocations does not equal total U.S. figure because of rounding process.

police and fire protection by adding personnel and equipment. Some communities have allocated funds to increase salaries for police and fire personnel. Statistics give evidence that 24 percent of every revenue sharing dollar has been spent for public safety.

 Approximately 22 percent of revenue sharing money has been spent on education. Because the Revenue Sharing Act prohibited local governments from using revenue sharing funds for this purpose, educational expenditures are accounted for by state government's expenditures for higher education and revenue sharing funds passed along from the state level to the local level for use in public schools. Hence, although local governments were prohibited from using their own portion of shared revenue for education, they were permitted to increase educational expenditures at the local level if state governments turned over to public school districts some or all of the state's revenue sharing funds.

The third major use of revenue sharing funds has been for public transportation systems. Transit expenditures have accounted for a reported 13 percent of allocated funds. In addition to public safety, education, and public transportation, state and local governments have expended revenue sharing funds for environmental protection, social services, health, and a host of other programs. It is no mystery, therefore, why the revenue sharing concept is enthusiastically supported by governors and mayors across the country.

THE FUTURE OF REVENUE SHARING

Although Congress has provided for a continuation of the revenue sharing program through September, 1980, the long-range future of the revenue sharing program as it currently exists is highly uncertain. In light of what has already been said regarding program financing, it is apparent that either much larger sums of money must be allocated by Congress or a different distribution of funds will be required in the years ahead, or both. Given President Carter's philosophy toward intergovernmental fiscal policies, both an increase in funding and a change in the allocation system are possible. President Carter is on record as favoring a revenue sharing program whereby revenues would go directly to local governments, by-passing the state governments almost entirely.

In early 1978, the Administration's advisers drafted a proposal that reflects the President's view of proper distribution of revenue sharing funds. Although only in the preliminary stage, it does indicate the stance the Carter Administration is likely to take when the current program expires in 1980. The plan calls for the separation of states from the existing revenue sharing program except for carefully designed payments for problem areas. The thrust of the plan is to provide states with up to $1.5 billion a year as an incentive for states to take a bigger role in bailing out troubled cities. Revenue sharing with states would be phased down by gradually taking money from state revenue sharing and increasing grant funds for only those states that effectively take steps to rescue fiscally troubled cities. States that do not would be penalized by sharp reductions in federal revenue. As envisioned, the state incentive fund program would increase over a three-year period to a total of $1.5 billion, financed by $600 million in new money and a 50 percent reduction in state revenue sharing funds.

At some undetermined point in time the incentive fund program would eventually terminate. States then would have to show evidence that they were spending their share of general revenue sharing funds to aid distressed and declining communities in order to continue receiving revenue sharing funds.

What this approach amounts to is a series of restrictions as to how states could spend revenue sharing funds and a greater share for local governments. Since state officials are likely to apply pressure for the incentive program funds without any loss of present revenue sharing dollars, the exact outcome is uncertain. It does appear, however, that revenue sharing in the future is to be more urban-oriented than at present.

CONCLUSION

Revenue sharing is no longer merely an academic exercise. It is now a working program which has been received enthusiastically by many officials at all levels of government. The present strong support of revenue sharing stems from the realization that if state and local governments are to provide for the needs of their constituents, new ways must be found to enable them to do so. The traditional fiscal tools in the hands of state and local governments are generally deemed inadequate.

Hence, revenue sharing is being received as a viable means of providing needed financial assistance through the distribution of general purpose funds from the federal government to states and localities. It also is looked upon as a productive way of distributing future fiscal dividends.

However, the two State and Local Fiscal Assistance Acts have been sharply attacked by critics. Included among the critics are individuals who support revenue sharing in general but object to certain specific features of the Acts.

One major objection relates to the method whereby funds are distributed. Why, critics ask, does a program intended to alleviate the ills of major urban areas in heavily populated states culminate with a bias in favor of generally low-income and sparsely populated states? It is apparent, they contend, that sound economic judgment has fallen victim to political compromise.

Also, critics raise an interesting issue related to public works expenditures. Since there is no restriction as to how revenue sharing funds may be used for public works, what will prevent localities from using these dollars for what critics believe to be low priority expenditures, such as stadiums or arenas?

The revenue sharing program is due to terminate as of September 30, 1980. As the program comes to a close, Congress will be faced with many conflicting pressures in determining whether to continue revenue sharing in the future. These pressures include the reduction or even elimination of state participation in the program, an increase in the appropriation level, additional restrictions on the use of funds, a change in the distribution formula, and the elimination of the revenue sharing program completely.

It seems likely that revenue sharing will be continued beyond 1980. Perhaps as more data become available for evaluating the program, many questions relating to the efficiency of revenue sharing will be answered. In the long run, however, the success of revenue sharing will in large part depend upon how well its advocates have accurately surmised the program's benefits and costs.

MAJOR ISSUES

1. Do you believe that the need factor in distributing funds is a drawback to the revenue sharing program?
2. Since general revenue sharing has become operative, should special grant programs be eliminated, reorganized, or maintained in their present form?
3. Should smaller-sized communities that are financially well off be eligible for revenue sharing funds?
4. Should local governments be restricted in the manner in which they spend revenue sharing funds?

SUBISSUES

1. Do you believe that revenue sharing will increase the efficiency of state and local government expenditures?
2. Do you agree with the proposition that state and local governments are faced with a fiscal crisis?
3. If need be, would you favor raising federal personal income taxes to provide sufficient revenue to share with the state and local governments?
4. Should state governments be excluded from the revenue sharing program?

SELECTED READINGS

Beer, Samuel H. "The Adoption of General Revenue Sharing: A Case Study in Public Sector Politics." *Public Policy*, Vol. 24 (Spring, 1976).

Blair, Patricia W. *General Revenue Sharing in American Cities: First Impressions*. Washington: National Clearinghouse on Revenue Sharing, December, 1974.

Caputo, David A. "General Revenue Sharing and American Federalism: Towards the Year 2000." *The Annals*, Vol. 419 (May, 1975).

Comptroller General of the United States. *Revenue Sharing: Its Use By and Impact On Local Governments*. Washington: U.S. General Accounting Office, April 25, 1974.

Dommel, Paul R. *The Politics of Revenue Sharing*. Bloomington: Indiana University Press, 1974.

Myers, Will S., Jr. "A Legislative History of Revenue Sharing." *The Annals*, Vol. 419 (May, 1975).

Nathan, Richard P., and Charles F. Adams, Jr. *Revenue Sharing: The Second Round*. Washington: The Brookings Institution, 1977.

Pechman, Joseph A. *Federal Tax Policy*, third edition. Washington: The Brookings Institution, 1977.

Reuss, Henry S. "Should We Abandon Revenue Sharing?" *The Annals*, Vol. 419 (May, 1975).

Thompson, Richard E. *Revenue Sharing: A New Era in Federalism?* Washington: Revenue Sharing Advisory Service, 1973.

The U.S. Dollar — 13
Can It Be Rescued?

During most of the past fifty years the U.S. dollar has been the strongest currency in the world. Americans and foreigners found its purchasing power, in the U.S. and abroad, to be strong in relation to other currencies. It became the world standard against which to measure other currencies and it served as the prime unit for settling international payment balances. For a time the U.S. dollar was considered more valuable and useful than gold itself.

Today the purchasing power of the U.S. dollar has dwindled, it can no longer be redeemed for gold, and its purchasing power compared to some other key currencies has depreciated. Other currencies are sought in preference to the dollar and some international transactions are now being determined in terms other than the U.S. dollar.

Although the U.S. dollar has been buffeted severely in the tempestous seas of international finance in recent years, it is still afloat. Attempts are being made to prevent it from capsizing and, perhaps, to restore it to its premier position among world currencies.

What knocked the dollar off its pedestal and tarnished its image? How does it stand in relation to gold and other major currencies? What are the strong currencies in the world today? What can or is being done to restore the prestige of the U.S. dollar? To better understand the current plight of the U.S. dollar, it is necessary to trace its history and its relation to gold and other world currencies.

HISTORY OF THE U.S. DOLLAR

Gold has been the elixer of humanity since the early days. It has been exchanged, hoarded, coined, and used for both industrial and decorative purposes. It has been instrumental in the winning of wars, bringing wealth and culture to nations, and causing jealousy and disaster. People have worked for it and fought for it. Its greatest uses have been as a medium of exchange and as a store of value. Even when not used as currency, it frequently has been used to give backing and value to the money supply. It has been coined since ancient times.

In spite of attempts by various governments in the past to limit its use as a money supply, it still holds a prominent role in determining the value of money. Its wide use as money, or backing for money, results from its general acceptance throughout the world. Its limited total supply, the relatively stable annual production, and its durability add to this acceptance. It is an important determinant of exchange value between currencies of different nations. It is an ultimate means of settling international balances of payment. Consequently, the amount of gold that a nation may have for the support of its money supply has been of major, if not critical, economic importance. Thus, when the United States established its monetary system, it gave gold an integral role.

The first coinage act in the United States in 1792 set up a bimetallic money standard. It defined the dollar in terms of both gold and silver. A dollar was defined as 371.25 grains of pure silver or 24.75 grains of pure gold. Thus, the mint ratio of the two metals was 15 to 1. When the market ratio subsequently deviated from the mint ratio, a shortage of gold coin developed. Then the mint ratio was changed to 16 to 1 when the gold content of the dollar was reduced to 23.22 grains by the Currency Act of 1834. Unfortunately the new ratio over-valued silver at the mint, which resulted in a shortage of silver coin. The virtual disappearance of silver from our monetary system was further hastened by the Subsidiary Coinage Act of 1853 by which the government stopped the free coinage of fractional silver. Subsequent demonetization of silver took place when the Coinage Act of 1873 practically eliminated the coinage of silver dollars. In 1879 the United States abandoned the inconvertible paper standard adopted at the outbreak of the Civil War and established a gold standard by giving the dollar its prewar gold content of 23.22 grains and making the dollar convertible into gold.

The Gold Standard

It was not until the turn of the century, however, that Congress established a singular gold standard for our money supply. Although for a few decades we had been on a *de facto* gold standard, it was not until the passage of the Gold Standard Act of 1900 that we went on a *de jure* gold standard. This ushered in the so-called golden age of the gold standard, which lasted until the outbreak of World War I. During this period, not only the United States but also most other major nations were on the gold standard. The most important of these nations were on the gold-coin standard, while others were on a gold-bullion or a gold-exchange standard. The heyday of the gold standard, however, was interrupted by the outbreak of World War I. As the war commenced, all belligerent nations abandoned the gold standard by refusing to redeem their currencies in gold and by prohibiting gold exports. In many cases, gold coin and bullion were called in by the government or the central bank. This was done to prevent the nation's gold supply from falling into the hands of the enemy, to conserve the gold supply for the purchase of essential war materiel, to continue operations in the foreign exchange markets, and to maintain enough gold reserve to preserve confidence in the nation's money supply.

In spite of various problems involved, most nations returned to some form of gold standard during the 1920s, with the United States leading the way in 1919 by establishing the prewar gold content of the dollar. Britain, Switzerland, France, Germany, and other nations followed some years later. Gold coin, however, virtually disappeared except in the United States as most countries adopted gold-bullion or gold-exchange standards. In general, these postwar standards were managed to a greater extent than were the prewar gold standards. High tariffs and other restrictions, heavy war debts, an unstable flow of international lending, and other disturbances made the operation of the gold standard more difficult, especially in serving its function in settling the international balance of payments.

With the beginning of the Great Depression in the early 1930s, countries abandoned the gold standard in great numbers. The United States and France were the only major nations left on the gold standard at the beginning of 1933, and the United States went off it later that year. The general abandonment of the gold standard was precipitated in large measure by an international financial panic that was caused by foreign creditor demands for repayment in gold of short-term liabilities such as bank deposits, and short-term government and commercial obligations. In most cases, the total credit demands exceeded the gold stock held by individual nations. Since they did not have the ability to redeem these obligations in gold, many nations were naturally forced to go off the gold standard.

Devaluation

With a 50 percent drop in the GNP between 1929 and 1933, an increase of unemployment from 1.5 million to 12.8 million, widespread bank failures, and a rash of commercial bankruptcies taking place, foreigners began large-scale withdrawals of short-term liabilities from the United States. Although our gold supply, then about 40 percent of the world total, remained above $4 billion, we lost over $270 million in February and March of 1933. Under these conditions, we abandoned the gold standard on March 6, 1933, when the President placed an embargo on gold exports. Subsequently we returned to a gold standard, but it was feared that reestablishment of the dollar at the old gold content with full convertibility would lead to such an extensive gold drain that it would seriously affect the abilities of the banks to issue credit and would jeopardize our opportunity for domestic economic recovery.

After calling in practically all of the nation's gold held by citizens, businesses, banks, and other organizations, the United States returned to the gold standard on January 30, 1934. The new gold standard, however, differed substantially from that in operation prior to March, 1933.

1. According to the Gold Reserve Act of 1934, the value of the dollar in terms of gold was reduced. The gold content of the new dollar was 13.71 grains

compared to the previous content of 23.22 grains, a reduction of approximately 40 percent. Consequently, the price of gold was increased from $20.67 to $35.00 per ounce. This meant that the gold supply, then worth nearly $4.2 billion, increased in dollar value by $2.8 billion to $7 billion.

2. Gold was, in effect, nationalized with some minor exceptions, and no currency in the United States was to be redeemed in gold.
3. The coinage of gold ceased, and all existing gold coin in the hands of the Treasury was converted into bullion.
4. Individuals and firms were prohibited from holding, transporting, exporting, or otherwise dealing with gold except under regulations specified by the Secretary of Treasury.

Although a number of other nations, such as France, Belgium, Holland, and Switzerland, subsequently returned to the gold standard, each had devalued its currency and introduced considerable management into its monetary system. By the outbreak of World War II, gold had lost much of its appeal, and most of the gold standards were of a gold-bullion or a gold-exchange type. No major nation had returned to a gold-coin standard, and most nations of the world were on an inconvertible paper standard. Of course, during World War II the entire world went off the gold standard. After the war, many nations returned to a form of the gold standard under the auspices of the International Monetary Fund. Most of these gold standards were limited and, with the exception of the United States, the redeemability of currency for gold, even for international purposes, was severely limited in most nations throughout the world.

The Gold Avalanche

Although gold economizing measures, such as the use of gold-bullion and gold-exchange standards, were prevalent in the early and mid-1930s, a wave or avalanche of gold hit the world, especially the United States, in the latter part of the decade. The causes for this increase in the gold supply were multifold. First, the increase in the price of gold encouraged its production. During the decade of the 1930s the annual physical output of gold more than doubled, and the value of the newly mined gold during the decade more than doubled the world's supply of gold. A second cause of the increased gold supply resulted from an increase in trade with the Orient, which paid for its imports in large part with gold. The gold supply was further increased by the melting of scrap gold, which brought a greater monetary reward to the seller.

While the world was experiencing a substantial increase in the gold supply, the United States was enjoying an even greater influx in its supply of the precious metal. The amount of gold held in the United States rose from approximately $7 billion immediately after devaluation of the dollar in 1934 to $22 billion at the end of the decade. It continued to increase in the 1940s, peaking at $24.5 billion in 1949. Although our economy did obtain some of its newly acquired gold from increased production and the melting process, the bulk of its increase, more than $16 billion, resulted from gold imports. This was due not only to a favorable balance of trade, but more so to the flight of capital that took place in Europe because of unsettled economic and political conditions preceding World War II. By 1949 we held 69 percent of the world's gold supply.

Dollar Shortage

Due to the scarcity of goods and services in many nations throughout the world after World War II, especially in the war-damaged nations, there was a great demand for American dollars as foreigners sought dollars to buy American products and to settle their international balances of payment. During this time of dollar shortage, there was a greater demand for American dollars than there was for gold. The Marshall Plan and reconstruction loans made by the United States to other nations were helpful in alleviating to some extent the dollar shortage.

Moreover, a number of foreign nations began to accumulate dollar reserves for future use in purchasing goods and settling trade deficits. Since the dollar could be converted readily into gold by foreign governments and central banks, it was as good as gold. It addition, American dollars could earn an interest income when held in deposit.

Surplus Dollars and the Decline in U.S. Gold Stock

Circumstances favorable to the U.S. dollar changed, however, in the decade of the 1950s. As war-torn nations rebuilt their economies and increased their production of goods and services, as our prices rose making our products more expensive to foreigners, and as we encountered more competition in world trade markets, our favorable international balance of trade was made less favorable. As we spent more money to maintain military installations overseas, granted more foreign aid, and Americans increased their investments abroad, the dollar shortage shrunk and our international balance of payments became negative, in spite of a continued favorable balance of trade. The dollar shortage was eased and many foreigners began converting American dollars into gold. This caused a gold outflow from our nation that continued until 1971. By the late 1950s our deficit balance of payments exceeded more than $3 billion annually. In fact, in the period 1958–1960 our adverse balance of payments exceeded $11 billion, and during that time we lost about $5 billion in gold and financed the rest of the deficit by increasing foreign holdings of short-term dollar assets. By the middle of 1972 our total gold reserve had dwindled from its peak of $24.5 in 1949 to $10.5 billion. This change in our gold holdings and those of other nations are shown in Table 13-1.

This table indicates that the world's gold supply increased from $35.4 billion to $43.2 billion during the period 1949–1965. During that time, however, the gold holdings of the United States dwindled by almost 50 percent, and the percent of the world's gold supply we held decreased from 69 to 32 percent. Increased production and shifts in gold holdings resulted in sizable amounts of

Table 13-1

GOLD RESERVES OF CENTRAL BANKS AND GOVERNMENTS, 1949–1977

Year	Estimated World Total[1] (Millions)	United States (Millions)	International Monetary Fund (Millions)	Rest of World (Millions)	United States (Percentage of Total)
1949	$35,410	$24,563	$1,451	$ 9,396	69
1950	35,820	22,820	1,495	11,505	64
1951	35,970	22,873	1,530	11,567	64
1952	36,000	23,250	1,692	11,055	65
1953	36,425	22,091	1,702	12,630	61
1954	37,075	21,793	1,740	13,540	59
1955	37,730	21,753	1,808	14,170	58
1956	38,235	22,058	1,692	14,485	58
1957	38,960	22,857	1,180	14,925	59
1958	39,860	20,582	1,332	17,945	52
1959	40,185	19,507	2,407	18,270	49
1960	40,525	17,804	2,439	20,280	44
1961	41,150	16,947	2,077	22,125	41
1962	41,275	16,527	2,110	22,640	40
1963	42,310	15,596	2,312	24,400	37
1964	43,060	15,471	2,179	25,410	36
1965	43,230	13,806	1,869	27,285	32
1966	43,185	13,235	2,652	27,300	31
1967	41,600	12,065	2,682	26,855	30
1968	40,905	10,892	2,288	27,725	27
1969	41,015	11,859	2,310	26,845	29
1970	41,275	11,072	4,339	25,865	27
1971	41,160	10,206	4,732	26,220	25
1972	44,890	10,487	5,830	28,575	23
1973	49,850	11,652	6,478	31,720	23
1974	49,830	11,652	6,478	31,700	23
1975	49,555	11,559	6,446	31,550	23
1976	49,129	11,598	6,311	31,220	24
1977 (Nov.)	48,964	11,658	5,825	31,481	24

SOURCE: *Federal Reserve Bulletin* (January, 1978), and *International Financial Statistics* (March, 1978).

[1]Excludes U.S.S.R., other Eastern European countries, and Mainland China.

gold flowing into such nations as Belgium, France, West Germany, Italy, the Netherlands, Switzerland, and even the United Kingdom.

Subsequent to 1965, gold reserves of central banks and governments dropped by more than $2 billion. This was due to the sale of gold by central banks and governments to private sources, especially through the London and other gold exchanges. Speculation regarding possible devaluation of the currencies of some major nations forced the price of gold upward in the free markets. The drain of gold out of central banks and into the free markets was arrested for several months when early in 1968 the 10 major nations of the world agreed not to supply the free market with gold. This was done in connection with the devaluation of the British pound at that time. The gold outflow from the United States resumed, however, and continued until President Nixon placed a ban on gold exports in August, 1971.

BALANCE OF PAYMENTS

The balance of payments was an integral factor in the relation to the gold outflow, and it is an important determinant today of the dollar's value in world markets.

There are several ways to show a balance of payments. Much will depend on the items included and the categorization of each item. A typical balance of payments statement for 1977 is shown in Table 13-2. It indicates the U.S. imported $31.4 billion more in merchandise than it exported. American tourists spent $2.9 billion more abroad than foreign tourists spent in America. The United States also had heavy military commitments abroad, and foreign aid totaled $2.9 billion. We also sent $2.1 billion in pensions and other unilateral payments to persons living abroad. On the plus side, the $25.6 billion in dividends and interest from abroad and the $7.4 billion in weapons sales to foreigners offset some of our deficit in the balance of payments for 1977. In total, however, the U.S. ended up owing foreigners $19.1 billion as a result of the deficit balance of payments.

Settlement of International Payments

Until 1971 gold was the ultimate means by which international balances of payments were settled. If there was a balance of payments due to the United States, foreign nations could make settlements in three ways: (1) by using their dollars previously obtained and held with American banks to pay the difference; (2) by selling financial assets to Americans, which amounted to borrowing U.S. dollars; or (3) by selling gold to the United States. On the other hand, if we owed a balance to foreigners, we settled by paying out dollars from our various accounts in foreign or American banks, by selling American securities in foreign markets and using the money to pay our trade debts, or by selling (paying) gold to foreigners.

Whether a foreign nation holding a balance of payments against the United States would increase its dollar holdings, its holdings of American financial assets, or would require payment in gold depended on many circumstances, such as its need for dollars, its current holdings of gold, and its desire to hold short-term financial assets for the purpose of obtaining interest income. Much depended on the practice followed in each country regarding its

Table 13-2

U.S. BALANCE OF PAYMENTS, 1977[1]
(In billions of dollars)

EXPORTS		IMPORTS	
U.S. merchandise exports....	$120.4	Foreign merchandise imports	$151.8
Foreign tourism in U.S.	7.3	American tourism abroad.....	10.2
Payments by foreigners for U.S. services..................	16.4	Payments to foreigners for services	11.2
Dividends and interest from U.S. corporations abroad..	15.1	Dividends and interest paid to foreign firms on U.S. investments......................	1.2
Dividends and interest received from personal investments abroad	10.5	Dividends and interest paid to foreigners on holdings of U.S. securities...............	11.2
U.S. weapons sales abroad ..	7.4	U.S. military expenses abroad...........................	5.6
		Foreign aid........................	2.9
Total balance of payments income............................	$177.1	Other payments involving pensions to people living abroad..........................	2.1
Total deficit in balance of payments	$ 19.1	Total balance of payments expense	$196.2

SOURCE: *U.S. News & World Report* (February 27, 1978).
Reprinted from *U.S. News & World Report.*
Copyright 1978 U.S. News & World Report, Inc.

[1]Does not include capital spending abroad by Americans nor capital investment in the United States from abroad. When these are included, the deficit amounts to approximately $28 billion.

reserves. Such countries as West Germany, France, Switzerland, Italy, and Belgium had a tendency to build up gold reserves. Consequently, any substantial increase in their dollar claims could easily result in a gold outflow from the United States. Other nations, however, preferred to hold part of their reserves in dollars and part in gold, while still others tended to hold most of their claims in U.S. short-term assets. An increase in dollar claims by countries in each of the latter two categories, of course, had less effect on the gold drain from the United States.

Not only was the gold flow affected by the action of individual nations, but it was also affected by the desire of foreign persons or firms to increase or decrease their dollar holdings. If they decided to decrease their dollar holdings, their dollars, through proper channels, could be exchanged for gold, resulting in an aggravation of the gold outflow from the United States. Even though they did not convert their dollars directly into gold, the dollars or dollar claims could be exchanged for domestic currency at banks, which in turn converted the dollars into gold.

Settlement of international balances of payment by the sale of gold from one nation to another could take place without any physical movement of gold stock. A foreign nation, for example, could purchase gold from the United States to resolve a deficit U.S. balance. Instead of shipping the gold to the foreign nation, however, it could simply have its newly purchased gold earmarked or segregated for its gold account at the Federal Reserve Bank of New York. This same nation could settle an adverse balance of payment with the United States by selling to the United States gold from its earmarked account. Early in 1978 the Federal Reserve was holding nearly $16 billion in earmarked gold for foreign and international accounts. This was in addition to the $11.7 billion gold reserve held by the United States. In addition, there was $45 billion in United States government securities and $416 million in deposits being held at Federal Reserve Banks for foreigners.

Changes in Gold Reserves

Prior to August, 1971, the U.S. settled its deficit balance of payments in part through the payment of gold in exchange for dollars held by foreign central banks and governments. Since August, 1971, however, payments by the U.S. to foreigners have not been made in gold.

Between 1949 and 1971 the United States had numerous, and sometimes sizable, deficits in its balance of payments and foreigners increased their dollar claims against the United States by a substantial degree. This caused a sizable increase in foreign holdings of short-term liquid assets and in some years a drain of gold exceeding $1 billion from the United States. As the United States lost gold despite the overall increase in the total world's supply, other nations increased their holdings of gold for a variety of reasons, including our own desire that they make their currencies freely convertible.

Nations that realized noticeable gains in gold holdings during the 1949–1971 period and subsequently can be observed in Table 13-3.

DOLLAR AND GOLD POSITION

The dollar problem is brought into clearer focus when the amount of gold is compared to our formerly required reserves and a study is made of the causes of the gold outflow.

U.S. Free Gold Reserves

In respect to our total gold holdings of $15.5 billion in 1964, for example, it should be remembered that approximately $13.4 billion was required as reserve behind Federal Reserve notes and deposit liabilities. This left about $2 billion in so-called free gold available for other uses, including the settlement of deficit balances of payment. This was quite a change from 1949 when we had over $12 billion in free gold reserves. Our free reserve position was made a little more precarious by the fact that foreigners in the mid-1960s held $24

Table 13-3

REPORTED GOLD RESERVES OF CENTRAL BANKS AND GOVERNMENTS, NOVEMBER, 1977

Nation	1949 (Millions)	1977 (Millions)[1]	Percentage Increase
Belgium	$ 698	$ 1,786	156
Canada	496	917	85
France	523	4,278	718
West Germany	—	4,978	—
Italy	256	3,490	1,263
Netherlands	195	2,300	1,079
Switzerland	1,504	3,515	134
United Kingdom	1,688	911	−46
International Monetary Fund	1,451	6,478	346
United States	24,563	11,658	−53

SOURCE: *Federal Reserve Bulletin* (January, 1978), and previous issues.

[1]Valued at $42.22 per ounce.

billion in dollar deposits and short-term American securities that easily and quickly could be converted into a demand for gold. This was offset to some extent by the fact that banks in the United States reported nearly $5 billion in short-term claims against foreigners. This meant that in 1964 foreigners had a potential $19 billion claim against our $2 billion free reserve of gold. Therefore, it was imperative that foreigners continue to hold dollars and short-term securities and settle future deficit balances against the United States by the use of dollar deposits and short-term securities if our gold supply was to remain free from jeopardy. This situation was eased considerably in 1965, however, when Congress voted to remove the gold reserve requirement behind Federal Reserve Bank deposits. This action freed an additional $4 billion of our total gold reserve. Finally, in 1968, when our free gold reserves dwindled to less than $1.5 billion, Congress removed the 25 percent gold cover on Federal Reserve notes. This freed all of our existing gold supply for international use.

Liquid dollar balances, rather than gold, have been held by foreigners for a number of reasons. Some are held for the purpose of receiving interest income, some as emergency reserves, and a certain amount is generally held as a working balance to carry on daily transactions of international trade. In addition to government securities, foreigners also hold several billion dollars in United States corporate and state and local government securities, which could be sold for dollars and, if the dollars were channeled to monetary authorities, eventually could be converted into gold.

Another possible discharge of the gold supply could result if there was a loss of confidence in the dollar. If, for example, Americans suspected that the dollar was to be devalued, it would behoove them to convert dollars to foreign currencies in anticipation of the devaluation, with the idea of converting the foreign currency back to dollars after the devaluation. In the interim, however, the American dollars held by foreigners could be converted into gold by foreign monetary authorities.

Role of International Monetary Fund

Those nations that are short of foreign currency or gold to meet a temporary deficit balance of payments can obtain some help from the International Monetary Fund (IMF). The Fund, established in 1944, has resources consisting of gold and the currencies of the 126 member nations, which were paid in by each nation on a quota basis. Quotas for each country are determined by the relative importance of the various countries in regard to international trade, national income, and population. Presently the IMF holds gold and foreign currency subscriptions in value equivalent to nearly 29.2 billion American dollars. Of this total, about $6.6 billion is in gold.

A nation desiring to borrow foreign currency or gold from the Fund may do so by depositing a like amount of its own currency with the Fund. Drawings from the Fund for an amount equal to 25 percent of the borrowing nation's own quota are almost automatic. Approval of additional borrowing is dependent upon the borrowing nation's efforts to take steps to eliminate its imbalance of payments. The borrowing nation has an obligation to repay its loan within a period not to exceed 3 to 5 years. Repayment is generally made by the borrower by repurchasing its own currency from the Fund with gold or convertible currencies.

Cause of Gold Outflow and the Weakening of the Dollar

One common way often used to find the reason for our gold outflow was to find specific categories of international payments that accounted for sizable portions of our deficit balance of payments. In 1974, for example, when our deficit balance of payments was $5.1 billion, some analysts cited our $4.9 billion in military expenditures as the major cause of our deficit balance of payments. Others pointed out that we spent over $8.1 billion on unilateral transfers, remittances, and pensions. On the other hand, some mentioned as inadequate certain categories on the credit side of the balance of payments, such as exports or the investment of foreign capital in the United States. In fact, many times such factors as high wage rates, high prices, or the Common Market were cited as causes limiting our export of goods and services and stimulating imports. Others using a chronological approach blamed the deficit on the last major phenomenon or two that occurred before or while we were shifting from a positive to a negative balance of payments. As the supply of U.S. dollars or dollar claims held by foreigners increased compared to the demand, the underlying strength of the dollar began to weaken. The one thing maintaining its strength was its convertibility into gold.

REMEDIES FOR GOLD OUTFLOW

Possible solutions for arresting the gold outflow and strengthening the position of the dollar have centered on remedying our deficit balance of payments. This, of course, would require a combination of adjusting both our debits and credits. But even without altering our balance of payments, the gold outflow could have been abated by inducing foreigners to hold more dollars and short- and long-term American securities. This latter method, however, would not have removed the potentially dangerous position of having excessive dollar claims that could be converted readily into gold. Some of the corrective measures suggested involved a greater degree of control or management over exports, imports, capital flows, the gold supply, and domestic economic measures. Here we would have to measure the advantage of a desirable balance of payments and a stable gold supply against the disadvantage of a certain amount of economic restriction. We also would have to weigh the merits of a favorable balance of payments against the possible adverse effect on our domestic economy of those measures adopted to obtain an improvement in the balance of payments.

Included among the measures suggested and/or adopted in the 1960s to arrest the gold outflow were the following:

1. Restrict imports.
2. Promote exports.
3. Reduce government spending abroad.
4. Reduce military spending overseas.
5. Reduce or eliminate foreign aid by
   a. using tying contracts, or
   b. encouraging other nations to help with aid.
6. Reverse capital outflows
   a. through higher interest rates,
   b. by paying higher interest rates on foreign deposits,
   c. by adopting an interest equalization tax, or
   d. by restraining credit on foreign investment.
7. Reduce required gold reserves.
8. Devalue the dollar.
9. Abandon fixed exchange rates.
10. Increase IMF lending ability.

During the throes of the gold outflow from the mid 1950s to 1971 we used each of the preceding measures. We restricted imports by the use of tariffs, quotas, and limited duty-free foreign purchases by American tourists. We promoted exports through trade shows and granted "E" awards to exporting firms. We found ways to reduce government spending abroad and cut back on overseas military spending, except for the war in Vietnam. In addition, we reduced foreign grants and loans by sizable amounts and encouraged other nations to help with aid to the developing nations. We endeavored to reduce U.S. capital flows with higher interest rates, paid premiums on foreign deposits in the United States, and imposed an interest equalization tax. In addition, the banks, through the Federal Reserve, voluntarily restrained loans for foreign spending. We also freed more of our gold for foreign payments by eliminating the gold reserve requirement behind Federal Reserve Bank deposits and Federal Reserve notes. In addition to these measures the International Monetary Fund created SDRs (Special Drawing Rights) to expand its lending ability, and rigid, fixed exchange rates were generally abandoned. When these measures failed to correct our deficit balance of payments and arrest the gold outflow, we finally devalued the dollar and stopped the convertibility of dollars into gold. A few of these measures require a closer inspection.

Devalue the Dollar

One proposal frequently made, and often bitterly opposed, for correcting our deficit balance of payments was devaluing the dollar or, in other terms, increasing the price of gold. Prior to 1972 the dollar was officially defined as 13.71 grains of pure gold. This meant that an ounce of gold was worth $35, which was the price at which the United States had agreed to buy or sell gold. The exchange value of the dollar in relation to foreign currencies was determined by the amount of gold in each of the currencies. Since the British pound, for example, was defined as 32.90 grains of pure gold, this meant that a pound exchanged for $2.40. If either nation were to devalue its currency, it would change the exchange rate between the two nations.

It was contended by some that the United States should devalue the dollar to lower its prices of goods and services in relation to prices in other nations. This, in turn, would reduce imports and stimulate exports. Furthermore, it would permit an increase in the domestic and foreign production of gold. In addition to these merits, the advocates of devaluation pointed out that prices of most commodities in our economy had increased in the previous few decades, but that the price of gold had not changed since 1934. In the previous 30 years, in fact, the free market prices of most commodities had more than doubled according to the Consumer Price Index. In the meantime, the price of gold as a commodity had remained constant by law.

Effect on Prices and Trade. To show how devaluation would help to correct the adverse balance of international payments, assume that the dollar was devalued by 33⅓ percent, or redefined as 9.143 grains of pure gold. This in effect would increase the price of gold by 50 percent to $52.50 per ounce, since there were 480 grains in an ounce (480/9.143 = $52.50). In fact, it was suggested by one noted British authority that the United States double its gold price. Such action would automatically make imports less attractive to Americans and American goods and services less expensive to foreigners.

This, of course, would tend to reduce imports and stimulate exports in the following manner. Assume that under the then current exchange rate of £1 = $2.40, British shoes were selling in both the United States and Britain at the price of £1 and that identical American shoes were selling in both countries for $3.00 per pair. Ignoring all tariffs and shipping costs, it would be cheaper for the Britisher to buy domestically produced shoes for £1 than it would be to buy American shoes at $3.00, which would cost £1 and 5 shillings to obtain. On the other hand, the American would find it more beneficial not to buy domestically produced shoes at $3.00, but to buy British produced shoes at £1. At that exchange rate the £1 could be obtained for only $2.40, thus effectuating a savings of 60 cents on the purchase of shoes. If shoes were typical of the prices of industrial commodities, it is easy to see how such a situation could result in a low level of American exports to Great Britain and a high level of imports from Britain into the United States. This, in turn, could aggravate a deficit balance of payments and possibly cause an outflow of gold from the United States to the United Kingdom.

If the dollar were devalued by 33⅓ percent, however, and no offsetting changes were to occur, the following reaction would take place. With the dollar then containing 9.143 grains of pure gold, the exchange rate between pounds and dollars would change to £1 = $3.60. This exchange rate is approximated by dividing the amount of gold in the pound by the amount of gold in the devalued dollar (32.91/9.143 = $3.60).

In such event the American shoes, if still priced at $3.00 a pair, would now be more attractive to both the American and British buyer at the new exchange rate. The Britisher would still face the choice of purchasing the domestically produced shoes for £1 or the American shoes for $3.00 a pair. But with the new exchange rate, it would be more profitable to convert the £1 into $3.60. The buyer could then purchase the American shoes for $3.00 and pocket the remaining 60 cents. Likewise, the American would now find domestically produced shoes more attractive. Since the buyer would now have to put out $3.60 to obtain £1 to buy the British shoes, it would be less expensive to purchase the American produced shoes for $3.00 a pair. Thus, both the American and Britisher would be inclined to buy American produced goods. Again, if shoe prices were typical of industrial commodities between the two nations, one can readily see how devaluation could reduce American imports and stimulate exports. A widespread flow of goods and services out of America could reverse the balance of payments and abate the outflow of gold. Indeed, it could even result in a gold inflow.

Effect on Gold Production. An increase in the price of gold through devaluation also would have the effect of bringing about increased gold production. Prior to 1972 the value of the world production of gold, exclusive of the U.S.S.R., other Easter European countries, Mainland China, and North Korea, approximated $1.4 billion annually at $35 per ounce. This amounted to approximately 40 million ounces per year. If the price of gold were raised above $35 per ounce, it would be more profitable for producers throughout the world to mine gold. In addition, increased production would result at many marginal sources of gold, which at current prices were not worth exploiting. Without any increased production, the value of gold production in terms of dollars would increase considerably. With it, it is very likely that the value of gold production would double its present rate.

One difficulty with devaluation was that it would benefit in large measure the Soviet Union and the Union of South Africa, the two major producers of gold. Another major objection to devaluation was the fact that any gains made toward correcting the balance of payments could be offset readily if other nations followed suit by devaluing their currencies or using other retaliatory measures. It was quite possible, also, that devaluation of the dollar might lead to anticipations of further changes. In such case this could lead to a further drain on our gold supply. Indeed, the mere suspicion that a nation is going to devalue its currency can lead to a flight of capital and a gold drain. Consequently, any move to devalue must be carried on as quickly and quietly as possible for best results.

Effect on Dollar Prestige. According to the critics, devaluation could also weaken or substantially reduce confidence in the American dollar and greatly impair our role as banker for the world. Countries holding dollars would find them less valuable in terms of gold and in terms of exchange value for other currencies of the world. Consequently, they may be reluctant to hold dollars as international liquidity. This, of course, could lower our international prestige and cause considerable disruption in the international financial world until a new currency for settling international debts was substituted for American dollars.

Furthermore, devaluation could be looked upon as an act of bad faith by those holding dollars, especially those caught unaware or those who did not have an opportunity to convert their dollars into gold or some other currencies before devaluation. If the United States devalued and other nations did not, the purchasing power of dollars and U.S. liquid assets held by foreigners would decrease; unless, of course, foreigners elected to spend the dollars to buy American goods and services, and provided the U.S. price level did not increase as a result of devaluation.

As a result of domestic and world monetary conditions, the United States in August, 1971, suspended the convertibility of dollars into gold, and early in 1972 devalued the American dollar 8.57 percent by raising the price of gold from $35 to $38 per ounce. The dollar was devalued again by 10 percent and the official price of gold raised to $42.22 per ounce in February, 1973.

Unpeg Exchange Rates

The exchange rates between the American dollars and foreign currencies for decades had been fixed or pegged at particular levels by a comparison of the gold backing behind each of the currencies. As explained previously, the exchange rate between the American dollar and the British pound prior to 1972 was £1 = $2.40 because the amount of gold in a pound was equivalent to the amount of gold behind $2.40. The relationship between gold and the currency of many other nations, including the pound, the deutsche mark, and the franc, however, was indirect insofar as these currencies were not directly convertible into gold. They could be converted into gold only through the exchange of dollar balances for gold. Thus, the fixing or pegging of the exchange rate prior to 1972 was tied to the willingness of the United States Treasury to buy and sell gold at a fixed price of $35 per ounce.

Fixed Rates. It should be mentioned, however, that exchange rates do fluctuate above and below the official par values in response to changes in supply and demand. Prior to 1972 these fluctuations, however, were limited to one percent as agreed upon by the International Monetary Fund, through which the exchange rates were set. According to agreement, it was the responsibility of the central bank or a government stabilization fund to prevent deviations greater than one percent. This was accomplished, of course, by purchase and sale of currency by the nation involved. If, due to heavy outflow of dollars to Germany, the deutsche mark rose in price from 37 cents to 37.3 cents, then it would have been expedient for the German Bundesbank to enter the market to sell deutsche marks (buy dollars) in an effort to prevent the exchange rate from exceeding the established limits. On the other hand, if the value of the deutsche mark fell, the bank sold dollars (bought deutsche marks) to maintain the price of deutsche marks. In this case, exchange rates were changed primarily by devaluation (depreciation) or revaluation (appreciation) of the various currencies rather than in response to supply and demand of foreign exchange. Differences in international balance of payments under such circumstances were settled by acceptance of foreign currencies at the fixed exchange rate or by the flow of gold.

Flexible Rates. It had often been suggested, however, that the problem of deficit balance of payments and the gold outflow could be corrected by adopting flexibile or unpegged rates. It was further suggested that using unpegged rates would avoid some of the difficulties involved with devaluation. If unpegged rates were adopted, the exchange rates between currencies would fluctuate with supply and demand to clear the market just like the price of any unregulated commodity. Such unpegged rates could be adopted simply by having the United States cease the purchase and sale of gold at a fixed price and by the elimination of the buying and selling of foreign currencies in exchange for dollars by the Treasury and the Federal Reserve. Furthermore, it would not be necessary for the United States to hold gold to stablize the value of the dollar or to settle international payments. Even with unpegged rates, however, a certain amount of gold would be desirable for the purpose of buying and selling foreign currencies to prevent sudden and severe shifts in exchange rates.

If the rates were not pegged, the value of the dollar in terms of foreign currencies would shift freely with changes in balances of payments. Naturally with a deficit balance of payments the value of the dollar in terms of foreign currencies would fall. Since foreign countries could not obtain gold in exchange for dollars, they would be forced to keep the dollars or convert them into U.S. liquid assets or to other currencies or assets. As the value of the dollar continued to decrease in terms of foreign currencies, however, it would make other currencies more valuable in terms of American dollars. This, in turn, would increase the purchasing power of foreign currencies in terms of American goods. Eventually this lowering of our prices and the raising of foreign prices relative to American dollars would bring about shifts in the balance of payments.

One strong objection to unpegged rates was that it was tantamount to going off the gold standard. Opponents of such a measure contended that it would damage our international prestige. Complaints would arise from foreign holders of dollars and U.S. liquid assets that the United States changed the rules of the game, and they would be prevented from obtaining gold at a specified price after having held American dollars and liquid assets in the good faith that they could be converted at any time into gold.

Those advocating unpegged rates answered this objection by pointing out that the United States could continue to sell gold at a specified price until it was all gone. At that time, since its gold stocks would be depleted, the United States would have to abandon fixed rates and move toward unpegged rates. It was pointed out further that if the United States were to make use of all its gold stock for settlement of its international balance of payments, it could satisfy most of the demand for gold by those who normally wished to convert dollar claims into gold. Consequently, no great loss would be suffered by the current holders of American dollars or short-term liquid assets.

It was also argued that unpegged rates would cause wide and excessive shifts in exchange rates and add a certain degree of instability to the balance of payments. This would result in considerable speculation in exchange rates. Proponents of unpegged rates, however, retorted that the shifts were desirable as a means of reversing the balance of payments. Another argument held that the nonfixed or unpegged rates would eliminate in large part the balance of payments restraint on the government to avoid inflation. Although we would no longer have to worry about the effects of inflation on the balance of payments, this would still not prevent the Administration from taking prudent measures to avoid inflation because of its other consequences.

The Crawling Peg. In one sense it was argued that fixed exchange rates may put an undue burden on a nation that is suffering a serious deficit balance of payments. It was contended that it may have insufficient reserves to go into the market and buy up its currency to prevent its exchange rate from falling. On the other hand, proponents of the fixed rate contended that completely flexible rates could cause such wide variations in exchange rates that there might be a loss of confidence in the international exchange system. Furthermore, it was contended that under the present fixed rate system, a nation may try as hard and as long as possible to maintain its fixed rate; but if it could not maintain it, the final alternative was to devalue its currency. This in itself, if it involved a major nation, could cause a serious disruption of international trade.

In an attempt to obtain the benefits of both systems, it was suggested that the band surrounding the fixed rate be widened to as much as 5–10 percent.

This, of course, would give a nation more time and latitude in adjusting its deficit balance of payments as a means of returning its exchange rate to its official fixed position. Opponents of this proposal suggested that it might cause a nation to become too complacent about correcting its adverse balance of payments.

A more recent recommendation was that of the so-called "crawling peg," which contains elements of the fixed rate, the flexible rate, and the wider band. Based upon the belief that there is one exchange rate that will equilibrate the supply of and demand for a particular currency, this system would permit the exchange rate to move, or crawl, toward this rate. One version would limit the rate of crawl over a given period of time, such as one sixth of one percent per month. Another version would make the crawl automatic. In this latter case the actual pegged rate at any time would be a band around the pegged rate within which the actual exchange rate could vary. If the rate were to move outside this band, either up or down, the nation would be obliged to buy or sell foreign exchange to return the rate within the band. The band, however, would move up and down with changes in the moving average. This would permit gradual adjustments in the exchange rate.

A big advantage of the crawling peg was that it would permit flexibility without allowing wide and sharp fluctuations in exchange rates that might occur under a completely flexible rate system. On the other hand, it would not require a nation to take drastic action to correct its balance of payments as soon as the exchange rate deviated from the offical narrow band.

Floating Exchange Rates

Although most exchange rates were fixed prior to 1972, a series of moves took place in late 1971, 1972, and 1973 that left exchange rates in a state of flux. The West German deutsche mark and other currencies were floated. Floating is the process of unpegging the exchange rate and letting supply and demand determine a new rate. The exchange rate may be fixed at this new, more realistic rate, or permitted to continue floating. Other measures which occurred included the suspension of gold convertibility by the United States, the imposition of an import surcharge by the United States, two devaluations of the American dollar, the revaluation of the Japanese yen, the widening of the band around fixed rates from 1 percent to 2.25 percent, and the adoption of the crawling peg by Brazil. Presently some rates are fixed and some are unpegged. Certainly all of them have greater flexibility today as a result of the recent international monetary changes.

Special Drawing Rights (SDRs)

During the decade of the 1960s world trade increased by more than 10 percent annually. In contrast, the total stock of international reserves, consisting primarily of gold, dollars, and pounds increased only 3 percent annually. Much of this relatively small increase in world reserves was accounted for by dollars since the United States, through its perennial balance of payments deficits, contributed to world international liquidity in the form of short-term liabilities to foreigners.

To overcome the world shortage of international liquidity, the so-called Group of Ten worked and deliberated over a period of four years on a system of Special Drawing Rights as a means of increasing world reserves.[1] In September, 1968, member nations of the International Monetary Fund unanimously agreed to the concept of an SDR plan.

Debtor nations, such as the United States and United Kingdom, were strongly in favor of the SDRs. Some of the creditor nations, however, were not so enthusiastic about the plan. Some nations, such as the United States, thought that the SDR amount should be a permanent addition to world reserves. Other nations saw the proposal only as a temporary expedient. In July, 1969, a compromise was reached when it was agreed at a meeting of the Group of Ten that $9.5 billion in "Paper Gold" would be created over a 3-year period. The new reserve asset became available January 1, 1970.

The final agreement called for the creation of supplementary reserves in the form of Special Drawing Rights (SDRs) established through the IMF. The SDRs were subsequently distributed to the member nations of the IMF according to each country's respective quota. Thus, the United States received nearly one fourth of the total SDRs created. Over the 3-year period the United States received an allocation of $2.3 billion. The United Kingdom could draw about $1.1 billion in SDRs, West Germany $542 million, and France $485 million, according to their respective IMF quotas.

Member nations cannot buy SDRs from the Fund but can use their assigned SDR reserves to settle balance of payments deficits. All member countries are obligated to accept SDRs from debtor nations. No creditor nation, however, can be compelled to accept SDRs in excess of three times its original allocation. For instance, since West Germany is allocated $542 million in SDRs, it cannot be obligated to hold more than $1,626 million in SDR balances or, in other words, its original allocations plus $1,084 million tendered by other nations. Since SDRs carry an interest rate paid by the debtor nation, a creditor nation may desire to hold a greater volume than that required.

Special Drawing Rights can be issued for balance of payments purposes and to protect a nation's reserve position. Upon mutual agreement, one nation can use its SDRs to buy currency of another nation. To encourage nations to accumulate other forms of reserves and not rely solely on their accumulation of SDRs, a provision in the agreement indicated that the average use of SDRs by a member nation must not exceed 70 percent of that nation's average accumulation over a 5-year period.

Special Drawing Rights can be used between nations either on the basis of bilateral agreement or at the designation of the International Monetary Fund. In the latter case the country desiring to use SDRs can request the IMF to

---

[1]The Group consisted of 10 world trade leaders including Canada, Belgium, France, Italy, Japan, the Netherlands, Sweden, West Germany, the United Kingdom, and the United States.

designate certain countries to receive (accept) SDRs and the amounts to be received.

The United States has been active in using SDRs for its exchange transactions, using them for both payments and receipts. In 1977 the United States was holding $2.2 billion in SDRs from other nations, while the second largest holding was that of West Germany with $1.2 billion in SDRs.

Although SDRs cannot be converted directly into gold, the unit value of an SDR initially was equivalent to the gold content of the U.S. dollar. Consequently, when the U.S. dollar was devalued and the price of gold raised from $35 per ounce to $38 per ounce, the value of an SDR was likewise increased to $1.09 per unit. Again, when the U.S. raised the price of gold to $42.22 in February, 1973, the transaction value of an SDR increased to $1.21 per unit ($42.22 ÷ $35.00 = $1.21). To improve the transferability of SDRs and move away from the exclusive reliance on the dollar price of gold as a means of determining the value of SDRs, the IMF, commencing July 1, 1974, widened the base of valuation by including currencies other than the U.S. dollar. Today the currencies of 16 nations provide a "currency basket" valuation for SDRs. The U.S. dollar is weighted 33 percent in the currency basket. At the end of 1977 an SDR was worth $1.22 per unit. Since the currency basket technique is the result of an interim agreement, this method of SDR valuation is subject to change at any time.

Eurodollars

One of the most mystifying forces affecting the value of the dollar, the price of gold, and the status of international liquidity in the past two decades has been the Eurodollar market. By simple definition a Eurodollar is a U.S. dollar on deposit in a foreign commercial bank. It can come into existence when someone transfers a dollar deposit from a U.S. bank to a foreign bank or when someone buys U.S. dollars in exchange for other currencies and then deposits the dollars in a foreign bank. Although there is a difference of opinion, Professor Milton Freidman maintains that Eurodollars are also created in the same manner that dollar demand deposits are created in regular domestic banking practice. More mystifying is the fact that most of the actual dollars underlying Eurodollar deposits never leave the United States. According to the Federal Reserve, "A bank accepting a Eurodollar deposit receives, in settlement of the transaction, a dollar balance with a bank in the U.S. A bank making a Eurodollar deposit or loan . . . completes the transaction from its U.S. bank balances."[2] Consequently, as Eurodollars are transferred around the world, the dollar balances supporting them are merely changed from one bank account to another within the American domestic banking system, or even within an individual U.S. bank.

Although the Eurodollar market is worldwide, London is the center of the market. Furthermore, large U.S. banks are the major holders and dealers in

[2]*Federal Reserve Bulletin* (October, 1969).

Eurodollars. The Eurodollar market, started less than two decades ago, operates under the supervision of the Bank for International Settlements (BIS); but to date there is little control or regulation over the Eurodollar market.

In recent years European banks have paid higher interest rates on deposits, including demand deposits, than those rates available on savings deposits in most American banks. Consequently, they draw from all sorts of investors including individuals, corporations, other commercial banks, and some central banks. On the other hand, customers, such as individuals, businesses, commercial banks, and governments, pay one percent or more above regular borrowing rates to borrow Eurodollars.

Since all free world currencies were convertible into U.S. dollars prior to August 15, 1971, and the dollar was so strong that it was acceptable for settling international payments even between two foreign nations, the Eurodollar pool flourished in the late 1960s and early 1970s. Moreover, Eurodollars can be transferred across national borders in large quantities on very short notice. Because of their great mobility, Eurodollars have been shifted readily into and out of accounts and across national boundaries to take advantage of higher interest rates.

In spite of their many advantages, however, the presence and use of Eurodollars can have a destabilizing effect on the world's financial markets. The hint of revaluation, for example, will create a massive exchange of Eurodollars for the currency expected to be revalued. This, in turn, raises the unofficial price of the currency, adding further to the speculation about revaluation. In the spring of 1971, for example, before temporarily closing its monetary market because of the dollar onslaught, West Germany had to purchase $5 billion in a matter of a few days because speculators thought that the deutsche mark was ripe for revaluation. More than $4 billion poured into the Japanese market for the purchase of yen during a 2-week period in the summer of 1971, just after the U.S. dollar was allowed to float. Speculators, of course, were counting on the revaluation of the yen.

Eurodollars were also a threat to the stability of the U.S. gold stock insofar as central banks and foreign governments, prior to August 15, 1971, could convert dollars into gold by selling dollars to the U.S. Treasury. Thus, Eurodollars added to the growing gap between foreign claims against the United States and the U.S. gold reserve. The recent and astonishing growth of the Eurodollar market is reflected in the fact that in 1958 there was no such market, while by the mid-1970s the Eurodollar pool had grown to approximately $130 billion.

In spite of all their impact, there is still some uncertainty as to how Eurodollars came into being, to what extent they may be created, and how much double counting may be involved in their numbers. It is estimated, for example, that the *net* Eurodollar amount for the mid-1970s was approximately $100 billion as compared to the gross figure of approximately $130 billion cited previously. There is even more uncertainty regarding the best way to regulate the Eurodollar market, if indeed it can or should be regulated at all.

Petrodollars

In the past few years there has been growing concern about the effect on international payments of the dramatic rise in dollar and other currency holdings of the Organization of Petroleum Exporting Countries (OPEC). The dollar holdings, often referred to as petrodollars, rose sharply as a result of the 1973 increases in the price of oil exported to the United States and other industrial nations. The consolidation of the Arabian oil producers into a unified body permitted them to set prices. Price pressure had been mounting from the devaluation of the dollar, the abandonment of dollar convertibility for gold, and inflation in the United States and other oil-using nations. In a typical recent year, for example, the gross transfer of purchasing power realized through import receipts of OPEC countries was estimated to be the equivalent of $100 billion, of which $95 billion was from the export of oil. After subtracting imports and grants to developing nations, and making a few other adjustments, the OPEC nations were left with a $60 billion surplus in their balance of payments.

Preliminary estimates indicate that, of the $60 billion, OPEC nations invested $11 billion directly in the United States. This amount was less than the increase the U.S. paid for oil imports from OPEC. About one half of the investments made in the U.S. were in the form of marketable government securities, $1 billion was used to buy real estate, and the remainder was placed in banking and money market liquid assets, such as large negotiable certificates of deposit. About $7.5 billion of OPEC's surplus was invested in the United Kingdom, $5.5 billion was lent to other industrial nations, $2.5 billion was given in aid to developing nations, and $3.5 billion went to international agencies. At least $21 billion of the OPEC surplus was held as Eurocurrency deposited in banks in London and other world financial centers. The remaining $9–$10 billion was invested in real estate and corporate securities in Europe and Japan, with many direct loans made to private industry.

The high price of oil caused substantial shifts in the balances of payments, especially of the oil exporting and importing nations. In addition, the "recycling" of petrocurrencies has had a substantial impact on various economies depending on the flow and direction of OPEC spending, lending, and investment. Moreover, petrodollar accumulation weighs heavily on the decision of the U.S. of whether to resume dollar convertibility into gold. Certainly petrodollar and Eurodollar conversion could bring heavy potential drains on the U.S. gold supply if the U.S. were to resume convertibility.

THE DOLLAR PRICE OF GOLD

Gold is not only bought and sold by governments and central banks throughout the world, but also in private markets. Until August, 1971, the world monetary price of gold was well established, especially by the U.S. Treasury, at $35 per ounce. In the private gold markets, the largest of which is London, the price of gold is free to fluctuate with changes in supply and demand. Other private markets exist in Hong Kong, Saigon, Macao, Bangkok, Beirut, Cairo, Kuwait, Johannesburg, Brussels, and Zurich.

From the time the London Gold Market reopened in 1954, after closing during World War II, until 1960 the free market price of gold stayed close to the official monetary price of $35 per ounce. The supply of gold for the free market is obtained from three major sources: (1) new production, especially from the Union of South Africa, which mines three fourths of the West's gold; (2) gold sales from communist nations; and (3) monetary gold of central banks whenever the free price of gold rises above its monetary price.

The Gold Pool

With increased industrial use of gold, limited supplies coming onto the market, and the speculation in 1960 that the United States might change its policy and devalue the dollar, the heavy demand for gold pushed the price of gold in the free market to more than $40 per ounce. At that time 8 major nations, including the United States and Great Britain, formed a Gold Pool for the purpose of stabilizing the free price of gold near the monetary price of $35 per ounce.[3] This was to be accomplished through the purchase and sale of gold in the free market by the Gold Pool, executed through the Bank of England. Technically, the Gold Pool consortium agreed to sell gold when the price rose above $35 per ounce and buy gold when the price fell below the $35 monetary value.

With the perennial heavy demand for gold for industrial uses, a modest increase in supply, and the continuous belief that the United States, Great Britain, France, or some other major nation might devalue its currency, the Gold Pool was a net seller of gold with its gold supplies coming primarily from the United States.

The Two-Tier System

As a result of its continuous balance of payments deficits and shortage of reserves, the United Kingdom, with the approval of the IMF, devalued the pound sterling by 14.3 percent, from $2.80 to $2.40, in November, 1967. At that time a wave of gold buying hit the free market. Gold hoarders speculating that the United Kingdom would be forced to devalue again or that the United States or some other major nation would subsequently devalue its currency drove the price of gold well beyond $40 per ounce. In the next 5 months the Gold Pool nations sold about $3.5 billion worth of gold, primarily from the United States, to the London market trying to keep the market price from rising too greatly. Faced with a continuous rise in the free price of gold in contrast to dwindling free gold reserves, the ability of the Gold Pool nations

[3]Other Gold Pool members besides the United States and Great Britain were Belgium, West Germany, France, Italy, The Netherlands, and Switzerland. France, however, ceased its participation in June, 1967, shortly before the Pool's heaviest gold losses began.

to supply the free market with gold was threatened. At that time, which was prior to its removal of the gold cover on its money supply, the United States' free gold reserves were $1.5 billion. Consequently, on March 17, 1968, the Gold Pool nations agreed to end the operation of the Gold Pool and endorsed the establishment of a two-tier gold price. By this agreement the Gold Pool nations ceased to supply gold to the free market. At the same time, they agreed to freeze world monetary reserves and stop buying gold for monetary purposes.

This action permitted the toleration of a two-tier system in which the free market price could deviate from the monetary price of gold without bringing about stabilizing measures by the major nations. It was hoped, however, that the freezing of world monetary gold reserves would force the producers to sell all their gold in the free market, thus driving the market price downward toward the monetary price of $35 per ounce. The Union of South Africa, however, contended that it should be able to sell in both the monetary market and the free market. This, of course, would permit it to split its gold in both markets to its most advantageous ratio. It would always have a stable market at $35 per ounce and could still take advantage of a free market that would yield a better profit on its production of gold. In reaction to the agreement, South Africa for a year or more sold very little gold to either the private market or the central banks. From March, 1967, until June, 1969, the price of gold on the free market fluctuated between $37.00 and $42.40 per ounce. The scheme initially worked as planned, however, because by December, 1969, the free price of gold was down to $35 an ounce.

Near Crisis of the Franc

As a result of the costly settlement of the general strike of French workers in the spring of 1967, along with other factors, France began to suffer a serious inflation in the latter part of the year. Consequently, French exports began dwindling and imports, especially from West Germany, rose rapidly. Rising prices caused some doubts about France's ability to hold its balance of payments position. Presuming that France might run such large deficits that it might not be able to support the franc and would be forced to devalue, the French and foreigners began selling francs and buying stronger West German deutsche marks and/or gold. Speculators, assuming that a possible devaluation of the franc would be followed by the devaluation of other currencies, even the pound and dollar, added more upward pressure to the price of gold in the free market. Between March, 1968, and November, 1968, France's gold supply was drawn from $5.2 billion to $3.8 billion, a drop of 27 percent.

To weather the storm against the franc, a $2 billion international loan of convertible currencies was arranged from the Group of Ten to help defend the franc at a value that many assumed would be reduced from its existing value of 20 cents American. This was in addition to the $985 million credit France previously received from the IMF for the purpose of buying francs to shore up the price. Money managers of the world's leading nations saw these loans as a move to buy time until a world monetary conference could be called after the new Nixon Administration took office in the United States.

In spite of the fact that the franc in some markets was selling at 15 percent below its monetary value, President de Gaulle of France expressed strong faith in the franc and gambled that general confidence in the franc could be restored without devaluation. Furthermore, he and others contended that the basic problem, especially between the franc and the deutsche mark, was that the deutsche mark was undervalued. He therefore called for the West Germans to revalue the deutsche mark upward to restore the balance between the deutsche mark and other currencies, particularly the franc.

Within a period of several days, Britain, to strengthen the pound and perhaps prevent a run on its gold, announced a heavy tax increase and the adoption of other measures designed to dampen domestic spending and reduce imports. Although West Germany refused to raise the value of the deutsche mark, it imposed domestic taxes aimed at reducing exports and increasing imports, especially between France and West Germany. De Gaulle astonished his own people and world financial experts when he announced that France would maintain the current parity of the franc. He then outlined a widespread austerity program calling for a reduction in the French budget deficit from $2.3 billion to less than $1 billion, an export expansion program, and other trade measures. From that time until mid-1969, the franc held its own, but there were many who believed that the French would be forced to devalue. With the defeat of President de Gaulle in the Spring, 1969, election in France, it was apparent that the new President, Georges Pompidou, would be less reluctant to devalue the franc. The franc subsequently was devalued by approximately 12 percent in August 1969. The franc-deutsche mark situation was eased further in October, 1969, when West Germany, shortly after a change in government leadership, revalued the deutsche mark (upward) by 9.29 percent.

The Demise of Gold

These currency readjustments, along with the creation of SDRs the following year and tight money and higher interest rates at home, took some of the burden off the U.S. dollar as a supplier of international liquidity. But the improvement of the U.S. balance of payments position was short-lived. The continuous inflationary pressures in the United States in the late 1960s and early 1970s aggravated the U.S. deficit balance of payments and the outflow of dollars. The task of reducing the flow of dollars abroad proved to be as difficult as before. Moreover, early in 1971 the United States experienced a substantial deterioration of its trade position and faced a deficit balance of trade for the first time in nearly a century. Speculation emerged that the dollar and/or some other currencies might subsequently be devalued. Consequently, the free price of gold began to rise substantially. By mid-1971 even nations that for years had retained "excess" U.S. dollars and refrained from redeeming them for gold in the interest of international financial stability began to question the wisdom of holding dollars as opposed to gold. By the end of July, 1971, it was estimated that foreign official institutions held between $40 and $50 billion in liquid claims against the United States. This was double the amount of a year earlier. On the other hand, the total U.S. gold stock was only $10.4 billion.

In the spring of 1971 many dollars were being sold in exchange for other currencies, particularly West German deutsche marks. On speculation that the deutsche mark would be revalued and thus worth more dollars, and that the unofficial exchange rate between the dollar and the deutsche mark would be moved away from the official monetary exchange rate (27.5 cents) in favor of the deutsche mark, the sale of dollars became so heavy that the foreign exchange markets in West Germany, Switzerland, Belgium, Austria, and The Netherlands were closed in early May, 1971. When the markets reopened, changes were made. Effective May 9, 1971, the Austrian schilling was revalued. The next day the West German government announced that the deutsche mark would be allowed to "float" (that is, the rate of exchange was unpegged) to permit the market to seek and establish new exchange rates between the deutsche mark and other currencies, particularly the U.S. dollar. At the same time, The Netherlands' guilder also was floated and the Swiss franc was revalued to 4.08 per U.S. dollar (24.5 cents). Within a short period the average appreciation of world currencies vis-à-vis the dollar was 6–8 percent and among major U.S. partners it was 10–12 percent. By July the deutsche mark had floated upward from 27.5 cents to nearly 29 cents and by July, 1972, had attained a market value of 31.6 cents.

It was under these circumstances that President Nixon, on August 15, 1971, announced his New Economic Policy. In addition to imposing a wage-price freeze for the domestic economy, the New Economic Policy (NEP) established a 10 percent surcharge on imports and suspended the convertibility of dollars for gold.

The Second Phase — Devaluation of the Dollar

It was evident that the U.S. dollar was overvalued in world markets and that currencies of several other nations, especially those with substantial balance of payments surpluses, such as Japan and West Germany, were undervalued. It was also evident that the United States could not continue forever as a major supplier of international liquidity for the world. In spite of this, the action of President Nixon on August 15, 1971, startled the international financial world and brought about serious repercussions.

The United States subsequently used the 10 percent surcharge as a wedge to encourage various nations to adjust their currencies and to take other steps for the improvement of world trade. In December, 1971, after numerous meetings, the Group of Ten, in cooperation with the IMF, agreed to the so-called Smithsonian Accord by which they pledged to work for an "effective" realignment of important world currencies. Some nations suggested that the United States devalue the dollar by 15 percent, but the United States still pushed for revaluation of other reserve currencies as well. Subsequently, in early 1972 the U.S. import surcharge was modified and the U.S. dollar was devalued by 8.57 percent when Congress officially raised the price of gold to $38 per ounce. As a part of the international accord, the Japanese agreed to revalue the yen and the deutsche mark and the guilder were to continue to float before setting new exchange values for them. The French franc and the British pound were to hold their previous par values.

While world traders, financiers, and nations were adjusting to these changes, the United States, the Group of Ten, and the IMF were analyzing their effects and studying a more elaborate agenda dealing with other issues related to the development of a new international monetary structure. Still to be considered were the future convertibility of the dollar for gold, the role of the dollar as a reserve asset, the future role of gold, the expanded use of Special Drawing Rights, the volume and control of international liquidity, and the possibility of moving from fixed to flexible exchange rates, with a "wider band" or a "crawling peg." Action on any of these issues would affect the role of the dollar, the U.S. flow of gold, and the United States balance of payments position, which was still in a sizable deficit position by mid-1972. Thus, it appeared that the gold outflow and related problems would be with us for some time, Furthermore, since the free market price of gold was driven up to over $60 per ounce by the fall of 1972, it was evident that speculators were unconvinced that the gold problem had been settled.

The United States balance of payments failed to improve to any substantial degree in 1972. Moreover, the international monetary authorities failed to come up with any further solutions to the world monetary problems and the relationship of the American dollar vis-à-vis foreign currency, especially the deutsche mark and the yen, continued to deteriorate. Consequently, in February, 1973, the United States again devalued. This time the value of the dollar was decreased by 10 percent and the price of gold raised to $42.22 per ounce.

A prolonged meeting of the Committee of Twenty (an enlargement of the original Group of Ten) in Kenya, Africa, in the summer of 1973 developed an outline of reforms and set a target date of July 31, 1974, to implement the reforms. The meeting, however, failed to produce any substantial remedies for the world monetary situation. In addition, the Arab oil embargo in late 1973 and early 1974 and the subsequent heavy increases in the price of oil had an adverse effect on the economies and balances of payments of the United States, Japan, West Germany, France, the United Kingdom, and other industrial nations. World financial conditions became more unsettled, and the OPEC nations began having more influence on world financial matters as a result of their accumulation of dollars and other currencies from sale of oil at the new, higher prices. This brought a new monetary problem to the international scene as the question now became how to invest or recycle these dollars back into the world money markets.

As world financial conditions became more uncertain, speculators bid the price of gold to more than $175 per ounce by the summer of 1974. With the announcement that the United States would permit its citizens to purchase and hold gold beginning December 31, 1974, the price of gold in the free market reached $200 per ounce by Christmas. When gold sales in America proved to be less vigorous than anticipated, however, the market price of gold dropped back below $200 per ounce in early 1975.

WEAKENING OF THE U.S. DOLLAR

Since the United States no longer converts dollars into gold for foreign treasuries and central banks, and foreign nations no longer fix their currencies in terms of gold or U.S. dollars, market forces of supply and demand play a more dominant role in determining foreign exchange rates. Meetings under the sponsorship of the IMF, the World Bank, and the Group of Ten countries in the past few years regarding the role of gold, the position of the U.S. dollar, the amount of SDRs, the widening of the band, the use of the crawling peg, the stimulation and expansion of economies, and other factors affecting exchange rates and international liquidity have produced little progress in the correction of disorderly exchange markets or in the establishment of a new international monetary system.

In the absence of a new international order, the currencies of many countries have been allowed to float. This means that the supply and demand for a particular currency affects its exchange rates. An increase in demand for a particular currency or a shortage of supply will strengthen the value of a currency and cause its price to rise in terms of other currencies. On the other hand, a decrease in demand for a particular currency or an increase in supply will weaken a currency and its value will fall in terms of other currencies.

Because the United States has experienced substantial deficits in its balances of trade and its balances of payment, as shown in Figure 13-1, the

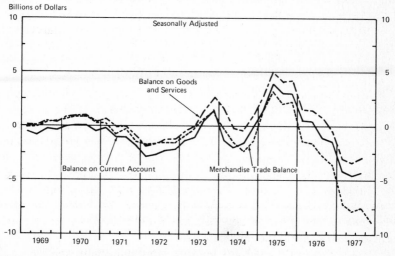

SOURCE: *Economic Indicators* (February, 1978).

Figure 13-1 **U.S. INTERNATIONAL TRANSACTIONS, 1969–1977**

supply of dollars abroad, or dollar claims against the U.S., has increased substantially in recent years. This has caused the value of the dollar to weaken vis-à-vis many other currencies of the world, as shown in Table 13-4. Although the U.S. dollar has strengthened in relation to some currencies, it has weakened relative to numerous major currencies. It weakened in particular against the Japanese yen, the West German deutsche mark, the Swiss franc, and other Western European currencies. The weighted average exchange value of the U.S. dollar against currencies of the other Group of Ten countries (excluding the U.S.) plus Switzerland, for example, declined 15 percent between 1970 and 1977. It dropped more than 5 percent in 1977 alone.

Table 13-4
**PERCENTAGE CHANGES IN FOREIGN EXCHANGE RATES,
1970–1977**

Country	Currency Unit	U.S. Cents Per Unit Of Foreign Currency 1970	1977[1]	Percentage Change[2]
Australia	dollar	111.36	112.70	+ 1.2%
Austria	shilling	3.87	6.25	+61.5
Belgium	franc	2.01	2.84	+41.3
Canada	dollar	95.80	90.14	− 5.9
Denmark	krone	13.33	16.33	+22.5
France	franc	18.09	20.61	+13.9
Germany	deutsche mark	27.42	44.63	+62.8
India	rupee	13.23	11.58	−12.5
Ireland	pound	239.59	181.78	−24.1
Italy	lira	.16	.11	−31.3
Japan	yen	.28	.41	+46.4
Mexico	peso	8.01	4.41	−45.0
Netherlands	guilder	27.65	41.37	+49.6
Norway	krone	13.99	18.33	+31.0
Portugal	escudo	3.50	2.46	−29.7
South Africa	rand	139.24	115.04	−17.4
Spain	peseta	1.43	1.20	−16.1
Sweden	krona	19.28	20.85	+ 8.1
Switzerland	franc	23.20	45.51	+96.2
United Kingdom	pound	239.59	181.78	−24.1

SOURCE: *Federal Reserve Bulletin* (June, 1971), and (January, 1978).

[1]As of November, 1977.
[2]A positive change designates a gain in value of foreign currency in relation to the U.S. dollar. A minus change designates a loss in value of foreign currency in relation to the U.S. dollar.

The falling value of the U.S. dollar, of course, acts as a corrective factor for the U.S. trade deficits. As the dollar falls in value, U.S. dollars cost less in terms of foreign currencies that are rising in value relative to the dollar. Foreigners, therefore, have to pay less for American goods and Americans have to pay more for foreign goods and services. This eventually will cause U.S. imports to decrease and its exports to rise in the absence of offsetting changes. Many other factors could also help reverse our trade deficits, such as a more rapid expansion in the economies of other major nations that may encourage them to import more goods and services, revaluation of strong or undervalued foreign currencies, a slowdown in the U.S. inflationary rate compared to other nations, and the establishment of a new international monetary system. There are also dozens of minor factors that could be used to limit imports and dollar claims against the United States.

CONCLUSION

The decline in the value of the U.S. dollar in foreign exchange markets has been attributable in large part to continuing large deficits in the U.S. balances of trade and payments. In 1977, for example, the trade deficit in merchandise alone amounted to over $28 billion. Two major factors contributed greatly to the U.S. trade deficit. One was our continued reliance on large scale imports of foreign oil. The second was the pace of our economic expansion compared to other major industrial nations of the world. The U.S. economic recovery from the 1974–1975 recession preceded and was more vigorous than that of the other industrial nations such as Japan, West Germany, France, and the United Kingdom. In addition, the U.S. money supply grew at a brisk clip and inflation turned upward again. So, Americans purchased more goods from foreigners than foreigners purchased from the United States.

As a consequence, some U.S. industries, especially the shoe and steel firms, were advocating the establishment of quotas against foreign imports. Many charges of "dumping" were levied against importers and some of them were found guilty by the U.S. Treasury Department. A system of target prices was adopted for the steel industry early in 1978 for the purpose of determining the intensity of dumping practices.

Our large trade deficits aggravated the fall in the value of the dollar in foreign exchange markets. At international monetary meetings, the U.S. and some others suggested that political leaders in such nations as Japan and West Germany, which had sizable surplus trade balances against the U.S., should stimulate their economies more vigorously. This, in effect, it was hoped, would encourage more U.S. exports, reduce the U.S. trade deficit, and stabilize the value of the dollar in foreign exchange markets. The foreign countries, of course, were concerned about the inflationary impact of further stimulation of their economies. They countered with the proposal that the U.S. develop a more positive energy conservation program and reduce its heavy dependence on petroleum imports.

In the summer and fall of 1977, as the dollar continued to fall in value, the Federal Reserve entered the foreign exchange markets. It sold deutsche marks, many of them borrowed on the swap line from the German Federal Bank, in an attempt to stabilize the dollar-deutsche mark exchange rate. The German Federal Bank, seeking to abet the cause, bought sizable amounts of dollars to help stabilize trading in some of its monetary centers. To the West Germans, of course, a further decline in the value of the U.S. dollar could mean a reduction of exports to the U.S. and an increase in American imports, which would lessen their trade surplus with the U.S.

As late as February, 1978, however, the U.S. dollar had not improved and was still declining vis-à-vis some currencies, particularly the West German mark, the Swiss franc, and the Japanese yen. The performance of the U.S. economy was more robust than that of the other major industrial nations, the U.S. inflation rate was between 6 and 7 percent, the U.S. money supply was still growing briskly, our reliance on foreign oil was undiminished, a definite energy program had not been adopted by Congress, OPEC members were considering raising oil prices and perhaps switching from a dollar to an SDR pricing system, gold was selling for $180 per ounce, and the U.S. was facing another merchandise trade deficit of $28–$30 billion in 1978.

MAJOR ISSUES

1. Should the U.S. be concerned about the decline in the foreign exchange value of its dollar?
2. Do you think that it was wise for the United States to devalue the dollar in 1972 and 1973?
3. Would you recommend that the United States resume the convertibility of dollars for gold?
4. Do you favor fixed or flexible exchange rates?
5. Suggest a program for reducing or eliminating the U.S. deficit balance of payments.

SUBISSUES

1. Do you think the United States should restore the gold reserve requirement (cover) for Federal Reserve notes?
2. It has been suggested by international monetary authorities that the band around exchange rates be widened from ±2.25 to ±10 percent. Comment.
3. Should the United States reduce or eliminate its foreign aid to correct its balance of payments?
4. What is your position regarding the creation of additional SDRs as a means of increasing international liquidity?
5. Do you see any serious economic consequences from the use of petrodollars or foreign currencies to purchase U.S. real estate and real assets, such as banks and manufacturing firms?

SELECTED READINGS

Allen, P. R. "Can the Eurocurrency Market Finance the Oil Deficit?" *Banker* (November, 1974).

Bleiberg, Robert M. "Back to Exchange Controls." *Barrons* (February 20, 1978).

"Can the Dollar Be Saved?" *U.S. News & World Report* (March 13, 1978).

Clarke, William M., and George Pulay. *The World's Money*. New York: Praeger Publishers, 1972.

Coldwell, Philip E. "The Growing Impact of International Forces Upon the Economy of the United States." *Business Review*, Federal Reserve Bank of Dallas (August, 1974).

Coombs, Charles A., and Scott E. Pardee. "Treasury and Federal Reserve Foreign Exchange Operations." *Monthly Review*, Federal Reserve Bank of New York (March, 1975).

Cutler, D. C., and D. Gupta. "SDR Valuation and Interest Rates." *Finance and Development* (December, 1974).

de Vries, Margaret Garritsen. *The International Monetary Fund 1966–1971*. Washington: International Monetary Fund, 1976.

"Foreign Exchange Markets: U.S. Dollar Buffeted." *Business Review*, Bank of Montreal (January, 1978).

"Foreign Exchange Operations: Interim Report." *Federal Reserve Bulletin* (December, 1977).

"Foreign Official Institution Holdings of U.S. Government Securities." *Monthly Review*, Federal Reserve Bank of Kansas City (September–October, 1974).

Friedman, Milton. *How Well are Fluctuating Exchange Rates Working?* Washington: American Enterprise Institute, Reprint No. 18 (1974).

——————. "The Euro-Dollar Market: Some First Principles." *Review*, Federal Reserve Bank of St. Louis (July, 1971).

Gray, R. Gary. "SDR's and the Oil Price". *New York Journal of Commerce* (December 10, 1977).

Haberler, Gottfried. *The Future of the International Monetary System*. Washington: American Enterprise Institute (March, 1975).

International Economic Indicators. U.S. Department of Commerce (December, 1977).

"International Economic Survey." *New York Times*, February, 1978 (special supplement).

International Financial Statistics. International Monetary Fund (March, 1978).

Johnson, Harry C. "The Case for Flexible Exchange Rates, 1969." *Review*, Federal Reserve Bank of St. Louis (June, 1969).

McDonald, I. "Monetary Fund Reform, Looking to the Future." *Finance and Development* (September, 1974).

McKenzie, George W. "International Monetary Reform and the 'Crawling Peg'." *Review*, Federal Reserve Bank of St. Louis (February, 1969).

"Monetary Effects of the Treasury Sale of Gold." *Review*, Federal Reserve Bank of St. Louis (January, 1975).

Mudd, Douglas R. "International Reserves and the Role of Special Drawing Rights." *Review*, Federal Reserve Bank of St. Louis (January, 1978).

"SDR's — A New Asset Supplementing Reserves for Growth in Free World Trade." *Business Review*, Federal Reserve Bank of Dallas (December, 1970).

"The Sick Dollar, From Bad to Worse." *U.S. News & World Report* (February 27, 1978).

"Stalemate on Recycling." *Economist* (December 14, 1974).

"United States-Canadian Economic Relationships." *Monthly Review*, Federal Reserve Bank of Kansas City (February, 1975).

"The U.S. Trade Gap: How Serious Is It?" *Business In Brief*. Chase Manhattan Bank (October, 1977).

Williamson, John. *The Failure of World Monetary Reform, 1971–1974*. London: Thomas Nelson and Sons, Ltd., 1977.

"The World Economy In 1977." *Economic Report of the President, 1978*, pp. 103–137.

The Energy Crisis — 14
Will We Grind to a Halt?

Without energy the economies of the United States and other industrial nations would come to a near standstill. National chaos would result, and after years, or perhaps decades, of deterioration we would revert to a primitive economy. Without energy the production of raw materials would be reduced to a trickle, industrial production would be minimal, manufacturing would all but cease, commercial activity would be localized, and transportation would be reduced to a crawl. Schools, churches, and hospitals would not function properly. Communications — via radio, TV, newsprint, and telephone — would be nearly dead. Agricultural production would absorb most of our time and labor. Without energy most of us would be reduced to a poverty level of living. No one, however, envisions a modern economy losing a large part, or all, of its energy. But it is not difficult to envision a modern economy with an insufficient amount of energy. It does not take much of a reduction in the energy supply to hamper a dynamic economy. In fact, it does not take a reduction of energy at all. A mere slowdown in the rate of increase in energy production is sufficient to distort severely the smooth operation of a modern industrial economy such as that in the United States. Witness, for example, the effect on the U.S. economy resulting from the periodic interruptions in the supply of energy in the 1970s from such factors as power failures, the oil embargo, severe weather, and the lengthy coal strike. In several sectors of the economy prices rose, production fell, travel slowed, shortages occurred, and jobs were lost.

PRIMARY SOURCES OF ENERGY

Over the years people have used various sources of energy to lighten their burden, increase their productivity, and improve their standard of living. In early years people learned to convert wind and water currents into energy to help them with their work. They also trained animals and harnessed their own energy to supplement animal energy. A major breakthrough came with the use of fire. Although fire was first used for heat and light, people eventually learned that fire and water could be combined to produce steam. Steam was subsequently used to power the piston steam engine and the turbine steam engine. This made it possible to manufacture many commodities in large factories at lower prices. These products could then be transported faster, farther, and cheaper in steam-powered ships and locomotives.

The production of energy was accelerated with the development and invention of the internal combustion engine, which used fire as a source of power. Among other things the internal combustion engine reduced transportation time, expanded markets, and reduced costs. Today autos, buses, trucks, locomotives, and some aircraft are powered with internal combustion engines. Internal combustion, moreover, is the source of power for most of our highly productive agricultural and construction equipment.

Today more than three fourths of the energy produced in the United States is generated by the controlled use of fire. Consequently, there is an enormous need for combustible materials. In early days wood was the main fuel for fire. Later wood was displaced in large part by coal, which remained the leading primary source of fuel until the middle of the twentieth century. Oil discovered in the United States over one hundred years ago was first used as fuel for lamps. The advent of the automobile increased the demand for oil tremendously, and by 1950 oil had become our leading source of energy. The continued exploration for and extraction of oil led to more uses of its by-product, natural gas. With its low price and fine combustible characteristics, the demand for natural gas increased; and by 1960 it had displaced coal as our second most widely used primary source of energy development.

Our newest source of energy is nuclear power. Developed initially for military uses during World War II, its application to peaceful uses is relatively new. Nuclear power comprises less than 3.5 percent of our primary source of energy, and most of this is directed to the development of electricity, which is considered a secondary source of energy. Water power, which also is used principally for the generation of electricity, represents only about 4.5 percent of our energy supply today.

Although there are several other minor sources, including solar energy and tides, five major primary sources of energy — oil, natural gas, coal, hydropower, and nuclear power — provide the energy that performs the bulk of our work in the United States.

USES OF ENERGY

In 1975 it was estimated that the U.S. economy was using 71.1 quadrillion BTUs of energy from various sources.[1] It was estimated further that by 1985 we will need 103.5 quadrillion BTUs, or 45 percent more energy in the next few years. It is projected that by the year 2000 we will require 163.4 quadrillion BTUs of energy to run our economy. The uses and sources of this energy for the year 1975 are shown in Table 14-1.

[1] A British thermal unit (BTU) is the quantity of heat required to raise the temperature of 1 pound of water 1°F at or near its point of maximum density.

Table 14-1
ENERGY INPUT TO U.S. ECONOMY, 1975

Source of Energy		Use of Energy	
Coal	18.8%	Residential & commercial	24.0%
Oil	45.9	Industrial	31.0
Natural gas	28.4	Transportation	26.0
Nuclear power	2.4	Conversion losses[1]	19.0
Hydropower and geothermal	4.5		
Total	100.0%	Total	100.0%

SOURCE: *Statistical Abstract of the United States*, 1976, p. 549.

[1]Losses caused by converting a primary energy source into a secondary energy source.

In addition to fuel use, primary energy sources can be directed into non-fuel uses. Oil, for example, is used for asphalt and road oil in the residential and commercial sector; chemical feedstocks are used in the industrial sector; and lubricating oils and greases are used directly in the transportation sector. It is estimated that another six percent of our energy sources is used in non-fuel capacities.

The portion of energy used by the various sectors of the economy will not change substantially in the coming years. But the sources of energy will change noticeably. By the year 2000 there will be a modest increase in the relative energy contribution from coal and a modest decline in the contribution from hydropower, whereas that from oil and natural gas will drop sharply, especially that of natural gas. On the other hand, there will be a dramatic increase in the use of nuclear power, as seen in Table 14-2. This expected change is based on the anticipated depletion of our oil and natural gas reserves. Conversely, the use of nuclear power is expected to spread due to technical developments and more favorable cost competition with other sources of energy.

Table 14-2
SOURCES OF ENERGY, 1975 AND 2000

Source of Energy	1975	2000
Coal	18.8%	21.3%
Oil	45.9	34.8
Natural gas	28.4	12.0
Nuclear power	2.4	28.2
Hydropower and geothermal	4.5	3.7
Total	100.0%	100.0%

SOURCE: *Statistical Abstract of the United States*, 1976, p. 549.

ELECTRICAL ENERGY

Enormous amounts of primary energy of all types are used in the process of generating electricity, which is regarded as a secondary source of energy. In fact, electric utilities rank second to the industrial sector in the use of primary energy. By 1985 electric utilities will be the major users of primary energy.

The demand for electricity is great and continues to grow because electricity is the most versatile form of energy. It is used for multiple purposes in the industrial, residential, commercial, and transportation sectors of the economy. The use of electricity is growing faster than the use of primary energy by those sectors. Projections indicate that by 1985 the overall requirements for electricity will be twice as great as they were in 1975. This means that electric utilities will have to gobble up about twice as much primary energy. Today a little less than one half of the electric utilities' energy needs come from coal, 16 percent from natural gas, 16 percent from hydropower, 15 percent from oil, and 9 percent from nuclear power. The first three of these will decline in importance by 1985 and the latter two, oil and nuclear power, will become more important in the generation of electricity. Again, a dramatic increase will take place in the use of nuclear power, as shown in Table 14-3. Observe, too, the growing demand for oil as a fuel for the generation of electricity. Naturally any restriction on the availability of domestic or imported oil will result in a greater usage of other primary sources of energy.

Table 14-3
THE USES OF PRIMARY ENERGY IN THE GENERATION OF ELECTRICITY, 1975 and 1985

Source of Energy	1975	1985
Coal	44.7%	29%
Natural gas	15.7	11
Hydropower	15.8	8
Oil	15.0	17
Nuclear power	8.8	35
Total	100%	100%

SOURCE: *Outlook for Energy in the United States to 1985*, Chase Manhattan Bank, Energy Economics Division, June, 1972, p. 26, and *Statistical Abstract of the United States*, 1976, p. 553.

As shown in Table 14-2, oil is the largest source of primary energy and it will continue to be so at least until the year 2000. Oil is the only one of the five primary sources of energy that is used by all the major marketing sectors — residential, commercial, industrial, and transportation. Moreover, it is presently the only source that can serve the needs of the transportation industry, which burns up about 26 percent of the total energy. Oil is expected to provide one half of the anticipated increase in energy demand between now and 1985. This is due in part to the dwindling supply of natural gas for which oil is a substitute.

Oil and natural gas combined represent the nation's major source of primary energy, accounting for three fourths of the nation's supply of primary energy. Unfortunately they are both now in relatively short supply.

ENERGY SUPPLY

The U.S. economy has been using energy at an astounding rate. Although the nation has been endowed with abundant supplies of energy, they are not limitless. In recent years some reserves have been dwindling to the point of concern and, looking into the future, it is not too difficult to project shortages in some sources that can have an adverse effect on our total energy output.

Coal

Coal is currently our most abundant source of energy. It is estimated that the United States is sitting on approximately 25 percent of the world's three trillion tons of potential coal reserves. Given the current state of technology, 150 billion tons, or a 300-year supply, is considered economically usable.[2] The total potential base, however, is nearly 800 billion tons, which would last 1,500 years at present consumption rates.[3] Although the estimates of our coal reserves vary, from all indications they are plentiful for hundreds of years to come.

In spite of this abundance, however, the United States is on the brink of a coal production shortfall similar to that of the petroleum industry. The coal industry over the past several decades has suffered from some severe financial setbacks. One of these was the loss of demand for coal as the nation's railroads switched from coal-fired steam engines to oil-fired diesel engines. Another sizable loss in demand occurred in the industrial and residential markets as a result of the availability of cleaner and less expensive natural gas. Economic conditions in the coal industry were aggravated further in the past decade as a large number of public utilities converted to nuclear-powered generating plants. Lastly, environmental requirements in this decade have hampered the production and use of coal and added to its cost of production. Consequently, the coal industry has not been keeping pace with the proper injections of capital to expand its capacity and technological advancement.

To meet the anticipated growth in demand between now and 1985 and beyond, the coal industry will have to nearly double its capacity. This task will be aggravated by the need to meet stringent environmental regulations for the industry. At the present time, for example, one third of the coal reserves has a sulphur content too high to satisfy current Environmental Protection Agency standards. In addition, the industry will have to rely heavily on strip

[2]"Enough Energy — If Resources Are Allocated Right." *Business Week* (April 28, 1973), p. 51.
[3]*Outlook for Energy in the United States to 1985*, Chase Manhattan Bank, Energy Economics Division, June, 1972, p. 46.

mining to meet its demand, and price of land restoration is becoming more costly. It appears that to meet the future demand for coal, which will accelerate as the output of oil and natural gas dwindle, the price of coal will have to rise markedly. But in the final analysis, coal today is an "ace in the hole" in the outlook for energy in the United States. Not only can it be used directly as a fuel, but continued improvement in the process of coal gasification will add to its versatility and demand.

Hydropower

Hydropower today is used in large part to generate electricity. Currently about 16 percent of the electricity produced in the United States is generated by water power. In some areas of the country, such as the western mountainous regions, more than fifty percent of the electricity is developed by water power.

The capital outlays for hydroelectric projects and equipment are high. Huge dams are required to control and direct the force of water to spin the large turbines that generate electricity. Although the capital outlays for such projects are high, operating costs are relatively low. A major advantage of hydropower in generating electricity is the absence of air pollution, which is so prevalent when other primary sources of energy, such as coal and oil, are used for that purpose. Some environmentalists, however, object to the construction of hydroelectric power plants on ecological grounds, such as the destruction of forests and the inundation of towns and villages.

Although hydropower is a clean and relatively inexpensive method of supplying energy, an expansion in the use of water power to any great extent is unlikely. It is expected that the amount of electricity generated by hydropower will not increase by more than 35 percent between now and 1985. At that time it is anticipated that no more than 8 percent of our total electricity will be produced through water power, and that water power will supply less than 4 percent of the total primary energy for the U.S. economy.

Nuclear Energy

The use of nuclear power, our newest form of energy, is expected to intensify and expand. It does, however, have a more narrow application than other forms of primary energy. Presently the peaceful use of nuclear energy is limited principally to the production of electricity by public utilities. Thus far it has had very little direct application in the industrial, commercial, residential, and transportation sectors of the economy. Its application to these sectors will grow indirectly to the extent that the utilities supplying electricity find it economical to substitute nuclear power for other forms of primary energy in the production of electricity.

In recent years exploratory activity has led to the discovery of additional uranium reserves, which are the source of nuclear power in the United States and elsewhere. Also, joint research efforts, by private enterprises and the federal government, have led to continuous improvement in the breeder reactor. When perfected, the breeder reactor will increase nuclear power capability and reduce the dependence on natural uranium as a raw material for the generation of nuclear power.

Time constraints present a major obstacle in the short-run conversion and expansion of nuclear power. Once it is decided to build a nuclear power plant it takes 7 to 8 years before its construction can be completed and the plant becomes fully operational. Consequently, it probably will be well beyond 1985 before we see any widespread adoption of nuclear power. Then, too, environmentalists have strong objections to the erection and use of nuclear power stations. This tends to delay the clearing of sites and the construction of nuclear power plants until all environmental and ecological standards have been met and the concerns of the environmentalists satisfied or appeased.

It is expected that by 1985 nuclear power will be used in the generation of 35 percent of our electrical output. It will, however, constitute less than 11 percent of the total primary energy required to run the U.S. economy.

Petroleum

As indicated previously, petroleum, including both natural gas and oil, constitutes our single most important source of primary energy. Natural gas, initially a by-product of oil discovery, has become more and more widespread in its use. At the present time both oil and natural gas are in relatively short supply. In large part the shortage of petroleum is due mainly to the artificially low price resulting from government price controls. For decades the federal government has set a ceiling on the wellhead price of all natural gas flowing into interstate commerce.

The general availability and low price of natural gas encouraged its use in many energy markets. Not only did the bulk of the growth market in energy fall to natural gas, but there was much conversion from coal and oil to the use of natural gas. This, of course, had a depressing effect on prices and profits for the oil and coal producers. All of this had an effect on the supply of natural gas and oil. The discovery and availability of petroleum is a function of exploration and drilling. Such activities are costly. Low prices and modest profits, however, limited the available funds that could be applied in the search for new sources of petroleum. In fact, the effect of price regulations on profits resulted in the diversion of some funds out of the petroleum industry and into other ventures where the potential returns on investment were greater.

If the market demand requires the drilling of a certain number of wells per year, but only a fraction of that number are drilled, there will be a shortage of petroleum. From 1955 to 1970, for example, the petroleum industry invested about $68 billion in search of oil. During that time it drilled about 650,000 wells. This resulted in the production of 50 billion barrels of crude oil and nearly 300 trillion cubic feet of natural gas. It has been calculated, however, that to satisfy growing demand the industry should have invested $50 billion more and increased its well-drilling activities by 75 percent. But because of the unfavorable pricing conditions, a long decline has occurred in oil-drilling activity. In 1956 a peak of 58,000 oil and natural gas wells were drilled, whereas in the period 1970–1974 a low of only 26,500 new wells were drilled annually. Figure 14-1 shows the relationship between the price of oil and well-drilling activity between 1960 and 1975.

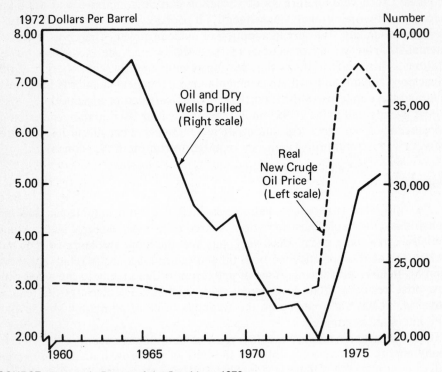

SOURCE: *Economic Report of the President*, 1978.

[1]Nominal price deflated by wholesale price index for finished goods.

Figure 14-1 **NEW CRUDE OIL PRICES AND DRILLING ACTIVITY**

The need for petroleum, both natural gas and oil, will be much greater between now and 1985. In fact, it appears that the industry must almost double its drilling efforts if it is to supply the needs of 1985. The cost of such activities will be nearly $150 billion in terms of 1978 dollars. Additional funds will be needed for laying pipeline, building transportation facilities, and constructing refineries. Analyses of the industry's financial structure and its ability to raise funds, both in the equity markets and the debt markets, indicate that it will not be able to apply more than $100 billion in these directions. Consequently, a shortage of petroleum relative to demand is expected in the future.

Natural Gas. The potential demand for natural gas in 1970 was 59.5 billion cubic feet per day, and we had a shortage of 3 billion cubic feet. By 1985 it is anticipated that demand will reach 107.0 cubic feet per day. Since domestic supply is expected to increase very little, the U.S. economy will end up with a domestic shortfall of approximately 41–47 billion cubic feet per day. Consequently, the need for an alternative source of energy will arise, which will likely be met through either additional imported natural gas or the production of synthetic gas.

More imports may be expected from Canada or as far away as the Soviet Union. But of course the farther away the source from the market, the higher the cost of transportation via pipeline, tanker, or freight car. Although natural gas can be liquefied and transported in liquid form, again it is a costly process when considering the use of specifically designed tankers to transport the gas. There is some hope of accelerating the development of synthetic gas from coal, which, as we have seen, is in plentiful supply. Coal gasification plants, however, are costly. Moreover, about one third of the energy content of coal is lost in the gasification process. Continued research and development in this field, however, may result in lower costs in the future. Oil also can be converted into gas by a gasification process. But it too would come at a much higher price than natural gas at the wellhead.

A projection to 1985 indicates a potential demand for 107.0 billion cubic feet of natural gas per day With total supply to be in the vicinity of 78.5 billion cubic feet per day, a shortfall of 28.5 billion cubic feet per day, as shown in Table 14-4, is anticipated. Thus, it appears the shortage of natural gas will continue for some time and other sources of energy will have to be used as a substitute for natural gas.

Table 14-4

ANTICIPATED NATURAL GAS DEMAND AND SUPPLY FOR 1985

	Billions of Cubic Feet per Day
Potential demand	107.0
Potential supply:	
Domestic production	60.0
Imports from Canada	5.5
Imports of liquid natural gas	6.5
Coal gasification	3.5
Oil gasification	3.0
Total gas supply	78.5
Shortfall	28.5

SOURCE: *Outlook for Energy in the United States to 1985*, Chase Manhattan Bank, Energy Economics Division, June, 1972, p. 43.

Oil. The expected shortfall of natural gas production will increase the demand for other forms of primary energy, particularly oil, since it is a close substitute. As a result, the demand for oil is expected to increase from 14.7 million barrels per day in the base period 1970 to 30.2 million barrels per day in 1985. It is estimated that domestic supplies will provide approximately one half of the necessary supply, or 15.0 million barrels per day by 1985. This will leave a shortfall of 15.2 million barrels per day which must come from other sources.

The domestic oil outlook could be improved by more investment in exploration and drilling. If this is not economically feasible, the industry will have to import more oil. In the early 1970s, U.S. domestic oil production was sufficient to satisfy 80 percent of our domestic needs. By 1985, however, it will be able to satisfy only 50 percent of our needs. Thus, greater dependence on foreign oil is in the cards. This decline in U.S. self-sufficiency is the crux of the current and near-future energy crisis. In addition, since a large portion of our current supplies of synthetic rubber and organic chemicals, such as plastics, are derived from oil, a secondary crisis could occur in these industries.

Projections indicate that the 15.2 million barrels per day shortfall expected in 1985 will be offset by imports, as shown in Table 14-5. Notice that the bulk of the imported oil will come from the Middle East and Canada. This puts the United States in a very vulnerable position. Presently the United States is more dependent upon oil than it is on any other primary source of energy. Any notable interruption in the supply of oil will distort the operation of our economic system. Substantial increases in the price of oil will also seriously affect the U.S. economy. Both of these forces, interruption of supplies and higher prices, caused considerable consternation for the U.S. in the early 1970s. Unstable political and military conditions in the Middle East are a threat to U.S. import supplies from that part of the world. Moreover, petroleum processing facilities are highly concentrated and easy targets for sabotage and military acts of aggression. A look at the factors leading to the 1973 oil embargo and the accompanying rise in the price of oil from the Middle East will throw more light on the precariousness of U.S. reliance on foreign oil imports.

Table 14-5
OIL IMPORTS EXPECTED IN 1985

		Millions of Barrels per Day
Total imports		15.2
From Latin America	1.5	
From Canada	2.1	
From Middle East & Africa	11.6	

SOURCE: *Outlook for Energy in the United States to 1985,* Chase Manhattan Bank, Energy Economics Division, June, 1972, p. 45.

THE ENERGY CRISIS

The price of energy in the United States historically has been lower than it is in most other advanced industrial nations throughout the world. For decades abundant supplies contributed to this lower cost. Low prices for energy and a sustained rate of economic growth encouraged the consumption of energy, directly and indirectly. Then, too, with low prices and ample supplies Americans were not prone to conserve energy. We were continually demanding more and more goods and services that required energy in their production. In addition, our high standard of living required much direct consumption of energy. More gasoline for more cars that were getting fewer and fewer miles per gallon, more fuel and energy for heating and air conditioning, and dozens of electrical appliances used in the home added to the demand for energy. Between 1950 and 1970 the consumption of energy in the United States doubled, and it continued to increase in the early 1970s.

Low Prices of Oil

Since the mid-1950s the Federal Power Commission, according to law, has regulated the wellhead price of natural gas sold for interstate transportation. Low prices were maintained throughout the 1950s and most of the 1960s. The artificially low price discouraged exploration and drilling for new sources of oil and natural gas. With the exception of the Alaskan North Slope and the Continental Shelf, there were no major discoveries of oil in the 1960s. On the other hand, the low price of petroleum products, particularly natural gas, accelerated their usage. This caused inventories to decline substantially by 1970. Because of shortages some suppliers were forced to curtail natural gas deliveries on interruptable contracts. Then in 1969 the regulated price of natural gas was permitted to rise in an effort to stimulate exploration and drilling.

As a result of the closing of the Suez Canal in 1956, a Mandatory Oil Import Program was adopted by the U.S. in 1959. This program imposed quotas on the importation of lower-priced foreign oil. The major oil producing states in America also established a maximum efficient rate of recovery (MER) for oil fields and limited oil output to some percentage of the MER. This limitation of output along with the import quotas helped to keep domestic oil prices somewhat higher than they otherwise would have been. With increased demand in the latter part of the 1960s, the allowable rate of recovery was increased by state agencies. Import quotas were also raised to permit more foreign oil to enter the United States. Available supply, however, failed to increase as rapidly as demand.

The use of petroleum products increased by two thirds between 1960 and 1972. Much of this increase was related to the transportation sector of the economy. By 1972 transportation was using more than one half of the nation's petroleum output. The slow growth of domestic production led to an increase in the importation of crude oil. In the four years prior to the embargo, imports rose from 22 percent of domestic consumption to 36 percent.

The Arab Embargo

In the meantime the various Middle Eastern governments of the major oil producing and exporting nations began to assume greater control of crude oil output and pricing. The Organization of Petroleum Exporting Countries (OPEC), formed in 1960, began to function more effectively by 1970. The Organization of Arab Petroleum Exporting Countries (OAPEC), a related group, was formed in 1968.[4] As excess capacity of crude oil began to dwindle in the United States, Canada, and Latin America, the market power of OPEC became stronger.

During the 1960s a move could have been made to improve U.S. petroleum self-sufficiency by permitting domestic prices of crude oil to rise. Instead of raising the price sufficiently to bring demand and supply into better balance, however, it was decided to permit increases in the import quota of foreign oil.

With the increased reliance of the United States and other nations on imported oil, particularly from the Middle East, OPEC could confidently raise its price and reduce its output. In October, 1973, OAPEC imposed an export embargo to support a jump in its oil price. Although the United States did some rationing to offset the adverse effect of higher prices, the price of oil and oil-related products rose rapidly. The price of Arabian and other OPEC oil increased from $1.10 per barrel, FOB, in January, 1971, to $1.62 per barrel by January, 1973. The price rose further to $3.15 per barrel in April, 1973, and finally to $7.11 per barrel in January, 1974. In one year, from January, 1973, to January, 1974, the price of Arabian oil increased 335 percent. By the time this Arabian oil entered the United States the cost was approximately $11.50–$12.00 per barrel, including the tariff and other landing costs.

Although the wellhead price of regulated domestic oil was $5.25 per barrel throughout 1974, the price of nonregulated oil increased substantially. When the embargo was lifted in the spring of 1974, imports began coming in at a faster pace, but the high price remained. The price of oil acquired by U.S. refineries from both domestic production and imports in late 1973 and into 1974 is shown in Table 14-6.

With the strengthening of its market position, OPEC took advantage of the world oil situation and raised prices. It was motivated to do so for a number of reasons: (1) there was a strong feeling that oil was underpriced in world markets; (2) there was some feeling that industrial nations for decades had an unfair advantage in their negotiations for the purchase of oil from the separate oil exporting countries; (3) for the first time in recent history the OPEC nations were in a position to do something about oil prices; (4) the Arab nations were concerned that the dollars and other currencies they received in exchange for oil had decreased in value as a result of inflation and devaluation; and (5) there may have been some attempt to demonstrate the importance of the Arab nations to the industrial nations in an attempt to win,

[4]Current members of OPEC include Abu Dhabi, Dubai, Ecuador, Indonesia, Kuwait, Iran, Iraq, Libya, Nigeria, Qatar, Saudi Arabia, Venezuela, and five lesser Arabian nations. OAPEC is made up of the Arabian countries in the group.

or force, political influence and support for the Arab position in regard to the Arab-Israeli conflict in the Middle East.

Table 14-6

REFINER ACQUISITION COST OF CRUDE PETROLEUM AND PERCENTAGE OF IMPORTED AND DOMESTIC CRUDE PETROLEUM IN REFINERY INPUTS, 1973–1974

Month	Cost (Per Barrel)			Percentage of Refinery Inputs[1]	
	Composite	Imported	Domestic	Imported	Domestic
1973: September		$ 4.54		28	72
October		4.91		29	71
November	$5.44	6.49	$5.00	27	73
December	6.54	8.22	5.95	24	76
1974: January	7.46	9.59	6.72	22	78
February	8.57	12.45	7.08	20	80
March	8.68	12.73	7.05	22	78
April	9.13	12.72	7.21	26	74
May	9.44	13.02	7.26	30	70
June	9.45	13.06	7.20	31	69
July	9.30	12.75	7.19	32	68
August	9.17	12.68	7.20	30	69
September	9.13	12.53	7.18	30	70
October	9.22	12.44	7.26	31	69
November[2]	9.41	12.53	7.46	32	68

SOURCE: *Economic Report of the President*, 1975, p. 76.

[1]Stocks are assumed to be in the refinery stream and do not figure in this calculation. The base is the sum of imports and domestic production.
[2]Preliminary.

Impact of the Energy Crisis

The problem of the current and pending energy shortfall of the early 1970s was aggravated to the critical stage by the Arab oil embargo. The reduction of imports from the Middle East and the skyrocketing price of energy highlighted the issue. The impact of this so-called energy crisis was felt in many sectors of the economy.

Curtailment of deliveries of natural gas became deeper and more widespread, both at the industrial and residential levels. Some plants had to shut down operations, others cut back their production schedules, layoffs increased, and payrolls were reduced. In many cases manufacturers, at great expense, had to convert their power facilities from the use of natural gas or oil to coal-fired equipment. Long lines appeared at gasoline stations as oil companies began rationing gasoline. Thousands of service stations throughout the country went out of business. There was much talk about coupon rationing of gasoline reminiscent of World War II days. Maximum speed limits were reduced to 55 miles per hour. The price of gasoline nearly doubled. There was a discussion in Congress about imposing a 30 cent per gallon tax on gasoline, and there was a substantial shift from the purchase of large cars to smaller-sized and compact cars getting more miles per gallon.

Government office buildings and hotel and motel establishments reduced room temperatures to 68 degrees. Utility bills rose substantially and families were asked to keep their lights and heat at reduced levels of consumption. The number of scheduled airline flights was reduced and car pooling was encouraged for travel to and from work. Higher prices for energy, of course, decreased the real income of Americans. As more was spent for energy, less income was available to spend on other goods and services. It has been estimated, for example, that higher oil prices in 1974 caused the consumer price index in the United States to rise between one and two percentage points. That meant American consumers lost $9–$18 billion in purchasing power in 1974 due to higher oil prices.

The Alaskan pipeline project, which had been stalled in Congress in large part because of environmental considerations, was finally authorized. The demand for coal, along with its price, rose significantly. Plans for nuclear power generation received renewed consideration. Increased investment flowed into the development and production of "shale" oil, particularly in the Rocky Mountain areas which have huge deposits of shale. More activity occurred in the development of oil from the "tar sand" fields, particularly in Canada. With higher prices more "stripper wells," those producing less than ten barrels a day and which were free of price regulations, were opened. Experiments in coal gasification were accelerated. The dates for meeting certain EPA standards were delayed or postponed in the interest of conserving or producing more domestic energy.

During this period the profits of large oil companies rose dramatically. In some cases profits doubled and trebled. Refinery profits for the entire petroleum industry increased 50 percent in 1973 and even more in 1974. Profits surged as a result of the shortages and the high prices of imported oil. The shortage permitted oil companies to sell gasoline and related products at premium prices, even those refined from the lower-priced domestically produced crude oil. Questions, of course, were asked as to whether the shortages were real or contrived. In answer to that it can be said that there certainly was a shortage and had the embargo lasted longer the shortage would have become more acute. It also can be said that oil companies took legitimate advantage of the market situation and raised prices substantially.

In response to the oil crisis, the President, by executive order, established a Federal Energy Office (FEO). It was given authority to develop and implement various policies and measures to alleviate the adverse effects of the oil shortage. During the days of the embargo, the FEO imposed a number of measures restricting the consumption of energy and sought ways to increase energy production. When the embargo ended in March, 1974, and oil imports were restored to former levels, the FEO was replaced by the more permanent, Congressionally-approved Federal Energy Administration (FEA). The FEA continues to operate today and is concerned with long-run measures to improve energy production and conserve its use.

Petrodollars

With the price of oil imports nearly quadrupling in a short period of time, a severe shock was created in world economics. Domestic output, income, and employment of oil-consuming nations were adversely affected. The high price of oil also had a drastic effect on the balances of payments between oil-consuming and oil-exporting nations. Purchasing power created in the oil-consuming nations was transferred through higher prices to oil-exporting nations. But the OPEC countries did not increase their imports proportionally. Thus, the aggregate demand in oil-consuming nations decreased.

It has been estimated that as a result of higher oil prices the gross transfer of purchasing power to the OPEC countries today is in the vicinity of $100 billion annually. All of this, with the exception of $5 billion, is from the exportation of oil.[5] On the other hand, the OPEC countries have increased their spending on imports by about $15 billion, raising their total import spending to $35 billion annually. This is about one third of OPEC's balance of payment receipts. After making certain adjustments for other items the OPEC countries have had an approximate $60-billion annual surplus in their balances of payments. An example of the drastic change in the total balance of payments between the OPEC countries and industrial countries is shown in Table 14-7.

The oil crisis in effect brought about a large capital transfer from countries with relatively high propensities to consume to countries with relatively high propensities to save. The OPEC countries at present have low propensities to consume due to their highly unequal distribution of income between

Table 14-7

BALANCE ON CURRENT ACCOUNT OF MAJOR AREAS, 1973–1974 (Billions of Dollars)

Area	1973	1974[1]	Change, 1973 to 1974[1]
OPEC countries[2]	5.0	60.0	55.0
Industrial countries[3]	2.5	−37.5	−40.0
Rest of world	−7.5	−22.5	−15.0

SOURCE: *Economic Report of the President*, 1975, p. 192.

[1]Preliminary.
[2]Organization of Petroleum Exporting Countries.
[3]The 24 countries of OECD.

[5]Revenues of the four largest exporters in 1974, for example, were Saudi Arabia, $19.4 billion; Iran, $14.9 billion; Venezuela, $10 billion; and Libya, $8 billion.

two extremes: the very rich and the very poor. In addition, the low economic stage of development of many of the countries' economies requires very little in the way of imports. Consequently, it appears that it may be many years before the deficit balances of payments of the oil-consuming countries vis-à-vis the oil-exporting countries are brought into a more stable and satisfactory equilibrium.

The accumulation of such large surplus balances, often referred to as petrodollars in comparison to Eurodollars or Eurocurrencies, poses a number of problems for both the OPEC countries and the large oil-importing nations. It poses a problem especially for the Arab nations in determining how to handle these petrodollars or petrocurrencies. Should they be spent, and if so, how and where? For answers they have in many cases relied on the advice of Western financial institutions, including some of the world's leading banks. Will the accumulation of such large masses of currencies lead to distortion and devaluation, which would further lessen their purchasing power? Can the world financial institutions properly handle such large flows of surplus currencies? What is to be the role of the International Monetary Fund (IMF) in this problem?

For the nations with large deficit balances of payments, a question arises regarding how they can overcome their deficits and how long it will take. What adjustments should they make in the meantime? Should they devalue their currencies? Should they shut off or curtail supplies of goods being exported to the OPEC nations? Should an individual nation try by various measures to shift its deficit to other nations? To prevent this last possibility, the 24 member nations of the Organization for Economic Cooperation and Development (OECD) agreed not to take unilateral action that would shift deficits to other member nations. There was concern also about the use of petrodollars to purchase real assets of the oil-consuming nations, similar to what the Japanese were doing a few years earlier when they had large surpluses in their balances of payments. Fears in this direction were highlighted when Arab investments were made in land, resort facilities, automobile companies, airlines, and even banks. It was feared by some that with billions in dollars and other currencies at their command, the Arabs could gain financial control of several of our leading business and financial establishments. Sixty billion dollars annually over an extended period of time could certainly buy a lot of assets!

Data for 1974 indicate that the OPEC countries invested about $11 billion of their $60-billion surplus directly in the United States. About one half of this investment was in U.S. short- and long-term government securities. Less than $1 billion was invested in U.S. real estate and private securities. The remainder was placed primarily in the form of large denomination certificates of deposit. About $7.5 billion was invested in Great Britain, $5.5 billion was lent to institutions in other industrial nations, $2.5 billion was lent to developing countries, and about $3.5 billion went to international financial institutions. About $21 billion of the OPEC trade surplus was held in Eurocurrencies deposited in banks in London and other financial centers. Most of the remainder was placed in European investment management accounts, in real estate and corporate securities in Europe and Japan, and in direct loans to private industry.

The task of "recycling" petrodollars has imposed a burden on world financial markets. At the present time the Committee of Twenty (C-20), composed of the leading financial countries of the world, is working with the IMF in an effort to smooth the process of recycling. Among other measures, they are encouraging the OPEC nations to channel more of their surplus funds to the developing nations.

PROJECT INDEPENDENCE

As a result of the energy crisis, the President in November, 1973, inaugurated a program called Project Independence. This project was designed to improve and expand domestic energy production to decrease and minimize our reliance on imports. In this way the U.S. economy would be free of disruptions and distortions caused by any sudden curtailment of energy supplies, particularly relative to imports. It assumed that the United States would have to rely on imports to supplement domestic production until the early 1980s. It was recommended that the risk of relying on imports could be reduced through the establishment of a nationwide energy storage program.

Project Independence also proposed the need for the government to supplement the efforts of private enterprise in the area of energy research and development. In a way it is almost necessary today to have some government input into the field of energy research and development if there is going to be a proper balance of energy policy and other national goals and policies. Federal goals for the environment, worker safety, mineral rights, dollar valuation, and import restrictions all have an effect on the production and delivery of energy. The project recommended expenditures of $10 billion over a five-year period dealing with the following:

1. Improving the efficiency of energy use and the conversion of fossil fuels to electric power.
2. Increasing the domestic production of oil and natural gas.
3. Expanding the use of coal.
4. Developing renewal energy sources.
5. Increasing the use of nuclear power.
6. Reducing the environmental effects associated with all stages of energy production and use.

The project deals primarily with the technological aspects of energy production and use. Unfortunately it says little about economic incentives. If private enterprise is to be expected to play a major role in the expansion of energy supplies, it must have the likelihood of profits to motivate it to do so. Moreover, prices and profits must be ample to supply, in part, the funds needed for continued research and development and the eventual expansion of U.S. energy capacity.

The Federal Energy Administration (FEA) estimates that the petroleum industry, for example, will need $223 billion in 1973 constant dollars for expansion in the next ten years if it is going to reduce its dependence on foreign oil. A major oil company, however, estimates that the industry will have to spend $411 billion in current dollars in the next ten years to minimize the dependence on foreign oil.

To insure the investments of such sizable funds, there has to be some assurance that the price of imported oil will not fall below the price of domestically produced oil; or, if it did, that there would be restrictions on the importation of foreign oil into the United States. In short, given the present conditions of instability and uncertainty, there has to be some feeling of confidence that the attempts of private industry to expand energy output will not be undercut by some adverse policy of the government.

Unfortunately there are many reliable sources that are skeptical of the chances for success of Project Independence. One Congressional study reported in 1975 that it would not be possible to achieve energy independence by the year 1980.

National Energy Plan

Since the OPEC embargo and price shock of 1973–1974, little progress has been made in the United States toward reducing energy consumption or increasing energy production. As a consequence, oil imports in 1977 were nearly double those of 1972 and foreign oil supplied about one half of the U.S. domestic petroleum demand. Although in recent years some upward adjustments in natural gas and oil prices increased exploration and the drilling of wells, production from new wells was more than offset by declining output from existing wells. As a result, crude oil production declined in the lower 48 states between 1970 and 1977. This decline in crude oil output was reversed in the fall of 1977 with the opening of the Trans-Alaska Pipeline System (TAPS) with its capacity of 1.2 million barrels per day. The lack of a pipeline linking the west coast with the industrial midwest, however, threatens to force shipments of Alaskan oil through the Panama Canal, which will increase its cost substantially.

With energy consumption rising and energy production decreasing there is a continuing imbalance between demand and supply, particularly of natural gas. The shortage of natural gas reached an acute level in the severely cold winter of 1977 when deliveries of natural gas, particularly to industrial users, had to be curtailed. These curtailments resulted in the closing of factories, schools, and other facilities, causing unemployment and loss of income.

In 1975 the Energy Policy and Conservation Act was passed to help conserve energy. Its major impact was to establish fuel efficiency standards for automobiles and trucks beginning with 1978 models.

A cabinet level Department of Energy (DOE) was formed by President Carter in October, 1977, to spearhead the administrative plans for energy. It began with a budget of $10.4 billion, planned for a staff of 19,500 employees, and was headed by Energy Secretary James R. Schlesinger. The new DOE consolidated the existing Federal Energy Administration, the Energy Research and Development Administration, the Federal Power Commission, and a number of smaller energy related agencies.

Faced with rapidly rising oil imports and more frequent shortages of natural gas, President Carter proposed to Congress in 1977 a National Energy Plan (NEP). This NEP contained several major elements:

1. To eliminate the subsidy on imported oil, the NEP called for a wellhead or a crude oil equalization tax (COET) to be implemented over a three-year period. By 1980 each barrel of domestically produced controlled oil would be taxed at the difference between the higher import price and the controlled domestic price. In addition, certain regulated oil prices would be permitted to rise more freely, and a tax would be levied on industrial and utility use of oil. Over a five-year period the tax would add $3 to the cost of a barrel of oil.
2. The plan proposed adjustments in natural gas pricing to stimulate its production.
3. The NEP suggests that the increase in oil and natural gas prices would encourage the search for alternative fuels. It proposed that firms be eligible for an additional 10 percent investment tax credit for the conversion to coal or other fuels.
4. A major feature of the plan is a fuel conservation package, which includes a blend of taxes, tax incentives, and regulatory requirements. The package includes a graduated tax on "gas guzzler" automobiles, tax credits for home and building insulation, and a large tax credit for solar heating and cooling equipment.
5. The NEP proposes the adoption in many cases of incremental or marginal cost pricing of utility rates to bring the price more in line with the higher level of cost associated with any diseconomies of scale associated with utility production.
6. The plan envisions growing reliance on nuclear power for the future, but cautions against uneconomic use or undue proliferation of nuclear risks.
7. The plan proposes the creation of a Strategic Petroleum Reserve (SPR). Current policy calls for the storage of 500 million barrels by the end of 1980. This would be supply enough to cover a 4-month import interruption of 4 million barrels a day, and prevent an oil crisis such as that which occurred with the oil embargo in 1973–1974.

The Department of Energy calculated that passage of the NEP as proposed by the President would reduce oil imports by approximately 4.5 million barrels per day by 1985. Furthermore, coal conversion programs, as proposed in the NEP, would increase the use of coal by approximately 200 million tons, the equivalent of 2.4 million barrels of oil per day, by 1985. Moreover, higher natural gas prices are expected to bring about increased production and result in the reallocation of natural gas to higher priority uses. Lastly, energy taxes and rebates are expected to encourage energy conservation. DOE calculated that the inflationary impact of NEP in 1978–1979 would be no more than 0.3 to

0.4 percent, and that by 1980–1981 it would fall within the 0.1 to 0.3 percentage range.

By mid-1978 Congress was still debating the NEP bill. Foreign nations were also charging that the continued heavy dependence of the United States on imported oil and the lack of a meaningful energy plan was aggravating the U.S. deficit balance of payments and causing a weakening of the dollar in world money markets.

CONCLUSION

From all indications, our nation's five primary sources of energy — water, coal, oil, natural gas, and nuclear power — will not be able to provide a sufficient supply of energy to satisfy our growing needs in the next 5–10 years. Consequently, we will have to rely more on imports, particularly in the form of oil and natural gas. This, of course, puts the United States at a disadvantage vis-à-vis the oil-exporting nations. Hopes that the OPEC countries may lower the price of oil or that the cartel may be broken or disintegrate seem remote. In fact, OPEC in the summer of 1978 was considering raising, once again, the price of its oil.

In the long run various adjustments and improvements can be made to move the United States closer to a position of self-sufficiency in the production of energy. In the interim we will have to conserve energy to ease the precariousness of the energy situation. On this score various suggestions have been made and a number of measures implemented by various government agencies. It is of interest to note in this regard that consumers are presently conserving energy. The Edison Electric Institute reported that the demand for electricity across the United States in 1974 dropped for the first time since the end of World War II.

In the long run policies and measures are needed to increase the total domestic production of energy from all sources. This is true especially if we desire to reduce or eliminate our dependence on foreign sources, particularly oil. If certain domestic sources of energy are going to dwindle or not keep pace with growing demand, then the yield from other sources will have to be accelerated. At the same time we will have to be less extravagant in our use of energy and continue current conservation practices. Moreover, if we are going to attain self-sufficiency in energy production, it will require the cooperation of industry, the federal government, the state governments, and the consuming public.

In regard to petroleum, in the absence of a deregulated price, or the absence of reliance on the market mechanism to determine price, an equitable price has to be permitted at the wellhead to promote exploration and drilling. Oil depletion allowances, too, or other forms of tax incentives, must be sufficient to permit a reasonably rapid recovery of investment costs. Although more oil and natural gas will flow from recent discoveries on the Continental Shelf and the North Slope of Alaska, additional reserves are needed. Some oil will flow from the North Sea discovery and the more recent discoveries in Mexico, but these will not promote self-sufficiency.

As we mentioned earlier, coal is our "ace in the hole." But here, too, a balance between environmental considerations and energy needs must be struck. The federal government owns the land on which 80 percent of the coal in the western states is located. EPA sulphur content standards and Congressionally enacted strip mining regulations will have to be adhered to before these lands become available to coal companies for mining. In 1975, the FEA detailed guidelines of its plan to force some power plants and factories to switch from natural gas and high-priced foreign oil to coal for their fuel. More experimentation, too, is taking place in the coal gasification process. A number of states are now taking action on this matter.

In the long run some help can be expected from the development and increased use of nuclear energy. Although plans for new nuclear power stations are in the works, it is a long process between planning and final operation. Moreover, nuclear power now provides a very small portion of our total energy. Even with a dramatic rise in the use of nuclear power, its use as a percentage of the total energy consumed will be limited because of its relatively narrow application. Its most feasible application is in the conversion of electrical power generation facilities from oil or natural gas to nuclear energy. But even here, as with coal and petroleum, environmental standards have to be reckoned with.

Water power provides a powerful and clean source of power. But in this case new sites have to be uncovered and it is a long-run process to construct dams and other facilities needed to generate electricity. Experimentation and development will continue with the harnessing and use of solar energy, tidal energy, and geothermal energy. But these sources require dramatic breakthroughs in their development and use before they become economically feasible on a large scale.

Even with conservation measures, the need for additional energy will increase substantially over the next few decades. If we wish to continue to operate our economy on a high level and provide a growing standard of living for even more people, we will have to develop a full complement of energy. Perhaps this will come in the form of a national energy plan.

MAJOR ISSUES

1. Should the federal government deregulate the price of oil and natural gas at the wellhead to encourage greater exploration and drilling?
2. To meet future energy needs, should the Environmental Protection Agency (EPA) standards be either reduced or postponed?
3. Should the construction of nuclear power plants be accelerated throughout the United States?
4. To bring the demand and supply of energy into balance in the future, is it best to emphasize energy production or concentrate on energy conservation measures?
5. Should the U.S. petroleum industry be nationalized?

SUBISSUES

1. If gasoline must be rationed, is it better to do it through a higher federal tax or by the use of coupons?
2. Should we have retaliated to the

OPEC oil embargo by curtailing shipment of goods, particularly foodstuffs, into OPEC member countries?

3. On the basis of the projected energy squeeze, in the future should the U.S. place an embargo or quota on the export of coal and oil?

4. Congress has considered imposing a special tax on automobiles that obtain poor gasoline mileage. Should such a tax measure be enacted?

SELECTED READINGS

Achieving Energy Independence: A Statement On National Policy. Committee for Economic Development, 1974.

"Can We Prevent Material Shortages?" *Business In Brief*, Chase Manhattan Bank (April, 1974).

Dialogue on World Oil. Washington: American Enterprise Institute for Public Policy Research, 1974.

"The Effects of the New Energy Regime on Economic Capacity, Production, and Prices." *Review*, Federal Reserve Bank of St. Louis (May, 1977).

"Energy Development and Policy." *Economic Report of the President, 1978*, pp. 179–194.

"Enough Energy — If Resources Are Allocated Right." *Business Week* (April 21, 1973).

"Harnessing H-Bomb for Energy: Breakthrough in Five Years." *U.S. News & World Report* (February 17, 1975).

The International Energy Situation: Outlook to 1985. U.S. Central Intelligence Agency, April, 1977.

Key Element of a National Energy Strategy. Committee for Economic Development, June, 1977.

"Less Worry About Oil." *U.S. News & World Report* (February 17, 1975).

Longworth, Richard C. "The North Sea Oil Rush Is On." *European Community* (April, 1975).

Mancke, Richard B. *Performance of the Federal Energy Office*. Washington: American Enterprise Institute for Public Policy Research, 1975.

Mitchell, Edward J., and Weitze Eizenga. "The Oil Crisis and World Monetary Arrangements." *Economic Quarterly Review* (June, 1974).

Nuclear Energy. U.S. Central Intelligence Agency, August, 1977.

"OPEC: The Economics of the Oil Cartel." *Business Week* (January 13, 1975).

Osborne, D.K. "Natural Gas — The Case For Deregulation." *Review*, Federal Reserve Bank of Dallas (October, 1977).

Outlook for Energy in the United States to 1985. New York: The Chase Manhattan Bank, Economic Energy Division, June, 1972.

"Schlesinger's DOE — Strangling at Birth." *U.S. News & World Report*, (March 6, 1978).

Starratt, Patricia. *The Natural Gas Shortage and the Congress*. Washington: American Enterprise Institute for Public Policy Research, 1974.

"Toward a Meeting of Minds?" *The Petroleum Economist* (March, 1975).

United States Energy Through the Year 2000. U.S. Department of the Interior, 1973.

"Utilities: Weak Point in the Energy Future." *Business Week* (January 20, 1975).

Volcker, Paul A. "The Challenges of International Economic Policy." *Quarterly Review*, Federal Reserve Bank of New York (Winter, 1977–1978).

Weidenbaum, Murray L. "Financing the Electric Utility Industry." *Challenge* (January–February, 1975).

The Population 15
Explosion — Can the World
Feed Itself?

Most of the chapters in this book have dealt with economic problems that are somewhat specific in nature. In the majority of the chapters, the problem considered was placed in the context of the United States economy and had a fairly clear-cut economic dimension. As such, most of the problems were amenable to economic analysis; and while there may have been several alternative solutions presented to each of the problems, the solutions themselves were couched in economic terms.

Unfortunately, such is not the case with the question of the population explosion. The problem of population growth cuts across national boundaries, academic disciplines, and cultural and moral systems, and becomes more acute with the passage of time. It is virtually impossible to restrict the question of population solely to economic factors because of this fact.

Given the all-pervasive character of the population question, we must therefore widen our view somewhat in the chapter to include not just the United States economy but the world economy. In addition, we must admit the testimony of various academic disciplines, such as demography, the physical sciences (particularly the ecological aspects), geography, and history. We shall consciously omit only one body of learning that bears heavily on the question of population, that being theology. The question of moral rightness or wrongness of artificial birth control measures will not be material for this chapter. We shall consider the limitation of the birth rate by artificial means as one possible solution to the problem of excess population, but the morality of this solution will be left to those more competent to comment on this exceedingly involved issue.

WHAT IS THE POPULATION EXPLOSION?

The word "explosion" has unfortunate connotations when it is used in the context of population. An explosion ordinarily describes a situation in which matter, under the impetus of some form of released energy, expands at an extremely rapid rate away from its center. When the word is used in connection with population, it usually connotes a rapid expansion of the world's population; an expansion that is proceeding at a faster rate than that in an earlier period. Such is the case today. The world's population is currently expanding at the rate of nearly 2 percent per year. Such a growth rate doubles the population in 35 years. Some countries, notably those in South America and some sections of Asia, are growing at the rate of 3 percent per year, a rate that would double their populations in 24 years.

The growth in world population has never conformed to a smooth curve indicating a regular rate of growth. Table 15-1 presents estimates of world population from the year 1 A.D. through 1968, and indicates the number of years necessary to double the world population for certain check-point years. It is quite obvious from the table that the rate of world population growth has accelerated considerably in the past 100 years or so.

Table 15-1

ESTIMATED POPULATION OF THE WORLD AND THE NUMBER OF YEARS REQUIRED FOR IT TO DOUBLE

Year (A.D.)	Population (Billions)	Number of Years to Double
1	0.25(?)	1,650(?)
1650	0.50	200
1850	1.1	80
1930	2.0	45
1968	3.5	35

SOURCE: Philip M. Hauser (ed.), *The Population Dilemma* (Englewood Cliffs, N.J.: Prentice-Hall Inc., 1963), p. 10; and Population Reference Bureau, Inc., Information Service, *World Population Data Sheet* (Washington: U.S. Government Printing Office, March, 1968).

The Resource Factor

Mere evidence of rapid population growth is not evidence of a problem. Certain nations — Canada, Australia, and New Zealand, to name a few — are seriously inhibited in their economic growth rates by a lack of population. To draw any reasonable conclusions about rates of population growth, these rates must be related to other factors. Among the most important of these other factors are food, space, energy resources, and natural resources. Of these, certainly food must be rated of primary importance. Thus, we might couch the problem of population in terms of the available world food supply. Is the world supply of food currently sufficient to feed today's world population at the necessary minimal nutritional level; and is the rate of growth in the world's food supply greater than, or at least equal to, the rate of growth in world population? If the answer to either of these questions is negative, then the problem of a "food gap" is very real.

The Problem of Distribution. Even affirmative answers to these questions do not remove the problem of excess population completely. Proceeding a little deeper into the question, we might ask, assuming that the world's food supply is adequate to feed the world population, is this food supply distributed among the nations of the world in an equitable manner so that all peoples have access to an adequate diet? If the answer to this question is negative, then necessarily the populations of some countries — or at least segments of these populations — are existing on substandard diets while other countries enjoy surplus food supplies.

People and Their Environment. In the final analysis the question of whether population is truly excessive, or whether current growth trends in population are too high or too low, can only be answered by examining the relationship between people and their environment. By *environment* we mean simply the sum total of all the available resources by which people seek to maintain themselves as a species. Since people exist in a finite (limited) environment (disregarding for the moment the possibilities inherent in extraterrestrial exploration), we must assume that there is some finite limit to the number of people the earth's environment can support at any given point in time.

All living organisms, plant and animal, tend toward a state of equilibrium with their environment. An ecological *equilibrium* state implies a situation in which the resources available to a given species are precisely equal to the amount of those resources necessary to maintain that species. Notice that we have used the phrase "tend toward" an equilibrium. A given species may or may not reach the equilibrium state, or may exceed it, depending on the changing character of the variables that determine the equilibrium state.

The Disturbance of Equilibrium

People have conformed to this basic "law of nature" during most of their sojourn on the planet Earth. Only in very recent times (on the historical time scale) have people been able to offset this law. With the advent of the Industrial Revolution in the late eighteenth century, people began to affect their environment drastically. They gained control of mechanical energy sources, broke the age-old dependence on animal or human energy, and thus were able to devote increasing amounts of time to devising ways to improve their own material welfare. Certainly the two most important developments affecting population growth that grew out of the Industrial Revolution were vastly improved agricultural machinery and methods and the highly progressive rate of advance in medical knowledge. The first of these two developments gave rise to large increases in the available food supply. The second development gave rise to drastically lower death rates, first in the so-called developed industrial nations and then in the developing countries.

The unfortunate fact is, however, that these two developments have not proceeded apace in all nations. In the industrialized countries, where medical advances first began to significantly lower the death rate per thousand, the application of an advanced technology to agricultural methods was generally successful in providing more than enough food for a burgeoning population. In those countries characterized as developing because of their relative lack of industrial activity (other than extractive), however, the application of technologically advanced agricultural production methods has lagged seriously behind medical advances. As a consequence, food supplies have not kept pace with growing populations that have resulted from a declining death rate and a stable birth rate. This phenomenon seems to be at the heart of what is referred to as the "population explosion."

In recent years, as the pressure of increasing population has begun to press against available food supplies, particularly in the nonindustrialized countries of the world, a great deal of effort has been put forth to isolate the causes of and solutions to the population question. But before we turn to an examination of causes and tentative solutions, we should gain some insight into the historical development of our current population expansion.

THE HISTORICAL DEVELOPMENT OF POPULATION EXPANSION

We have discussed the concept of an equilibrium between people and their environment and we have noted that people managed to disrupt this equilibrium through the Industrial Revolution. Prior to the Industrial Revolution the growth in world population proceeded at the figurative snail's pace. The lives of primitive people were fully occupied with looking for their next meal. They could gather seeds and fruit. An individual might kill small animals; in combination several people might kill large ones. Yet in very early years, people were as much hunted as they were hunters. Their food supply was uncertain. They had little or no protection against the elements. They had only the most primitive weapons. Their death rate, living in such a merciless environment, must have been very high. The discovery of fire and the improvement of weapons made life somewhat less precarious, but it is unlikely that the world supported more than a few million humans until people began to control their environment. This control of the environment began with the cultivation of crops and the domestication of animals.

The Agricultural Revolution

The agricultural revolution was the first recorded disruption by people of the relationship between themselves and their environment. It preceded the Industrial Revolution by about 10,000 years and permitted the human species to begin to increase in number for the first time. Ten thousand years later isolated societies still exist that have not participated in this revolution. Most of the human race, however, gradually forsook the role of the hunter and became farmers or shepherds. The relatively assured food supply permitted a somewhat lower death rate and a consequent rise in population. This newly acquired control of plant and animal energy permitted at least some humans to direct their activities away from the never-ending chore of providing the necessities of life. Pyramids were built, philosophers began to question the origin and purpose of people and their environment, new territories were discovered and exploited. Still, about three fourths of the population was engaged in agriculture. Only about one fourth of the people were surplus in that their efforts could, a least potentially, be invested in activites that tended to raise the standard of living.

The Industrial Revolution

The Industrial Revolution, with its associated improvements in food supply and medical knowledge, resulted in a sharp drop in the death rate. The consequent increase in population began in Western Europe around the end of the seventeenth century. From A.D. 1 until 1650, the average rate of increase in world population was about 150,000 per year. By the end of the nineteenth century a new, sharply higher rate of increase was well under way. In England, between 1800 and 1900, the population increased from 9 to 35 million, excluding the millions who emigrated. During the nineteenth century, the world population grew at an average annual rate of 4.5 million. Most of this increase occurred in Europe, the scene of the original Industrial Revolution, and in the new territories to which Europeans had emigrated.[1]

The existence of newly discovered lands served as an escape valve for the swelling populations of Europe during the eighteenth and nineteenth centuries. Between 1800 and 1924, when the United States brought a halt to its open immigration policies, almost 60 million Europeans left Europe for new lands. This tremendous outflow of humanity had a twofold beneficial effect on the countries of Europe. First, it relieved population pressures that were swiftly building as a result of the Industrial Revolution; and second, the virgin soil of the new lands provided food for the emigrants as well as for those who stayed behind to work the shops and factories.

The Twentieth Century

The beginning of the present century witnessed a new development that was to have a tremendous effect on the rate of growth of the world's population. Those countries with the more advanced medical technology began to export that technology to countries that could neither develop nor afford such medical care. Diseases that had previously ravaged entire populations were brought under control with a consequent dramatic drop in the death rate. The birth rate in such countries, however, continued at its existing pace and, as a result, population began to grow rapidly. By 1946 the world was adding to its

[1]Lord Boyd Orr, "Mankind's Supply of Food," in Fairfield Osborn (ed.), *Our Crowded Planet* (London: George Alwin & Unwin Ltd., 1963), p. 83.

population at the rate of 22 million people a year. By the early 1950s the rate of increase had reached 30 million a year. It is now estimated that world population is growing at the rate of at least 75 million people a year.

THE DEMOGRAPHIC TRANSITION

In an agricultural society, birth rates ranged from 35 to 50 per thousand, while death rates ranged from 30 to 40 per thousand. Such historical rates would normally result in a natural rate of population growth of about 0.5 to 1.0 percent per year. In actual fact, however, agricultural societies did not grow at this rate because of wars, famine, and epidemics. After the Industrial Revolution, death rates in Europe declined sharply. Currently many countries have death rates under 10 per thousand. Naturally this drop in the death rate increased the rate of population growth during that time.

Why then is population not increasing at the rate of 3 to 4 percent in industrialized countries today? The excess of births over deaths is now approximately the same as it was at the beginning of the Industrial Revolution. But note the time lag. It took much more time for the birth rate to fall than the death rate. This lag is commonly called the *demographic transition*, and it is the main reason for the increased rate of world population growth in the last two centuries.

The European countries were able to increase their standard of living during this period of rapid population growth because they enjoyed the fruits of the Industrial Revolution. Technology improved agriculture to the point that 10 to 20 percent of the population could now produce more food than the western nations could consume. This freed the energies of the balance of the population for the production of other goods and services.

The Lag in Developing Nations

The primary concern with population growth today is that the developing nations have reduced their death rates through the use of modern medical techniques, but have neither fully participated in the Industrial Revolution nor reduced their birth rates. In short, the time lag between reduction in death rates and reduction in birth rates is still present, the demographic transition has not yet taken place, and the resultant rising populations are pressing against available food supplies that are limited by obsolescent cultivation methods. Certain sections of the world are still caught in the dilemma of falling death rates and stable birth rates at a relatively high level. Notice particularly in Table 15-2 the birth rates and death rates that have prevailed in Africa, Asia, and Latin America. These areas of the world are characterized by very high birth rates and death rates that are higher than most other areas. But the figures take on even greater importance when one considers the fact that these areas have experienced little or no decline in the birth rate while the death rate has dropped sharply over time. A consequence of the time lag in the fall of birth rates is the relatively high rate of population growth in these

Table 15-2

ANNUAL RATES OF INCREASE IN POPULATION

Continent	Annual Rate of Increase 1965–1975		Birth Rate per 1,000 1965–1975	Death Rate per 1,000 1965–1975	
Africa	2.7%		47	20	
Asia (ex. U.S.S.R)	2.1		35	14	
America	2.0		28	9	
North America		1.0	17		9
Latin America		2.7	38		9
Europe	0.6		16	10	
Oceania	2.0		23	10	
U.S.S.R.	1.0		18	8	
World total	1.9		32	13	

SOURCE: United Nations, *Demographic Yearbook 1975* (New York: United Nations, 1976), p. 139.

areas that are most often characterized by their lack of industrialization and low agricultural crop yields.

The Aggregate Effect of the Demographic Transition Lag

To get some idea of the aggregate effect of the demographic transition we should look at total population by area over time. Table 15-3 presents such a

Table 15-3

POPULATION OF THE WORLD BY CONTINENTS, 1920–1975
(Millions of People)

Continent	1920	1930	1940	1950	1960	1970	1972	1975
Africa	140	157	176	207	257	344	364	401
Americas	208	244	277	329	412	511	533	561
Asia	966	1,072	1,212	1,384	1,684	2,056	2,154	2,256
Europe	329	356	381	395	426	462	469	473
Oceania	9	10	11	13	17	19	20	21
U.S.S.R.	158	176	192	181	214	243	248	255
World total	1,810	2,015	2,249	2,509	3,010	3,635	3,782	3,967

SOURCE: United Nations, *Demographic Yearbook 1960* (New York: United Nations, 1961), p. 142; *Demographic Yearbook 1963* (New York: United Nations, 1964), p. 118; *Demographic Yearbook 1967* (New York: United Nations, 1968), p. 97; *Demographic Yearbook 1970* (New York: United Nations, 1971), p. 105; *Demographic Yearbook 1972* (New York: United Nations, 1973), p. 119; and *Demographic Yearbook 1975* (New York: United Nations, 1976), p. 139.

picture. If we combine the world annual rate of increase of nearly 2 percent with the world population of almost 4 billion people, we can then project a world population in excess of 7.5 billion people around the turn of the twenty-first century. What are the chances that such a projection is valid? What factors can we expect to affect the validity of such a projection?

PROJECTIONS OF WORLD POPULATION

Any attempt to project world population into the future is necessarily fraught with difficulties. It is hard to imagine any event that would be subject to more forces than the rate at which the human race reproduces itself. Nevertheless, if one wishes to forecast future world population, an attempt must be made to isolate those forces that seem to bear most significantly on the rate of human reproduction. Having isolated what seem, to the forecaster, to be the key forces affecting population growth, an attempt to quantify these forces must then be made to get some idea of the dimension of their effect on population growth. In short, the population forecaster must try to construct a logical explanation of why population is growing at the rate it is to be able to predict what it will be in the future.

Even if the explanation does adequately explain past population growth, however, the forecaster has to guarantee that the forces affecting the past population growth will continue to act similarly in the future, or even act at all. Many individuals over the past 200 years or so have offered explanations of population dynamics (change). None of them has ever offered a theory of population growth that has been universally acceptable to all. Perhaps the most notable commentator on the population question was Thomas Robert Malthus, an English clergyman and economist.

Malthusian Theory

Essentially Malthus' theory was that in a given state of the arts population will outrun the means of subsistence if the food supply is based on the law of diminishing returns and if population grows by biological urge. Malthus believed that the population would increase to the limits of the food supply; but at those limits population growth would be restrained by powerful "checks." These checks are summarized as moral restraint, vice, and misery. These, in turn, are classified as "positive checks," which increase the death rate, and "preventive checks," which reduce the birth rate.

Malthus' positive checks were simply the cruel aspects of life. He included overwork, insufficient food, poor habitation, overcrowded urban areas, unwholesome foods and medicines, luxurious surroundings that sap the strength, sickness and disease, and war.[2] When Malthus wrote of preventive checks, he confined his recommendations to self-restraint and delayed marriage as the only acceptable preventive checks. He considered contraception

---

[2]Thomas Robert Malthus, *Population: The First Essay*, Foreword by Kenneth E. Boulding (Ann Arbor: The University of Michigan Press, 1959), p. 38.

to be an unqualified vice and refused to consider it as an admissible alternative to the positive checks enumerated above.

Malthus' writings on population have had a curious history. They have been both praised and criticized from the first, but they display an astounding ability to recover from criticism and remain at the forefront of writings on this question. It is literally impossible to pick up any book even vaguely concerned with population change without encountering some reference to his work.

Two basic criticisms have been made against Malthus' work. The first, which was particularly relevant in his time, was that his population theory was written as part of an argument against William Pitt's Poor Laws. Malthus believed that society could not effectively help the poor through charity since they would simply lose all incentive to work productively or to limit births and thus the number of poor would increase as a consequence while the supply of food would not be affected. He wrote that the net result of charity to the poor would be that ". . . the same produce must be divided among a greater number, and consequently that a day's labour will purchase a smaller quantity of provisions, and the poor therefore in general will be more distressed."[3] One can well imagine the hue and cry that arose against this seemingly heartless position which held that to assist the poor was actually to injure them in the long run.

The second major criticism against Malthus' theory is still heard today. He is charged with ignoring or not anticipating the tremendous increase in arable land in the newly discovered and exploited areas of the world; and more serious, with not anticipating the rising productivity per acre that resulted from the Industrial Revolution. One can well ask, however, whether these events have completely contradicted Malthus' theory, or whether they have merely postponed the attainment of a population equilibrium.

The Problem of Inherent Uncertainty

As can be seen from the Malthusian theory of population, long-range population forecasts are highly vulnerable to unpredictable forces. These forces can greatly alter the population growth rates for individual nations and for the world as a whole. For example, there is always the chance that the people of the world may accept a cheap and readily available method of artificial birth control. In addition, science may perfect a method of consciously controlling family size that is acceptable to the Roman Catholic Church and, thus, to a significant proportion of the world's population. On the more ominous side, previously unknown diseases may develop that could decimate large segments of the populations in countries unprepared to deal with them. Or equally horrible to contemplate, a nuclear war could rid the world of perhaps one half of its population in the initial onslaught and the aftermath. These are all possibilities, be they good or evil, that would radically upset the current growth rate of world population and possibly bring it to a complete halt.

[3]*Ibid.*, p. 47.

Thus far we have dealt almost exclusively with the broad forces that affect population growth. Fertility rates, mortality rates, supplies of food, public health measures, all of these factors are constantly acting upon the rate at which the human race is changing in number. Admittedly, we have not dealt specifically with the forces that motivate people to have children at one rate rather than another. There are a number of theories that purport to explain why a given nation's birth rate is higher or lower than that of other nations at a given point in time, or over time. Unfortunately none of these theories is completely satisfactory to the point that it will explain variations in birth rates for all countries over all periods of time. Nor should we expect to find such a generalized theory. Given the large number of cultures and subcultures that the world has experienced, the vastly different educational levels that exist in various parts of the world, the different attitudes of the world's major religions toward the question of conscious birth control, and other very basic economic and sociological differences between peoples, it would be too much to expect one explanation of the rate of population growth to fit all regions of the world.

The Doubling of World Population

Figure 15-1 presents a view of the world population trend from the time of the birth of Christ to the year 2006. There now seems to be little doubt that population will double to exceed the 7.5 billion level in one more generation, assuming that the necessary food supplies, shelter, etc., are forthcoming. But this is an important assumption. Can the peoples of the world hope to provide the necessities of life for almost twice their present number within this relatively short period? And further, will the provisions that are forthcoming be sufficient to raise that portion of the human race that is presently close to the margin of subsistence to a nutritional level that is considered adequate when measured against standards that presently exist in the wealthier, industrialized countries? And finally, the most crucial question of all, assuming that food supplies and shelter are produced that are sufficient to significantly raise the material living standard of people of the entire world, will these supplies be distributed in an equitable manner to all of the world's people so that presently existing large pockets of hunger, sickness, and privation can be erased? Consideration of these questions is material for our next section.

THE WORLD FOOD SUPPLY — FUTURE PROSPECTS

When dealing with the prospects for the world supply of food, and considering its adequacy for feeding the prospective future world population, we are confronted with something of a dilemma. World food supply and world population, when placed in juxtaposition, form a classic case of circular causality. Obviously world population cannot grow faster than the food supply available to sustain it; but on the other hand it is extremely doubtful whether the food supply will increase fast enough to outpace the population and yield surpluses. Should world population growth outpace the rate of increase in food,

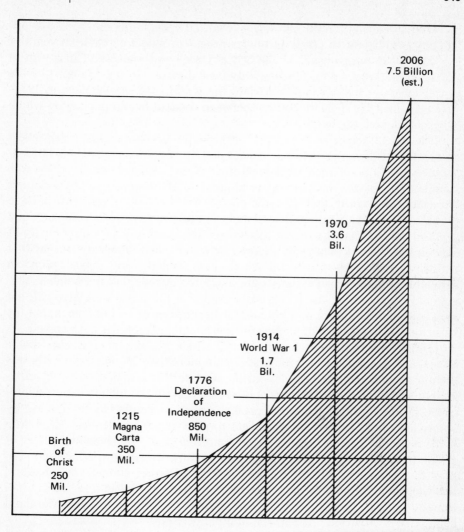

SOURCE: Adapted from *U.S. News & World Report* (November 9, 1970), p. 30.
Reprinted from *U.S. News & World Report*.
Copyright 1970 U.S. News & World Report, Inc.

Figure 15-1   **WORLD POPULATION: THE EXPLOSION AHEAD**

then the only result can be widespread worsening of nutritional levels and eventual famine and death for a considerable portion of the world's people. What are the prospects of feeding the forecasted world population of 7.5 billion in the year 2006?

Recent Problems

The present outlook for feeding the world's population in future years is ambiguous. At a time in which many nations of the world chronically face poverty, hunger, and starvation, other nations are in the envious position of being self-sufficient in foodstuffs. In addition, some nations are self-sufficient in certain years but food surpluses resulting from bumper crops are apparently insufficient to cover shortages in less productive years. In years of low crop yield, nations such as the Soviet Union and Mainland China turn to the world marketplace for foodstuffs to avert disaster. In fact the entry of the Soviet Union and Mainland China into the world food marketplace in 1972–1973 magnified the delicate balance between foodstuffs and population which exists throughout the world.

The world food crisis of the 1972–1974 period brought a greater awareness on the part of developed nations concerning the long-range challenge of feeding the world's population. Although most experts concur that the crisis was symptomatic of the inadequate production and distribution of foodstuffs throughout the world, they disagree on the extent of the future food shortage problem. Those who are optimistic about our ability to provide adequate food supplies believe that the recent food crisis was the result of a multiplicity of unfavorable factors which by chance occurred simultaneously during that period. In their view the world will resume its long-term upward trend in agriculture production. Pessimists are likely to concede that the number, timing, and magnitude of the forces responsible for the crisis were atypical, but they hold that the return to more normal circumstances will not mean that the basic long-term problem of feeding the world's population has been solved.

The world food crisis began in 1972 when the output of wheat, coarse grains, and rice declined for the first time in more than 20 years. Not only was there a decline in these cereals, but the decline was a major one — approximately 30 million tons. The impact of such a drop in production can be appreciated by the fact that the world production of foodstuffs has to increase by approximately 25 million tons per year to meet the rising demand. This drop in the output of cereals created a sharp shortfall in supply since it occurred at a time in which several North American countries were restricting their supplies to eliminate consistently large surpluses. Further complicating matters, this was the first time in recent decades that adverse weather affected production in several subcontinents simultaneously — the U.S.S.R., Mainland China, India, Australia, Africa, and Southeast Asia.

Although undoubtedly the primary factor accounting for such a precipitous turn in world food supplies was extremely poor weather conditions, other negative factors played a significant role. These supplementary factors included an unprecedented boom in economic activity in developed nations and worldwide inflation sustained by monetary instability and speculation. Consequently, world food prices increased sharply with the most devastating effects felt by developing nations.

In 1973 two other elements exacerbated the problem, namely fertilizers and energy. The cyclical production shortfall of fertilizer was worsened by the rise in world petroleum prices in 1973, causing both higher fertilizer prices and reduced output. Increased petroleum prices increased the cost of fuel for agricultural purposes and also led to shortages and high prices of feed stocks for fertilizer manufacture.

Having withstood the impact of such shocks, food producing nations, particularly those such as the United States which had artificially restricted the production of certain foodstuffs, reexamined their production policies. With an emphasis on increased production, it is expected that harvest yields will improve significantly over the next few years and that world food stocks will be replenished to safe levels. However, it is recognized that shortfalls in some areas of the world are not only possible but likely, in which case the matter of an equitable distribution of export supplies again becomes a major concern. Like world population, the world's food supply has become a matter of inherent uncertainty.

World Food Bank

The recent food crisis emphasized the need for some sort of stop-gap solution to cope with the reoccurrence of such short-term food problems. One proposal which has gained wide support in many quarters is that of a world food bank. Proponents contend that the creation of an internationally managed world food bank would provide stability in the world food economy and perhaps substantially reduce the pressures of international competition for available food supplies. It would also diminish the world's dependence on the United States for the production and distribution of excess foodstuffs.

Although there are many variations of the world food bank proposal, the plan of the United Nations' Food and Agriculture Organization (FAO) serves as a general model. This plan calls for all governments, including food importers as well as exporters, to maintain specific minimal levels of food stocks to meet international emergencies. Government representatives would meet regularly to review the adequacy of existing food stocks and take whatever action they deem necessary. Developed nations would be assisted in establishing and maintaining the reserve crop necessary for self-protection against crop failures by international agencies such as the World Bank, the International Monetary Fund, and the FAO.

Despite the many complex political and economic problems associated with a world food bank plan, many believe that it offers the best promise of ameliorating short-term pressures on foodstuffs. However, it is recognized that the basic problem is of a long-term nature and that the race between foodstuffs and population must be ultimately dealt with by effectively increasing agricultural output or reducing population growth.

An Optimistic View

Thus far our discussion of the prospects for future world food production has been primarily on the pessimistic side. But such a pessimism is not shared by all commentators on the population question. Colin Clark, a noted British economist, takes a much more optimistic position on the future of the world's food supply. Clark believes that the population problem is being exaggerated. There is a population problem, but according to Clark it is not a problem of too many people in the world, but rather one of too many people in one place.

Clark concedes that since 1940 there has been an unprecedented increase in world population, but taken country by country, the picture is different.

Clark states that the countries with the highest rate of population increase are the countries with the greatest rate of economic growth. Clark also points out that the converse is true since the countries with declining populations have been those countries with the lowest economic growth.

Clark asserts that the agricultural situation is far better than it may appear. New agricultural discoveries are constantly reversing old predictions of food production. In fact, Clark says, the phenomenal rise in agricultural output has resulted in a food surplus problem. The current food problems center around the efficient distribution of food rather than production. Given improvements in food production efficiency, Clark foresees no shortage of agricultural products. Even if there were no agricultural advances beyond what we have, Clark believes there is no possibility of a real population problem for several centuries.

Potential vs. Actual

But potentiality is not actuality. Because the arable land of the world is limited by geographical characteristics and climate, other productive inputs, such as mechanized farm equipment and particularly fertilizer, will have to be substituted to increase production to feed the world's growing population.

Investment. In recent years there has been a growing awareness on the part of developing nations of a need for greater resource allocation to the farm sector. To a large extent this realization has been fostered by the fact that the necessity of importing foodstuffs to feed increasing populations is costing valuable foreign exchange that could be better used in buying farm machinery and equipment. Greater effort is now being directed toward the construction of a chemical industry that would be capable of satisfying the tremendous need for fertilizers. The production potentiality of intensive application of fertilizers in the developing countries is pointed up by the fact that over the past four decades output per acre in North America and Europe, where fertilizer and machinery are extensively used, has more than doubled while in Asia, Africa, and Latin America it has risen by only approximately 10 percent. Obviously if the latter areas begin to adopt the modern, highly productive techniques of agriculture, their farm output will increase dramatically.

The great disparity in fertilizer application that exists between the developed and developing areas is evidence of the immense task facing those who would raise the agricultural productivity of the developing areas. Thus, while Clark is undoubtedly right in his belief in the potency of the earth to produce more food, the task of actualizing this potency through the application of more efficient farming methods and the usage of more fertilizer is easier written about than accomplished.

The achievement of successful developmental breakthroughs in agricultural productivity is generally thought to be the responsibility of the developed nations. One such agricultural development may exist with hybrid wheat. Still in the experimental stage, major seed producers in the United

States are attempting to develop a commercially viable hybrid wheat which ultimately could bring abundance to granaries throughout the world. The new wheat could allow a farmer to increase wheat yields 25 percent or more immediately. As the hybrids are improved, yields could double within a few years. Since wheat is the world's largest crop, the benefits derived from hybrid wheat may significantly lessen hunger throughout the world.

In addition to wheat, agricultural researchers are trying to boost yields of soybeans but thus far have been frustrated in their attempts to do so. Agricultural scientists see this research as a major means of providing enough protein for the burgeoning world population. World consumption of soybeans is increasing by about 7 percent a year, faster than the beans can be grown in the United States, which provides 90 percent of the world's supply. Although soybean production in the United States had increased over 400 percent since 1950, much of this increase has been achieved by quadrupling soybean acreage. Soybean yields per acre, however, have increased by only 6 bushels an acre since that time. Therefore, the discovery of a superproductive soybean is being given high research priority in the hope of providing sufficient soybeans to meet the world's protein needs.

Obviously if the previously mentioned research proves successful, world farm output could increase dramatically. Those who are optimistic about the future see such efforts as a hopeful indication that in the not-too-distant future some of the developing nations of the world will become self-sustaining as far as foodstuffs are concerned.

Aquaculture. Another recent development has excited the imagination of many commentators on world food problems. Research scientists in the U.S. Department of Agriculture have developed a method for converting rough ocean fish, a type that had been previously considered inedible, into a palatable, high protein food. This conversion process opens up almost inexhaustible supplies of a high protein type of food that is badly needed in many of the world's food shortage areas. The potential food resources contained in the world's oceans have barely been touched to the present time, and this new method of exploiting them is a manifestation of the quickening interest in utilizing the virtually inexhaustible resources of the sea. So much interest in the potential of the sea as a source of food has developed that a new term, *aquaculture*, has emerged to describe scientific methods of harvesting the ocean's riches. Many experts feel that if the sea can be exploited scientifically as a source of foodstuffs, and if aquaculture can be used to supplement agriculture, then the problem of shortages in the world food supply will be largely solved.

Redistribution of Food Supplies. It goes without saying that some areas of the world are better endowed with the prerequisites for agriculture than are others. Soil conditions, climate, length of the growing season, and the amount of arable land will all influence the ability of any given nation to become self-sufficient in foodstuffs. Certain areas of Africa, for example, offer little hope of developing an efficient agricultural sector because of the lack of sufficient rainfall. This being the case, it becomes necessary for such nations to cultivate those resources that they do have in abundance (in the case of the African nations adjacent to the Sahara, this would be petroleum) and trade them to the more fortunately endowed agricultural nations in exchange for foodstuffs. A famous case in point is Great Britain, a poorly endowed nation as far as agricultural resources are concerned, that grew to economic greatness by utilizing its facility for the fabrication of goods.

It must be made quite clear, however, that most of the nations of the world do have the potential for developing a viable agricultural sector. In any discussion of the redistribution of foodstuffs from food surplus areas to food shortage areas, one always encounters the danger of emphasizing too heavily the responsibility the surplus areas have to the shortage areas. It is certainly true that it would be morally inexcusable for the surplus areas to refuse foodstuffs to nations in need, but it is equally true that the persistent subsidizing of food needs by those nations with surplus food supplies may remove any incentive the shortage areas have to develop efficient agricultural sectors in their own economies.

Pessimistic Consensus

Not all experts agree that the long-run solution to feeding the world's growing population lies in increased investment or the redistribution of excess foodstuffs. Pessimists point to several critical factors which they believe will undermine attempts to increase the supply of foodstuffs at a rate required to sustain the population of the world.

They argue that the use of fertilizers and technology to increase per acre yields may be reaching a point of diminishing returns, where it costs more to increase production than the added production is worth. As for aquaculture, many oceans already have been overfished, as is evidenced by the fact that despite more time and money invested in ships and equipment, fish production has been declining since 1970.

The world is also running out of new lands to cultivate, and in many countries land is being taken out of production quite rapidly as urbanization expands. Fresh water for use in agricultural production is becoming scarce, while most rivers that form convenient sources of fresh water already have been tapped.

A final factor is the growing affluence of the developed nations. In Western European and North American countries the demands for foodstuffs are increasing out of proportion to population. People consume more beef, poultry, eggs, and milk as they become more affluent, and grain that would be directly consumed in poor countries is indirectly consumed as food for livestock in developed countries.

Consequently, those who maintain this point of view contend that the only viable alternative to rapid increases in food supplies is to slow down world population growth rates. The question of conscious control of the birth rate, and thus population size, is a thorny one indeed, but it cannot be ignored in view of the increasing sentiment all over the world in favor of it.

POPULATION CONTROLS

Since rates of population growth are, in a broad sense, determined by the relationship between birth rates and death rates, it follows that measures to control population size must operate on one or the other, or both of these variables. To a large extent, the last 50 years or so have seen an almost exclusive attention to efforts designed to affect death rates. A great deal of research effort and public health activity has been devoted to alleviating the suffering and death in developing nations whose populations regularly have been decimated by diseases that were historically endemic to the area. Probably the outstanding effort in this regard has been the worldwide attempt to eradicate malaria through mosquito control and the administering of drugs that impart immunity to this dread disease. Massive efforts to improve sanitation levels through the construction of sewage systems and water systems that would ensure the delivery of pure water to the population have significantly increased the overall health level of populations and thus reduced death rates. In Ceylon, for example, the expenditure of $2 per person on a public health campaign resulted in the reduction of the death rate by 75 percent in a 10-year period.[4]

These widespread efforts to decrease death rates have not been matched by measures that would induce similar downward trends in birth rates. The result, as we have seen, has been to accelerate population growth rates to the point that, in many countries, population is beginning to press heavily upon the available food resources. Only in the past 25 to 30 years has much attention been focused on the question of spiraling population growth, and only in the past 15 to 20 years has significant research effort been instigated in an attempt to deal with the problem. This is not to say that the problem was completely ignored for a long period of time, but the commentators on population problems were largely voices in the wilderness during much of that earlier period.

Now there are indications of a growing awareness of the very real problems posed by rapid population growth the world over. This awareness is being accompanied by positive programs of action in many of the developing nations. Efforts to disseminate knowledge and methods of artificial birth control are proceeding apace in India and South America, as well as other areas of rapid population growth. The effectiveness of such programs cannot be validly appraised, but the combination of money, time, and human effort that is being devoted to them seems to indicate that eventually they will begin to significantly lower birth rates.

Of course, the obstacles to the success of such programs loom very large in many areas of the world. The relatively low educational level of the people,

[4]Eugene R. Black, "Population Increase and Economic Development," in *Our Crowded Planet, op. cit.*, pp. 67–68.

the social stigma attached to the small family in some areas, the active opposition to artificial contraception that is present in predominantly Catholic countries, and finally, the almost overwhelming immensity of the task of spreading birth control information to literally billions of people give rise to serious questions as to whether birth control is really a solution to rapid population growth, at least in the all-important short run.

Because of these obstacles, the subject of population control is a highly emotional one in many countries throughout the world. Consequently, the United Nations and other international bodies, such as the World Bank, have approached the problem of population control with great caution. Recognizing the diversity of interests among nations, global organizations are seeking ways to present the case for population control in terms of national social values. Interests are easy to antagonize and emotions can become aroused at either the private or public level. For example, the alarmist Malthusian-style position that focuses attention on rapid population growth in developing countries may be interpreted as being neoimperialistic in nature. Distrust and possibly fear may result if developing nations suspect an ulterior motive on the part of developed nations, which could lead to open opposition to any birth control program. Thus, international organizations must relate population control to the national interests of developing nations and convincingly show that they will be the principal beneficiaries of any control program.

It is possible that such attempts to check the current rate of population increase will succeed, and in a much shorter period than is currently envisioned. Should this happen and birth rates begin to decline toward a more normal relationship with death rates within the present generation, then much of the potential danger inherent in the aggregate population problem will be removed.

POPULATION TRENDS IN THE UNITED STATES

Up to this point we have confined our discussions of population questions primarily to a world context. We have examined the forces influencing population growth and food supply on a worldwide basis for the simple reason that such forces operate for the planet as a whole and only secondarily for particular nations. In this section, however, we shall turn our attention to the United States, that most fortunate of nations if judged by material standards, to give some insight as to how its people will fare as their numbers increase in the coming years.

Bureau of the Census Projections

The Bureau of the Census has recently published revised estimates of the population through the year 2025. These estimates were constructed under three different sets of assumptions regarding the birth rate, death rate, and net immigration in the United States for the relevant time period. Table 15-4 shows these different projections.

Table 15-4

PROJECTIONS OF THE U.S. POPULATION, 1980–2025
(Millions)

Year	Series I	Series II	Series III
1980	224	222	221
1985	239	233	229
1990	255	244	236
1995	269	253	242
2000	283	260	246
2005	298	268	249
2010	315	275	251
2015	335	283	253
2020	354	290	253
2025	373	296	252

SOURCE: U.S. Bureau of the Census, *Projections of the Population of the United States: 1977 to 2050*, Current Population Reports, Series P-25, No. 704.

Virtually all of the differences between the three series of estimates can be assigned to differing assumptions regarding the birth rate. Series I reflects a growth rate based on a moderately high fertility level of 2.7 children per woman. Series II is linked to a zero population growth rate of 2.1, while Series III projects population under the assumption of a fertility rate of 1.7. The last rate would eventually lead to a declining population.

It is obviously impossible to predict which of the three estimates will ultimately be correct, if any. Since actual population in 1977 was almost 216 million, even if we accept Series III, the most conservative of the three, we can expect an increase of about 30 million people in this country by the year 2000 and an increase of about 36 million by the year 2025.

Zero Population Growth

In recent years many Americans concerned with population growth have advocated population control policies for this country. As an outgrowth of such concern, an organization known as Zero Population Growth (ZPG) was formed in 1969. The organization now has chapters in nearly all 50 states. The basic argument for population control, the organization argues, is that although the United States has a small population problem compared to other countries, a rapidly growing population increases environmental pollution of all kinds and thus will result in a sharp reduction in the quality of life for most Americans. It is also pointed out that each child born in the United States consumes 30 times more of the basic life support systems of the earth than the average child born in India. Therefore, the average American places inordinate stress on the world's irreplaceable natural resources, and members of

ZPG find it difficult to envision any large-scale success in offsetting the increased use of such support systems.

As a means of controlling population growth, a policy of zero population growth is advocated. According to this plan, population can be stablized, not immediately, but over the next 60 years or so. To accomplish this feat, the total fertility rate of American women would have to be 2.1 for each generation to replace itself exactly. Thus, 1,000 women would have to bear 2,100 children so as to replace themselves with 1,000 women of childbearing age in the next generation. The extra 100 children allows for mortality and the fact that more than half of the children born each year are male.

As this childbearing rate is maintained over several generations, a stabilized population would result, ignoring increases in population due to immigration. Consequently, even if the zero population growth policy is adopted at the present time, the nation's population will increase significantly by the time stabilization is attained.

The benefits of pursuing a policy of zero population growth have been assailed by its critics. In some cases, the extent of the benefits claimed are challenged, while in others the assertion is made that the costs of the program may well exceed the achieved benefits.

Population Characteristics. One of the most obvious results of reaching a stabilized population by the year 2040 is the fact that the average age of the nation's population would be significantly older. The Bureau of the Census reports that in 1970 the median age of the U.S. population was slightly over 28 years. The consequences of a policy of zero population growth over a span of 70 years would culminate in a population with a median age of 37, an average increase of 9 years.

Critics of ZPG argue that an older population is likely to resist change and be less innovative than a younger population. This would only serve to lessen technological growth. Supporters of ZPG contend that an older population, such as the one projected for 2040, would resemble the present age distribution in Sweden and England. There is little evidence, they contend, that the Swedes and English are any less progressive and innovative than are their younger counterparts in America.

Labor Force. An older population would bring about noticeable changes in the participation rate of the labor force. Female participation rates would swing upward as women had fewer children and thus would be free to enter the labor force in larger numbers at an earlier age. On the average, the rate of participation for males is likely to be unchanged, except perhaps in the 20–24 and 55 and over age groups. Young males are expected to continue delaying their entry into the labor force due to the trend for more advanced education and training. The participation rate of males 55 years and older is more difficult to analyze because of the unknown effect of such factors as medical advances, work-leisure choices, technological advances, and early retirement.

Members of ZPG contend that the labor force of 2040 would be of greater quality and thus more productive. Stabilized population growth should lead to better medical facilities and treatment. The result would be a healthier and more efficient work force. Workers would also be better educated and more skilled. Critics respond to such purported advantages of ZPG by indicating that in all likelihood the aforementioned increases in productivity could readily occur with a growing population as well as with a stablized one.

Environment. By stabilizing population growth, society, according to ZPG, would be come much more livable because environmental pollution would be drastically reduced. This view is based on the fact that population growth and density are key factors in accounting for our present rate of environmental decay. Critics claim this view is oversimplified. ZPG, they argue, would only make a minor dent in solving the environmental crisis, for it is affluence, not population, that is the major factor contributing to pollution. Even with a stabilized population our demands for the kinds of goods and services that are responsible for much of the environmental pollution would increase rapidly in the future because of increased affluence. ZPG, in itself, would not serve to stem the tide of pollution, for even with the attainment of ZPG, a much greater amount of resources would have to be allocated to the public sector than is presently allocated to launch a meaningful attack on environmental decay.

Public Sector. ZPG supporters point to the reduced economic pressures on all levels of government that would result from a stabilized population. With an older population, there would be a record number of taxpayers, while at the same time the number of school-aged children would be significantly less. These trends might lead to an unprecedented number of fiscal surpluses in the public sector. These surpluses could be prudently allocated so the quality of life in America would be substantially enhanced as a result.

Skeptics question the effects that an older population would have on the already burdened Social Security System. The System currently relies on large numbers of working taxpayers to finance the old age and retirement needs of those who no longer are in the work force. What will happen as the System becomes increasingly top heavy with older people? It appears that as the young adult population decreases while the elderly population increases, the federal government may experience major fiscal difficulties. This certainly would be true of the Social Security Trust Fund.

Also, critics doubt the ease with which resources can be easily adapted to other uses. Their concern rests, to a large extent, in the number of institutions that have been built or are in the process of being completed on the basis of an expanding population. Schools, hospitals, and other institutions will have to be put to effective use in some other capacity and in a manner in which there is a net benefit to society. The problem is likely to be difficult for many of the individuals who have been specially trained, such as teachers and nurses. What kind of a transition are these people likely to make? The transition, undoubtedly, could be made over a long period of time, but not without some hardships to individuals and society as a whole.

Private Sector. The attainment of ZPG in the next century would necessitate adjustments in the private business sector. But, overall, national output and income per capita should be considerably higher than would be the case if higher population growth rates prevail. Higher incomes with a stabilized population will lead to increased sales for business people, for it is the number of spending customers and not total population that is critical in determining the level of business activity. It is also recognized that an older population would affect various industries differently. Detrimentally affected industries, however, will have more than ample time to adjust to predictable changes that are slow in materializing. Many of these firms could diversify their product lines without undue difficulty.

Opponents argue that the degree of transition is of much greater magnitude than is supposed. Some industries would be hit almost immediately and would have but little time to adjust. Those industries that produce goods and services for preschool children, such as dolls, toys, tricycles, and diapers, would feel the impact first. Soon thereafter, the impact would be felt by the elementary school group. One would expect the demand for toys, games, bicycles, school equipment, clothing, and children's furniture to fall off appreciably. Eventually as the number of teenagers decreased, producers of records, motorcycles, and perhaps automobiles would be affected. As the years pass, the diminished rate of new family formations would affect the housing, appliance, an durable goods industries. Through all these phases, producers of services, as well as goods, would also be affected. For example, in the field of medicine, obstetricians would be first affected, followed by pediatricians and then orthodontists. As a result of lower birth rates throughout the 1970s, many of these industries are already experiencing declining sales activity.

Should the momentum of the ZPG movement continue, population growth rates will continue to decline. The biggest question for demographers is whether the reduced birth rates of the present reflect a position of long-run stabilization or whether they are merely short-term experiences.

Surpluses, Social Obligations, and Survival

Our discussion of the United States cannot end here. Precisely because we are so well endowed with the goods of the world, and because we have taken advantage of our good fortune, we are in a very vulnerable position. There is no deeper envy than that felt by the hungry person outside the house of the well fed. Thus, we Americans are the envy of a considerable portion of the world's people, simply because we are among the world's best fed people. Envy is a destructive emotion and unless it can be satisfied, the consequences are likely to be disastrous. Thus, the United States cannot be satisfied simply to feed, clothe, and house its own increasing population; it must also be prepared to aid materially those areas of the world that are not so well endowed.

Probably the most important export of the United States in the coming years will not be its surplus food supplies, but rather technology and capital. While the United States could perhaps increase its output of foodstuffs enough to feed the hungry of the world in the short term, it is doubtful whether it could long sustain them given the rate of population increase. The only viable long-run solution lies in the development of efficient agricultural systems by those countries that are not self-sufficient in foodstuffs. It is in the development of such systems that the United States can be of greatest service, both to the world's people and to itself.

THE ALTERNATIVES BEFORE US

Since the question of world population is so multifarious and complex, and since we have been able merely to scratch the surface of the problem, perhaps it would be best to consider a series of alternative approaches for dealing with population pressures. Admittedly some of the proposed methods for dealing with the problem of population pressure do not touch upon all facets of the problem, but by presenting several alternative proposals we should be able to highlight virtually all of its aspects.[5]

Ultimately the rate of growth of world population rests upon the rate at which children are born and the rate at which the population as a whole is dying. As a corollary of this statement, control of the rate of growth in world population must work upon either of these rates, or both.

History, ecology, and reason tell us that eventually population growth will return to an equilibrium with the growth in the economic environment. There seems to be little doubt that the world's population is currently growing faster than the environment, especially in the developing nations. It is impossible to predict at this time at what point stability will be reached, but the fundamental choice seems to be between achieving it by lowering the birth rate or allowing the death rate to rise. If one objects to limiting births, one must be prepared to favor increasing the death rates unless another development, such as the Industrial Revolution, is believed to be imminent in the developing nations. Until such a revolution comes to pass, we shall be forced to witness and participate in a remorseless return to equilibrium. The question is not whether the equilibrium is to be reestablished but by what means this is to be achieved.

A Significant Increase in the Death Rate

There are relatively few serious advocates of a return to higher death rates. Our entire medical research effort is oriented in precisely the opposite direction. Nations throughout the world are involved in public health programs designed to prevent premature deaths caused by diseases arising from unsanitary living conditions, disease-carrying insects, or outright ignorance of

[5]We do not pretend to have presented an exhaustive treatment of this issue. Some aspects such as the psychological, the political, and the theological have not been covered at all; our only defense is that this book is concerned primarily with the economic issues.

the lifesaving capabilities of modern medicine. A few economists have suggested that developing nations postpone public health expenditures and, in this way, prevent the drastic fall in death rates that always accompanies the undertaking of such expenditures. These economists suggest that such a measure would hold the population fairly steady and allow resources that would have to go to feed a burgeoning population to be allocated to investment goods that would quicken the pace of economic development. Aside from the moral aspects of this suggestion, one can question the effectiveness of a stable population if it continues to be wracked by disease because of the absence of public health expenditures.

Another proposal that might fit in this category is legalized abortion. A few countries have adopted this method, but there seems to be a great deal of opposition to such a remedy over most of the world. The idea of taking the life of an unborn infant, as a matter of individual choice, runs directly against the concept of the worth and dignity of the individual that pervades most cultures. It is somewhat doubtful whether such a remedy would ever find widespread acceptance on a worldwide basis, although that does not mean it is impossible.

There does not seem to be much hope for a solution to population pressures in the area of increasing the death rate. People have been exposed to the opposite kind of effort for too long to consciously permit efforts to shorten life expectancy. Thus, we must look elsewhere for a solution.

Emigration

The movement of masses of people from overcrowded areas to places where living room is available has long been one solution to population pressure. The out-migration from Europe in the eighteenth and nineteenth centuries was one of the relief valves following the rapid population growth generated by the Industrial Revolution. It is questionable, however, whether emigration is still a viable solution in the last quarter of the twentieth century. The money costs involved in moving literally millions of people from, say, Latin America to Canada would be prohibitive, to say nothing of the almost impossible human difficulties that would be involved.

As with an increasing death rate, emigration does not seem to be a reasonable short-run solution to overpopulation. The money costs alone would be so large that a fraction of their total spent to increase agricultural productivity in low crop yield areas might well result in a much more efficient expenditure of funds. Such a possibility leads directly to the third alternative solution to the problem of excess population.

Raise Production to Meet Growing Needs

This alternative seems to present the greatest possibilities for a short-run solution to the population problem because most of the increase in food production has taken place in the agriculturally advanced economies. Many of these nations have been burdened with heavy surpluses of foodstuffs while the developing nations have barely been able to keep pace with the needs of their rapidly growing populations.

We have already discussed the difficulties of raising agricultural production in the food shortage areas of the world. We would emphasize once again, however, that the exporting of surplus foodstuffs from the haves to the have-nots does not seem to be a viable long-run solution to the problem. The emphasis must shift to the exporting of agricultural expertise and capital to allow the food shortage nations to develop their own efficient agriculture. Certainly this does not mean that all exports of foodstuffs should be immediately cut off. Such a move would likely prove disastrous for some of the developing countries. But unless there is a massive effort on the part of all the nations of the world to develop self-sufficient agricultures in food deficient countries, by the year 2000 we could well witness that most terrible of all population checks, famine.

Thus, rapid increases in agricultural productivity hold the most immediate hope for the problem of excessive population precisely because, most often, populations are excessive with respect to the food supply available to feed them. Realization of this fact is spreading rapidly among nations faced with the problem, and the growing emphasis on the development of efficient agricultures is cause for hope that the world need not face widespread famine.

The importance of improving agriculture in developing countries was highlighted in the Report of the World Bank's Commission on International Development in 1969 when it stated, "Agriculture growth is indispensible in order to raise levels of living for large majorities of their population. . . ." The report indicated that more aid will be necessary from the developed nations to help the developing nations solve their food and production problems.

On the other hand, Professor Colin Clark, British Economist and Director of the Institute for Research in Agricultural Economics at Oxford University, to whom we alluded earlier in the chapter, takes a more optimistic view. Clark feels that starvation and malnutrition are not as widespread as reported. He disagrees with some of the data published by the United Nations and others on this matter. According to Clark, we still have vast unused areas throughout the world available for agriculture products. In fact, Clark suggests that population pressures have stimulated technological development in agriculture to such an extent that agricultural productivity increases on a worldwide scale are running ahead of population increases.

Birth Control

With this alternative probably rests one important long-run solution to the problem of excessive population. There is some finite limit to the number of people that can inhabit the earth, if only because of spatial and resource restrictions. World population cannot grow without end; an equilibrium must eventually be reached between the people inhabiting the earth and the resources available to sustain them. It is reasonable to suggest, then, that world population should stabilize at a point somewhat short of the absolute limit imposed by the above restrictions. If we have any concern at all for what has been termed the quality of life, then this suggestion must be admitted. By the quality of life we mean the manner in which people live; the composite of material and nonmaterial things that are available to use and to enjoy during an individual's sojourn on earth. Food, clothing, shelter, elbow room, the right to acquire knowledge or enjoy beauty, the right to be left alone, all of these things rest in large part on the number of people that inhabit the world at any given time.

Certainly the most discussed method of controlling population is birth control, or the conscious limiting of family size to some chosen number. Whether such control is exercised by use of artificial methods, or whether it results from late marriage, continence during marriage, or some natural method, the results are the same — a decrease in the number of children.

But birth control is not the panacea that it might seem. There are serious difficulties involved in the implementation of birth control programs, especially on a national scale, and many experts on the subject remain to be convinced that such programs can significantly affect the birth rate. The reason for this uncertainty is readily seen. Birth control concerns what is probably the most intimate and personal facet of human relationships, and the problems in rigidly ordering this relationship make practically all other difficulties pale by comparison. But this is not to say that birth control does not hold out real hope for stabilizing population growth in the long run. As the educational and economic level of the world's people rises, and as methods of birth control acceptable to all groups are developed, it is likely that more people will accept this solution.

We must be careful, however, when speaking in this context to emphasize that birth control must be considered, at best, a long-run solution. Not tomorrow, nor next year, or even the next generation will likely witness the world wide acceptance of efficient population control. Perhaps the demographic transition will be under way by the time birth control methods become a more widespread check on world population. At any rate, eventually some mechanism must act to check the growth in world population. Hopefully it will be controlled by people and thus be humane in its effect. If people are not successful in developing such a check or in eliminating the food gap, the result will be famine.

CONCLUSION

With this study of the alternative solutions to the population explosion, we hope that the reader has acquired some grasp of the immensity and complexity of the problems facing us as a result of rapid population growth. To be aware of and to understand a problem is to be along the road to its solution.

Ultimately the hope for a solution to this problem lies in the intelligence and ingenuity of people. We became the dominant species on earth precisely because we alone among the vastly diversified life forms on earth have such powers. To deny that we will use them in the solution of this problem is to deny the one characteristic that differentiates us from all other life forms. We are not prepared to make such a denial, and thus we can predict that an acceptable solution to the problem of population pressures will be found and implemented in the not-too-distant future.

MAJOR ISSUES

1. What political and economic obstacles would have to be overcome to organize a world food bank such as the one the United Nations proposes?
2. What role, if any, should the newly rich oil-producing nations play in purchasing food for the malnourished people of the world?
3. What political implications do you foresee if the people in food shortage areas are forced by rapid population growth to remain at the margin of subsistence?
4. Do you think the developing nations will be able to develop efficient agricultural systems with help from the developed nations?
5. To what extent should the United States concern itself with the world's supply of nonrenewable resources?

SUBISSUES

1. Under what conditions should the United States limit exports of foodstuffs to foreign nations?
2. Would you agree with the assertion that the United States is capable of feeding the world's population for the foreseeable future?
3. Can you think of any short-term solutions for the famine and starvation currently taking place in developing nations?
4. Is it likely that the developing nations will adopt a policy of zero population growth during the next decade?

SELECTED READINGS

Bird, Caroline. *The Crowding Syndrome*. New York: David McKay Company, 1972.

Brown, Ray E., and Joe D. Wray. "The Starving Roots of Population Growth." *Natural History* (January, 1974), pp. 46–53.

Chamberlain, Neil W. *Beyond Malthus*. New York: Basic Books, 1970.

Commission on Population Growth and the American Future. *Population Growth and America's Future*. Washington: U.S. Government Printing Office, 1972.

Cripps, Edward J. "The Church Faces World Population Year, 1974." *America* (November 17, 1973), pp. 370–372.

Darwin, Sir Charles G. *The Next Million Years*. London: Rupert Hart-Davis, 1952.

Demographic Yearbook. New York: United Nations, 1948 to Present.

Ehrlich, Paul R., and Anne H. Ehrlich. *Population, Resources and Environment*. San Francisco: W. H. Freeman and Company, 1972.

Greir, George. *The Baby Bust*. Washington: Washington Center for Metropolitan Studies, 1971.

Moraes, Dom F. *A Matter of People*. New York: Praeger, 1974.

Population Reference Bureau, Inc. *World Population: Growth and Response, 1965–1975*. Washington: 1976.

Ross, Douglas N. *Food and Population: The Next Crisis*. New York: The Conference Board, 1974.

Index

A

B

C

0